THE SACRED ORDINARY

OTHER BOOKS BY ARTHUR O. ROBERTS

Prayers at Twilight
Poems that capture the variety
of questions and concerns surrounding death.

Exploring Heaven
Arthur O. Roberts distills the best
Christian thought and speculation to answer
age-old questions about the life that comes after this one.

Look Closely at the Child
Take a new look at the first Christmas through
poetry about the people and events connected to the nativity.

Messengers of God
Discover more about the way in which
hearing, seeing, smelling, tasting, and touching
are receptors of God's presence in your life.

Drawn by the Light
The autobiographical reflections
of Arthur O. Roberts.

Back to Square One
With beauty and insight,
Quaker poet and philosopher Arthur O. Roberts
encourages us to turn our losses into spiritual gain.

Sunrise and Shadow
A collection of poems that ask deeply and
move us powerfully with their concrete vision of truth.

Move Over, Elijah
Sermons in poetry and prose that offer
vivid commentary on God, man, life, and the Bible.

These books are available at
www.barclaypress.com

THE SACRED ORDINARY

SERMONS & ADDRESSES
by Arthur O. Roberts

BARCLAY PRESS
www.barclaypress.com

THE SACRED ORDINARY

© 2006 by Arthur O. Roberts

Published by
Barclay Press, Newberg, Oregon 97132
www.barclaypress.com

All rights reserved.
No part may be reproduced by any method
without permission in writing from the copyright holder
except for brief quotation
in connection with a literary review.

Scripture quotations from:

the *Holy Bible: New International Version* (NIV), copyright © 1973, 1978, 1984,
International Bible Society, used by permission of Zondervan, all rights reserved;
the *New Revised Standard Version Bible* (NRSV), copyright © 1989,
Division of Christian Education of the National Council of the Churches of Christ
in the United States of America, used by permission, all rights reserved;
the *New Revised Standard Version: Anglicized Edition* (NRSV, Anglicized edition),
copyright © 1989, 1995, Division of Christian Education of the National Council of
the Churches of Christ in the United States of America,
used by permission, all rights reserved;
The New English Bible (NEB), copyright © 1961, 1970, Oxford University Press
and Cambridge University Press;
and *The Jerusalem Bible* (JB), Darton, Longman & Todd, Ltd. and Doubleday,
a division of Bantam Doubleday Dell Publishing Group, Inc.,
reprinted by permission.

ISBN 1-59498-008-X

Cover by Donna Matichuk

Contents

Foreword	vii
Introduction	1

Sermons 1967-1990

The Quiet Revolution	3
Saying Yes and No	9
Situation Grace	13
Jesus and the Burdens of Work	19
Poem: Fire on the Beach	*24*
Hope	25
Waiting	31
The Kingdom Is Among You	35
Poem: Samantha Smith Speaks	*40*
How the Spirit Proves the World Wrong	41
Christ, the Key to Mystery	53
Right Standing	65
Poem: Pentecost	*73*
Back to Square One	77
Fruit of the Light	83
Filioque, a Latin Commentary on the Meaning of Pentecost	89
Reflections: Jack Willcuts Memorial	95
Poem: A Tribute to Our Friend Jack	*100*
"How Can we Know the Way?"	101
Vocation	109

Sermons 1991-1999

Toward the Third Millennium	117
Poem: Trek Toward the Third Millennium	*121*
Silence	123

Egypt To and Fro	129
Poem: Egypt To and Fro	*131*
The Leadership of Christ	133
To Give You Hope, and a Future	145
A Voice Immeasurably Majestic	153
Poem: The Transfiguration	*155*
The Thing with Feathers	159
Circles	163
Stories of Faithful Local Friends	171
Poem: Love in Sunday School	*175*
Receiving an Inheritance	181
The Burdens of Discovery	185
Caesar or God?	191
Justice and Mercy	199
A Job Well Done	205
Poem: A Job Well Done	*206*
"Blessed Are the Peacemakers"	207
Marking Time	211
The Crisis of Faith	221
On Being Christ-Centered: Jesus as Lord	227

Sermons 2000-2006

Adventure in Contentment	233
The Day of the Lord	239
Poem: On Your Agenda?	*241*
Poem: Either Way	*241*
Poem: Especially My Arrogance	*242*
Poem: I Wish They Would Learn	*242*
Poem: Has George Found Billy?	*243*
Poem: Touch Would Help	*244*
Exploring Heaven	245
Poem: Putting it Together	*246*
Poem: A Reasonable Requirement	*248*
Poem: A Comfortable Lap	*250*
Poem: I Feel Spiritual	*251*

Be Strong in the Lord	255
Halloween	263
Poem: Perpetua	*263*
Patience	269
Metaphors of the Atonement	273
Gratitude	279
Poem: We Remember	*279*
Poem: Foliage Isn't Everything	*280*
Poem: Blows the Fog Away	*281*
The Kingdom of Light	283
A Call to Holiness	289
Bible "ABCs"	295
Remembering	299
Poem: Egypt To and Fro	*300*
Poem: Swings in Heaven	*301*
Poem: The Really Important Things	*301*
God's Comfort	303
Poem: Let the Spirit Soar	*305*
"C'mon, Kyle!"	307
"Outside the Box"	311
"Kinda"?	313

Foreword

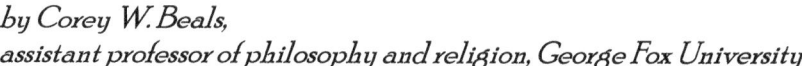

*by Corey W. Beals,
assistant professor of philosophy and religion, George Fox University*

One may wonder whether there remains a place in our world for sermons. Are we not in an era that despises sermonizing—an age where the ego is often fed with advice like "Look within yourself for truth"? And when we listen to a sermon, how often do we hear the joke that it is forgotten before Sunday dinner is finished?

This collection from Arthur Roberts put these skeptical questions to rest. For example, one of these sermons was given during my college baccalaureate service at George Fox College fifteen years ago. Not only do I still remember it, but it has served as an inspiration and guide over the last decade and a half. I asked Roberts for a copy of the sermon after the service, and he sent me a copy that I have reread on multiple occasions.

The sermon he gave then ("Toward the Third Millennium," p. 117ff) is an example of what is found in many of these sermons—soaring idealistic reflections alongside down-to-earth, practical advice, followed by plain-speaking poetic verse. For example, he has high, lofty words such as "every vision will come true." At the time of hearing those words, my vision was to become a professor like the speaker of those words. I took those lofty, idealistic words to heart and eventually my wife and I moved across the country with our two cats to pursue graduate school. But those moves also gave opportunity to draw upon the practical words contained in the same sermon. During each of the eight moves since hearing that sermon, I have kept in mind his advice to "Travel light." In verse, he writes, "Anticipating a major move ask yourself forthrightly, 'Do we really need this stuff?'" Although we need some things like friends' addresses, clothes, and prized books, he writes, "Take these things with you. But first, junk the junk and share the rest."

This book of sermons, I would suggest, should be one of those prized books that you take with you each time you move. It reveals Roberts's deep respect for the ordinary and shows us that it is there we encounter the sacred. For example, he writes about a man he admired who understood the "sacramental character of ordinary, earthy things" (p. 173). And Roberts also delights in revealing mysteries. But as you read through this volume, you will come to see that when Roberts reveals a mystery, he doesn't explain it or demythologize it. Instead, he points to the mystery, and helps to awaken our awe in the face of that mystery (see for example p. 53ff).

I invite you to read this contemplatively. You may find, as I did, that it is hard to just rush through it. Or perhaps, as a house church or small group, you could read out loud one of these sermons per week, providing a year's worth of sermons. Alternatively, you might use it as a reference, or as a model in how to craft a fine sermon. It is a book worth having and reading and absorbing.

Introduction

The sermons in this collection date from 1967 to 2006. They were preached during my tenure as a professor of religion and philosophy at George Fox University (formerly College) and in retirement years while my wife, Fern, and I were living in Yachats, Oregon.

During earlier years as an active pastor I usually preached extemporaneously from notes rather than from manuscripts. Fourteen written sermons, however, were published in 1967 under the title *Move Over, Elijah* (Barclay Press). These are not included in the present publication.

Reading a sermon isn't quite the same as hearing it in the context of a worshiping community but does offer alternative values. Any book, including this one, lets you learn something about the writer; but there are other and better values to be gained. A book of sermons lets a reader see biblical truth through the lens of another person. It provides a window through which to view the witness of the church in recent decades. It is a tool for personal spiritual reflection, especially valuable if accompanied by prayer. I would feel amply rewarded if the book so ministers to you.

How, and to what extent, these sermons affected the lives of hearers is difficult to measure. I prepared them prayerfully, with particular congregations in mind, and am confident that the Holy Spirit, who guided me in preparing and delivering the sermons guided others in responding to God's message through them. I pray the Holy Spirit will do so through this format also.

Arthur O. Roberts
Newberg, Oregon
April 2006

The Quiet Revolution

Newberg Friends Church, Easter, March 26, 1967

Because we live comfortably within Christendom, in this year of our Lord, 1967, we get complacent about our faith. "Ho, hum, another Easter." "Doesn't the choir sing well, though?" "How many did you say were coming for dinner?" And so it goes. I warn you, however, a worldwide repudiation of Christianity is taking place. The church is under purifying attack. Either it shapes up or phases out. The reinforcements to a Christian society that we take for granted are falling away.

Well, what about us? If we are honest, we must admit that faithlessness is not just something flouted by brazen hedonists and exhibitionist preachers. It is a real temptation to us as well. In moments of pressure we yield to it, usually without saying anything to anybody, scarcely admitting it to ourselves. It may be we sit in church listening to the hymns and looking at the minister. And suddenly we wonder if all the refinements and decency couldn't take place without this church bit. Would the world be different? Would people be just as kind? Perhaps you are singing, "There is a fountain filled with blood," when the anachronism of the language hits you. A storm of unbelief finds a crack in your faith. You shake it off like a recurring bad dream that leaves you out of sorts in the morning. The vultures circle round, waiting for Christianity to stumble and fall and die.

Acknowledge it! Acknowledge that sometimes even Easter seems unreal, a kind of quaint play reenacted out of convention and featured annually as writers and television men might feature an antique automobile show. When the shafts of doubt pierce us we wonder if it isn't a good play with a poor third act for our scientific age. What comes to us is a scenario with barefooted men in robes padding about looking solemn—and a credit line to Concordia films.

We are tempted to feel let down by Christianity, at least those of us in the heat of the day who have struggled hard. We may even feel disillusioned, like Judas. But I bet we don't think of identifying ourselves with him! He was disillusioned with what he thought would be a sure thing, a real revolution. Only we aren't bitter, like he was, to the point of self-destruction. For we have Walter Cronkite heralding the twenty-first century for us. We see the golden age looming before us, with vacations in space and exciting trips to Mars for someone—probably someone else. But at least we can read about these exploits in the comfort of robot-managed homes, with air conditioning to screen out the contaminants and a redwood fence to screen out the neighbor kids.

Beyond Vietnam the golden age looms. Both Communism and Western materialism think so. The big revolution is on with lots of news and excitement—lots of blood and splash. And somehow, the church isn't with it— bypassed with polite tolerance.

The doubts of the disciples

When we stop to think about it, the followers of Jesus had the same feelings. Imagine! But it's true. On that Easter morning, before it meant anything more than a weary mop-up after the brutal pogrom, Mary Magdalene thought only of the apparent sacrilege that had deprived her of doing homage to the body. "They have taken away my Lord," she sobbed, "and I don't know where they have laid him." When reports of Jesus' resurrection reached the apostles they pooh-poohed the stories as "idle tales"—so much nonsense. They simply refused to believe. Such was the skepticism of a swarthy Palestinian whose mode of transportation was not a mustang but instead a donkey plodding on dusty roads. Such was the skepticism of an unsophisticated fisherman who never took a course in comparative religion or yelled at a football game. But he had listened to Jesus. He had watched him heal the sick and show the world how to love unselfishly. He had watched Jesus die, sagging on the Roman cross, nails forced through hands and feet. This is the fellow who called the resurrection report "idle tales."

Doubt characterized certain other followers of Jesus who discussed Jewish politics while traveling to Emmaus. "We had hoped," they confessed to a stranger who joined them, that Jesus would be the leader to liberate the country, "but...," and they shrugged their shoulders in a gesture of disappointment. They had lost the election. The revolution had fizzled, apparently, or Jesus wasn't the leader they had imagined him to be, or Rome was just too clever. Oh, they could second-guess the campaign all right; they were clearly the losers. So they resigned themselves to yet another generation of indignity, injustice, and insult. They would suffer some more under the Roman tyrant who sat upon the seven hills of Rome and dominated the Mediterranean world.

"We had hoped!" We had hoped. We had hoped. This refrain drums its beat through time. It's the sound of faith crushed, of goodness hammered to a cross, the sound of brute power, of cleverness laughing in the face of God. It's the sound of right sacrificed to vengeance seekers, of flames crackling in war-torn villages, of soil falling on the bodies of war-dead thrown into a common grave. It's the sound of revolutions. We had hoped! Every generation hears it. One more effort and then peace....

But the noisy revolution is only the penultimate sound—the next to the last. God has the last word and his word is: a *quiet revolution*. That's what Good Friday and Easter are all about. For the stranger who joined the Emmaus losers was Jesus. The risen Christ jogged their memories about the quiet revolution by which God changes ordinary folks like you and me. These travelers had invited the stranger to dinner that evening, and in the breaking of the bread their eyes were opened. Christ lives! Wonder of wonders! Like them, our hearts burn within us when first Christ becomes known to us and the world opens its meaning to us for the first time.

Those skeptical followers who had scoffed at "idle tales"—they, too, learned the resurrection is true. Christ appeared to them, ate with them, talked with them, and promised that his Spirit would be with them. Mary's frustrated cry evoked the response of Jesus himself, as he spoke her name. Now no one could take away her master! Even Thomas, who had clung to his scientific attitude, came to exclaim "My Lord and my God!" when Jesus appeared and said, "Thomas, thrust hither thy hand into my side.... be not faithless, but believing." And he believed. As a result of his belief and subsequent witness, several million Asian Christians today trace their spiritual legacy to Thomas.

Well, Peter, Thomas, Mary, and the nameless travelers along the Emmaus road are long dead. As is Paul, who had killed Christians because he thought they were obstacles to God's program of revolution—that is, until Christ appeared to him some years later on the Damascus road. Paul learned then and there about the quiet revolution. Here are the words about that encounter:

> And now, my brothers, I must remind you of the gospel that I preached to you; the gospel which you received, on which you have taken your stand, and which is now bringing you salvation. Do you still hold fast the Gospel as I preached it to you?...
>
> First and foremost I handed on to you the facts which had been imparted to me: that Christ died for our sins, in accordance with the scriptures; that he was buried; that he was raised to life on the third day, according to the scriptures; and that he appeared to Cephas, and afterwards to the Twelve. Then he appeared to over five hundred of our brothers at once, most of whom are still alive, though some have died. Then he appeared to James, and afterwards to all the apostles.
>
> In the end he appeared even to me....(1 Corinthians 15:1-8 NEB)

Such is the church's great testimony. Christ lives! The testimony that clinches the words of Mary and of Thomas and of Peter is so aptly expressed by Paul: "In the end he appeared even to me." Isn't this really *your* testimony? We know the Sriptures are true not only by their coherence and authority but because Christ comes to us. "Even to me" caught up in sin and shame, aware of failure and limitation, he appears.

The resurrection is a mystery of faith. Not a myth, but a mystery—a mystery more profound than the mystery of galaxies and the building blocks of life. Those realities that we do know are dwarfed by a context of meaning we glimpse fleetingly and seek to grasp. That the disciples believed Christ died for the sins of the world and that the resurrection gives cosmic vindication of such, we freely affirm.

As the Lord renewed the faith of those who were dismayed and terrified, beaten and defeated, then, so he will do now. Indeed, as we come to the end of ourselves, come to the point of throwing ourselves into remorse, Christ comes and calls us to new faith. He points beyond Vietnam and civil rights struggles, the future of America or Western civilization, beyond the stability of our jobs and homes. God calls the signals in history and nature. Christ is God's word to us. The cross and the resurrection tell us what life is about and where it is going for us and for all humanity. The last enemy, death, cannot be overcome by human revolutions.

How can we know Christ as did the disciples? He does not confront us in tangible ways. We cannot touch his side. Jesus' words to Thomas help us: "blessed are those who have not seen and yet have believed" (John 20:29 NIV).

Well, we read these words. Can they mean something to us? The matter is more than verbal direction. Words run out and fall back mute until God's spirit gives them life and meaning—until God himself comes through this testimony and says to you: "It's true. Christ lives, and you too shall live." Our senses are God's messengers. Remember how Jesus stressed really hearing with our ears, really seeing with our eyes? So let's ask how God speaks to us, how we touch him, how the Holy Spirit is with us.

How do we respond in faith?

We know something about the meaning of Christ by having experienced suffering. Oh, I don't mean just reading about poor Indian children starving, or pain-wracked people in hospitals, or injustices inflicted upon illiterate migrants, and the like. We can get closer to the cross than that, even though we may well come under a burden for a torn and bleeding world. Let's start more simply. What of your own experiences? Anyone who has fallen over the furniture amid amused glances of onlookers, or blinked back tears over a thoughtless remark, or suffered the pains of a toothache has sufficient ground to sense the meaning of the cross. Whoever has the common grace to blush can respond to Jesus' agony in Gethsemane. Experiences of isolation, loneliness—these tell us life is less than what it could be. To these reflections add a few years and see incompleteness, loss, and finally death wipe out all struggles to achieve and to be. No wonder Paul said that if in this life only we have hope in Christ we are of all men most miserable. We feel acutely the serpent's sting upon the heel. And when this happens we see human revolutions toppling to the ground like the legendary Achilles.

It's not enough to say, well, this is how we got the world, so let's tidy it up. The flaws are endemic. They adhere to human sin. All our towers of Babel end in confusion of language and meaning. No prophet is needed to note the breakdown of words today, for sin always wrecks the trust involved in using words with integrity. With the linguistic foundation destroyed superstructures soon topple.

Redemption is called for. The cross and the resurrection are God's gifts. "As in Adam all die, so in Christ shall all be made alive." There's nothing parochial about *this* truth. Nothing limits Christian emphasis to one day a year. It's a mighty shout from God to creatures made in his image.

It's not enough to blame others or ourselves for failures, for the eroding of lives, for sickening disasters caused by ignorance, stupidity, greed, lust, hate. Even those who love us may sin against us in ignorance, as we do to them. The cross goes beyond suffering to make *sacrifice* sufficient for the sin. The cross stands square for forgiveness. God has forgiven us! Let's forgive each other. Get alone with yourself now. Let the ugly things you've thought and said and done and been sweep before your eyes. No role-playing now. Just you in the presence of God. Can you understand now why Jesus said to forgive seventy times seven? Why he rebuked Peter for wanting to spare him the cross?

Penitently we pray with the psalmist, "Wash away all my iniquity and cleanse me from my sin" (Psalm 51:2 NIV). Risen with Christ we become the new humanity, for we have identified ourselves with the worst criminals, acknowledging "we have all sinned." As George Fox described it, "The ocean of light is greater than the ocean of darkness" (*Journal,* ed. Nickalls, Cambridge, 1952, p. 17). It overcomes it.

That's why Christ is such good news. Is goodness worth the price? Should the blush fade? Should calluses cover the hurt? Should we become self-centered? Or do we discover a meaning to suffering, to ignorance, to guilt? In Christ, failure can be redeemed. Love is better than hate, unselfishness than selfishness. Truth is better than falsehood. Jesus tells us to live in faith that this is *God's world*—that it is worth the suffering, the sacrifice. Our captain has shown us an attainable goal.

We resonate with Isaiah's prophecy (chapter 53 NEB, emphasis mine) about the Messiah:

> Surely he has borne our griefs and carried our sorrows. We did esteem him smitten, stricken of God; he was wounded for *our* transgressions, bruised for *our* iniquities, and upon him was the chastisement that makes *us* whole. With his stripes *we* are healed. All we like sheep *have* gone astray, we have turned every one to his own way and the Lord has laid upon him the iniquity of us all.

In some unfathomable way the sufferings of Christ become the sacrifice that makes us whole. It was our cross, really, as surely as the dying boys in Vietnam unite us in a common obligation to be our brothers' keepers. And the blood cries out from the ground until Christ once and for all makes the sacrifice for sin. He writes his will upon our hearts and remembers our deeds against us no more. This is the new covenant (see Hebrews 10).

The way of the resurrection is a new and living way. We belong to the new order of things. God loves us. Christ is the offering for our sins. He is our intercessor, the one who understands. God turns suffering into redemptive sacrifice. Long ago a prophet, tormented by sin and a desperate need for atonement, in agony cried out, "Shall I give the fruit of my body for the sin of my soul?" Not good enough. Only the sinless one suffices. It's God's way.

This redemptive sacrifice is not just in the past. Christ reaches us from the future. His first coming is linked with his second. In the resurrection we learn the good news that Jesus has crashed through the barrier of death and the running down of physical force. The new heavens and the new earth are no sop of poetic imagery but a symbol of a new order. This world has scarcely touched the meaning of the resurrection. God's sacrifice is for the redemption of the *world*, and the church is witness to that love.

The quiet revolution is not just suffering and sacrifice, but good news—like the first ripe strawberry that portends a greater crop, like spring daffodils and crocuses. Christ, the new Adam, leads us into powers beyond imagination. Budding maples do not mock us by saying "one more year closer to the end." No. They point us to God's process. Life is more than a deteriorating party, more than making Kewpie dolls out of teenagers and selling them to the carnival crowd.

The quiet revolution is good news for those who crave justice. It tells them that vengeance is God's, not man's, and to patiently work for righteousness without compromise. The quiet revolution is good news for the loveless. True love *can* be found despite misrepresentations and caricatures peddled to the most perverse tastes.

The quiet revolution is good news to the tender fainthearted ones tempted to escape into drugs. It's good news to the tough fainthearted ones tempted to escape via exhibitionist garb, greasy hair, and dirty clothes. It's good news to the steady old middle class whose routine can also become escapist. Good news, Joe! Life is more than ten years of swagger, twenty of brag about the swagger, a medal for years on the job, nowhere to go, and one mad dash for the concrete abutment. You don't need alcohol to drown the vision of what life might have been. Life may be filled full of God, so filled with beauty that the senses don't have to become jaded with coarse shows.

Join the quiet revolution

Young people, join the quiet revolution! This is where things happen. Good news, professor, join God's revolution! Is this the ending of civilization or the beginning of a new golden age with other worlds discovered? Whichever, God measures the meaning. Christ teaches us how to live changed lives in changing worlds. He beckons us into the future and sends history bouncing homeward down the years.

So, friends, live by the gospel with its call for love, forgiveness, reconciliation, and peace. Why should we still live as though dragged down into the net of sin? Don't fret as if this were the world's last night, as if one more violent revolution will stave it off. Don't place all your bets on the United Nations, the United States, or the Republican party of 1968. What really changes things is the quiet revolution, as we turn and find God's focus, as we join the eternal throng of those who love God wholly.

Good news, Dad. Good news, Mom. Good news, Sister; good news, Brother. Christ is risen. Trust him. Believe him. Live for him. Watch the quiet revolution. Did you see the grass grow yesterday? It made no headlines. One day in a hundred years a windstorm tears through our countryside and makes headlines. But every day, this one included, the ground pulsates with life. The stars continue in their orbits. The "sun of righteousness," our elder brother, with healing in his wings, gathers a family to himself. Look up! It's God's world. His sovereign will is at work, and in our freedom we may choose that way and unite with it. Look then to your high moments and not to the doubts that sometimes storm within and rage without. Trust Christ now, and through the wall of death into the eternal life beyond. Say "yes" to the risen Lord.

Saying Yes and No

Reedwood Friends Church, Portland, Oregon, November 1, 1970

On this first day of November we come to worship the Lord and to inquire after his will for our lives. On several occasions of legal proceedings, I have been tendered the oath and have requested instead the affirmation. Each time I have wondered about the tenacity of our Quaker forebears. They insisted this testimony made a difference. They paid dearly for their refusal to take the oath—often loss of property or jail sentences. Why did they take it so seriously, I wondered. Upon reflection I realized for them it was a time of civil war. The oath was used politically to coerce loyalty, first by the king and then by the Commonwealth. In this kind of muddle early Friends were able to hear Jesus' words, and to take them literally, "swear not at all."

James is a very practical New Testament writer. Honesty and prayer for him are interrelated. Receive his words to you, from chapter 5.

As I read this you may have recognized a number of common ventures of our lives in which prayer plays an important part. This talk could be entitled, "Saying Yes and No through Prayer," because in this section James prefaced what he says about prayer with a strong admonition to integrity in speech—in current parlance, to "tell it like it is." James talked about moods, about health, about sins, about general human concerns, and about those who fall.

Scripture reading
James 5:12-20 (NEB)

Above all things, my brothers, do not use oaths, whether by heaven or by earth or by anything else. When you say, yes or no let it be plain "Yes" or "No" for fear that you expose yourselves to judgment.

Is anyone among you in trouble? He should turn to prayer. Is anyone in good heart? He should sing praises. Is one of you ill? He should send for the elders of the congregation to pray over him and anoint him with oil in the name of the Lord. The prayer offered in faith will save the sick man, the Lord will raise him from his bed, and any sins he may have committed will be forgiven.

Therefore confess your sins to one another, and pray for one another, and then you will be healed. A good man's prayer is powerful and effective. Elijah was a man with human frailties like our own; and when he prayed earnestly that there should be no rain, not a drop fell on the land for three years and a half; then he prayed again and down came the rain and the land bore crops once more.

My brothers, if one of your numbers should stray from the truth and another succeed in bringing him back, be sure of this: any man who brings a sinner back from his crooked ways will be rescuing his soul from death and cancelling innumerable sins.

So let's share our own experiences. *First, about our moods.* Notice the contrast between the person who is troubled and the person who is happy—in "good heart." Think about it. Where do you fit in today? To be honest (which is what James insists upon) I must acknowledge being on the troubled side. It isn't necessary to explain the reasons. I expect some of you are troubled also. Others aren't, and that is good for us troubled ones to realize. One purpose of worship is for troubled persons to receive strength from those whose hearts are full of praise to God. So right now we will pause in silence so that those of us who are troubled may hear words of praise, and your happiness will not be a prideful thing, but a source of strength to us. Will two or three of you give us a word of praise? [audience participation]

Thank you! Now those of us who are troubled are often quieter than those whose hearts are bubbling with joy. But there may be some of you who would stand with me to acknowledge honestly your mood, and speak about it if you wish. Are there others besides me who are troubled? James insists: "Is anyone troubled? He should turn to prayer." So, we will turn to prayer. Will some of you pray for those of us who are troubled? [audience participation in prayer]

Thank you! We troubled ones face the sin of discouragement as you cheerful ones face the sin of pride.

Second, about our health. James also talks about health. Sometimes illness and discouragement are related, aren't they? Do some of you need to *say yes and no in respect to health?* To take the admonition of James to face things squarely may require that some of you ought to admit your problem and seek medical aid. There is a kind of bad faith that pretends things don't exist. We fear that acknowledging a condition will make it worse. The highest form of faith is to say yes to illness, or to sin, or to discouragement, or to combinations of these conditions. But faith also says yes to hope. Faith says yes to ourselves and to God, and no to discouragement and despondency. Otherwise we become fatalistic and say, "well that's the way it is." The Lord always wills to heal us, although we do not always understand the means. Even death finally heals although that is the last enemy and we fear it and bow to it only reluctantly. Finally God will say to us all: "Well, it is time for a new body, a new place, a new realm of reality." This too can be a healing, but for now we pray on behalf of the various ailments that take away the radiance of life as it should be. I ask you now to be honest about your health, bring your needs to God and receive his healing as I pray:

Heavenly Father, you know all about our needs. We pray now on behalf of all who are ill, whether present this morning, or absent, for those in our families and among our loved ones. Raise them up. Give knowledge and discernment that we may honor the bodies you have given us, that they may be kept by the power of the Holy Spirit. Let our bodies be your temple. May we use them wisely and well. Forgive us for having used them badly, or treated them ignorantly. Make the temple clean again, a good place for your Spirit to dwell. Amen.

To be honest before God in a spirit of prayer consists also in *saying yes and no in respect to sin.* This is the hardest kind of honesty. James writes: "Confess your sins to one another and pray for one another, then you will be healed." Maybe it is our sense of rugged individualism, that in America one's life is one's own business. Or a feeling that to confess sin is to confess weakness, and that at all costs we must give forth an image of strength. Frankly, I am tired of the effort at image building, aren't you? It is almost as if we have to hire a PR person to make us look good to others. I think that attitude carries over in respect to God. It is as though we could fool God. But we know we cannot. If we take simplicity of speech seriously we can and must face sin. *Sin* can be defined as the willful transgression of the known will of God, or more broadly as anything by which we commit an evil against God or a neighbor. Maybe the best way to identify sin is in the phrase from the Lord's prayer: "Forgive us our sins, as we forgive those who sin against us." How have others sinned against us? How have we forgiven them? Reflect upon the past week. Test your self in respect to God's standard, and ask his forgiveness in a time of silent prayer. [pause]

Some of you may have been uncharitable, unkind, have held grudges against others. How about asking God to forgive the attitudes as well as the actions? Ask God to point out the unclean way and lead you in the way everlasting.

Heavenly Father, we pray for your forgiveness for the sins we have committed, the sins against others, the sins against you. Where there has been jealousy, forgive. Forgive the violence we have done others whether by physical strength or through our words and influence. Forgive us, we pray, for the dark thoughts we have had, for our lack of love for others and for you; for the inordinate satisfactions we take in our material wealth. Help us accept your forgiveness as we forgive others. Help us hear Jesus' words "go and sin no more." In Jesus name, amen.

Finally, consider James's teachings *about our concerns*. Elijah was an amazing person, yet with human frailties like our own. I feel intimidated by his kind of faith that could change the weather! No rain for three-and-a-half years and then rain when he prayed. Amazing! A real prophet of God. And yet we are exhorted to identify with him. How? Perhaps in his passion for truth. What was he concerned about? The idolatry that swept the land, Baal worship fostered by Jezebel and condoned by Ahab. Can you see the parallels? Paganism hasn't disappeared. This morning's *Northwest Magazine* features an article about witches and witchcraft. I can remember when we thought that sort of thing was all back in the remote past when our colonial ancestors were ignorant and naive. Maybe these people weren't any more pagan than we are. Admit it, this is a pagan society in many ways and America is a pretty pagan nation. It is hard for us now to accept God's judgments upon a people, like it was in the Old Testament times. But maybe we should say that our drought is Vietnam, that God is judging our nation for our sins. Our country needs to be healed of its wickedness. The church, also. The Society of Friends has been fragmented, partly, I think, as a judgment of God for our unfaithfulness, our apostasy, our unbelief, our carelessness and indifference. God judges every church. My concerns today are that our church may be healed and that through judgment that begins at the house of the Lord our society may also be brought back from its wickedness.

James brings accountability right to us. He writes: "My brothers, if one of your number should stray from the truth and another succeed in bringing him back, be sure of this: any man who brings a sinner back from his crooked ways will be rescuing a soul from death and cancelling innumerable sins."

So, I suggest we concern ourselves with those who fall. And look upon their fall as an opportunity to be priests on behalf of the fallen. On this day we think about the Protestant Reformation. At the heart of that Reformation is the conviction every one may be priest to his neighbor in love. You may be the means of grace on behalf of another. So let us pray for the fallen, for apostasy in the church, for paganism in our nation and ask for divine restoration.

Heavenly Father, we think now of those who have fallen in sin. We think about those dear to us, well known to us. We pray for those in the fellowship of this church. We ask that as we think about them you will prepare our hearts to be instruments of their renewal. Give us faith. Thank you for teaching us about honesty from the book of James. Give us greater power in prayer because of the forthright character of our faith. We ask for some measure of the power of Elijah in our own day of idolatry. In Jesus name, amen.

Situation Grace

Reedwood Friends Church, May 19, 1974

This is a time to ask questions about morality. Old standards are shaken and the revolution won't go away. In the text I infer that Christians are expected to do good deeds that have the characteristics of light and salt—to illumine and make palatable. In America, at least, it appears that the influence of Christianity from without as light and from within as salt is not as apparent or working as well as it once did, at least in accustomed forms. The parable Jesus told about yeast that makes the whole lump of dough rise, is also pertinent. It teaches of the permeation of society that Christianity can or should provide. It is easy today to be gloomy and figure that the salt has lost its savor, that the yeast isn't working, and that the lights are burned out. That's not altogether true, is it? In coming together in worship we recognize that it is not true, and yet we are humbled by how token some of our deeds have become and how sanctimonious some of our praise to God appears to many people. Jesus said

Scripture reading
Matthew 5:13-16 (NIV)
You are the salt of the earth. But if the salt loses its saltiness, how can it be made salty again? It is no longer good for anything except to be thrown out and trampled by men.

You are the light of the world. A city on a hill cannot be hidden.

Neither do people light a lamp and put it under a bowl. Instead they put it on its stand, and it gives light to everyone in the house. In the same way, let your light shine before men, that they may see your good deeds and praise your Father in heaven.

---

our righteousness must exceed that of the scribes and Pharisees. Furthermore, Jesus said he didn't come to abolish the law, but to fulfill it. In our low mood Jesus comes off sounding harsher than Moses or Paul. For example, Jesus said it isn't enough not to murder; whoever is angry with his brother is liable for judgment. It is not enough merely to avoid slander; whoever denounces his brother as a fool hazards hell fire. Avoidance of adultery doesn't make one righteous, even a look of lust condemns. It isn't enough just to honor formal oaths; we are to be so truthful that oaths aren't needed. To assume liability for damages, eye-for-an-eye, isn't enough;

Jesus tells us to exceed legality by going the second mile. Even religious activity wilts before his gaze. It is not enough to give to the poor. Do it without getting ego badges. As for prayer and fasting, do it, but don't count on religious merit—no social recognition to pay us back for being religious. Good deeds are to give God praise and not to provide social advancement among our peers. So Jesus puts it on a high shelf. Or so it seems if we forget Golgotha, for Jesus did practice what he preached. That is important, for his death and resurrection lays upon us both the burden of discipleship and a promise of victory, a promise that Pentecost appropriates. And so I confess to you that sometimes I feel like Mary in *Jesus Christ Superstar*, "Jesus scares me so, yet I love him so."

How have Christians responded to Jesus' high moral code?

(1) One response has been to *accept the teachings but postpone them*. Proponents of this view reason that the ethic is obviously too hard (*impractical* is often the word) in a sinful world, but when Jesus returns this will be the way to do it. In the meantime read Hal Lindsay's latest books, speculate on whether Kissinger is the anti-Christ, and get ready for the rapture. Such dispensationalist views distort sober biblical expectations about the future life. Ethically they're a cop-out. Jesus did not say let your light so shine that men may see your predictions about the anti-Christ and glorify God. He talked about good deeds. I hope you will resist succumbing to prophecy-addiction. Do rather what Jesus said: occupy until he comes.

(2) The second response is to *suppose that Jesus bargained for more—expecting to settle for considerably less by way of acceptable conduct*. There is some basis for this view. After all, God is merciful and Jesus often spoke in paradoxes that are difficult to translate into actual moral conduct. Whenever one takes time, however, to decipher paradoxes—like "whosoever loses his life shall save it"—if anything, the moral force comes through all the more strongly. If Jesus were given to exaggeration on morality he might also be given to exaggeration about forgiveness or about heaven or about other important doctrines. "You must be born again" is as figurative as "going the second mile." So I suggest we take Jesus seriously on all points. As Mark pointed out, Jesus spoke with authority and not as the scribes who played word games with religion, making it a hobby rather than a life.

(3) A third approach is to *emphasize attitudes and not actions*. To teach the people to have clean hearts at least, if not clean hands. Well, this has some plausibility. Out of the hearts are the issues of life, said Jesus. Paul proclaimed eloquently that if we gave our bodies to be burned but didn't have love, it was nothing. The very passages in the Sermon on the Mount that I just summarized transcend actions and reach to attitudes—not to hate, for example. In practice we acknowledge that intention makes a difference. Manslaughter is much less punishable than first degree murder, and so on. Jesus didn't think intentions substituted for good deeds, however. That's what is meant by the law not being dispensed with but rather fulfilled in particular actions. My friend Richard Taylor—a Nazarene theologian—is wrong to imply, however, that motives can make actions right. For example, he insists that soldiers can kill the enemy with perfect love in their hearts and on proper occasions (that is, just wars) ought to do so. This is an attempt to preserve holiness as a set of right attitudes even if it polarizes morality between public and private situations. The Jesuits tested this theory over the centuries, and from their experiences I think we can say it is found wanting. They became such studied manipulators that certain countries banned them lest they steal away the minds of the young! Jesuits became adept at circumlocution, which consists of telling it like it isn't. So much so that *jesuitical* and *casuistry* found their way into the dictionary as common words. How interesting, then, that a Jesuit

advisor defends vulgarity and profanity as good ways to keep the presidential cool—to relieve tension. I wonder if he might not also advise marijuana, or Roman circuses like Nero used. The term *mental reservation* was a Jesuit way of breaking a command of God while keeping your fingers crossed. It was reasoned that God needs some hatchet men in this corrupt world; therefore a group of dedicated people who wouldn't consider their own advantages could serve the church under obedience to the Pope and thus help God set up kingdoms and take them down.

Well, it isn't hard to draw parallels, is it? Draw some in your own lives, and ask if you don't sometimes think God needs some deceit and violence to protect his and your interests. Jesus really did put it on a high shelf, didn't he?

(4) Let's look at another approach: *dividing private from public goodness.* For several centuries now the church has done this. It began when Constantine made Christianity legal and other religions illegal. It became easy to think of Christendom instead of Christ, to consider that Christians had a mandate to rule the earth, forgetting how Jesus contrasted servanthood with pagan domination. With morality neatly divided, the Old Testament became a guide for public morality with emphasis upon refining the eye-for-eye principle of justice; and the New Testament became a rule for personal ethics, with a portion of it postponed, of course. Romans 13 was appealed to as carte blanche for governments to do as they pleased. Submission to government was distorted into idolatry as if government made divine law. In some ways this worked better when empire and church were united than when nation-states developed. At least in the Middle Ages it was easier to liken the whole empire to Israel than to try to figure out why one nation was an elect nation and others weren't. At least in the age of chivalry people stopped fighting at sundown and rested on the Sabbath; and they hadn't developed "overkill"!

At a historic conference in 1550 the Spanish Catholic Church decided—dredging up Aristotle's theory of society—that Indians were natural slaves and could be coerced before converted, and, if recalcitrant, slaughtered. The best of the American missionaries, like Bartolome de los Casas, implored the church not to listen to such reasoning. But the greed of the *conquistadores* won out and thus an Inca chief preached the Word before he was killed and his kingdom plundered. Lest you think Catholics were the only Christians involved, consider our American forefathers who hanged Quakers, shot Native Americans, and defended slavery. Consider also all who argue that military intervention in Southeast Asia was necessary to protect the church or to enable it to evangelize. It's the same thing—coercion the precondition of evangelism—and death to the infidel. But our country has had the leaven of the gospel; and so we have not rested easy in conscience thus to divide the ethic between private and public morality. We don't really want to destroy the unregenerate. The problem is, we have wanted to claim this only for people of our land, and now God asks whether we're willing to look across the world and extend this gospel principle worldwide. William Penn said that whoever would not be ruled by God would be ruled by tyrants. In our day the tyrants are paper tyrants. It's hard for us to determine and be responsible for our corporate selves, our public selves.

If Christ fulfills all covenants, then there are really not two ethics but one, however difficult and costly it may be. It makes us squirm (as it did Peter when Jesus asked him, "Do you love me more than these?") when we begin to apply one ethic to all peoples around the world. God has forced us American Christians to the wall. By landslide victory, America elects Richard Nixon, a public pragmatist and by heritage a private Quaker Christian. Now he may soon resign or be removed from office in a scandal that rocks the nation. See the tragedy of it! Many of us, including Christians, wanted it this way. Now that God has shown us the consequences of a double ethic we cannot bear it. Weep with the modern day Hannah, Hanna Nixon, over her sons—Edward, sick; Don Jr., dealing with Vesco the king-maker; and Richard, scion of the Whittier pioneer stock—all of them spiritual descendants of Fox, Woolman. Can this be the product of Scripture Light Press and Quaker Sunday schools? Weep and pray, for we are caught up in the same judgment. May God have mercy on us all, and restore to us the power to illumine, to salt, to leaven, to free us from a split ethic.

(5) A fifth option is to *ignore the Sermon on the Mount and focus on winning people to Christ*, spiritualizing the difficult portions of the Scripture, using all the helps put out by Christian commercial enterprises that avoid offending anybody. Keep the Sunday school children crossing the Dead Sea innumerable times so they won't ask what it means to live in the holy center of God's will now. It won't work. Cynicism erodes; science takes over explanations, first of the outside world and then of the mind. Youth play the religious games but soon find more exciting entertainment. Artificial standards lead to revolt.

(6) A sixth option is to *accept sinfulness within Christianity, that is, to suggest that salvation is a way of keeping us saved in the midst of sinning*. Quakers and Methodists and others within Holiness traditions abhor this kind of treatment of the gospel and rightly dub it cheap grace.

(7) *Situation ethics* is another option, an attempt to face the law from the standpoint of love. A few years ago Fletcher popularized this view in a book by that title. He sought to avoid rules—legalism on the one hand and antinomianism on the other hand; everyone is his own judge. His view of love seemed too permissive to people, and though he talked about *agape* or self-giving love, people inferred license to do what they pleased, in the name of love. Well, Fletcher left love loosely defined and weakened the authority of God by considering the commandments as general statements lacking veto power. Nevertheless, the questioning brought about by situation ethics has made us ask ourselves about principles of morality and especially again about love as its base. Too many people, unfortunately, feared only that situational ethics would give sexual license to the young. They weren't concerned about whether it would make middle-aged people greedier. This phenomenon may say something about our times. Situation ethics *has* turned the spotlight upon all of

these other views. In its own way each is situational. Why does turning something public change its morality? Is it right to band together to kill, but not to band together to steal? Or to covet? Or to commit adultery? In its searchlight the super-puritan views have been seen as too punctilious, like weighing out the tithes of garden herbs and neglecting racial justice. The old badges of holiness that once marked our communities are gone—black-suited men, women with no jewelry and with hair tied back in buns. Unfortunately, reaction has set in. Some who were youth in our churches during the transitional fifties and sixties now feel pride in being able to smoke a pipe or drink champagne or go to X-rated movies. It's a search for equilibrium again. Let's pray to God for something more than reactions.

(8) That leads me to the final position: *situation grace.* Situation grace acknowledges that there are hard circumstances that face us and that we are limited, finite, and fallible. It also acknowledges the law of God as sovereign. Fletcher apparently weakened the law in deference to existential human choice. Bonhoeffer says it would be better to act out of love on behalf of a neighbor even if you incur guilt before God than not to act at all. Perhaps there is tragic moral choice, not theoretically speaking, but where we live. And so I would rather agonize with guilt because I don't know how to love successfully without sinning or to love one neighbor without hating another, than to wash my hands of responsibility or narrow morality to minutia. I have more sympathy for the person who kills in a situation of fear than one who divides the killing into approved public slaughter and private pacifism. Everyone has a breaking point. We live within limits. Thus, grace. We do not have to accept God as some inexorable force, but as a Father who gives us new starting places; over and over and over again, if necessary. The discovery of Jesus' way is like finding the world's most valuable pearl, like finding treasures hid in a field, like a full day's pay for an hour's work. This is righteousness beyond that of the Pharisees. Our salvation doesn't depend upon some foolproof system.

Jesus' statements in the Sermon on the Mount are not intended to put morality out of reach, but rather to teach the ways of love. Indeed, all have sinned and come short of the glory of God. All. The object lesson is Jesus' treatment of the woman caught in adultery. Jesus was more concerned to destroy self-righteousness than to destroy persons. The Sermon on the Mount is not designed to make us super-puritans who develop increasing scruples on this and that, but rather to accept the meaning of grace and the awesome respect for a holy God.

After all, salvation is from the Lord. Sanctification is the work of the Holy Spirit and not our own achievement.

Therefore, my stand on morality is this. First, I accept the law as greater than all codes. I honor the Decalogue as establishing boundaries of morality and all the other biblical statements as ways by which I should love my neighbor as myself. I recognize that God's will is greater than rules. He is, after all, the heavenly Father, and not some traffic cop hidden in the willows. If through ignorance or will, I fall short of what God wants, I know that I have an advocate with the Father, even Jesus Christ, the Righteous. He is my elder brother.

Second, I accept love as the best word. This is the way to hold God's ethical choices together. I would rather fail in love than to accept hate or violence or greed. I will do all I can to apply love within the structures of society, family, commerce, and nations. I will try to simplify my life in order corporately not to violate other people.

Third, I will acknowledge grace. After all, I have limits of knowledge and limits of power. I will therefore be more compassionate upon those whose power and knowledge is less than mine, or whose circumstances differ. I will seek to follow those who are exemplary and be less censorious of those who are not. I will not confuse grace with relativism. God's way is good. He gives good gifts. As a giver and as a receiver I would be like Christ. I'll try to translate that compassion publicly. I would set the prisoners free. Why shouldn't amnesty be granted to all persons who don't actually endanger their fellow men? Consider politics from the standpoint of the family, the community, the region, and the whole world, demonstrated as acts of love and kindness. This leads to the elevation of persons, not their lowering.

Fourth, I will accept discipleship in God's kingdom now with all the risks and dangers involved, not calculating consequences by man's wisdom, but joyously sharing in life-shedding light and sprinkling salt wherever I can. I invite you to join me in the jubilee of God. Let the Light shine. Don't so calculate probabilities that you effectively postpone the kingdom. Love, serve, offer hope in hard times. Let your family be a place of joy and of happiness, a place of forgiveness, of restoration. Let your church extend that family. Maybe we can't do much as an empire, but God doesn't need empires. Let them crumble away. Maybe the empire of America will be redeemed, maybe it won't. Maybe America will become poor in this world's goods, maybe it won't. But Portland needs you. Portland needs your light. The kingdom is here; live in it. Accept situation grace.

Jesus and the Burdens of Work

Reedwood Friends Church, September 2, 1984

Today we apply Jesus' teachings about the burdens of work to those in the labor force. Last Sunday's message spoke to those who labor through study. We speak now to those who get paid for work instead of paying for it. Reflect upon the Scripture reading. How interesting that Jesus' first disciples were commercial fishermen. Oregonians can relate to that—we know the uncertainty of the catch and whether the season will or will not be profitable.

The scene is Lake Galilee and Jesus has already made himself known to the people. The call to these first followers comes from an ordinary workplace. Here are people who understand nets. They had been out all night with their nets and caught nothing. When they came in there was Jesus preaching from a borrowed boat. He looked at the tired workers and told them to try it again. It was his word that sent them back, but he sent them back on their boats and it was their nets that filled to capacity.

Scripture reading
Matthew 11:28-30 (NIV)
Come to me, all you who are weary and burdened, and I will give you rest. Take my yoke upon you and learn from me, for I am gentle and humble in heart, and you will find rest for your souls. For my yoke is easy and my burden is light. (See also Luke 5:1-11.)

Whether the miracle consisted of bringing in a school of fish or inspiring confidence to try again we will never know. Maybe something of both. In any case the incident caused these commercial fishermen to follow the One who said henceforth they would net people, not fish. At first glance this incident might inspire those who assume that if work gets hard one could go to preaching. Although Jesus did take these particular fishermen out of their occupation I don't think that is the main point. The main point is about nets.

The word *net* aptly describes how we connect with each other. A net simply is a reasonable way to organize space and time so some things are retained and others excluded. There are all kinds of nets. It is an *in* word, really. Long distance telephone calls go via "Save Net." Hours of radio time are preempted by a few mouths and many ears. "Talk-net" offers financial, psychological, and medical advice. And then there are the "networks"—those media channels that glean the oceans of facts for what become newsworthy events.

This is Labor Day and we are reminded that the labor force is a network, a net that works. Sometimes the selective character of media networks is lost on us, and we forget the human bonding called work and the grid of relationships it supports. Oh, there are many other kinds of nets too: food nets, clothes nets, hair nets, music nets, power nets, political nets, trade nets, sports nets, religious nets. One can become a net nut in all kinds of ways.

We are so caught up in nets we do not know whether we are the fishers or the fished, netters or netted. After getting on 35 new mailing lists in a year one wonders. We feel like the psalmist who lamented: "They spread their net for me." So we identify with frustrated laborers and their nets—they were caught in the snares of Rome, in its political and economic web. We know the burdens of work and the anxieties produced if our labors are economically insufficient. Whether it is pumping gasoline or waiting tables or filling out slips of paper—whatever—our labor does connect us with others.

Consider the burdens of work.

For the words of the text assure us that Jesus understands our burdens. What are they? Well, the first burden is *physical weariness*. "They toiled all night" says the text about these fishermen. Who doesn't understand toil?

The second burden is *regimentation*. The kids in school aren't the only ones under orders, not the only ones to be evaluated, not the only ones to face "put downs" by those over them. After years of labor it can become a burden to have to show up weary-eyed on Monday morning at eight o'clock.

A third burden is *drudgery*. I have been thinking a lot about it (having mentioned it in connection with school work). Some things are just boring, whether in school or on a job. Let me offer you a tip for handling drudgery. Think of it this way: Your performance requires so little attention your mind can be busy elsewhere. Your work gets done with little effort and full remuneration. So you get paid for daydreaming. Think what you can do with all your spare brain power. You can fantasize constructively. You can pray for people whom the Spirit brings to mind, you can make plans for family projects. What a wonderful opportunity to use your mind. Try it! It beats going through the day like a zombie, half asleep. And it's less frustrating.

A fourth burden of work is *ethical accountability*. This is somewhat more serious. When is action an accommodation to reality and when is compromise? Each one of you faces ethical issues on your job. Sometimes it involves moral problems within the workplace itself. Did I remember to pay for the stamps I used for the personal letters? Am I robbing the company or only reimbursing myself for money or time spent beyond the call of duty? Am I paying my employees what they really deserve or what I can get by with? These are the internal moral problems. But there are also moral problems dealing with the work enterprise itself. Is what I am doing—the network of which I am a part—helpful to human life, or is it predatory? Is my whole company stealing? Exploiting? Cheating?

A September 1984 issue of *Wilderness* magazine described how vast areas of jungle are being cleared for pastureland so we may have more hamburgers at the local fast-food restaurant. A Panamanian farmer, interviewed, said, "Yes, I think about the jungle. I think about the animals that die when I burn the jungle and how they're destroyed, and I regret it. But I look at my children and then I look back at the forest and I ask, 'Who do I choose?' You Americans who buy the beef, you should be asking some questions yourself." He puts the question poignantly. Through our net of work we find it hard to avoid complicity in evil.

There is a fifth burden of work: *stress.* We all face it. The community of faith at worship provides for many of us the occasion for getting release from its bondage. To keep stress constructive instead of destructive is difficult at best, without worship hardly tolerable.

A sixth burden of work is *alienation*—being distanced from the consequences, rewards, and significance of our labor. This is Karl Marx's most telling indictment of industrial capitalism. Oh, it is more than just having to overcome sweatshops and other exploitive utilization of human labor. Specialization itself alienates us from the whole purpose of an enterprise. We are just doing our jobs, not creating anything, because the enterprise is too vast and too impersonal for us to feel like a craftsman.

The seventh burden of work is *marginalization.* Many people in the world have to say to themselves, if not to others, "Nobody wants my skills." Marginalization occurs most devastatingly in third-world countries as the poor and unskilled leave the villages and flock to the cities where they live in shanties at the edge of the urban world. In Latin America these shacks are called *favellos.* Five thousand people a day, no longer useful under agribusiness, flock to Manila and find nothing to do but to search the dumps for food or saleable goods.

Jesus understands these burdens. He worked as a carpenter and drew commercial fishermen to himself. It is easy for the church to become a haven for those who have made it in the economic world and to be impatient with those who have been marginalized— even those who in old age "catch nothing."

Consider how Jesus offers rest to the overburdened.

Last Sunday I spoke about the yoke of the Law and how this term was used by the rabbis to describe the precepts of Moses. Well, the yoke had become a galling instrument to many people. Jesus often lashed out at those who inflicted moral demands on others but never lent a helping hand. Looking the Pharisees steadily in the eye Jesus said the Sabbath was made for man and not man for the Sabbath. He deliberately broke some of the heavy-handed rules about Sabbath keeping.

For those in the workforce the galling, ill-fitting yoke is economic necessity. "They toiled all night and caught nothing" can be said today of millions of people whose labor barely supplies their needs. This is the case whether the economic network is capitalism or socialism. Those who work with hand and wit are everywhere overburdened. To them, to us, on this Labor Day, Jesus offers us rest. We celebrate Labor Day by not working. That is appropriate. It reminds us of what is owed. That labor earns rest, not just physical respite from work, but adequate reward. Every labor trek across the desert deserves its Canaan. The promised land is justice. What the gospel offers to those who labor is liberation from whatever of sin oppresses, whether that be inward or outward bondage. Let the church, therefore, be in the forefront of every effort for justice for all who work, and especially for those who bear the most of its burdens.

At this point I must acknowledge that the powerful and the wealthy work, also, and not just the powerless and the poor. The wealthy have their own burdens—to sustain what they have received, as either their due or their destiny. The rest Jesus offers the rich is *simplicity*. To learn from the flowers and the birds that God cares. To not be hung up on privilege and money.

The rest Jesus offers all who are alienated from their labor, whether by inadequate compensation or stressful complexity is *community*. How fascinating that the same root word appears in the following three terms: *koinonia*, *communism*, and *community*. The very word by which Christians describe their most intimate fellowship contains the root used by terms expressive of the search for a network in which people are linked with each other and linked with God. To belong to each other credibly, responsibly, and accountably is what humankind seeks. The old philosopher Aristotle said that community is basic to economic equality. But he couldn't quite come up with the bond for community. And Marx, who studied Aristotle, thought this was a weakness in the old philosopher that he must correct. So he made economics the basis of equality. The collective hardly achieved community, but it is not difficult to imagine that the coffee picker in Latin America might think it worth a try.

The task of the Christian is to leaven the workplace with diligence, and also with compassion. It is to leaven the political network with integrity and Christian conviction about values and their priorities. Jesus offers us his peace when we struggle for justice and self-fulfillment through prayer and not through power plays. This leaven occurs both in personal work and in our corporate responsibility. Labor Day is a tribute to the efforts to find community on the part of all who work. It is a tribute to those who have stood up for justice, for the dignity of the laborer and against all oppressors, even when the oppressors have the upper hand and write the laws and the history books.

Consider how Jesus works with us.

Each of the presently competing world systems is part of the yoke of economic necessity under which people live and work. It can be a heavy yoke, for we are bound up into networks that demand our time and energy, and sometimes we come up empty, if not for others, at least for ourselves. Both of these systems—capitalism and socialism—flounder because they are human-centered and inadequate to the subtleties of human nature, both its capacity for evil and its capacity for good. Marxism rightly understands that the worker should not be alienated from his labor, and that labor should be basic to value. But the Marxists generally fail to understand that there is no inexorable economic law (dialectical materialism). They fail to understand it is not inevitable, not like gravity. They fail to understand that a socialist system does not prevent or justify greed or exploitation. They fail to understand that capital held by officials, even in the name of workers, guarantees neither efficiency of effort nor fairness of distribution.

Capitalism rightly understands that the stewardship of the earth requires freedom sufficient for human creativity. But capitalists generally fail to understand that there is no inexorable economic law (supply and demand). They fail to understand it is not inevitable, not like gravity. They fail to understand that a capitalist system does not prevent or justify greed or exploitation, that capital held by private individuals and their surrogates (corporations)—even if in trusteeship for the workers—neither guarantees efficiency of effort nor fairness of distribution.

Both systems constitute a "work net." Let both bow the knee to Jesus. They now bow the knee to Baal. Workers of the world are overburdened by systems that have become deified. In both systems are Christians who take their faith into the workplace. Let's pray they will be leaven. What Jesus means concerning labor is learned allusively—like in a parable. Reflect with me about the second incident involving fish. It is found in John 21, where the disciples decided to return to normalcy—resume fishing—now that the Jesus event was over, as they thought. Jesus showed himself to them in the morning light. Again, they had caught nothing, and when Jesus called out from the shore, "Have you caught anything, friends?" they answered, "No." To this he replied, "Throw the net to starboard and you'll catch something." The second miracle of the great catch followed. And Simon Peter jumped overboard in his haste to get to shore as the others came dragging the catch of fish behind them.

On the shore they saw that Jesus had already prepared breakfast, with bread, and fish frying. "Come have breakfast," Jesus said, and no one had to ask who the host was for they knew it was the Lord.

Fascinating! At the beginning Jesus called his disciples out of the workplace in a scene of frustrated labor. And now, after the resurrection, he calls them again. This is significant. And here are the signs I find: First, *Jesus' resurrection appearance is reinforced in the workplace.* Remember, says Jesus, I lifted your burdens before; I will lift them again. I will always be with you. Second, *Jesus' resurrection supports us in finding creative solutions.* Having heard Jesus, having seen the cross and witnessed the resurrection, must we go back to an evil world with its grinding burdens? The world stands on the brink of nuclear war. Let the workers of the world rise up and take their cues from Jesus. Then the nets will be full. Apply this personally. If you are in a slump, a midlife crisis, or just feeling blah, hear Jesus call you to cast the nets on the other side. Jesus promised to give us his Spirit, who is the spirit of truth, of creativity. Give him power in your mind, and on your job, and in your company.

Finally, this incident teaches *the sacrament of Christ's presence in an ordinary breakfast for working people.* Why try to artifice the spiritual? The workplace is where people best experience the sacrament of Christ's presence, not in some liturgical abstraction. This is communion at its finest, and, I think, as Jesus intended it.

Fire on the Beach

Fire on the beach,
a charcoal fire
with crisp fish broiling
on the coals,
and broken bread,
for toiling souls
who hear their risen Lord
call "shoot the net
to starboard!"

Fire on the beach,
God's fire;
Christ serves the fish,
Christ breaks the bread,
His gracious bounty
after days of dread
and empty nights
to celebrate.

Fire on the beach
one gray morning…
"It is the Lord!"
whose altar coals
now purify the love
of toiling souls
who hear anew
His call to fish
for men.

(from *Sunrise and Shadow*, Barclay Press, 1985)

Hope

Reedwood Friends Church, November 4, 1984

"Hope springs eternal" is an old saying, based upon the common perception that life can and will be better than it is at the present moment of reflection. Or at least not diminished, not "hopeless." We have all experienced the fading of hope, to be replaced by despair, cynicism, or fatalistic resignation. "Win a few, lose a few" is a response by one for whom expectations are realized about half the time. Why is hope such an important aspect of life? Because we are of limited understanding and power, because time goes forward irreversibly, because we can compute probabilities imperfectly, and because our wills, and the wills of others, are subject to change (they are fickle, even).

And so I ask you to do a quick inventory of your specific hopes. Don't dress them up, or rank them—just list them in your mind for now, so that the Scripture text can have some practical application for you. For the text suggests that salvation is not just a Christian

Scripture reading
Romans 8:18-27 (NIV)
Our text is verse 25 "If we hope for what we do not yet have, we wait for it patiently."

I consider that our present sufferings are not worth comparing with the glory that will be revealed in us. The creation waits in eager expectation for the sons of God to be revealed. For the creation was subjected to frustration, not by its own choice, but by the will of the one who subjected it, in hope that the creation itself will be liberated from its bondage to decay and brought into the glorious freedom of the children of God.

We know that the whole creation has been groaning as in the pains of childbirth right up to the present time. Not only so, but we ourselves, who have the firstfruits of the Spirit, groan inwardly as we wait eagerly for our adoption as sons, the redemption of our bodies. For in this hope we were saved. But hope that is seen is no hope at all. Who hopes for what he already has? But if we hope for what we do not yet have, we wait for it patiently.

In the same way, the Spirit helps us in our weakness. We do not know what we ought to pray for, but the Spirit himself intercedes for us with groans that words cannot express. And he who searches our hearts knows the mind of the Spirit, because the Spirit intercedes for the saints in accordance with God's will.

---

beginning through forgiveness of sins, nor a final resurrection, but also a process. Salvation is our response to a bent world, a response of hope. A response so important Paul lists hope along with faith and love as the cardinal Christian virtues. The principles drawn from these words of the apostle Paul seem to me as follows:

The whole of creation is in a condition of expectancy.

"It groans," said Paul. The figure is that of a pregnancy coming to term. Human redemption is a sign to creation that its labor will be rewarded. The sufferings of the creation can be summarized briefly as *ecological abuse* (desertification, acid rain, erosion of soil, pollution of air and water). Greed and ignorance put the earth in bondage, resulting in streams of refugees both psychological and geographical fleeing from drought or violence. The "wasteland" as Eliot rightly noted, is neither the desert nor the jungle, but rather the bondage to decay produced by sin. It is a social wasteland. Earth, said C.S. Lewis, is the "silent planet." Over this incredibly beautiful globe, with its awesome capacity for sustaining us if rightly treated, gallop from horizon to horizon the four horses of the apocalypse: conquest, war, scarcity, and death. The rest of the cosmos is waiting. It is groaning for humanity to find its new Adam—Jesus Christ, who can lead it and us back through the flaming sword, into a renewed paradise of God.

Our own hopes are part of that expectation for renewal.

We groan also, we people of God who have the firstfruits of the Spirit. For we have envisioned what will be. We have seen the peaceable kingdom. We know the redemptive power of divine love. Jesus has looked down at us from the cross and we trust those eyes. For us the gap between what could be and what is looms large.

Therefore we await the redemption of our bodies. We want to experience in our bodies, whether now or after death, the universe as God wants it to be, as it can be, as it *will* be. We want things to turn out right. We want the arrow of time to carry us with it, not speed it away from us. We long for what Paul calls "the redemption of our bodies." (*The Jerusalem Bible* renders it, "to have our bodies set free.")

There is a tendency toward cynicism among the young: The world will probably get worse—wars are inevitable, therefore we must get what is coming to us and not raise our expectations too high. We must settle for "hard" solutions, such as separating public from personal morality. Some youth have a religious hope of heaven and a secular hope for earth. Or so it seems to me. This may explain the extreme militancy of young Christians, many of whom apply *Christian hope* only to a very narrow circle of personal meaning.

This scriptural passage indicates, however, that it is *through* our own hopes, based upon what Jesus Christ has done and is doing in the world, that the whole creation will be released from its bondage. We are joint heirs with Jesus Christ. If we do not have this kind of hope in his name, then the world continues to groan in travail, in exhausting labor. If we have hope then we speed the day when the whole cosmos is given new birth. God deals with us contingently. He has no binding flight schedule. The plane awaits the passengers. God works through our hopes not in spite—or independently—of them.

Such hope is difficult to sustain, but we do so with the help of the Spirit.

"The Spirit intercedes for us with groans that words cannot express." It is hard for us to make specific the character of the world renewal our faith teaches; the odds are so overwhelming and the variables so numerous. So we ask the Spirit to accept our yearnings for the life that could be, and to sustain our hopes for it.

This is more than a general yearning for the peaceable kingdom in some dim future. We yearn to contribute our own small steps toward that kingdom. We are confronted by confused political systems, by a threat of nuclear annihilation, violent aggression in society, breakdown of families, personal failures, and diminishments of health, aging, and loss of loved ones.

We recognize a need for divine help. Without the Spirit we sink slowly into cynicism, despair, predatory use of others, or into fatalistic submission—to be tossed like driftwood upon the churning waves of time.

The promised Holy Spirit helps us in our hopes. "The whole creation has been groaning in the pains of childbirth right up to the present time." Do you see it? A universe is in the process of birth and we are a part of it. Our lives enter into its shaping. We are actors on a cosmic stage, spotlighted by heavenly light and accompanied by music from the stars. We human beings, created in the image of God and renewed by the mind of Christ, constitute a mighty cast in a great drama! Our roles contribute to the whole. Our lines are important. The one who notices even the fallen sparrow surely listens to our hopes. Consider then some of the things hoped for, your lines in the script. Here are some categories. Do they include your hopes?

1) Political hopes
- That there won't be nuclear war.
- That justice will prevail in our country.
- That justice will prevail among nations.
- That resources and human need might be fairly matched.
- That Russia and the United States will work together.
- That Russia will quit its aggression.
- That the United States will quit its aggression.
- That justice and peace will come to Central America, Poland, Afghanistan, Lebanon, Haiti, India, Ireland, etc.
- That tyranny will be reduced. And terrorism.
- That our city officials will be honest.
- That Oregon's economy will improve.
- That our schools will do a better job.
- That large nations won't make pawns of smaller ones.
- That our taxes will go for important things.
- That the gospel of Jesus Christ might leaven the nations.

Does all this seem impossible? Consider the hopes of Isaiah, as recorded in chapter 19. With the country facing probable invasion by Assyria, this prophet expressed his hope that one day there would be a road between Egypt and Assyria, each having access to the other, each worshiping Yahweh, with Israel in the center. The Lord will give this promise, said Isaiah, "Blessed be my people Egypt, Assyria my creation, and Israel my heritage." Don't be discouraged because the Camp David Accords failed. See it as a significant step. Renew your hopes. Envision the people of God, not secular Zionism, standing between the great powers on the left and the right. Thank God Billy Graham knows that God loves the Russians and that our Russian brothers and sisters love God and share similar hopes with us and all peoples.

What are your political hopes based upon? Pragmatic calculations, national or state interests, expectations of personal gain? Or upon a righteousness God has promised will flow down as the waters cover the sea? Upon a promise that the nations of the world will be gathered to Christ?

For too long Christians have been living like the Holy Spirit hadn't been given, like Christianity made no real difference. Once people had hopes for the United Nations, now Christians are in the forefront of those clamoring to abandon it. Maybe it lacks the leaven of the gospel. George Fox and John Wesley would be ashamed of us! I suggest we look again at Jesus. Consider what the resurrection is all about. Jesus' way works. It does triumph over evil. The blood of the Lamb and the word of our testimony—this is how we overcome.

2) Philosophical hopes.
- That science will be an ally, not an enemy of faith.
- That technology will be my servant not my master.
- That I can handle bad luck and personal misfortune.
- That psychology doesn't make our faith out of date.
- That Jesus' ways make sense now in our complex world.
- That I am not just programmed by my environment.
- That humankind in space is in divine ordering.

If we see the big picture, the whole universe awaiting our redemption, then we can handle change. We grasp a reality unfolded by change. "There is no eternal city for us in this life," said the writer to the Hebrews, "but we look for one in the life to come" (see 13:14). Principalities and powers bow the knee to Jesus. Psychology and technology are only tools, means. Love working within us is greater than these tools—it will use them for good. Are you as interested in the cosmos as Carl Sagan? Outer space is as much the realm of Christ as this meetinghouse. Why settle for Luke Skywalker? This myth is but a shadow of a larger reality.

3) Personal hopes
- That I will be able to live out a normal life span.
- That I will have good health and sufficient financial resources.
- That my contributions to society will be honored and appreciated.
- That I can live according to Christian standards of morality.
- That I will be loved by family and friends.
- That I will have family and friends to love.
- That my faith in God will be sustained throughout life.
- That I will be able to handle adversity and suffering.
- That my actions won't compromise my Christian testimony.
- That I can forgive others as God has forgiven me.

Your personal hopes may be expressed more concretely. Some you hardly dare whisper to yourself. In any case, let me exhort you to maintain these hopes. Not your wants, or wishes, but your hopes. When related to the Christian hope, for which the resurrection is the earnest of our inheritance, these hopes become indeed anchors to the soul. We live by hope, not just by hope in general, but by specific sorts of political, philosophical, and personal hopes. Take courage! Through your faithfulness and that of others like you God is bringing to birth a new world.

You have not yet seen this New Jerusalem, but you live by its vision. Your choices and actions can be in accordance with such hope. We call it faith; and it subdues kingdoms. Be assured, also, that hope reaches beyond this life. Your efforts are not lost, nor are you discarded. Any sufferings you endure now are not to be compared with the glory that will be yours in the eternal kingdom of God. A nineteenth-century hymn-writer, Henri Malan, offers us this prayer:

O that thy holy fire were burning,
Savior, in every waiting heart!
Still all thy people's anxious yearning,
That they adore Thee, King and Lord.

Cleanse and revive, unite thy people,
All who thy holy name adore
That by the light of thy salvation
Souls may be saved, yea, more and more.

Fountain of life, forever flowing,
Breath of the mighty, living God!
Thy holy flame of burning passion
Kindles a fire that quenches not

Fuse all discordant hearts together;
Thy kingdom's mighty temple build.
Spread thy bright flames of love and mercy,
That all the world be glory filled!

[Prayer for the congregation, by age groups, interests]

Waiting

Reedwood Friends Church, April 21, 1985

Our experience with waiting

"Wait a minute!"
But the minute stretches into hours,
and the hours into days,
and months, and years.

Man is born to wait it seems.
Waiting until Dad comes home from work,
waiting to be six and go to school,
waiting to get out and play at recess,
waiting until vacation comes,
waiting for Christmas,
waiting to go visit Grandma.
Waiting to enter high school,
waiting to drive the car,
waiting for the Valentine formal,
waiting to go to college,
waiting for the war to end.
Waiting to be asked or
waiting to ask the loveliest of questions.
Waiting to get married,
waiting to get that new job,
waiting to get a promotion, to move,
waiting to get well,
waiting to take a vacation,
waiting for the kids to come home,
waiting for the kids to come visit,
waiting for the kids to write,
waiting to retire,
waiting to die,
waiting....

Scripture reading
Acts 1:1-10a (NIV)

In my former book, Theophilus, I wrote about all that Jesus began to do and to teach until the day he was taken up to heaven, after giving instructions through the Holy Spirit to the apostles he had chosen. After his suffering, he showed himself to these men and gave many convincing proofs that he was alive. He appeared to them over a period of forty days and spoke about the kingdom of God. On one occasion, while he was eating with them, he gave them this command: "Do not leave Jerusalem, but wait for the gift my Father promised, which you have heard me speak about. For John baptized with water, but in a few days you will be baptized with the Holy Spirit."

So when they met together, they asked him, "Lord, are you at this time going to restore the kingdom to Israel?"

He said to them: "It is not for you to know the times or dates the Father has set by his own authority. But you will receive power when the Holy Spirit comes on you; and you will be my witnesses in Jerusalem, and in all Judea and Samaria, and to the ends of the earth."

After he said this, he was taken up before their very eyes, and a cloud hid him from their sight.

They were looking intently up into the sky as he was going.

Waiting is more than inactivity, or a rhythmic rest from labors. We wait in the spiritual meaning of that word because the mind moves forward in time at the speed of light while the body (and lots of other bodies) lags behind. The mind says "hurry up" and the body says "give me time; I am coming." To wait is to anticipate, to look forward to a happening our mind has already turned into an event for which it has already written the news story: "John Doe graduates June 1 if not at the head of the class at least with decent grades after a lot of work." This is one kind of waiting: call it *expectant waiting*. Psychologically, we spend a lot of time in this kind of waiting, for the biological processes of life operate in such a way that it takes a lot of thought and energy to synchronize our personal agenda with the rest of life.

So it is then that there are expectant mothers, expectant students, expectant citizens, and expectant workers. As with birth, gestation periods provide the stage settings for innumerable private dramas. Your mind holds the program notes for several of these private dramas right now, and your spirit rises to an emotional crescendo as the particular period of waiting moves inexorably toward a climax. Some of these little dramas you brought with you into this meeting for worship, and between times of singing or listening, you bring these to mind, perhaps praying about them.

The ministry of Dallas Willard last week was so important to us because waiting is not passive—we are not driftwood on a random tide, but navigators of the ship. How well our shores are reached, or even if they are reached at all, is partly in our hands and partly in the hands of God. So we search for guidance in often murky weather. Wise Christians, according to Doug Gwyn's analogy, use the Bible for the map and the Spirit for the compass.

Two weeks ago we celebrated Easter. This is God's great drama. The world was waiting for its Savior, and its Savior came. "Up from the grave He arose, With a mighty triumph o'er His foes. He arose a Victor from the dark domain, And He lives forever with His saints to reign." Such is God's doing, a wonder groped for in primitive rituals and symbolic state ceremonies; a wonder grasped by the prophets, scholars, and shepherds. The world was waiting for the birth of its true king; the resurrection proved he was no usurper.

The resurrection of Jesus signifies our own ultimate victory over death, that final enemy. Because he lives, we too shall live. Here is our vision of Zion, the city of God. We see a place where God shall wipe away all tears, where swords will be turned into plowshares, where no one shall make anyone afraid. It is as if the clouds parted briefly and we saw—snowcapped and magnificent—what the smoggy, bloody world will become. And our spirits soar to its magnificence. We are there, even though our bodies ache with fatigue and our feet are blistered from the rocky climb over the path we look back upon and call history. Glimpsing that peak we are content to calibrate our journey by shorter segments—finding a mate, rearing children, getting through school, changing jobs, and so forth. We are free. The rock has been rolled away. We have hope, and we can wait.

But there is another kind of waiting. It is different from that expectancy for which Easter is the true symbol. Call this other kind *reflective waiting.* This is a different kind of waiting. It is the kind of waiting Ralph and Cynthia Gilliam are experiencing now that the expected baby has been born. It is the kind of interval experienced by those of you who graduated from college last year, or switched jobs, or retired, and are not sure where the trail of life leads next. You have been on the mountain and must go down to the valley, or perhaps ascend other peaks revealed from the perspective just attained. It is this kind of reflective waiting of which Luke writes in the Scripture lesson.

Let's review the scene, but first a reminder. Although *we* know how it all came out, because we have the scriptural record, the people who *experienced* that fifty-day interval between the resurrection and Pentecost didn't have such knowledge. Kierkegaard was right—life is lived forwards and explained backwards. I suppose one could say of these followers of Jesus that they were between jobs. And they suffered disorientation like all persons who don't know what to do next.

Luke summarizes the situation: *First, for forty days the Risen Christ showed himself alive to the believers*—to as many as five hundred at one time, adds Paul (1 Corinthians 15). This served to affirm his followers and to deny the allegations of his opponents. Jesus appeared, perfectly healthy and able to move in and out of physical dimensions. *Second, Jesus talked to the disciples about the kingdom agenda.* He had, after all, reclaimed the earth for the meek. It was the most important coup in the history of humankind. So the agenda of the kingdom was important although not then nor now easily understood. People would have a Christ, said William Penn, but not to rule over them. Even after the resurrection the disciples wondered if the kingdom was about to be restored to Israel. Peter and John were wondering about Judea when Jesus had the world in mind for them. They had forgotten what Moses and Elijah had said on the Mount of Transfiguration. Wouldn't you suppose the "suffering servant" talked about Isaiah's prophecy of a universal, peaceable kingdom?

Third, Jesus commissioned the disciples for their own work in the kingdom. We know now about Pentecost and in a couple of weeks will celebrate this historic outpouring of the Holy Spirit upon Jesus' followers. It would make revolutionaries out of reformers and set the world ablaze with the flame of their passion for righteousness. But at the time they didn't understand this. Furthermore, in the midst of difficult talk about a kingdom that couldn't be shaken, Jesus left. Abruptly, in the clouds. He had told them to wait in Jerusalem for a new baptism with the Holy Spirit and then to fan out to the ends of the earth, beginning at Jerusalem—right where they were. Forget about the next election, he had said in effect, and don't worry about putting the end times on a countdown. You've got work to do; but first, wait.

The disciples were left staring at the sky, like we are when the great moment comes and goes and we have to decide what to do next. Waiting. Waiting with eyes skyward, a crick in the neck, and a sinking feeling in the pit of the stomach. The old fears slither in: Was it all a chimera, a bad dream, some hypnotic trance induced by living too long on old hopes? It was the highest of all high moments, for themselves, and—they had been led to believe—for the people of God. And then, poof! Bad enough the defeat of the crucifixion, but then to get their hopes up again! The resurrection seemed so reinforcing to the expectations of this revolutionary political action committee, warmed by the charisma of Christ's presence, briefed on the agenda of the new government, and alerted to the forthcoming commissioning ceremony.

They must have been as disconsolate as the Democratic National Committee after last November's election. What to do now? Fortunately for them (that is, for this apostolic political action committee), a couple of angels told them the separation wouldn't be forever, and that they should head into town from the Mount of Olives. There was, after all, a promise from the One who had never failed them, so why not just wait?

Well, wait they did, occupying the time, like we do yet in church, with prayer, scriptural exegesis, and business matters. At this point I could say "sermon continued until Pentecost Sunday," but I would like to make some applications of this second kind of waiting, *reflective waiting.* The Lord may have something to teach us from this fifty-day interval. What if they had thrown in the towel at that point? What if Peter had said, "Enough is enough. I've been a yo-yo long enough. This time I am really going fishing"? What if James and John had played *Waiting for Godot*? What if you and I miss out on some personal Pentecost because we can't handle the absent Christ so we turn to the comfort of psychological analysis to manage our highs and lows? Or we decide, like the Grand Inquisitor and the other religious manipulators, to just substitute ritual art for the fire of heaven? Either out of pity for the masses or out of prospect for easy money?

They waited, these early followers of our Lord Jesus Christ. Thank God they waited. When presence turned to absence they waited. The glory would return. When the agenda bogged down in management procedures, they waited. They would understand the kingdom. When their commission to witness to the world began to seem pretentious in the stuffy air of an overcrowded upper room, they waited. They would learn how to get from Jerusalem to Portland.

Significantly, they did not wait for Jesus' return but for his promise. When clouds obscured the divine presence they left the mountain. Ecstasy is an unexpected aftermath of obedience, not its precondition. Spiritual power comes through prayerful waiting. Just as the historic resurrection fulfills our yearnings for significance and meaning in the ascendant mode of life, so the historic Pentecost fulfills our yearnings for significance and meaning on the downhill slopes of life's high moments.

There is an upper room for you when business complexities cloud an earlier idealism. Or when the baby cries all night, and sickness, rather than health marks your marriage. Or when the one who promised to love you until death do us part has fudged on the sacred vow. Or when happy college days give way to dutiful clock punching. When the new job turns out to be not what you expected, or the new friendship. When you are just a little nobody in the new class at school. When the Herods and the Pilates of the world throw your kingdom agenda in the wastebasket and even people at church think Jesus was not very practical, at least not until he comes back through the clouds. There is an upper room for you when the children all leave home, or you have had the retirement party, or you have to sell the house and move into a nursing home. And Jesus promises to be with us, to the end of the age. Christ's presence becomes all the more real when we are baptized with his Spirit. That presence is no longer just a report in a book by the ones who put their hands in his wounded hands and with their ears heard him say to wait. That kingdom agenda is not just ancient history. That commission is not just a drama enacted each year to remind us of what might have been. The presence is real. The agenda is dated today, April 21, the year of our Lord, 1985. The commission is real in an earth whose ends are under our feet and at our fingertips. Jesus has not left us nor forsaken us. He is with us now.

The Kingdom Is Among You

Reedwood Friends Church, October 20, 1985

Like the quiet clicking of a clock when the conversation breaks off, or the children have become quiet, or the television sits grey and still, is Jesus' teaching about the kingdom. This teaching gives the Gospels a thematic melody played out in variations of exquisite force and beauty. Jesus began his ministry saying to people, good news, the time has come, the kingdom is near! He told parables about it—weeds sown in a field, a lost coin, and a parent's yearning for delinquent children. He answered puzzling questions about this kingdom. Even though his followers were rather fuzzy about its meaning, they believed Jesus; on one ecstatic occasion they put him on a donkey and sent their new David into Jerusalem under an arc of palm branches, proclaiming "Blessed is the king who comes in the name of the Lord."

It is reported that after his resurrection Jesus spent forty days instructing his followers about the kingdom. Although he warned them not to misunderstand the nature of that kingdom, not to set dates and hand out appointments, he so baptized these disciples with his Spirit that they went out to witness this kingdom to the ends of the earth.

The persistent beat of this teaching about kingdom continues to drum out truth to us whenever we quiet ourselves, or are by circumstances made quiet, in the presence of the Inward Christ. "Kingdom" is always high on the agenda when that still small voice commands our attention to what the gospel is all about.

There was some uncertainty back then about the nature of this kingdom. Matthew called it the kingdom of heaven (a typically Jewish circumlocution); Luke explained it as the kingdom of God. The apparent ambiguity of the term, and its lack of tangibility frustrated the early followers of Jesus. Nevertheless they had its melody in their hearts and its tune in their heads. And so like seedlings growing in the cracks of cement after spring rains, this kingdom took root in a totalitarian regime, spread along its roads, and eventually flourished amid its ruins.

This haunting, melodic line of kingdom teaching, however, tends to get lost in a cacophony of other sounds, sometimes even those of its own accompaniment; and in its absence, fumbling improvisation distorts the clarity of the original composition. So the kingdom that supplanted cruel Rome becomes itself a new cruel Rome, the worse for wearing false colors. So Jesus' vision for a new and righteous order becomes transposed into this or that theocracy in which men, with a passion to remove its ambiguity and provide greater tangibility, first accommodate, then compromise, and finally sell out this kingdom to the princes of this world. Their remorse when they learn they cannot manipulate Jesus leads to statues in the parks (like for Mary Dyer, the Quaker grandmother, hanged in Boston), to holidays for slain prophets (Martin Luther King, Jr.), and to belated and entangled efforts at compensatory justice on behalf of peoples who were exploited by folks who thought they were acting in the interests of the kingdom.

It *is* hard to affirm the kingdom. Apply it too firmly to the here and now and it gets distorted into the dictatorship of the proletariat, or the gospel of wealth and health, or some kind of narrow nationalism. Apply it too firmly to the future and it gets distorted into a cryptic puzzle, the preoccupation with which keeps Christians from being effective and relevant witnesses. One group of Christians supports machine guns for the contras and another group for the Nicaraguan army, but most of us stand somewhere in the middle wishing we could better understand *how* the kingdoms of this world are to become the kingdoms of our God and of his Christ. Its like trying to get gum off one shoe with the other: we're stuck with problems either way.

Receive then with me the text of the day with an expectation that Scripture will teach us, rebuke us, correct us, and train us in righteousness, as Paul advised Timothy (see 2 Timothy 3:16-17).

Scripture reading
Luke 17:20-25 (NIV here and in subsequent texts, emphasis mine) reads:

Once, having been asked by the Pharisees when the kingdom of God would come, Jesus replied, "The kingdom of God does not come with your careful observation, nor will people say, 'Here it is,' or 'There it is,' *because the kingdom of God is among you.*

Then he said to his disciples, "The time is coming when you will long to see one of the days of the Son of Man, but you will not see it. Men will tell you, 'There he is!' or 'Here he is!' Do not go running off after them. For the Son of man in his day will be like the lightning, which flashes and lights up the sky from one end to the other. But first he must suffer many things and be rejected by this generation.

Consider some of the implications of Jesus' teaching about the kingdom of God.

Kingdom is a word about kinship.

Jesus taught very publicly. In this episode he was answering questions posed publicly by the Pharisees, and also instructing his disciples. The key phrase in Jesus' discourse here is "the kingdom of God is among you." Scholars have argued whether that should be translated "within you" or "among you." The Greek doesn't help much, the meaning depends upon the context. Because the word *kingdom* usually connotes interpersonal, rather than personal meanings, "among you" seems the best translation.

So to understand the kingdom, think first about groups, about kinship. In the South the word *kinfolk* refers to relatives. We speak of our immediate family and of those social extensions of our biological unit: our friendship circles, our schools, even sometimes proudly "our kind of people," in contrast to other groups disdainfully addressed as "those kinds of people." We play the game of "us and them" skillfully, as do children who have grown up with a soccer ball in their hands. Sociologists call this human penchant for group identity "ethnocentricity," and its dysfunctionality, "ethnocentrism."

Mostly we overrate our people and underrate other people although some persons reverse the order, to the discomfiture of all us joiners, cheerleaders, partisans, and loyal patrons. Nationally, we are now on a binge of overrating our kind of people, having found intolerably hard to handle even a few years of sober reflection upon our political and economic sins and shortcomings.

Sometimes we hedge our egoistic bets: putting down one group while adulating another. Teenagers often underrate the biological family circle and overrate their peer circle. For young adults the denominational family sometimes suffers at the expense of political, commercial, or other religious affinities. For all of us there is a tendency to put down what is not far enough away (geographically or socially) to be exotic and thus attractive, nor close enough to be emotionally bonding. For example, I think Newberg is a fine little town and George Fox College an excellent institution of higher learning. But some Portlanders who lack strong social bonding to the college have to overcome the geographic barrier (can anything good happen in Newberg?). For them George Fox College suffers intermediacy—it should be either closer or farther away.

What has this to do with the kingdom of God? The kingdom of God is not some exotic entity unrelated to ordinary events. Look around you. Look at kinship. These circles of affinity, although they bear the marks of sin, do point to the kingdom, and when infused by Christ's spirit, become part of the kingdom of God.

Once, reports Luke, Jesus' mother and brothers came to see him but couldn't reach him for the crowd. Someone passed the word along that they were waiting for him, to which Jesus—always alert to the teachable moment—said: "My mother and brothers are those who hear God's word and put it into practice" (Luke 8:21). I like to picture Jesus saying this as he parted the crowd, touching one and smiling at another until he reached and greeted with deep affection his kinfolk.

People remembered that saying, so we should ponder it too. Who are the people closest to me? Those who hear God's word and practice it. They are family, the family of God. To accept that kind of kinship breaks down all kinds of ethnic walls, doesn't it? Not just race or national origin, but also political, social, and cultural walls. It makes family, the paradigm of social bonding, a metaphor for the kingdom. It rebukes our tendency to underrate or overrate. The kingdom unites those who are nearby and those who are far off. And although we may prefer our family to the one next door, the Kansas City Royals to the St. Louis Cardinals, or George Fox to Linfield, or Quakers to Baptists, or Portland to Los Angeles, Democrats to Republicans, capitalism to socialism, the United States to the Soviet Union—or any other combination of these affinities—the words of Jesus remind us that these are all secondary.

The kingdom of God is among us because Jesus is among us. He is King of kings and Lord of lords. These other circles, these other kingdoms, are for the Christian client states to the Empire of God. The kingdom is not an organization for religious hobbyists but the primary social structure to which all other social structures should be and eventually will be subordinated. Before Jesus every knee shall bow. Christians are people who know this to be the case and witness it to others. Christians know that people of the earth are by creation of one blood, and that by the blood of Christ they can be restored to the unity of divine intention.

Kingdom is a word about power.

Whether it be as saplings slowly making rubble of rock walls or lightning arcing from earth to sky, the picture Jesus gives of the kingdom is one of power. Even the scenario of people running first here and then there to be present at the inaugural day of the Lord depicts power. One reason Jesus warns us against chasing after those who shout that they have cracked the divine code for the second coming is that we may fail to see Christ at work presently in our midst.

A decade ago the Lausanne Conference on the Kingdom announced as one of the signs of the kingdom, exorcism—the casting out of evil spirits. Considerable discussion occurred before the conference reached unity about this matter, partly because exorcism had been so narrowly construed—releasing unsophisticated people from psychic bondage. But if exorcism is understood more broadly as God's power breaking the grip of Satan upon people within **all** social structures, then we realize that exorcism is a sign of the kingdom, and we rejoice in that evidence of divine power.

Jesus was once accused of being in league with Satan because he cast out evil—a patently illogical accusation that Jesus quickly refuted, and then added: "If I drive out demons by the finger of God, then the kingdom of God has come to you" (Luke 11:20).

The finger of God! Look at it this way. Slowly the force of kingdom teaching reaches South Africa. First, unheralded missionaries and ministers, worship, the reading of the Scriptures in Christian homes—black and white—becomes leaven in the dough. Then Alan Paton's *Cry the Beloved Country*. Then the public ministry of persons such as Bishop Tutu. Then pleading by churchmen for the South African Christians to repent the sin of apartheid. Then the election of Allen Boesak as president of the World Federation of Reformed Churches (90 million members). Then the pronouncement by that body that South African Christians, particularly the *bruderbond*, had in apartheid embraced heresy essentially by denying the efficacy of Christ's atonement and its implications for breaking down walls of separation. Then ugly scenes of rioting and repression, with the whole world looking on. The finger of God arcs like lightning from earth to sky in piercing judgment and reverberating mercy. Satan's grip upon a social system is broken. Christ stands there, one foot in Johannesburg, another in Soweto, and asks them to recognize him as Lord. Will they? Let us pray to God they will. And pray also for ourselves that the finger of God will pry away clenched fingers of deceit, coercion, psychological manipulation, sloth, and indifference and thus exorcise the demonic within the circles of our affinity.

Kingdom is a word about destiny.

Clearly our text indicates that looking for signs about the completion of the kingdom is to be on the wrong wavelength. The coming is certain; the time is not. The kingdom "does not come with your careful observation," or, as other translations say, "visibly." Literally, you can't discover its purpose and destiny like a spy pinching secret evidence. There is no cryptic message to decode.

God acts so fast we are caught looking backward, as in the days of Noah or Lot, as succeeding verses illustrate. If we want signs, look backward, at the wake made by humanity upon the sea of life. Such signs, like the sign of Jonah, tell us how myopic we get in respect to God's will, how prone to confusing

God's kingdom with our own favorite kinds of kinship, how tempted to substitute our methods for his.

It is hard for us to see the silent buildup of kingdom power until the lightning is upon us. So it is with the small judgments, the small mercies, the little ecstatic moments when the fire of the Lord burns intensely within and among us, and in surprise we say to each other, surely the Lord was present with us. So it will be, we imagine, in that final day of the Lord when all provisional judgments and mercies are authenticated by a new heavens and a new earth, fully characterized, as Paul said, by "righteousness, peace, and joy in the Holy Spirit" (Romans 14:17).

Jesus warns that our patience will wear thin. Disciples will long for even one of the days of the Son of Man and will not see it, and will be tempted to go after theatrical or ethical shortcuts offered us by people, who, to use a second-century Christian phrase, "trade on Christ."

I have great respect for Benjamin Weir, held captive in Beirut for sixteen months, mostly in solitary confinement. Wrote he (*Oregonian*, 10/13/85):

I used the simple materials of my barren room as images to reinforce my confidence that I was in the care of God. There was a light cord hanging from the ceiling from which the bulb had been removed. It occurred to me that it was something like Michelangelo's hand of God reaching down to Adam, reaching down to me in communication and support.

This man understands Jesus' teaching about the kingdom of God. I said earlier I preferred the translation "among you" to "within you." Actually, Benjamin Weir's experience helps us understand why both terms are appropriate. During his enforced solitude, this Presbyterian elder—snatched by terrorists as he was en route to a board meeting—developed a cycle of prayer for people and places in the 22 countries of western Asia and eastern Africa that he had visited, summoning up to his mind's eye congregations of these people. Surely the kingdom of God was *within* him because he understood how the kingdom of God is *among* us. Weir glimpsed a highest circle of paradise—one envisioned by Dante in *The Divine Comedy*—a circle with only light and love for its boundary, encompassing all the rest of the universe.

Kinship, power, destiny—this is what the kingdom of God is all about. Perhaps it is best to conclude by thinking about children. Once Jesus gathered little children to him and told his very officious disciples to not hinder them, adding, "Anyone who will not receive the kingdom of God like a little child will never enter it." Children see the world with fresh eyes; the earth is pregnant with promise of adventure. They know kinship and are willing to extend it indefinitely. The power of love and truth they sop up as trustingly as sponges. For them the future is wrapped with the ribbons of the present. They have a word about the kingdom to us who have become jaded in life and dull of heart.

Samantha Smith speaks.

In my tribute on her behalf [on the next page], Samantha Smith has the last word. She was the girl from Manchester, Maine, who tried to get Russia and the United States to be friends, and who died, unfortunately, August 25, 1985, in a plane crash, along with her father.

Samantha Smith Speaks

I am speaking to you,
Mr. President.
Are you listening?
I will shout if necessary
to be heard above the voices
of your advisors.

But I would rather talk quietly
using ordinary words,
for when I shout I sound angry,
and angry voices
make your guards suspicious.
They will move you
(or more likely me) away.
You only have to lift your hand
and everyone will be quiet.
And you can look at me and say
"well, I am listening."

At this point my mouth will dry up,
and probably my mind, too.
There will be no problem of shouting.
And you will look at your watch
(for you are a busy person)
and say, "speak up, please."

That's how it will be;
so I will write my speech
and fold it in my pocket
for the day when you are listening.
And this is what I will say:

"Sir, the world is a neighborhood,
so why don't we spend more time
visiting our neighbors?
Neighbors organize softball games
and clean up trash every now and then.
Neighbors have picnics
and walk to church together.

They bring food over
when someone is sick
or has a house fire.
So, Mr. President,
why don't we do these things
with our neighbors in the world
instead of pointing bombs at them
from behind closed doors?"

I hope you really listen,
and do not just pat my head
and tell me how nicely I spoke my piece
and ask what is my name
and where do I live,
because if you do
I will answer you with a riddle,
so after I am dismissed
you will say to your advisors,
"now what did the kid mean by that?"

This is what I will say:
"I have a new name and I live
by the banks of the river
lined with trees,
in a garden
where the towers of the city
point to the sky."

How the Spirit Proves the World Wrong

Reedwood Friends Church, June 6, September 9, 1986, and February 15, 1987

How the Spirit proves the world wrong about sin

Sin in general isn't a particularly popular topic. This is the case in church as well as at office coffee breaks or on an evening with friends. You can't say that about sin in particular. It is a popular topic. Humanity, you might say, has a phobia about sin—a kind of love-hate relationship with whatever theologians subsume under the word *sin*. Consider the hype given in the movie section of the newspaper, or the entrepreneurial uses made of the term. There is even a perfume labeled, "My Sin." Against such slick advertisement that makes sin look good it is hard for the church to make it look bad—even by television evangelists whose lifestyle certainly doesn't suggest Elmer Gantry or a 1930s tent meeting evangelist, or some other spoilsport labeled "Puritan."

Why bother to talk about sin? Well, if we are to know the gospel as "good news" it may be useful to reflect on the bad news. Obviously, Christianity comes across as

Scripture
John 16:5-11 (NRSV)

Now I am going to him who sent me; yet none of you asks me, "Where are you going?" But because I have said these things to you, sorrow has filled your hearts.

Nevertheless I tell you the truth: it is to your advantage that I go away, for if I do not go away, the Advocate will not come to you; but if I go, I will send him to you. And when he comes, he will prove the world wrong about sin and righteousness and judgment: about sin, because they do not believe in me; about righteousness, because I am going to the Father and you will see me no longer; about judgment, because the ruler of this world has been condemned.

---

deliverance from bad things, wicked people, or horrible events. What is so special about being saved if you have never been lost, or released from bondage if you were never trapped? A deliberate study of the dark side of life may be better then whistling or crossing our fingers. We all know this dark side is to be reckoned with, whether we have pondered adolescent degeneracy in *Lord of the Flies*, or adult degeneracy in the novels of Walker Percy, or have just watched the evening news on TV. Actually, we know sin is to be reckoned with when we turn on our inward monitor and pass sentence upon ourselves.

From the words of Jesus in John 16, I infer that without divine help our understanding of sin will be distorted, just plain wrong. John uses the term *world*, which I take to mean attitudes and judgments about values that ignore or spurn God's will. (Parenthetically, we probably ought not to think of the "world" as "them." Worldliness as I have defined it doesn't demonstrate class-consciousness.) Actually, Jesus consoled his followers that his ascension was needed. Then they could receive his gift—the Holy Spirit, whose guidance, as an inward counselor, can give a right understanding of things. Specifically, he implies we can have a right understanding about sin, about righteousness, and about judgment.

It is enough today to consider the first: sin. What does the world say about sin? If it is wrong, as the text indicates, we need to know the shape of that wrong. Admittedly, what I have to offer is a kind of composite formed from Bible study, personal experience, and observation. Actually, it is not so hard to be an authority on sin. Now, I don't think it is important whether the word *sin* is used or not. Most people agree there are attitudes and actions that are reprehensible, revolting, cussed, antisocial, bad, defective, depraved, malevolent, or whatever. A commonly agreed upon list may be hard to come by, but that is not so with common consent that evil is around and that people have contributed to its being here.

From where I stand these are some of the ways the world looks at sin. The list isn't exhaustive; if it were it would be more than we could bear.

The world considers sin excusable. Now I should qualify that a bit. Generally but not always sin is excused more readily for oneself, or in relationship to one's interests, than it is for others. That is, one is more inclined to rationalize one's own defection from moral norms than the defections of others. "I was upset," or "had a hard day," or "needed a few more strokes than I get at home," and so forth. But because we know that subjective biases are in effect, we have to come up with systems (if we are acting worldly) that can handle this, and still give us room to negotiate our judgments in respect to the judgments of others. There are three such systems of explanation:
a) heredity, b) environment, c) fate.

The first system excuses sin on the basis of genes, chemistry, biological urges, and the like. The human being is a "naked ape" whose aggression as a killer of kind is excused (although lamented) by reductive reference to the evolutionary chain. Sometimes I think this explanation has something going for it. Like when I observe the spitting rituals of youth in certain subcultures, and remember my own wanton killing of birds.

Depth psychology and anthropology can help sort out irrationalities that seem to be built into the human psyche, but can they excuse sin? No! The second system excuses sin on the basis of environment. Satan comes as an angel of light, it seems, encouraging folks to blame sinful conduct on bad home conditions, social pressures, or economic needs. It is true, unfortunately, that some folks become victims, but their retreat into a psychosis of victimhood constitutes a moral abdication of responsibility. The third system excuses sin on the basis of bad karma, seeking to avoid accountability by limiting or denying one's freedom to choose—"the devil made me do it." This system, like the others, fosters self-deception instead of penitently facing up to one's sin. [Portions of the preceding paragraph have been edited to make up for original text that is no longer available.]

How the Spirit Proves the World Wrong about Righteousness

The Holy Spirit, said Jesus, will "prove the world wrong about sin and righteousness and judgment" (John 16:8). He also promised that this Spirit would guide his followers into truth. Actually, the second promise appeals to us more than the first. Tolerance encourages us to talk about the Holy Spirit as teacher rather than as critic. But maybe we should follow the order of the discourse and try to understand Jesus' first promise before tackling the second.

Consider the context of Jesus' promise: Jesus is consoling his disciples, who are distraught about his announced and impending absence. They don't comprehend the cross; they fear when Jesus leaves everything will be lost. After all, what confidence could the world put in a defeated messiah? Jesus assures them that his going will work to their benefit (although, as we learn later, Judas remains unconvinced, turns to compromise, and is finally shattered).

Jesus understands his followers' anxieties and promises them the baptism with his Holy Spirit. He also assures them he will be more convincing to the world through his Spirit than through his earthly life alone. From the Scripture we gain the insight that the world will try to discredit Jesus as an authority on sin, righteousness, and judgment, first because he disappears, and second because his goodness puts on public display the evil of those who would lord it over the earth and its people.

In a sermon last spring we considered the Spirit's correctives to worldly views of sin. Subsequently, we will consider correctives to views about judgment. Today we consider unspiritual (worldly) perceptions of righteousness and how the Spirit proves these perceptions wrong.

This list of unspiritual perceptions about righteousness is neither exhaustive nor free from contradiction. It merely reveals some of my judgments. These intuitions arise from my own experiences of the world, both the one within and the one outside my heart.

Don't worry too much about nuances to the word *righteousness*. Basically, the word means "conforming to God's will," or "doing what is good." We are not concerned today with dictionary definitions but about meanings people load on the word. So consider this list of worldly views about righteousness, and how the Spirit proves them wrong.

1. The world believes that righteousness is an ideal for persons but not practical in the public domain.

What is an unspoken premise of this view? That being good didn't work for Jesus, so how can it work for the rest of us? In the Christian centuries the Spirit has exposed the erroneous alternative: that human social covenants thrive on public unrighteousness. Where, now, is the Roman Empire that crucified Jesus and quashed the hopes of Judas? It lies in the tomb of history, buried by those who heeded the words of Jesus to seek first the kingdom of God....Followers of the Galilean understand that labeling a human agency "public" does not license it to use evil means for good ends. The Holy Spirit has also proven the world wrong in trying to sanctify evil means, or to limit righteousness to the private sector, by the expedient of pasting

Christian labels onto public enterprises such as empire, nation, company, religion, or party. Righteousness means right ordering. Working through providences and through the church, the Holy Spirit teaches that Christ is Lord of the earth, and that being spiritual is more than a pious attitude or lofty personal ideals.

2. The world believes that investing leaders (particularly deceased heroes) with righteous halos is a useful educational fiction.

The Spirit exposes the sham of such merchandized virtue. People who hunger and thirst after righteousness (and they do) are not impressed by flaunted displays of exemplary virtue. And they are bruised by the cynicism that follows such sophistry. (Jesus warned us against making a show of our charity, didn't he?) People who hunger for holiness know goodness when they see it in persons of good will who love God, and who love their neighbors as themselves. They are reminded of Jesus and a succession of people who have followed his ways of love. Furthermore, the Spirit shines into the quiet, dark center of the soul; and in that Christ-light we know—all of us—that we have sinned and come short of the glory of God. The Spirit corrects the world within us by opening it to the righteousness of God demonstrated on the cross. Forgiveness for our sins characterizes God's goodness and prompts our forgiveness of the sins of others. In such redemptive acts the Spirit cuts through that petty pride by which we would preempt virtue for partisan purposes, until at last we acknowledge ourselves to be one with humanity—equally dependent with others upon God's mercy and grace.

3. The world believes that righteousness is a kind of religious word for circumspect, interpersonal, moral behavior.

Your righteousness has to be more than that of the scribes and Pharisees, said Jesus. Secular as well as religious legalists abound in our time too. Together they select a moral agenda for others, mostly concerning the appetites of the flesh (probably because society spends so much public energy stimulating them). Lawlessness is worse, of course. And it has its own set of advocates. But the Spirit teaches a form of righteousness higher than mere ethical conformity and more satisfying than moral anarchy. We don't just refrain from theft, murder, or adultery in Jesus' kingdom of light. Hate and lust have been replaced by love. Abstract duty has been replaced by personal loyalty to Jesus, who calls us his friends, and gives us his Spirit for an inward counselor.

The Spirit applies to our world Jesus' parable of the dutiful, sulking, elder brother resentful of the prodigal's home welcoming. The Spirit makes relevant Jesus' conversation with the dutiful young ruler burdened by a full financial portfolio, an impeccable moral reputation...and an empty heart. The Spirit reminds us what James learned from Jesus: mercy triumphs over judgment. Without the will and the power to love God and our neighbor, law imprisons us behind barriers of prohibitions and restraints. The Spirit provides us the will and the power to live righteously, to enter freely into that covenant with God to which the law witnesses.

4. The world believes that righteousness is much less exciting than sin, especially for adults.

But the Spirit teaches that the wages of sin is death. Despite an expensive ad campaign by a Babylonian horde of public relations advisors, God's message keeps getting through: Sin is an ugly and a costly business. Ask the victims. Admittedly, righteousness of the prison-bars type would make any release seem exciting, even sin. Whoever knows the thrill of friendship and love, however, or the creative adventures of work, or the aesthetic satisfactions of play; and, supremely, whoever has tasted the ecstasy of divine encounter can never find sin anything but dull and insipid. What marriage is to husband and wife so is God's covenant with his human creatures—a relationship of joy and creativity.

5. The world believes that strong claims of personal righteousness probably mask insecurity, or even neurotic tendencies.

Well, they might be right about some of us neurotic Christians! But the world misunderstands, or refuses to know, the meaning of righteousness as a gift. People who win a prize or receive a generous award are not called neurotic for jumping up and down with joy. Neither are Christians neurotic for receiving joyfully the gifts of God. Actually, the world projects its human face upon God, making him a grumpy boss, or a sinister cosmic dictator zapping people for no reason. Contrary to the world's understanding, the gospel means good news: People are welcomed into the Father's house. We prodigals don't have to buy our way back home! Theologians describe such giftedness as imputed righteousness—that is, Christ the sinless one opens the door and lets us sinners in. Think of it this way: God says to Jesus, "Come over for dinner and bring your friends!" And Jesus writes our RSVP.

Something about entering God's house makes us want to clean up our act, to be good, even righteous. Especially when it is Jesus who invites us. Maybe it is the dinner that does it. Maybe it is the Father's voice, or his arm about the shoulders, or the magnificence of his house. Call it the convicting and convincing power of the Spirit witnessing to our spirits that we are children of God. Slumming around in sin, we had forgotten how beautiful God's place is. Coming home after having been away makes us realize what it means to belong to God's human family. And so we let the Spirit cleanse our desires and purify our wills. We love him because he first loved us. Incredibly, coming to God's house, we discover that his home is within us. He dwells with us.

Theologians refer to the cleaning-up process as imparted righteousness, or sanctification. This kind of righteousness, said the early Quakers, is what being a Christian means. Why stand around in the doorway like a stranger, they said, when you can be at home in the house of God? These are my sentiments. Why, indeed?

We've looked at how the Spirit proves the world wrong about righteousness in five ways: to think righteousness an impractical personal idealism, a socially useful fiction, an imprisoning duty, or a dull or neurotic pretense. The Spirit, however, reveals a righteousness taught by Jesus, which is practical, honest to human aspiration, motivated by love, exciting, and obtainable by God's gracious invitation. We will note briefly a few other worldly notions and their correctives.

6. The world believes that if righteousness exalts a nation, its converse is also true—whatever our nation exalts is righteousness.

You can easily spot the fallacy: false conversion of categories. The Spirit teaches a right ordering of relationships. Nations are subordinate to the reign of God, not the reverse. One day, when the gospel is witnessed to all the peoples, nations will be gathered to Christ. The church lives (and sometimes dies) by this conviction. Nations will bow the knee to Jesus. George Fox urged Oliver Cromwell to cast his crown at Jesus' feet. Bishop Tutu preaches the same prophetic admonition to President Botha.

7. The world believes nobody can tell other persons what is right for them but only what is legally tolerable.

William Penn said that those who will not be ruled by God will be ruled by tyrants. Persons who think righteousness is a purely private, subjective matter fall into a sink of moral anarchy that precipitates legalistic tyranny. The Spirit's answer: kingdom righteousness.

8. The world believes that righteousness, like other value-laden terms, is socially conditioned.

They may say they believe that way. But the Spirit, working through conscience, tells them otherwise, especially when they take their eyes off others and begin to look within. The Spirit also helps them separate mores from morals, standards from principles, and idolatrous motivations from divine ones.

9. The world believes that codes of righteousness reflect the interests of people in charge.

On the surface the world is right on this one. The Spirit, working through the providences of history or within personal conscience, however, will teach them that even selective codes of righteousness, selfishly chosen to maximize power over others, draws from universal principles such as fairness and truth. The Spirit of God is the Spirit of Truth.

10. The world is more interested in receiving the results of righteousness than in being the agents of righteousness.

Descriptively, the world is correct; but prescriptively it is wrong. Through the events of history the Spirit teaches that evil must be overcome with good. To the church the Spirit offers power to be agents of reconciliation. Those who would like to live off the earnings of the godly will discover themselves soon bankrupt, themselves becoming agents of unrighteousness. Subject to divine wrath, they will need to hear the Spirit beckoning them back to the Father's house, there to receive his mercy and to learn his righteousness.

Conclusion

It may be that you, like I have done, can acknowledge false understandings of righteousness in the world discovered around or within you. Is your list a bit different? No matter. Let the Holy Spirit correct them. The Spirit will take the things of Jesus and make them plain to you. Have the confidence and courage to grasp what the apostle Paul described as "a righteousness from God [that] comes through faith in Jesus Christ to all who believe" (Romans 3:22 NIV).

The Spirit Will Prove the World Wrong about Judgment

We repeat the Scripture text for this series, John 16:8-11. "When he comes, he will prove the world wrong about…judgment…because the ruler of this world has been condemned." A few weeks ago news cameras focused upon Ferdinand Marcos, clad in jungle garb doing boxing feints to show the world he was ready to take over the Philippines again. Actually, he looked pathetic—a washed-up, deluded old man, his only power being wealth others will use. Obviously, before Aquino's campaign unseated him he stood condemned. We do not yet see the prince of this world reduced to such pathetic proportions; but Jesus saw it, saw the end of an age. Satan stands condemned.

Consider the Scripture context: Jesus is consoling his distraught disciples. They don't comprehend his announced, impending crucifixion. They fear when Jesus leaves everything will be lost—what confidence could people have in a defeated messiah? Jesus understands their anxieties. He promises his followers a baptism with his Holy Spirit and assures them he will be more convincing to the world through this Spirit than by his earthly life alone. The world, he warns, will try to discredit Jesus as an authority on sin, righteousness, and judgment, first because he disappears and second because his godly sacrifice exposes those who would use evil means to manage the earth and its people.

In two previous sermons we considered the Spirit's correctives to worldly views of sin and righteousness. Today we consider how the Spirit corrects our notions of judgment.

People in power are being deposed all the time. It is par for the course. Good, bad, or indifferent, this world's leaders serve their time and are supplanted. Idi Amin is nearly forgotten. Some, like Somosa and Marcos, are overthrown. Presidents are voted in or out of government and out of corporate, educational, or professional offices. Cultural style setters and fashion designers share the same transitory rule and fall from power. Sometimes these cultural forces are long ranging, sometimes of short duration. (I wonder how long-minus-length sideburns will continue, or black dresses for high school girls.) Merchants and presidents, their patrons and their devotees, seek to perpetuate power through mythologies of one sort or another, using various forms of force, ranging downward from prayer to persuasion, to legal incorporation, to manipulation, to coercion, and finally, to violence. One could say that evil carries with it the seeds of its own destruction. Or one could say that the Holy Spirit provides the insights that turn us from evil and toward the good.

Jesus' words declare that Satan, the ultimate oppressor, has been defeated. The second Adam has crushed the head of the serpent. Once, after his seventy-two disciples returned triumphant from a preaching mission, Jesus said "I saw Satan as lightning fall from heaven." His words are borne out by the resurrection, which is his guarantee to us that the rulers of this evil world have overreached themselves in crucifying the Lord of Glory. Enough is enough. A new era has dawned. Jesus has succeeded in his coup d'etat; and if people cannot see the new day, or grow restless awaiting the gathering of the peoples into God's kingdom, they have only to ask the Spirit within. The Spirit will confirm what Jesus' death and resurrection mean. The

Spirit will prove the world wrong and Jesus right.

Judgment may be considered in these ways: l) as a moral decision—what is right or wrong, 2) as an interpretation of historical events, 3) as a legal settlement of conflicting claims, and 4) as a political choice. My previous sermons dealt with moral decisions. Today we consider judgment in other ways.

How then does the Spirit prove the world wrong about judgment?

1. The world interprets historical events from a circle of limited interest. The Spirit teaches us to interpret history according to divine purpose.

That purpose offers the larger circle: "For God so loved the world...."
Tolstoy wrote:

> People whom fate or their sin or mistakes have placed in a certain position, however false that position may be, form a view of life in general which makes it seem right and admissible. In order to preserve this view, these people instinctively keep to the circle of those who share their outlook. This surprises us, where the persons concerned are thieves bragging about their dexterity, prostitutes vaunting their depravity, or murderers boasting of their cruelty. This surprises us only because the circle, the atmosphere in which these people live, is limited, and we stand outside. But don't we observe the same phenomenon when the rich boast of their wealth, that is, robbery; the commanders in the army pride themselves on their victories, that is, murder; and those in high places vaunt their power, that is, violence? We do not see the perversion in the views held by these people, only because the circle formed by them is more extensive, and we ourselves are moving inside of it. (*Resurrection*, Oxford, 1916, pp. 166-167)

Earlier this month in Portland, Jesse Jackson urged Russia and United States to acknowledge that together they make up only one eighth of the world's population. The world is our circle of moral accountability.

Jesus' death and resurrection move us outside our limited circles. This we learn from listening to the Holy Spirit, who is God permeating personal time and space. Political, ethnic, or cultural walls cannot stop the Spirit. Under the influence of the Spirit we interpret U.S.-Soviet relationships or family relationships in terms of the cross and the resurrection. We interpret events of our own lives on God's terms. Not only will we stand before God after death, we stand before him now. The cross is the courtroom and the resurrection the verdict. We cannot do evil that good may come. The cross has triumphed over such attempts. The resurrection vindicates truth and goodness; Satan and evil are dethroned. The assurance of life eternal and a renewed cosmos keeps us steady. If the world were to go on its way indefinitely, with no hope of change except what we can engineer, we would despair. But we treasure a hope of glory in these earthen vessels of ours. They are like signs of spring, symbols of hope we can use this time of year and this time of civilization:

> What is as sure as death and taxes?
> What as certain as ebbing tides?
> Predictable as the common cold?
> This: a dull grey gloom that slides
> like sluggish slime into the soul
> and dutifully attacks us.
> We name this monster, February.
> What is as sure as birth and taxes?
> As determined as the flooding tides?
> Predictable as a tale retold?
> It is that the foggy phantom glides
> away at earth's first hint of gold—
> How quickly its grip relaxes.
> Oh divine apothecary!

2. The world adjudicates conflicting claims on the basis of laws established for local or national interest. The Holy Spirit whispers to us that rights and privileges are not limited to parochial legality.

The Spirit reminds us that the meek will inherit the earth. Through the Spirit we understand that God owns and we lease. Thus every transaction of law is a triangle involving two parties and God. The Prince of Darkness does not want God on that plane of neighborliness. In the cross such selfishness is judged wanting. The world is wrong in thinking there can be good social order on the basis of privileged and unprivileged classes, whether these be internal or external to our culture. The Spirit tells us that loving neighbor as oneself is a universal ethic. The Golden Rule lays a tape measure clear around the globe.

3. The world makes political choices as if evil were the compelling necessity in life. The Spirit assures us the good is the compelling necessity in life.

Through people of conscience everywhere, the Spirit assures us that lowest common denominator political choice only brings government to anarchy. In a recent issue of *Christianity Today,* Charles Colson reluctantly concludes that in this evil world governments must resort to deceit; the prince of this world still reigns, he thinks. We sympathize with him, we feel his anguish. But the Spirit reminds us that Jesus' vision is otherwise: "I saw Satan fall like lightning from heaven."

At this point experience confronts the theoretical. Some may say "That's nice religious teaching, but what has it to do with me?" In Potok's book *Davita's Harp* (Fawcett Press, 1986, pp. 315ff), a loving, Jewish Communist mother—a passionate worker for justice—tries to explain to her perceptive little girl, who has drunk deeply from the well of spirituality offered by good people in her life, Jewish, Christian, and agnostic, why she thinks religion is an illusion. "This is a terrible century, Ilana. So many people are being hurt in it." The mother had recounted her rape years before and the death of her old grandfather who tried to stop the soldiers. Her father had been away at a religious meeting. "Is this why you don't like religion, Mama?" presses the daughter, "because of your father?"

"That and other things. It made a slave of my mother."

"Not everyone is like your father," persists Ilana. "Mr. Helfman isn't. Mr. Dinn isn't."

To which the burdened young widow replies sadly, "I only know my own life, Ilana. In my life there was my father not Mr. Dinn or Mr. Helfman. You can't forget the bad things that are done to you by telling yourself that the world isn't all bad. We really can know only the people and the things that touch us. Everything else is like words in the dictionary. We can learn them but they don't live deep inside us. Can you understand that, Ilana?"

Are sermons just "dictionary words" to you? Abstract, distant from the troubled story of your soul? If so, read the Holy Spirit's lines within your story, spoken through an Aunt Sarah's goodness or a Mr. Dinn's—a goodness that speaks truth to your suffering and your loss. The Spirit highlights Christ's message with compelling force: The good is life's compelling necessity and love its real direction. It is not as distant observer but as active participant that the Crucified One cries out, "I saw Satan fall as lightning from heaven!" It is *his* verdict that the prince of this world stands condemned.

"I saw Satan fall like lightning from heaven!"
I hear you, Jesus, but evil seems
not to have been damaged much
with or without Satan.
At least where I live.
In the world I experience
a dark cloud of knowing
chills the air wherever I go,
in whatever neighborhood I live,
on every job, every day.

It's not just the terrorists, Lord,
although that's bad enough,
nor headlines about Satan cults,
child pornography,
or teenaged children
who slaughter their parents,
or well-dressed people
who make millions selling drugs
to unemployed kids
or young people determined
to be ultimately happy—
or executives at thirty-three.

"I saw Satan fall like lightning from heaven!"
I hear you, Jesus, but evil seems
not to have been damaged much
with or without Satan.
It is not just that comedians
turn happy humor into sick jokes,
or that script writers debauch
the little early risers
with Saturday morning cartoons
instructing in violence
and how to buy toy tanks
(each piece sold separately,
batteries not included).
Or that con artists bilk the aged
of their life earnings,
or that the rich and clever
prosper at the expense of
the poor and ignorant.

Nor is it just this demonic fixation
upon war and how most expeditiously
to deal death to enemies.

"I saw Satan fall like lightning from heaven!"
I hear you, Jesus, but evil seems
not to have been damaged much
with or without Satan.
At least where I live.
In the world I experience
a dark cloud of knowing
chills the air wherever I go,
in whatever neighborhood I live,
on every job, every day.

That evil is not just out there
generally in public places.
It is in my world.
I thought I had life together,
but the whole thing fell apart.
The serpent entered my tent,
(and our folk "the better sort").
In my family the apostasy occurred,
the maiming accident,
the hardly hushed scandal.
Mine the alcoholic uncle,
the neurotic sister,
the sadistic brother,
the ungrateful child,
the unfair boss,
the faithless spouse.
Mine, mine the nights of regret
and the daytime fantasies
of what might have been.

Oh, my Lord God,
I confess more:
in the chilly world
where I live
the evil is not just around me,
it is within me!

How the Spirit Proves the World Wrong

In my heart I have hosted
the prince of this world,
and finally let him rule.
His sly greed is mine,
his carefully curtained hypocrisy,
and his bartered love.
He taught me hundreds
of euphemistic labels
to paste over selfishness.
The prince of this world
taught me the insinuated threat,
the exploitive maneuver,
a smothering benevolence,
a wandering eye
and a hurtful tongue.

"I saw Satan fall like lightning from heaven!"
I hear you, Jesus, but evil seems
so much a part of me
that until you crush the serpent head
within my heart, I stand condemned.
With contrite heart and Spirit-led
I pray, forgive me, gracious God;
restore a right spirit within me. I repent!
Draw back the curtains of my soul
to let your love and truth shine in.
Show me, Jesus, your vision
of the good raised up,
of the evil put down.
In joyful music, art, satisfying labor,
children's play;
at home and away,
imprint on my heart, O Lord,
what you want me to learn:
that good has come to stay.

Let Michael Stoops and Mother Teresa,
a physician's healing touch,
and the thoughtful acts of friends,
become sacraments of your resurrection
and of my own, someday.
Send your Holy Spirit
to teach me how to read
between the headlines,
and how to translate editorials
and world affairs reports
into the language of Pentecost.
Teach me how and whom to touch
in love and friendship.
Oh, my Lord, whisper Good News
on forest and sea breezes;
let the sun's warmth
announce your presence.
Give me the good sense
to recognize your followers
however they may be clothed
and wherever they live.
Put my hand in anyone's hand
who hungers for righteousness,
in whatever neighborhood I live,
on every job, every day,
until we are all gathered
around heaven's throne,
and the creatures
of the whole creation
(including me),
become what you
have called us to be.

In Jesus' name, amen.

Christ, the Key to Mystery

Reedwood Friends Church, fall, 1987

"Mystery Revealed," part one

From its beginning Christianity faced competition from other contenders for the hearts and minds of humanity. Although the earliest believers were Jews, most of their ethnic kin rejected Jesus as the Messiah, clinging rather to the mystery of their Abrahamic covenant. Gentile Christians faced competition from devotees of the imperial cult, who deified their leader. It was an understandable act of populist politics, for upon Rome—the "eternal city"—poets, generals, philosophers, and politicians for centuries had fastened a halo of mystery. Add to covenant and empire a third contender—the mystery religions, such as the cult of the Great Mother, whose non-political devotees tried to appease the gods through bloody rituals (bathing in the blood of a slain bull) or to manipulate divine power through psychic force. Against these contenders the Christians proclaimed their understanding of divine mystery and its revelation in Christ.

Today Christianity faces similar competition for the hearts and minds of humanity. Zionism and Islam offer militant versions of the Abrahamic covenant. Nationalism elevates its heroes to imperial status in countries around the globe, whether in the Soviet Union, the United States, South Africa, Nicaragua, or Libya—sometimes with Marxist, sometimes with capitalist mystique. Mystery religions from Satanism to Scientology leverage the guilt and hopes of non-political devotees in an awesome display of modern priest-craft.

Given our social nature Christians find it hard not to accommodate to these contending ideologies, difficult not to invest Zionism or nationalism or cultic gurus with some measure of the mystery that belongs to Christ. These two sermons consider the Christian mystery that flowered from Jewish seed, overran the Roman Empire, and left Gnostic religions as footnotes to history. These sermons aim at giving you confidence as faithful Christians confronted by secular or religious challenges.

Scripture reading

Our primary text, Colossians 1:26-27 (NIV here and in subsequent texts), states the theme. God's word in its fullness is:

the mystery that has been kept hidden for ages and generations, but is now disclosed to the saints. To them God has chosen to make known among the Gentiles the glorious riches of this mystery, which is Christ in you, the hope of glory.

Introduction

In this sermon we consider how the mystery of life is made not only bearable but glorious in response to Christ within. Our text offers this outline:

1. The saints are charged with illuminating the mystery of God.

2. Such mystery is glorious ("treasures of wisdom and knowledge").

3. The key to that mystery is Christ within.

What is the mystery of God the saints must illuminate?

First, let's ask what the word means, then why mystery needs illuminating, and finally its dimensions.

We use the word *mystery* to describe circumstances or events we cannot fully explain or control. Reality eludes our grasp in some way. We mean more than simple puzzle-solving. People read a mystery novel until the wee hours of the morning not just to find out who committed the crime. That could be accomplished long before bedtime by turning to the final chapter. Scientists are more forthright about unveiling mystery than fiction writers—making experiments as expedient as possible and not delaying significant findings just to titillate the imagination. Yet they too receive satisfaction from the process of the unveiling itself, from the experiments, and not just from the results.

By *mystery*, then, we mean more than unsolved mathematical, social, or philosophical puzzles—more than elusive data or missing premises from which to draw reliable inference. We mean that the whole of what we experience is greater than its parts; that neither inductive analysis nor deductive logic fully captures meaning. We imply that our intuitive reach exceeds our rational grasp. So we use the word *mystery* to signify meanings about things, persons, and events that elude explanations, even scientific ones.

Think about holding your baby for the first time. No wonder we refer to the miracle of birth; facts about weight and height won't reach. Consider the opaque pools of sexuality, or the rippling streams of friendship. Think about watching someone die. Violently. Peacefully. Reflect upon entering an abandoned forest cabin, littered with ancient debris. Or looking at a family album reaching back several generations. Feel the mystery of life and death.

Ask about your feelings as you watch the waves break incessantly against the rocks, or listen to the crickets on a summer evening, or scan the night sky. Think about your inner dialogue, those "I/me" conversations, about the little mental probes you send out to others—strangers or friends—some subtle and others not so subtle, seeking entrance into their being. Consider political leaders, who as individuals would spurn voyeurism, but who corporately scheme to peek into the bedrooms and offices of opponents.

Consider the tenacious loyalty people feel for *their* families, *their* ethnic origins, *their* political systems, *their* colleges, *their* automobiles, *their* music. Can you feel the mystery of loyalty?

Mystery begs illumination.

We're ambivalent about it. We strive to understand God, nature, and other people; we struggle to diminish ignorance and increase rational control; yet justifiably we fear that with such understanding life will diminish. We fear it will lose its punch. To avoid such loss some people feed imagination with paperback or film fiction, stereotyping good and evil. Others preen the ego with daydreams, or act out these fantasies by manipulating others, often in religious guise.

But most people busy themselves in commodities exchange, buying and selling, trying to substitute the mystique of invented things for that grander mystery of the heavens set in place by the hand of God. (A glance at the advertisement industry confirms that judgment. *Creation* means this year's clothing fashions, not the galaxies.) If we let all hidden things (both within us and outside us) be exposed to scientific light—we say begrudgingly—we can still cherish illusions, still retain an aura of the unknown. We invest artificed culture with a mystique of reality. A continuously minted coinage of social respectability, fostered by education and other social forces, contributes to a tacit agreement to preserve this mystique.

But we cannot have mystery without God. Without God mystery is only useful social fiction aimed at jazzing up an otherwise dull (or disappointing) world. The mystique of invented things is a contemporary opiate of the people. Cynical consumer managers understand this. The bold confidence of this secular priest-craft is symbolized by T-shirts that people buy to advertise what others sell them—"This Bud's for You!" Mystery yields to marketing. Have you noticed the full-page advertisements for Virginia Slims lately? The model, in various poses of youthful rapture, looks about the age of our granddaughter—sixteen.

God's judgment on such mystery is spelled out in the book of Revelation, chapters 17 and 18, where the city rich in gold, silver, and silk becomes a lodging for every foul spirit; and merchants rich through debauching the public lament a loss that heaven, the prophets, apostles, and saints celebrate as gain. Babylon symbolizes the seductive force in society—evil imbedded in structure—which finally people see through and pull down in outrage.

A secular historian, Barbara Tuchman, illustrates this Babylonian syndrome. In an article about America's deteriorating ethic (*Oregonian*, September 21, 1987), she implores people to wake up to the deceptions of our visual culture. "Public acceptance of the pictured image without regard to the reality underneath" is for her the greatest sign of America's ethical decline—a seduction comparable to eighteenth-century French monarchy. Then it was "curled wigs and elegancies" that masked decadence. Now it is our preoccupation with looking good. "Television has become our monarch." She contrasts the passionate interest in Gary Hart's amorous adventures with flaccid reaction to lost lives and broken laws resulting from incompetence or deceit by public officials.

Consider the dimensions of mystery.

The "saints," according to our text, shed light on mystery. The domain of Satan must and will yield to the domain of Christ. Consider mystery in each of its three dimensions: the created order, the social order, and the personal order—the self.

A Christian accepts the mystery of created order.

The natural order is neither a mindless process nor a warehouse of raw materials. The Christian retains awe at nature's treasures and gives glory to God as maker and sustainer. Proverbs 8:22-31 (JB) extols this mystery in describing wisdom as God's master craftsman, "delighting him day after day, ever at play in his presence, at play everywhere on his earth, delighting to be with the children of men." This sense of awe gives humility to our science and opens the universe to us. Job's question: "Which is the way to the house of light, and where does darkness live?" is a good prelude to discovery. We might ask it this way: How can we explore to their source supernovae and black holes?

Job's conclusion at the end of his time of troubles reminds us of human limitation and discourages us from trying to be lords (read "tyrants") of the universe rather than its stewards: "I am the man who obscured your designs with empty-headed words. I have been holding forth on matters I cannot understand, on marvels beyond me and my knowledge."

Are you a scientist, a mechanic, an engineer, a farmer, a builder? I speak this word to you: Receive the mystery of creation as a steward of great riches, as caretaker of divine bounty and goodness. Does technology only hasten entropy—move the world faster toward famine, pestilence, and war? Christ is the word that this need not, and will not, forever be so. Be a faithful person: probe creation's depths, reshape its parts for the healing of the nations, offer it as a sacrament to the Creator. Adventure in natural things like a reborn Adam or Eve, led by the hand of God through fiery swords of disease, decay and death, nuclear arsenals, and chemical pollution, toward a renewed Eden. Field and city belong together, nature and society. To fulfill this vision God enlists your brain, your heart, and your hands.

A Christian accepts the mystery of society.
Society is both a means of common grace and a network for the demonic. Tyrannies on the right and on the left imprison flesh and spirit; but God works through them, raising leaders like Moses to let the people go. Even in the harshest political soil the human spirit flowers and bears seed. Just as the martyrs seeded a church that triumphed over the Roman Empire, so in every country and culture of the world God is at work, judging evil and raising up people of faith.

Accepting the mystery of God in history, the Christian submits to social order as God-ordained but will not allow any particular government or social structure to usurp conscience or displace Christ as Lord. The Christian loves and seeks the highest good of the other whether that neighbor is inside or outside family or political, social, or cultural circle. Accepting the mystery of divine providence, a Christian shares material possessions with a brother or sister in need (as James writes—3:17) because he or she has needs. A Christian's reasons for sharing are not reasons of commercial or national interest. A Christian rejects both anarchy and tyranny in favor of social participation, even though social systems and organizations flounder and often fail, waste time and energy—often bringing frustration and despair, especially for those who offer leadership. No wonder the Christian feels like an alien in this world and would often opt for the hermit stance, either literally or figuratively—let others run things.

I have a word for you, my brothers and sisters who serve on community councils or school boards, hold elective or appointed political office, teach in or superintend schools, work in stores, give music lessons, serve as waiters or waitresses, counsel or manage other people, or keep a company's books. Receive the mystery of human society. Accept it as Eden—flawed, but under God, recoverable. Learn from father Abraham, of whom the writer of the Hebrews spoke thus: "By faith he made his home in the promised land like a stranger in a foreign country; he lived in tents, as did Isaac and Jacob, who were heirs with him of the same promise. For he was looking forward to the city with foundations, whose architect and builder is God" (Hebrews 11:9-10). Accept your tents but look frequently at the blueprints of God's future city. You make a better citizen of this country for being a citizen of the world to come.

A Christian accepts the mystery of personal order.
The mysteries of the natural and social orders intersect

within the self. If I ask the question "who am I?" outside the boundaries of mystery, nature and society immediately respond. Reduced to the lowest level of analysis it comes down to this: You are an animal that talks and manipulates things skillfully, a pawn to be moved about, or even dispensed with, for national interest. The mirror of society tells us who we are; it measures our lives by a scale of social utility and achievement—good, bad, or indifferent. Some of us get high marks and public acclaim; others are blamed, criticized, used, ignored, remanded for social repair, marginalized, or even removed. Actually, there are so many social mirrors we get confused. As in an arcade, we see ourselves tall and short, wide and narrow, one time this way and another time that. Which one is truly me? The mirror our family holds out? That of our peers? Those with whom we work? The government? The fashion pacesetters? Film and TV personalities? At best the mirror of society gives a limited view of the self, at worst a warped one. All of us eventually will be forgotten by society, or tucked obscurely into its records.

But if I ask "who am I?" within the boundaries of mystery, then I find a different mirror, the mirror of creation. With the psalmist I commune thus with the Creator:

> I look up at your heavens, made by your fingers, at the moon and stars you set in place—ah, what is man that you should spare a thought for him, the son of man that you should care for him? You have made him little less than a god, you have crowned him with glory and splendor, made him lord over the works of your hands, set all things under his feet....(Psalm 8:3-6 JB)

The psalmist gained perspective on the self by looking at creation. Urban people find that mirror of creation hard to find. Sometimes we have to go to the park, to Tilikum, to Twin Rocks, to the sea, or to the mountains to find that mirror. My brothers and sisters, young and old, look in God's mirror of creation, what he has made and what he has given to be shaped by your hands. See yourself as little less than a god, crowned with glory and splendor, one to whom God has entrusted his wonders. Don't be a preening Lucifer; be an earnest child of God, captivated by a tidepool or a star, a tree or a tower, an automobile or a poem. Enjoy the Father's world.

From time to time gaze deeply into your own eyes. Not at the mole on your face or the wrinkle in your forehead. Look into your eyes. Do it prayerfully. Find reflected there the image of God. Let the Spirit be your tour guide. Oh, you will not like everything you see on this inward journey. You may discover conflict between the self that delights in God's law and the self that fights that law (see Romans 7:21-24). That Light that shows your self as flawed will also show your self restored. Having seen yourself in God's light you can better look into eyes of other persons. Maybe you could practice on your friends. The mysteries of creation and society become burdens of joy rather than burdens of despair once you accept the mystery of your own being.

Time moves us forward, inexorably, mysteriously. We do not know what will happen tomorrow. But we can anticipate certain things. We will change and so will everything around us. We ride time's rocket all the way through death into the reality that lies beyond. But one's self remains, crowned with God's glory and splendor. Don't look at the timetable constantly or you won't enjoy this trip. Don't count the wrinkles and the aches, don't fight a rear-guard action against time. Be a trusting child of God. You are time's passenger; enjoy the trip!

Sadly, in the midst of good the mystery of evil appears; chaos intrudes on design, chance wreaks havoc on purpose. But the converse is also true. In the midst of evil, good spouts like flowers in spring. Chaotic happenings suddenly reveal beautiful design in the character of people, and purpose weaves random events into significant social change. It's God's world!

Accept mystery in joyous, adventuresome, Abrahamic faith! It's the first step. The revealing of mystery is the second. The mystery of life is made not only bearable but glorious in response to Christ within. The next sermon will consider how Christ within gives mystery meaning and makes God's riches available.

"Mystery Revealed," part two

Our primary text is Colossians 1:24—2:8. Verses 26-27 state the theme: God's word in its fullness is "the mystery that has been kept hidden for ages and generations, but is now disclosed to the saints. To them God has chosen to make known among the Gentiles the glorious riches of this mystery, which is Christ in you, the hope of glory."

The first sermon considered the glorious mystery with which the saints are charged; this one considers how Christ within makes these treasures available. Last Sunday I urged faithful acceptance of mystery within nature, society, and the self. I charged you to be good stewards of the "treasures of wisdom and knowledge" embedded so mysteriously in nature, society, and the self.

The key to mystery

Christ within is the key to mystery.

To reveal mystery is not the same as to offer an explanation. Just as the whole novel is needed and not just a line from the final chapter, so the mystery of life wants more than explanation. It is not enough to say: "God knows," or "God has it figured out." Suppose late at night you hear a strange rattling on the roof. By acute listening and clear reasoning you determine it is nothing mysterious but only a squirrel getting acorns from the gutter. This is mystery explained. M*ystery revealed,* on the other hand, continues to be allusive and opaque. But we can handle it, in hope, not in despair, just as we live in marriage with a person we never fully know but whose mystery is revealed to us in tender and ecstatic moments. The philosopher Wittgenstein said mystery is not *how* the world is but *that* it is.

Our biblical text states that what has been hidden and obscured for centuries is in Jesus Christ *revealed*. This revelation is not just for covenant people, but also for Gentiles (read "pagans," or "non-church-goers"). It is their hope of glory too. God has tipped his hand and the saints have seen it. Waking early they have glimpsed the sunrise of the world's new day. Its magnificence takes their breath away before the colors fade. Paul writes that if the saints bind themselves in love and stir up their minds (2:2-3 JB) they can exhibit before the world God's "jewels of wisdom and knowledge." This Scripture implies the saints can be argued out of being message-bearers. Out of fear or greed they can maintain a closed shop with secret religious passwords, ritual taboos, and legalistic monopoly over magnificence.

Christians bear the burden of discovery: The world is not flat with brutality and misery. It is not dull with decadence and death. It flames, rather, with beauty and purpose along multiple radial lines. Forces that speed outward from a divine center also surge among us and within us, inviting participation. But discoverers find home folk sleepy, skeptical, unadventuresome, or chained by routine. And they wonder if what they glimpsed in Christ was the dawning of a new day or one more bursting bubble. Thus Paul's exhortation to the saints, the discoverers, "to live your whole life according to the Christ you have received" (2:6 JB).

My fellow discoverers, consider what the phrase, "Christ within, the hope of glory," means within nature, society, and the self.

Christ reveals purpose in nature.

Our scientific mode of thinking makes this claim difficult. We view nature mechanistically, as scientifically predictable. This has made life comfortable, and we hesitate to give more than a poetic nod to the notion that Jesus has anything to do with the natural world. We don't mind a miracle now and then but get nervous when material things get loaded too heavily with things spiritual. We fear dishonest science and hypocritical religion. Naiveté and stupidity don't make life easier. Do you remember the play *Waiting for Godot* in which two friends engage in random conversation awaiting the arrival of their friend, who never shows up? This is how the modern world considers God, at least in scientific terms. A no-show.

Examine things, analyze causes, develop systems, combine components as you will—secularists argue—and God never shows up. Why wait? Furthermore, random events and a violent food chain seem so at variance with Jesus' character that it's easier to keep the natural separate from the spiritual. Even Christians often limit divine agency to cosmic beginnings and endings, rather than to affirm that Christ is present and busily at work within nature. Or they think the work of Christ is limited to the human, mental part of nature, which natural scientists are happy to let preachers and psychologists quarrel over, so long as they don't tamper with real things.

Is such skepticism or dualism adequate to the mystery of life? No. How *does* Christ reveal the mystery of creation?

First, in Christ human redemption is linked with creation.

Call it a theological unified field theory. In Colossians 1, Paul teaches that "all things...in heaven and on earth" are created in Christ, a conviction echoed in John's Gospel. Salvation isn't limited to changes inside human minds. Christ within is not only our hope of glory but that of the heavens and earth. Even minor disasters such as poisoned streams and desertification reflect a need for larger wisdom and better will; and the minor mercies such as renewed rivers and reforestation reflect God's redemptive purposes. Is it fair to say that when Christians are "encouraged in heart and united in love," as Paul exhorts (2:2), they reveal the glories of God's creation? Yes. Isaiah's prophecy of the peaceable kingdom is echoed by the final book of the Bible, Revelation, which pictures Christ bringing about cosmic renewal.

Second, Christ reveals the mystery of nature by showing the meaning of time.

We *explain* time by various measuring devices. These "clocks" calibrate interactions of energy and mass, cycles of birth and death, dissolution and reformation energized by light. But time is a mystery experienced in many forms. And why only one direction? Earlier I mentioned *Waiting for Godot*. A recent cartoon shows Godot waiting alone in an empty airport carousel for baggage that hasn't arrived! God not only waits for mishandled baggage, he waits for fickle passengers. In the midst of time Christ reveals its mystery—the mystery of the eons of waiting. Through Christ, muted nature gains a voice. And although ignorance and sin delay the world's flight, it will arrive. Creation yearns for human redemption.

As Paul states, it still retains the hope of being freed, like us, from its slavery to decadence, to enjoy the same freedom and glory as the children of God (Romans 8:18-25). Loren Eiseley once wrote (*Night Country*, Scribner, 1971, p. 223):

> There comes a time when the thistles spring up over man's ruins with a sense of relief. It is as though the wasting away of power through time had brought with it the retreat of something shadowy and not untouched with evil. The tiny incremental thoughts of men tend to congeal in vast fabrics, from gladiatorial coliseums to skyscrapers, and then mutely demand release. In the end the mind rejects the hewn stone and rusting iron it has used as the visible expression of its inner dream. Instead it asks release for new casts at eternity, new opportunities to confine the uncapturable and elusive gods.

Before his death Eiseley accepted Christ as the focal point of that inner dream questing for eternity. Something can be said for thistles. They were, after all, Jesus' crown.

Third, Christ reveals the mystery of nature by linking human effort and cosmic future.

Scientists understand the observer effect. The presence of the observer affects how we take hold of reality. Consider Christ the ideal observer. Having come into the world, which his word created, he gives it direction. Does it make a difference how we look at nature? The elements appear to suffer random rearrangements in mute disinterest. Or is it that our senses are too dulled to read the signs? Having experienced Christ within, we no longer consider the cosmos as just a bag of rocks to build things with or make into projectiles. Having experienced Christ within, we no longer think our actions have no bearing on what the cosmos will become, nor can we believe that ours are the only hands on the controls. Love and truth give coherence to all creatures, individually and together. This love and truth have been demonstrated to us, historically, in real time. Christ is prototype humanity and Lord of the earth. Through him we regain constructive stewardship of the earth. Neither artificial intelligence nor hyper-drive can release the universe from the imprint of Christ. Love and truth are the language of the universe, personified in Christ. To be Christian is to be more not less creative. A renewed earth awaits a renewed humanity.

Christ reveals the meaning of the social order.

Last Sunday I said the Christian affirms and submits to social order as God-ordained but allows no particular structure to displace Christ as Lord. Any reflection upon history shows the tremendous impact Jesus has had upon society.

First, Christ reveals meaning within the home.

Within the home Christ has lifted the status of each member. Women and children are not family property, to be bought or sold; people are not pawns to be moved about by a political or economic sovereign. Outrage against apartheid in South Africa has less to do with wages than with family breakup resulting from separated housing. What is the mystery of sexuality hidden beneath layers of the world's mythologies? The masculine/feminine complementarity. Social wholeness. Masculine and feminine together delineate God's image. This is more than biological and economic role definition; it's the Edenic model of human fellowship with the Divine. By example and teaching Jesus lifted manhood and womanhood and childhood from cultural tyranny. Religion isn't just synagogue ritual for men or church ritual for women. Jesus freed faith from gender bias and made it gender rich. Patiently the Holy Spirit cuts through cultural incrustations to recover glory for the family. One year soon Roman Catholic priests will be allowed to marry. One year soon Baptist churches and the Reformed churches will let women minister to home as well as to foreign congregations. And someday predators who prey on families (Quaker, too), merchandising breakup, will weep over the destruction of Babylon and the loss of revenue. But the people of God will sing hallelujah! Christ who dandled children on his knee and wept over Lazarus' death—the Lamb of God who takes away the sin of the world—is with us now. Such is the mystery of Christ within the home!

Second, Christ reveals meaning within political structures.

Tony Campolo has alleged (*Partly Right*, Word Publishing, 1985) that the modern church capitulated to secularism on every social issue except that of the family. He may be mostly right! Many Christians want the family—and maybe business—but not government, to follow Jesus. Christians are leavening political structures, however. They submit to Caesar but they follow Christ as Lord. This preeminence of the lordship of Christ involves good education, economic freedom, and the right uses of power. These believers may be a minority but they are vocal. They challenge the old double standard for personal and public ethics.

Increasingly Christians want government to approximate the ethics of Jesus. This is embarrassing. It might be okay for a city council but it would surely impede national efficiency. Christians are becoming a nuisance. Talking about Jesus as Lord in the political realm alarms political realists. Christian interest in the political process makes good election copy especially if Christians trip up morally or hold a selective moral agenda. Suppose we elected a president with Robertson's personal agenda, Jackson's social agenda, and Sister Theresa's compassionate moral agenda? That combination would make even Christians uncomfortable! We trust morally flawed practicality more than technically flawed idealism.

Sometimes Christians have been too utopian, but more often we have lacked faith in the combined power of love and truth. The gospel seems to fade out like FM stations once we get beyond local boundaries. I read about a man who was killed by protective devices he installed in his own home. What a parable for humanity's global house! Are our technicians really so wise?

Christ leavens the political framework of human society. Not by organizing a Christian party (these degenerate) but by infusing all systems with confidence in love and truth and the power of the Spirit to take Jesus' teachings and make them effective. We want a witness to be truthful. We look for fairness by county commissioners and the school board. We do not want corporations to cheat or to kill their competitors. Although political units are larger, our witness is the same. The pagan nations *will* live by Christ's light (Revelation 21:24) at Jesus' triumphant second coming, the timing of which depends upon faithful Christian witness. We hasten the day of the Lord by showing secularists the riches possible in human society *now*. Consider the impact Quakers, Methodists, and Baptists had upon society. They offered freedom and dignity to all persons. Family structures, peer relationships, ethnic customs, national pride can all be enriched when Jesus Christ is worshiped as Lord. The mystery of human society is thus revealed.

Christ reveals purpose within human personality.
Last Sunday I mentioned the struggle within the self, as depicted in Romans—living contrary to moral law affirmed. There are many reasons for that inner war. Basically, without it the human person would usurp divine prerogatives. Something within rebels against divine order. We fear loss of freedom so we disobey God, only to become trapped by our own devices or by persons stronger than ourselves. Theologians call it *carnality*—this disposition to spite God. God's response they term *grace*. Salvation comes when we accept that forgiving response, are cleansed by his spirit, and are enabled to do what is right. Such infusion of power and purity is the essential baptism. Let's consider more fully how Christ within reveals the mystery of the self.

First, Christ within provides a true center to the self.
It is a modern maxim that self should be autonomous, that is, compelled or judged by no outside force. But the same technologies that free the self can also bind. People have been herded like ants into armies and spent as ammunition, or worked to death like drones for the benefit of their oppressors. Small wonder people grasp at whatever promises release from social bondage.

But danger lurks. Without God the self becomes a hollow shell. One has to take the place of God. As Sartre said, one is "condemned to be free." There is no exit from responsibility and no external guidelines. To make the universe revolve around me is more than I can handle. It's more than anyone can handle. Trying to do it produces illusion both for the successful and the unsuccessful. Emptiness can be as terrible for the rich as for the poor. On either side of life's road hope and despair extend endlessly toward an ephemeral horizon yielding no boundaries but life and death. No natural law or cosmic purpose, no national glory stretching over centuries, no enduring values such as truth and justice. Only the self, wrapping tiny fingers about the earth until they weaken, slip, and fall. Sigmund Freud considered religion a dangerous illusion because it shielded the self from reality and sheltered hurtful complexes. Some religious culture does that—it offers avoidance fantasies. But secular culture offers the more dangerous illusions, for it leaves the self not really empty but full of sin, like hidden formatting on a word processor that needs to be selected out and canceled.

Jesus Christ cancels self-centeredness but does not destroy self-identity. The rim finds power at the hub. The paradox of mystery remains—one has to lose self to find it, die to personal interests to discover them, give life away to save it. By becoming a slave to righteousness instead of unrighteousness we discover freedom and never again want sin's bondage. Kierkegaard once said truth isn't truth until it's true for me. To be evangelical means experiencing Christ at the center of my self, beyond explanation, in the silence of divine mystery—an experience ecstatic beyond words, an eternal weight of glory. If you are self-centered and feeling empty, I invite you to discover Christ there.

Second, Christ within forms the basis for social interaction.
People get frustrated trying to make the universe revolve around themselves. They seek alternatives. Most can't be hermits. They have to socialize to know who they are. Without others they have no identity. Tennis partners, gangs, devotees, cliques, clubs, corporations, families, ethnic groups, hobbyists, lobbyists, patriots—in the social self we seek the individual self. Of course social interaction is good, but "joiners" can become mere aggregations of solitary individuals, as lonely on leaving the group as on arriving. So rituals invest social circles with the garments of God. The flag, the company logo, fraternity regalia, or Kiwanis hymns evidence a groping after mystery—too often becoming idolatrous substitutes for God. But these ritualized circles of loyalty are not enough.

We crave authenticity. Like adolescents we want to be unique but cannot find a way to do so without mimicking socially prescribed behavior. Or we fear betrayal: Having bent our backs and sometimes our consciences for the company or the country we want more than songs, uniforms, and badges. Our souls seem at auction, with family, peers, school, culture, business, government, or religion trying to buy us at the lowest bid. The human quest for freedom of the self apart from God litters history with revolutions and successive tyrannies. And pioneers who search new lands or new levels of education to escape them, soon load burdens on others or find themselves enslaved by the next wave of immigrants.

Christ within does not destroy the powers that shape our common lives but redeems them. The family becomes a fit model for marriage and the church. Schools begin to educate on behalf of truth, not manipulation. Socializing becomes a feast of good things where laughter is not at the expense of another. We become drunk with the Spirit instead of liquor. In music and the arts we recreate the world in joyous play. Commerce becomes a way to enrich each other through special skills and shared work. In this kingdom, the best of capitalism and the best of socialism merge, for labor has been redeemed. On the great day of the Lord people from every tribe and tongue and nation will sing praises to the Lamb who was slain from the foundation of the world, who has gathered his people unto himself.

The church of Jesus Christ keeps this vision alive. It is good news. Weary statesmen welcome it although, like the ruler who came to Jesus by night, they scarce believe humanity can be born again, that old things can become new. But gospel leaven works within the world. Each new destructive technology exposes Satanic purpose and makes Jesus' way look good. "Ready or not, here I come," calls Jesus, as we scramble to hide ourselves. And he finds us! He finds us together! Russians and Americans, Contras and Sandinistas, Republicans and Democrats, communists and capitalists, Muslim and Christian and Jew, secularist and believer. Christ calls us to live in expectation of a heavenly Zion where Christ, the slain and risen Lamb of God, reigns over a united and redeemed people. Keep that vision before your eyes like Mount Hood above the city, like the morning star in the darkness, like a passport to the coming world. Christ within offers personal dignity and social significance.

Third, Christ within gives meaning to time.
Infancy becomes childhood, childhood moves to adolescence, adolescence to youth, youth to maturity, maturity to seniority, seniority to old age, old age to death. The signs are everywhere that our time is brief and swift. Our toys have been discarded, the school grades forgotten, the new house now needs repair, shrubs once planted have been replaced. The grown children hold Christmas festivities at their places now. Shoulders sag, eyes grow dim, disease strikes, friends die. Oh, there are the interruptions to the rhythm—premature deaths, accidents, calamities, wars. But the clock ticks on for each of us. The last enemy *is* death. The death of others diminishes us and symbolizes an unknown experience that lies ahead for us.

We are all passengers on time's rocket. But Christ gives meaning to time because, as our elder brother, he has gone through the portal of death before us. He knows the way. He has cleared the path. He has spied into that eternal Canaan toward which we ride. His resurrection promises ours. Oh what a wonder, this life and heaven too! To enjoy earth and to know it will be renewed. To treasure friendship and know it will endure beyond death. To love another and to know this love will not be snuffed out. To paint a landscape or build a house or write a book and feel the pulsebeat of eternity. To venture into space and know we will live across its magnitude.

My brothers and sisters, Christ within is good news. We shall be raised, like flowers from seed, after the winter rain. The mystery hidden for ages is now revealed, "Christ in you, the hope of glory." What glorious wealth in God's word to humanity! Hallelujah!

Right Standing

The Carey Lecture, Baltimore Yearly Meeting of Friends, 1988

Introduction

Thank you for inviting me to the 317th sessions of Baltimore Yearly Meeting to give the Carey Memorial Lecture. It is an honor to be chosen, and to be a guest speaker again after a dozen years. As a recorded minister under Northwest Yearly Meeting I have accepted your invitation for Spirit-directed ministry. So I have prayed that I might be faithful to you and to those who established this continuing memorial to past leadership. It's twenty years since consolidation of your two yearly meetings. I know that you continue to struggle for spiritual unity. I ask you to reach past the limits of my understanding in this particular lecture. Let Christ be your teacher through my words.

Once at age thirteen I slipped on wet schoolhouse stairs and bounced down each step until I reached the lower hall floor, scarcely able to breathe and unable to respond either to mocking laughter or solicitous query. I had lost my voice as well as my footing. In that embarrassing situation I appreciated a student friend who simply held me steady until agony subsided and speech returned. Consider this a parable for life's larger situations in which we lose our footing and our voice. Consider it a parable for Baltimore Yearly Meeting, an application of theme, "Seeking a place to stand."

I address your spiritual standing as individuals and participants in a shared spiritual journey. When one part suffers, the whole body hurts. Maybe you are striding through life buoyant in physical, mental, and spiritual health. It is my discernment, however, that the parable *does* apply to Baltimore Yearly Meeting, to Friends generally, and to some of you personally. What are my expectations for this address? That my remarks will help some Friends catch their breath, stand erect, and tell the world who they are.

Right standing

So join me in considering what "right standing" may mean to you personally, to Baltimore Yearly Meeting, and to Friends generally. I elaborate the yearly meeting theme as 1) standing against evil, 2) standing for the right, 3) standing forth in faithful commitment, and 4) standing by to receive divine grace.

1. Standing against evil

Imagine this kind of "standing" as *good footing.* Picture preparing a concrete base for a house foundation or for a bridge. Think of placing your feet on a starting block for a race, or getting ready for a golf stroke. Recall leaning into a raging storm. We struggle against many opposing forces—inertia, ignorance, lethargy, tragic blunders, compromised principles, malice, and demonic power. Knowing its subtlety and terrors, with the psalmist we thank God for rescuing us from all evils. "My feet were on the point of stumbling," he said, "a little further and I should have slipped, envying the arrogant as I did, and watching the wicked get rich" (Psalm 73:2-3 JB).

Today I urge you to stand against three evils—well, actually four: pollution of the earth, pollution of the body, pollution of the mind, and pollution of the spirit.

First, pollution of the earth
Lamenting it doesn't suffice. We've got to stand against it. Pollution results from a mix of ignorance, adventure, quest for sustenance, and greed. I applaud efforts by scientists to check global pollution and am grateful for publicity arising from the recent Toronto conference. The problems are enormous and complex. But we can hold each other accountable to stand against pollution with appropriate technology applied by conscientious persons in just societies. "Do you avoid waste?" That's a good query isn't it? So is "can you find a less polluting technology?"

Simplicity may indeed mean reduced wants. This is easier in respect to clothing than health care. But simplicity also involves better industrial and social design. Accordingly, I ask Quaker scientists and Quaker college administrators to give priority to this concern. Let hope characterize their search, remembering that Jesus' promised Holy Spirit is the spirit of truth. Pray that scientists can stand against patronage that overtly or covertly contributes to earth's pollution. Pray that scientists may demonstrate courage as well as skill, and consider research a spiritual calling.

Second, pollution of the body
"Substance abuse" can become a euphemism for drugs other people get hooked on. What about yourself? Tobacco and alcohol are killers. So is overeating. So is fouled water and air. Abuse of prescription drugs models chemical dependency. Historically Friends have testified against tobacco and alcohol abuse, sometimes pleading moderation, more often abstinence. Recently, social pressure and reaction against legalism have muted the abstinence testimony. Beer and wine appear on Quaker tables and at Quaker colleges and gatherings. Woolman said exhausting labor contributed to alcohol abuse. For our era I would add entrepreneurial culture. So I put this query to you: Do you abstain from harmful, addictive, and unnecessary drugs—including alcoholic beverages, tobacco, marijuana, and cocaine?

Let's also continue to stand against commercial dumping of carcinogens, food contaminants, and dangerous herbicides and pesticides upon poor countries.

Third, pollution of the mind
Because we cherish freedom for others as well as for ourselves we are caught between the evils of censorship and mental pollution. Quaker demonstrations haven't included vigilante raids on high school libraries. I don't think they should, although a bit of Carry Nation hatchet work on hard-core pornography offers an attractive temptation! To protect our children from mental pollution we will have to find ways to go between the horns of this dilemma. Putting our own children in private schools isn't enough, nor does it protect other families. Media leaps over the walls. Pornography is only the most blatant form of mental pollution. Like a child plastering french fries with ketchup, contemporary printwriters and screenwriters drench their work with profanity, vulgarity, and violence. It sells. It then worms its way from popular or avant-garde culture into socially approved art forms. We get used to it and figure our kids can handle it. But at what cost? Cynicism? Sometimes. But more often a tragic loss of the holy. Mental pollution fogs our senses; we no longer see Sinai nor hear God shout "You shall not take the name of the Lord your God in vain!" No longer can we touch a neighbor and

trace the image of God. Technological jargon as well as gutter speech makes it hard for the phrase "the finger of God" to be an effective metaphor. Language, the coinage of humanity, is becoming debased. Teachers, elders, help our families stand against mental pollution.

Fourth, spiritual pollution
Behind pollutions of earth, body, and mind is a demonic force early Quakers labeled "deceit." It's hard to keep our footing spiritually, not just because of mean people, corrupted language, or systems loaded with greed, lust, sloth, envy, and ignorance, but also because the dark source of these evils crouches within. Because of deceit. Call it sin, depravity, the demonic. Call it what you will, deceit dogs our journey. When Christ's light penetrates the center of the soul in quiet judgment we know that it is so. We feel sullied, betrayed, spiritually polluted.

"Put on the full armor of God" urged Paul, "so that you can take your stand against the devil's schemes" (Ephesians 6:10, NIV here and in subsequent texts). Of course it is better to light a candle than curse the darkness, but first one must acknowledge the darkness. George Fox had confidence the ocean of light would overcome the ocean of darkness. But first he acknowledged the darkness. "Principalities and powers" aren't just governments, but also educational and cultural organizations, even religious groups, including liberal ones. All the powers get demon infested. We become better agents of the Light if we keep a wary eye on this wily tyrant.

Consider deceit as idolatry, as demonic force masked in false light. Deceit pollutes our common life. Shall I detail its idolatrous fallout? Statements by public officials, calculated, or evaluated, for effect rather than for truth. TV sports commercials, aimed at young men, that legitimate getting drunk on beer (Miller Lite). A computer company (Radio Shack) ad that steals a folk hymn and twists its lyrics into "You've got the whole world in your hands." That's profanity. On glittering avenues we name Public Relations (although God calls them Babylon) psychologists prostitute their skills under bondage to commercial pimps. That's idolatry. Even benevolent institutions hover at the edge of deceit in highlighting image over substance.

Here are some cult forms of this idolatry: personal vanity preened by consumerism, national sovereignty hallowed by bloody mythologies, and religion wrapped in cultural icons that portray contemporary experience as the test of truth and consider Deity as just a projection of social need.

We need good footing to stand against such evils. Leaders of the seventeenth-century Quaker Christian Awakening identified a "persecuting spirit" and "Ranterism" as evidences of deceit. Today we stand firmly against the persecuting spirit but not so firmly against Ranterism. Disguised by euphemisms such as "the autonomous self," "personal liberty," and "individualism," Ranterism strikes us from behind. It decimates Quaker ranks and mutes our historic testimony. It turns meetings from Christ-led churches into groups engaged in psychological ego struggles labeled "consensus."

Our culture makes it easy to typecast people for easy reference and utilization, treating them as diverse publics to be enlisted in a cause, rather than as brothers and sisters in the family of God. We Quakers aren't immune from using people for promotional purposes, instead of loving them for themselves. Beware deceit. A young friend of mine left a meeting a few hundred miles from here because the kids there were sleeping around, taking dope, and engaging in petty theft. Does a strong peace witness exempt us from personal moralities? No. Given the breakdown of Quaker marriages during the past two decades, perhaps we should put on sackcloth and stand penitent before the meetinghouse. Scandalized by the moral defections of popular televangelists we come under the same judgment. Did power blind their eyes to morality? What has blinded our eyes? Vanity? Greed? Sloth? Pride, probably—pride in our custodial role over social ethics. Spiritual deceit casts a dark shadow over a people of God historically known as "Children of the Light." O God, forgive us. Elders, ministers, leaders, theologians, help us stand against such deceit! Our feet have slipped.

2. Standing for the right

Consider this kind of standing as measurement against a plumb line, as a grandparent measuring a child's height against tape pasted on a closet door, as an adolescent asking "how am I doing?" as a grade card, as a professional evaluation, a medical or bar examination, a book review, a medical prognosis, a judicial opinion, or as a statistical trend line.

Paul's well-known imagery depicts the Christian armor as "the belt of truth," the "breastplate of righteousness," and "feet fitted with the gospel of peace as a firm footing" (Ephesians 6). Peace as firm footing, I like that! Today I urge you to stand for three right principles—well, actually four: education appropriate to the universe God has given us, healthy families in a well-tended earth, peace as the means appropriate to justice, and faith in Jesus Christ as Lord.

First, education appropriate to the universe God has given
We are God's stewards of the cosmos and not squatters contending for ownership. Let education flow from that principle. Good education aims at responsible community, national and international citizenship. It must also teach accountability to the Creator for the universe placed in human trust. On this issue aboriginal peoples can be included among our teachers. God has given us a role in shaping reality, however, as well as ecological harmonics. To some extent God lets us plan the future. Fox said the whole earth took on a new smell when he found spiritual peace. This statement symbolizes a Quaker understanding of earth's sacral character. This conviction, along with legal restraints, gave science and the practical arts a strong place in the Quaker education, at least until cultural demands renewed a classical curriculum. In the past Quakers pioneered many educational ventures and reforms. We need imaginative and pioneering minds now. So I ask Quaker educators to strengthen the network of public school teachers and to support legislation and philanthropy designed to educate the world's children, so that neither ignorance nor arrogance shall mar humankind's appropriate stewardship of God's cosmos.

Quakers started more schools and colleges than we probably should have, and when our outreach failed to keep pace with our institutions, we shifted from educational stewardship for our own children to educational trusteeship for other people's children. Both missions can be defended but need reexamination. Like the Jesuits we have justified elitism in the name of educating future leaders. In so doing have we rationalized and eroded purpose? And will the Quaker schools in Africa and Latin America also follow that route and lose touch with Quaker families and with the poor? Many Quaker youth are locked out of our schools, financially or academically, and sometimes spiritually. And then we lament loss of Quaker identity. The Friends Educational Council and the Friends Association of Higher Education provide a national network of educators. Will they address these issues? Pray that they will.

Second, healthy families in a well-tended earth

Specialization alienates unless checked by compensating forces. Young professionals' families face enormous corporate pressures. Moving up often means moving out. And splitting up. Age groups get segmented and loyalties realigned. It's the rock group for the kids, professional associations for the parents, and the retirement village for the grandparents. It takes spiritual commitment and discernment to overcome these diverging forces.

In practical terms how can we sustain strong families on a healthy planet? By choosing whatever keeps the biological family unit central to human society: family economic enterprises, shared recreational and service activities, a legislated healthcare and childcare system, an international nutritional network, jobs that support family stability, and, for us, Quaker meetings serving as an extended family.

During open worship recently a seven-year-old lad arose and spoke movingly about his grandfather, who was dying. This lad felt at home enough in worship to be a vessel of ministry, supported by his parents, of course, but also by other children and adults. Biologically unrelated persons of this church function as siblings, as uncles and aunts, as grandparents. It is a tribe of the Lord. Unfortunately, not all our meetings offer children and their parents such helpful extended family support. Some are simply too small. Is that why many Quaker families look to other churches for the nurture of their children, or maintain Friends membership while worshiping elsewhere? It could be. For some it's a case of competing, not intersecting, circles of loyalty. Remain Friends and lose the family or hold the family together and lose the Friends connection. Is that why traditional Quaker families are leaving our meetings more rapidly than newcomers are joining? It's one reason. Friends bear heavy responsibilities toward outsiders, expending energies in commendable mission and service projects. Meanwhile our family base erodes. Numbers remain constant or decrease. How might your own meeting strengthen families and nurture them in Christian faith? Sometimes a homeowner has to suspend other activities in order to put a new foundation under the house. The family of Friends is at that critical point now.

Third, peace as the means appropriate to justice

Peace is obviously an essential way to sustain strong families on a healthy planet! With other peace churches Quakers believe peacemaking includes reconciling people to God and neighbor to neighbor. Peace is part of Christian discipleship, a testimony sustained by the community of faith.

A word to activist Quakers: I appreciate your efforts to put deeds above words, and to affirm humanity against partisan interests. You expose subtle connections between injustice and violence. Against great odds and frequent criticism you labor for economic and social justice. Some of you have suffered imprisonment or sacrificed financial security in order to live out your witness. You may be tempted, however, to overlook Golgotha's agony, tempted to substitute the just revolution for the just war, to approve violence by the oppressed but not by the oppressor. You are tempted to substitute political compromise for gospel leaven, to accept lesser evils as instrumental good. Subconsciously you may conclude Jesus is too impractical for the real world. This attitude sustains those who look for other saviors, deify the state, become power brokers, or embrace cynicism. I call you back to the cross, to the agony of God, and to the mystery of redemptive suffering. I remind you of Simon Peter. Although under pressure he denied Jesus, he still refused Judas' option—violence as the route to the kingdom. I remind you, also, that Peter finally turned his eyes from others and heeded Jesus' words, "Follow me!" Is this a word to you?

Our peace testimony will be stronger for being Christian and not merely pragmatic or prudential. There are three kinds of peace, said Luis de Leon, sixteenth-century Spanish mystic. The first takes place "when a man is subject to God, and has accepted God's will, obeying divine laws in their entirety, and God, accepting man's submission, treats him with sweetness and love and sends him the gift of grace." The second is the rule of reason over human senses and passions; the third is justice to each individual "without struggle or delay." "Each type of peace gives mankind a great deal of prosperity and when they are all present at the same time man reaches happiness and serenity" (*The Names of Christ*, Classics of Western Spirituality, Paulist Press, 1984, p. 216). Quakers can applaud de Leon's vision of *shalom*.

Fourth, faith in Jesus Christ as Lord

Someone once asked why we should use religious language to explain the dynamics of social interaction. Why not talk about personality integration instead of being "converted" or "in Christ"? This person misunderstood Christian truth claims, misunderstood Christ's own understanding of his mission. Early Quakers believed in the reality of both inward experiences of Christ and outward historical events testified to by the Scriptures. Revelation by the Spirit certified the historical incarnation through the Scriptures. Revelation by the Spirit also confirmed Christ within. It is abundantly evident that the Quakers affirmed that Jesus Christ and the Light are one. The Quaker awakening offered the world a distinctly Christian doctrine of the Spirit—Jesus Christ teaching his people himself. We are inheritors of that robust faith, some of us by a lineage three-and-a-half centuries long, others by recent convincement. Jesus Christ stands at the center of the cosmos, at the center of history, and at the center of the human spirit. Don't succumb to unbelief. Jesus speaks to you, "don't be faithless, but believing." Experience the crucifixion and the resurrection, receive Christ's Spirit. In the same paragraph that the apostle Paul said "Do everything in love," he also said "Stand firm in the faith" (1 Corinthians 16:13).

If seventeenth-century witness seems antiquated, catch Teilhard de Chardin's vision (see *The Divine Milieu*, Harper, 1960, and *Building the Earth*, Dimension Books, 1965). The late Jesuit paleontologist sees all creation being gathered to Christ, the Omega point. The central point of the universe is not a formula, nor a place, but a person—Jesus, the Christ. By virtue of the creation, and especially of the incarnation, Chardin declares, nothing can be considered profane. The earth slowly moves toward the grand *parousia* when all life and thought shall be brought under the sovereign power of Christ. The church lives as a witness to this future.

3. Standing forth

Imagine this kind of "standing" as a *position* within an order of reality: as a family member, as an employer or employee, student or teacher, artist or patron, public official or citizen, national or foreigner. Picture these orders encircled by the divine order. Circles within circles. In each circle find your vocation (to use a Lutheran term)—ways to serve your neighbor in love. Such is the priesthood of believers. Through what Elton Trueblood called "the common ventures of life" one can activate effective relationships with God and others. In New Testament language (Romans 12:1), one can become a *living sacrifice,* mind renewed, holy and pleasing to God, an acceptable offering on the altar of the world. Not as a victim but as a friend.

"Standing forth" means seizing opportunities for faithful actions. Such actions flow from knowing who you answer to, knowing who beckons you from the future. Lewis B. Smedes writes in *Love Within Limits* (Eerdmans, 1979, p. 41): "We have an undeniable right to be what we truly are and to be known as what we are. What we are is the image of God. I need not prove that my existence has some 'redeeming social value' to demonstrate that I am a member in good standing of God's image-bearers. I need merely be, as a person...a creature with the dignity and destiny of God's own child and partner."

Today I urge you to stand forth in respect to three kinds of actions—well, actually four: principled use of science and technology, artistic use of material treasures, imaginative international cooperation, and witness to the kingdom of God.

First, principled use of science and technology

Many of us find our vocations within science and technology. Information exchange is America's largest commodity. The apocalyptic vision in the final book of the New Testament pictures the future not as pristine Eden but as a garden city. We can learn from the past but will never live there again. Augustine envisioned the city of God over against the city of man. The French sociologist, Jacques Ellul, has warned us against the Babylonian allure of civilization's demonic power. But the city can give humanity a place to stand. Jerusalem the golden beckons us. God invites us to help create it. Historically Christians have been in the vanguard of history's great discoveries and adventures, sometimes rationalizing conquest, but more often moderating abuses or sowing the seeds for God's kingdom. I applaud Baltimore Yearly Meeting's emphasis upon the right sharing of the earth's resources. Can we go cosmic? Are we prepared to be salt and light and leaven for the human adventure into space? Why not!

Second, artistic use of material treasures

Historically, we Quakers have been too Puritan in regard to the arts. Fortunately that's changing. Discerning the sacred within ordinary things, we ought to lead in artistic interpretation of reality. Why be so Platonic, taking perverse pride in the plain and ugly and rationalizing aesthetic failure by appeals to duty? Do we assume God speaks only prose? Have we substituted a ritual of physical silence for an awesome, joyous, silence of creature before Creator? Beauty surrounds us and invites us to participate. We don't have to succumb to high-art snobbery any more than to intellectual snobbery. The aesthetic best often does become enemy of the ethical good. But it doesn't have to. The creation isn't just raw material for food, shelter, and commerce. The creation is also for making sand castles, sculpting from stone, painting pictures, and fashioning flutes. It's for enjoying earth's creatures who share our journey. A Continental contemporary of George Fox, the "cherubinic wanderer," wrote (Angelus Silesius, *The Cherubinic Wanderer*, Paulist Press, 1986, p. 51):

> Creatures are God's echo,
> Nothing is without a voice:
>   God everywhere can hear,
>   arising from creation His
>   praise and echo clear.

The terrible seriousness of technological society is not always well-relieved by consumer entertainment. It lacks imagination. Can we Quakers help recover artistry in the material wealth of the universe? I hope so. We might start with worship. It doesn't have to be ritualistic to be artistic. But it can be artful and joyous. Many of us need help in feeling at home aesthetically, allusively, within God's created order. Quaker artists—poets, painters, dramatists, novelists, musicians—unite! You've nothing to lose but our chains.

Third, imaginative international cooperation

On this point I will be brief. I applaud Quaker efforts at internationalizing the conscience. Let's keep it up, finding new and imaginative ways for cultural interchange and non-political cooperation. Let's also actively support the United Nations. It represents, although imperfectly, a unique forum. Quakers have lobbied politically for greater international participation, for the law of the seas, for international health efforts. We have an additional task, a neglected one—getting local Christian communities of faith to affirm the United Nations, or indeed any kind of global community, including worldwide Quaker fellowship. For years the Friends World Committee seemed to be a kind of international religious jet set. Thanks to good leadership that has changed. As a result of some of its conferences and activities, patronizing practices by mission and service agencies have been replaced by shared participation. Not long ago the World Reformed Churches judged their South African counterparts to be heretic because apartheid denied basic Christian teachings. We applaud that. Recently Latin American Quakers chided North American Quakers for an inarticulate or muted Christian testimony. We applaud that too. Quakers are becoming intercultural. Chiquimula and La Paz, Nairobi and Kotzebue are as central to the Quaker wheel as London and Philadelphia, Richmond and Newberg. Accepting Christ as the hub of this wheel helps us overcome provincialism.

Fourth, witness to the kingdom of God

In this kind of standing the kingdom of God is our destiny and the Scriptures its map. Let that map chart and correct our course. In the swirl of ideologies and loyalty circles it remains the impelling vision. Like Abraham in the wilderness, we put one foot before the other and plod toward the city with foundations, whose builder and maker is God. We leave ethnic homelands knowing that Christ has chosen us. We avoid the traps of religious and cultural ceremonies because we belong to God's royal priesthood. We are loyal but critical patriots because we belong to God's holy nation— a company of faithful people who have been called out of darkness into God's glorious light (see 1 Peter 2:9-10).

In faith's journey glimpses of the kingdom will occur at awesome and fruitful still points intersecting life's rhythms. To use science-fiction lingo, in these moments we are snagged and held against all known powers of resistance, by "a wandering instability, a knot in time and space, a ripple in the between that came wandering through our safe solar system and sucked us up" (C.J. Cherryn, *Port Eternity*, Day, 1982, p. 47).

The "Day of the Lord" isn't just a messed-up time to be lamented or lobbied against. It's divine visitation. The kingdom of God flashes like a supernova across a darkening sky. For the Society of Friends, and for you, personally, such a day can be Pentecost revisited.

Pentecost

"Blood and fire and drifting smoke,"
forecast of the world's weather.
But wind leaped a fence, blew
open a door, filled the house.
Curtains trembled. "Who's there?" creaked
the floor. The windows all rattled
the answer, "He's here! Whoever
can hear, throw off the night's cloak!"
"Come on out! Come on! Why
drapes and walls, you sleeping folk,
on this beautiful day? Wouldn't you rather
wake up? It's five minutes 'til nine!"
The kids came alive. "Hey, He's here!"
"Get up, Dad, what a great morning!"
And Mom banged the kitchen pans. With her
breakfast commotion the neighbors awoke.
Inflamed now with imploding wind
we looked, we laughed, we loved.
Each heard the language the other spoke.
Man, woman, boy, girl—together.
"Blood and fire, and drifting smoke,"
forecast of the world's weather.
But we shouted yes to God, to ourselves,
to neighbors, the day the wind called.
"He's here; come on out,
come on...He's here!"

(Arthur O. Roberts, *Sunrise and Shadow*, Barclay Press, 1985)

4. Standing by

Imagine "standing by" as a TV message stating that the network signal has been lost but technicians are working to restore it. Think of waiting helplessly for a tow truck to pull you from a ditch. I urge you to stand by in three circumstances—well, actually four: in the midst of demographic change, in times of personal tragedy, in diminishing power, and in time of death.

First, in the midst of demographic change

When I was in grade school the world population reached two billion. Currently it is five billion. Next year the total will be increased by a hundred million persons. My identity as a transplanted Welsh-Dutch ethnic is impacted by these demographic factors. Not directly, but indirectly, through rapid social, political, and cultural changes.

For some these changes bring favorable circumstances—good jobs, new suburbs, better education, adventure, global travel. Not so with others. Choked by constricted traffic, obsolete factories, and political neglect, neighborhoods deteriorate and sometimes die. As a result support groups dwindle, cultural customs change, and youth move elsewhere to find jobs commensurate with professional skills. Conditions no longer favor the lifestyle to which we have become accustomed. After a fifth robbery or a third mugging even idealistic families abandon the city. In these circumstances we discover helplessness.

Currently some Friends meetings are experiencing such diminishment. Crowds don't flock to the meeting now like they do to other religious groups. Routine burdens fall on fewer—and aging—members. Quaker testimonies simply appear quaint to others. Discouragement sets in, or we make desperate compromises to preserve identity, at the cost of Christian faithfulness.

In such times we need others to stand by and steady us. To help us bear the pain and regain our breath. To help us stand erect again. The Methodists did this once for some Friends meetings. Baptists and Pentecostals and Catholics stand by for some Friends families now. Sometimes it's easier to accept help from casual neighbors than from relatives, or borrow at heavy interest from mercenary strangers rather than from generous friends. I am glad Quakers are becoming more willing to receive help from each other. Friends who have lived before us are also our helpers, through the legacy they have left us. Gratitude for all who steady us in hard times may be a condition for standing on our own again.

Second, in times of personal tragedy

Children and grandchildren get caught in drug addiction or cult power, crib death takes a firstborn, drunken driving a teenager. Meetings are destroyed by petty and unforgiving factions. Elders sue each other in court or commit adultery oblivious to its cost in cynicism for the young. In all such circumstances we depend upon others. Guilty and innocent parties alike—and those in both categories—come to know the forgiving grace of God. "Tears shed in common," I once read, "constitutes a sign of true community." I find God's tears in Jesus' eyes and it helps me mingle my tears with the tears of friends dying of cancer. Have you noticed the renewed sense of divine grace in those meetings that took in boat people, aided refugees, or set up care centers for the homeless? We can deny tragedy, rage at it, or like Job or Jeremiah find God in a deeper way. We can understand the meaning of a cup of water offered in Jesus' name. An ancient psalm writer proclaims that the Almighty who gives each star its name also heals broken hearts (Psalm 147).

Third, in diminishing power
Our influence wanes because other leaders emerge. We become burned out trying to push projects of human betterment against a tide of greed and winds of political stupidity. Strokes and senility mute voices once depended upon. Conflict shatters romance. Poverty dulls the face of hope. Quaker influence seems to be ignored now rather than admired. Neither nostalgia for past glory nor gratitude for prophetic faithfulness by others can overcome a sense of loss at being bypassed in religious leadership. It's good to know there are 200,000 African and 25,000 Central American Quakers—Quaker leadership doesn't have to be Anglo-Saxon. In a dark funk these numbers don't heal our sickness, but the Holy Spirit can teach us to trust them to be torchbearers on our behalf. We like the term "Friends" as a mark of intimacy with Christ. This intimacy doesn't connote preferential rank but rather deferential servant-hood. Sometimes servants are in the public eye, at other times not. We seek faithfulness, not public acclaim. Consider Milton's phrase from "A Sonnet on His Blindness," "They also serve who only stand and wait." Waiting doesn't mean exchanging hand-wringing for fatalistic acceptance. It means preparing ourselves for new baptisms of the Spirit.

Fourth, in the time of death
We experience death standing by another. In turn ours will be thus experienced. We face death as diminishment. Not as the end of identity but as transition to life eternal.

> The seed comes first
> ...and then the flower.
> Diminishment of seed
> is death's dark hour.
> But there remains a thirst
> for life, a hidden shower
> of Light; now freed
> by resurrection power
> that Light has burst
> death's hold. Its hour
> is past. Mortal seed?
> No, immortal flower!
> O Lord Christ,
> O glory, glory!
> (Arthur O. Roberts, *Sunrise and Shadow*)

The one we honor as Lord has prepared a home for us, the dimensions of which beckon us with hope and startle us with adventure. God offers us new clothing for an even more fulfilling life, where the stars sing for joy, and there is peace in the City.

I conclude with an early Christian admonition (Galatians 5:1) "...Stand firm, then, and do not let yourselves be burdened again by a yoke of slavery." Standing against evil can become an enslaving burden. So can standing for the right, and standing forth in faithful commitment. Life itself at last becomes a burden to be laid down. But God and the faithful community will always stand by us. So let us cherish divine grace, experiencing it sometimes in mystical or ecstatic worship but more often through persons who love us and stand by us.

Howard Macy expresses it well in *Rhythms of the Inner Life* (Revell, 1988, p. 65): "God is the Wholly Other, the Mystery that comes to us but over-reaches our comprehension and control, the crackling Power that steals our breath away. To encounter this Holy One leaves us awestruck, overcome by the Light, melted by unthinkable love."

Back to Square One

Reedwood Friends Church, February 26, 1988

Introduction

The theme of this sermon is handling losses in order to achieve spiritual gain. In certain board games players may be forced back to "Start" because of the throw of the dice, the strategy of others, or their own mistakes. The game appeals to us because it imitates real life experiences. When we find ourselves in a conversational impasse we may say "let's get back to square one," and when directions sent are not the same as directions received we say "maybe we should just start from the beginning." Remedial discipline does the same thing, only more forcibly. These games and social practices reflect the fact that life flows by fits and starts, sometimes moving smoothly, at other times with erratic gains and losses.

Trials common to human experience

What sorts of things send you back to square one, burdened by loss and failure? How do you persevere under trial in order to win the crown of life that God has promised those who love

Scripture reading

James 1:12 (NIV here and in subsequent texts)

"Blessed is the man who perseveres under trial because when he has stood the test, he will receive the crown of life that God has promised to those who love him."

---

him? Consider with me seven sorts of trials common to human experience and then hold them up to the light of biblical teaching. I'll illustrate each one and offer biblical perspectives.

1. Misfortune

You are unlucky; the windstorm blows the oak onto your roof instead of the neighbors. Your car falls apart just after the warranty expired. A rabid chipmunk bites your child.

2. Exploitation

Someone gains at your expense. You get mugged, your house or your marriage gets broken, your self-esteem shattered, your body maimed. Through little or no fault of your own, destruction comes your way. Perhaps, like Job, thugs (individual or corporate), destroy what fire and tornado miss. In short, you are a victim.

3. Inept Performance

Your plans don't work. With all good intentions you bumble the committee assignment and commit social blunders, embarrassing family or friends. Hindsight reveals this to you with startling clarity.

4. Second-rate competition

You are bypassed for promotion; another is chosen president of the class. You don't make the athletic team or the honor society. The company that urged your application regretfully informs you someone else has been chosen. A rejection slip instead of a check arrives from the publisher.

5. Silent partnership with evil

Influenced by others and with fuzzy acquiescence you become a silent partner in what turns out to be a morally flawed enterprise. Exciting new friends get drunk at the high school prom and wreck your parents' car. You hire on for a lucrative sales program, featuring successful looking Christians, and end up aiding and abetting a pyramid scam.

6. Natural attrition

Things you value disappear, like heirlooms in a house fire, like friends forever leaving. The utility company cuts the roots of a favorite curbside tree and it has to be taken down. Your golf score deteriorates, so does your health. Loved ones die.

7. Moral turpitude

Masks of self-deception get ripped away to reveal a pattern of deceit, sexual immorality, greed and/or covetousness. You realize that you are an oppressor: other persons can or should consider themselves your victims.

Biblical exposition

Which kind of loss are you experiencing? Misfortune, exploitation, ineptitude, second-rate competition, complicity in evil, natural attrition, or moral failure? Does the Spirit nudge your conscience at one of these levels and say, "Listen up, now, I have a message for you?" Here are some biblical perspectives to help us cut our losses and to regain the crown of life the Lord has promised.

1. Misfortune

The mystery of suffering deserves more attention than this sermon can give. We think of Job, of course, when we consider misfortune. Actually, he was also a victim. Heavily tested, he became neither bitter nor sanctimonious. He avoided neurosis. The Epistle of James, from which our text was drawn, exhorts us to consider Job, praising him for such perseverance that God's compassion and mercy were clearly demonstrated (James 5:11). In case you lack Job's consummate skill in facing up to God and his courage to rise from the ashes with integrity intact you might consider the case of the lame man at the pool of Bethesda (see John 5). Now here is one *practiced* loser—for thirty-eight years others always got to the miraculous moving of the water before he did. Jesus had a strong word for him, "Get up and walk." If you are a practiced loser Jesus has that word for you. So hike back to square one, put on your thinking cap and roll the dice. Even five or ten years is too long to nurse grievances at bad luck.

2. Exploitation

There are lots of victims in the Bible—from Abel to Stephen. Plus unnamed martyrs like those Hebrews 11 mentions, people who were flogged, stoned, and sawn in two for their faith. Like the disappeared persons of our times, individually they made no headlines. Nor do many abused people today, bearing up silently violence heaped upon them by others. Joseph is a biblical victim to learn from. Sold into servitude by jealous brothers, in godly faith he resisted toadying up to his owners—no slow-footed shuffle, no obsequious speech, no downcast eyes. Joseph neither abandoned his moral standards nor wreaked vengeance on his persecuting kinfolk once the tables were turned.

Are you a victim? Consider Joseph. You can read about him in Genesis 37 through 47—ten whole chapters. He could tell you about years of family neglect! You may not become a powerful political figure (although in our time of global distress we could do with a few public Josephs) but you can learn a lot about what Jesus meant by turning the other cheek, and returning good for evil. We know Jesus did this but sometimes we need some less awesome models—like Joseph—for our own actions.

If Joseph seems out of your league, consider Hagar, invited by her rich but barren owner, Sarah, to become a surrogate mother. A jealous Sarah thought the pregnant servant looked smug, and Abraham too solicitous; Sarah abused Hagar so badly Hagar fled into the desert. There the twice-victimized girl received a special visit from the Lord, who had heard her cries. The angel promised that her baby, Ishmael, would be father of a great nation.

No, Hagar didn't prosper as well as Joseph. She remained a slave. But Abraham loved their son, however, and marked him with the covenant sign (circumcision). Those who call Abraham father ought to remember God's words to him: "As for Ishmael, I have heard you: I will surely bless him; I will make him fruitful and will greatly increase his numbers...I will make him into a great nation" (Genesis 17:20ff). History might have been different if Sarah hadn't driven Hagar away. In any case, offer a few cheers for Hagar, who handled exploitation reasonably well, with God's help. Give kudos for Ishmael, too, to whom Abraham gave goods if not the inheritance, and who joined favored brother Isaac to give Dad a proper burial (Genesis 25); for Sarah, too, who finally quit laughing, listened to God, and returned to square one. Can we applaud you, also, for standing strong in the face of exploitation?

3. Inept performance

Certainly the Old Testament character Saul stands head and shoulders among the world's worst bumblers, even though—or perhaps because—he was a king. Samson, another bumbler, at least ended the tragic game with a triumphant flourish. I'm not sure what we can learn from them, other than to take seriously loving the Lord God with the mind as well as the heart.

Would it surprise you to include Moses, a liberator of enslaved people, among inept performers? His courage in rejecting the perquisites of privilege was unmatched strategically. He showed remarkable ineptitude in starting a revolution no one supported. What's remarkable is that after a long time removed from the game of setting captives free, and following a remarkable "burning bush" experience of the holiness of God, he put his counter back on square one and let God guide his moves. All burned-out reformers could profit from such a "Mosaic" vision. Nicaraguan mediator Orbando might recommend this biblical reading for Undersecretary Abrams, the Contras, and Daniel Ortega.

You would probably name Peter one of the biblical bumblers who got put back to square one and still reached the finish line. We don't know whether he stumbled over the kitchen stool every day, like some of us, but we do know Peter made dumb remarks at sacred moments. In a burst of zeal he also tried to walk on water. This must have embarrassed his children as well as his mother-in-law. But all that doesn't matter given Peter's response to Jesus' challenge. Do you recall the story? After resurrection excitement had died down, ashamed of his evasions and denials at Jesus' trial, Peter was ready to pick up the old life again—beaten in the kingdom game. Or so it seemed, until Jesus met him on the beach one morning, fixed breakfast for him, looked him in the eye, and asked, "Peter, do you love me?" (see John 21).

Do you consider yourself inept, meaning well but living ineffectively? Put yourself now in the place of Peter and let Jesus ask you that question, "Do you love me?" With the keys of the kingdom in your hands and Jesus' spirit in your heart you can return to square one. People may even liken you to a rock because of your strength. You can win the crown of life.

4. Second-rate competition

We live in a competitive society where self-worth is too often measured by job rating. In our hearts we know the Master doesn't measure heart devotion by hand and head performance. We recall how Jesus rebuked his disciples for making leadership power plays before they even understood kingdom business (see Luke 10:35-45). And yet as stewards of creation we want to excel, not just for social acceptance but also for sheer exuberance of creative effort. After all, sloth is a deadly sin, as well as pride. So our competitive losses give us the blues and at times spiritual depression.

Is this so with you? Then consider Jesus' parable of the talents. A second-rate competitor received the Master's commendation and an offer of a job, and the third rate competitor would have gotten an Olympic bronze if he had not been a poor loser griping at the management (see Matthew 25). Ah! maybe we are on to something; remember the superb artistic performance by 1964 Olympic ice dancers, Torvill and Dean, at Sarajevo? Perfect 6s all across the board! Every performance after that is second-rate, from kids at the Lloyd Center rink on up to Calgary participants. They may be second-rate but they are not losers.

Consider also Jesus' parable about the employer who offered employment throughout the day, and paid each worker a full day's wage. If God loves us this much we can start over again, and again, not so much competing with others to be "the best" as working against a personal Spirit-given par for the course.

5. Silent partnership with evil

Abraham's son-in-law Lot illustrates such unintended complicity in evil. Greedy for the best land, he overlooked the moral environment surrounding his business relocation, and when Sodom and Gomorrah were destroyed it took Abraham's spirited intercession before God to spare this one who had gradually slipped into a silent partnership with evil. Even with a last minute reprieve from fire and brimstone Lot didn't really get back to square one. The cave to which he retreated in the shock of bankruptcy hardly qualified for a new beginning, nor did the desperate, drunken, incestuous scheme connived by the daughters he had offered the men of Sodom instead of his male guests (see Genesis 19).

The apostle Paul is a more instructive example, fortunately. Devout, zealous for Israel's messianic destiny in bringing righteousness to the whole world, he persecuted Jesus' followers, whom he thought misguided and dangerous. Then Christ met him on the Damascus road and hauled him back to square one. I think an earlier episode awakened his conscience. He had held the coats for those who stoned Stephen to death, and I think he couldn't get Stephen's ringing testimony and serene visage out of his mind at night when he tried to sleep (Acts 7—9).

I know it's difficult to avoid being coat holders in our complex, technological world. Our citizenship, our taxes, our employment in impersonal organizations, all this brings indirect involvement in the misery of many people. I don't know how to resolve these issues for you. But I can offer Paul to you as an example of one who really got into the kingdom game as a winner after he included himself, proud son of Abraham, champion of God's covenant, in the acknowledgment that "all have sinned and come short of the glory of God." It is instructive to note that he spent three years in the wilderness before the Lord brought him forward into public leadership in the Christian community he had abused. Paul named square one "grace": a better way to handle failure than searing the conscience, becoming narrowly legalistic, or drugging the mind by conspiracy theories of evil.

6. Natural attrition

Having turned sixty-five I find my interest beginning to quicken in what is called the third age. Don't just fob us seniors off with heavenly talk. Young people die too, and middle-aged ones. The resurrection promise is so incredibly wonderful that it makes insignificant the span of life, but not its quality. We celebrate this resurrection promise soon, at Easter time. But for now, what can we learn from the Bible about the crown of life during the penultimate years? Well, we could refer to Abraham and Sarah again, as past prime progenitors of Jew, Muslim, and Arab. But I would rather commend you to Simeon and Anna, two old saints who had the prescience to understand that the baby Jesus was indeed the Messiah and were content to die having envisioned what that would mean for the world (see Luke 2). I think Luke must have had them in mind when he recognized in the Pentecostal baptism of the church a fulfillment of an ancient prophecy, which included old people who would "dream dreams" among those upon whom the Spirit would fall.

A few weeks ago I thought of that verse when Elise Boulding, a world-famous Quaker sociologist and sixty-eight-year-old grandmother, came to George Fox College to talk about imaging a world without war. My granddaughter listened in rapt attention. The talk by this practical idealist reinforced my granddaughter's youthful hope for a reasonably safe world. A few years previously I had heard her crying for fear the world would blow up before she had a chance to really live. So, third-age people: Dream the dreams, keep our young people from succumbing to the cynicism that fosters alcohol abuse and reckless hedonism. Help them see in Jesus the author and finisher of their faith. Let them know that the dice are not loaded against their hopes and aspirations any more than they are loaded against your own.

7. Moral turpitude

Consider Jesus' commendation for the prayer of a broken man who cried out penitently, "God be merciful to me, a sinner." Jesus said God preferred this prayer to the rhetorically polished invocations by respected and successful religionists. (I wonder whether Jimmy Swaggart in his dramatic public confession shouldn't have read this penitent short form rather than King David's long and dramatic penitential Psalm 51.)

Has moral failure moved your counter off the board? Jesus will listen if you come with humble and contrite spirit and not just out of shame at being found out. And he will give you a place to begin again. I said "to begin again"...with all the struggle, reparation, and spiritual discipline required to make it back up the board—no cheap grace. Such is conversion. All sorts of sinners have experienced this renewal, which is so profound that until the press queered the term, Christians referred to it as being "born again." Actually, the metaphor fits well the recovery of those who have made a mess of themselves morally. Is moral failure where you really experience loss? if so, plead the mercy of God and accept his forgiveness.

Conclusion

I do not know which losses are hardest for you to handle right now: misfortune, exploitation, ineptitude, second-rate performance, complicity with evil, natural attrition, or moral turpitude. But I do know that we don't get so far away we can't resume the kingdom journey. The crown of life may again be ours. Although clock time moves forward, God's grace transcends time and space. Judgment moves us back, mercy moves us forward. Perhaps the most beautiful exultation about hope appears in Lamentations 3:22-24 (JB). "The favors of Yahweh are not all past, his kindnesses are not exhausted; every morning they are renewed; great is his faithfulness." Face your losses forthrightly. With divine grace you can recoup your losses—and turn them into spiritual gain.

Fruit of the Light

An exposition of Ephesians 5: 2-21, Reedwood Friends Church, September 4, 1988

Introduction

Recently I removed a piece of driftwood that had been used as a temporary windbreak for ground cover planted in the spring. Underneath, where the wood had covered the ground, I discovered pale and sickly plants, struggling for survival. They resembled strings of noodles or stretched-out tubeworms. In only a few hours, however, this condition changed. Sunlight turned these poor things green and whole, enabling them to lift unfolding leaves in verdant praise to their Creator, fulfilling their genetic purposes.

Before your mind gets sidetracked analyzing photosynthesis, or contrary-mindedly countering my metaphor with examples of roots hidden in soil, let the illustration bind you to the text of holy Scripture: God's light makes us whole persons, beautiful testaments of praise to our Creator. Such human nobility recovered by divine grace, however, can be endangered by impediments such as sexual immorality, rage, thievery, foul speech, grudges, slander, spite, and greed. Don't get trapped in the darkness again. You were in darkness once, the apostle Paul wrote to the ancient church, and I paraphrase it for you now: don't be trapped under driftwood again. Take a moment to remember times when you felt more like limp noodles than a living plant. More like a thing creeping in darkness than a tree lifting leaves to the sun and offering its fruit in love to others. Remember, and be grateful for God's forgiving grace. The certificate of divine forgiveness, however, isn't a license to sin at Christ's cost.

For some of you it may not be a memory, but rather a picture of your present miserable condition. Darkness smothers you. Your spirit lies trapped under a log of your own or another's devising. In either case, hear God's message about living in the Light, about fruitful personhood made possible by Jesus Christ, our Savior and our Lord.

Being children of God means to love like Jesus did, to become a fragrant offering, a living sacrifice to God. The biblical admonition clearly implies a lifestyle very different from the general pattern in the world. As verse 16 in *The Jerusalem Bible* version reads, "This may be a wicked age but your lives should redeem it." Not just by sensible morality, but also by spiritual exuberance. Don't be drunk with wine, writes the apostle. Alcohol abuse is the world's ritual sign. Be "filled with the Spirit." Listen to that, you Children of the Light, this is your sign! Be filled with the Spirit! Don't let novelists, moviemakers, and cultural trendsetters tell you otherwise. You want adventure, mystique, and the good life? The Holy Spirit, not spirits, offers stimulus.

Last Sunday Pastor Thornburg spoke of not grieving the Spirit by whom we are set free from burdens of rebellion and hypocrisy.

Today I continue this kingdom-of-God theme by looking at the effects of Christ's light (*photizo*) upon our lives, by examining God's photosynthetic activity upon the human part of creation.

Fruit of the Light

I've given you the context, now the text: Ephesians 5:8b-9 (NIV), "Live as children of light (for the fruit of the light consists in all goodness, righteousness and truth)." The New International Version puts the subordinate clause in parentheses, maybe to warn us against wearing religious labels without understanding character implications.

What are the effects of divine photosynthesis? Goodness, righteousness, and truth. Superficially these words seem dull and undramatic until we reflect upon great literature where they shine like jewels in diverse settings, sometimes in mirrors of satire and irony, but more often in straightforward dramas of human struggle between virtue and vice, justice and injustice, truth and deceit. Flawed people struggling toward the Light may be heroes; depraved persons aren't. Goodness, righteousness, and truth *are* more exciting than their opposites. Ask any victim of vice, injustice, and deceit. Ask any friend of the victim. Wouldn't you agree with me, remembering life under the log? So, consider the fruit of the Light, the effects of divine photosynthesis upon the human spirit.

> First, goodness. If this word's too vague, consider virtuous character.
>
> Second, righteousness. Translate this term to mean right living and fair actions.
>
> Third, truth. Interpret this to mean understanding things, events, and people as they really are.

Let's look at each of these fruits, or effects, of being Children of the Light.

Goodness

We properly fear self-righteousness and boasting if we look at ourselves, so let's think about people worshiping with us today. Say to yourself about someone you know well, "This is a good person!" Don't judge superficially, like what they wear, or how they speak, or what kind of job they have, but in reference to quality of character. This person constitutes a standard of what people ought to be—humanity at its best. The Hebrews talked about wise persons, the Orientals about sages, the Greeks about virtuous persons. All described humane qualities basic to specific actions and reasoned judgments. Our Scripture text contrasts wisdom and foolishness. I know it is difficult for us not to think of goodness as the cumulative effect of right living and good reasoning. There is a kind of reciprocal cause-effect relationship between character and action (philosophers and psychologists argue about it), but for now think of goodness as spiritual source rather than cumulative effect. As fertile ground open to divine planting and tending.

If you were to ask them, persons you nominated for goodness would be hard put to answer how they qualify, and would probably mumble embarrassed disclaimers. So I suggest you look around for clues. Philosophers speak about the indefinability of the good. That is, we can define other qualities as being good but no easy way finally appears to say what the good is. It's a kind of ultimate word. Where reason's road ends, intuition guides us to the peak of moral definition. So look for the signs pointing toward what we call "good" and the human quality we call "goodness."

Our Scripture reading mentions an important sign. Note verses 10 and 18-20. *It is characteristic for a good person to find out what pleases the Lord.* The Hebrew poets called this the "fear of the Lord," and "delighting in the Law." The creature checks in with the Creator. The good person also revels in the Spirit Christ has sent. These are God-intoxicated people, worshiping together, making music in their hearts, giving gratitude for God, and lifting up the name of the one who has called them into the kingdom, the Lord Jesus Christ. Now a word of warning: new believers, like the newly rich, sometimes confuse show for substance and haven't learned humility. Saying "Lord, Lord" all the time, or "Praise the Lord" for every little thing, from a compliment to a flat tire—this isn't necessarily lifting up the Lord's name, but rather making an unctuous nuisance of themselves and bringing offense to the gospel.

From that principle of wanting to please the Lord we can draw some inferences about how good people draw upon the divine Light. You may think of others.

1. They are authentically spiritual, in joyous relationship with the Creator. They don't play church. The sacred infuses their ordinary life—family affairs, play, work.

2. They nurture that spirituality in public and private worship.

3. Prayer for them means much listening to the heavenly voice.

4. Their love follows Jesus' example.

5. Their morality relates responsibly to their faith.

6. They cherish truth and bear its weight responsibly.

7. They subordinate themselves to needs of others without loss of autonomy.

Righteousness

What about righteousness? We said this term has to do with right living and fair actions. In the Scriptures the word *justice* is often a correct synonym. If character is inward, righteousness is outward. A good tree, said Jesus in good rabbinic fashion, bears good fruit. You don't get figs from thorns.

Our Scripture reading gives us a good cue on this quest also. Note verse 11.

Characteristically a righteous person makes the most of opportunities, redeeming evil days. Rather than merely lamenting them, we might add. There is some confusion in Christian theology about this word *righteousness*. In the Middle Ages the Roman Catholic Church got to merchandizing salvation—you venerated the bones of this saint, said the Hail Mary x number of times, contributed to the pope's building campaign, and certain spiritual rewards followed. Martin Luther raged against this abuse, especially the selling of indulgences to poor, pious Germans to benefit rich and greedy Italian clergy. (Such blatant "selling of the gospel" has appeared again in our times, sometimes with Protestant evangelists the culprits.) In any case, the Reformation wouldn't have any part in "works righteousness"; they emphasized that no amount of good deeds could earn salvation. An unforeseen consequence developed, however, to mar the needed emphasis on salvation by faith alone: the separation of saving grace from appropriate kingdom morality. It took people off the hook, as it were, from considering moral actions, particularly public ones, as part of their spirituality.

The Quaker movement recovered a morally accountable Christian faith. Theologically speaking, it recovered the doctrine of sanctification from monastic obscurity, ritual distortion, and Protestant neglect. Friends believe God wants to make our hearts pure and our hands clean. This is what the gospel is all about—good news that it can be done. If our eye is focused, our whole body can be full of Light. Our movement was first known as Children of the Light, a term drawn in part from this passage of Scripture. Friends wanted to live in the Light, even if that meant going to prison for refusing to go to war or to make obsequious deference to rulers, or going to the gallows for religious liberty, like the Boston martyrs. They knew that love means actions in accord with divine purpose.

You know these stories. Reedwood Friends follow the same torch, in activities on behalf of the homeless, for justice in Central America, for equity and peace in the Middle East. The Light leads us into compassionate care of the aged and infirm, good education of our youth, to integrity in professional endeavors and dedicated public service. Such an activist role isn't easy. It's tempting to become narrow and harsh reformers, or follow Jesus in private morality and follow the opinion polls in public morality. We get tired of being called "knee-jerk liberals" or "do-gooders" by Christian brothers and sisters who witness to Jesus on talk shows while advocating capital punishment and more aid to the Contras. But we persist. We are convinced righteousness hasn't much to do with prayer in public schools, but it has a lot to do with a fair wage, humane living conditions, family and legal equity, nondiscrimination, freedom, economic and educational opportunities, and justice to the oppressed—worldwide. Bringing in the kingdom doesn't just depend upon us, but God has entrusted part of the creative process to us. Jesus told us to seek first the kingdom of God, and its righteousness—and not to worry about tomorrow. That's good advice, for when people start the probabilities game, they end up deciding Jesus is just too impractical, so they abandon the cross for the sword and deny resurrection power.

What are some cues about righteous persons? How do they make the most of opportunities and redeem the evil day? Here are some characteristics of righteousness derived from the divine Light. You can think of others.

1. They do kingdom things wherever they are, but within a global context.

2. They cooperate with others in a way that lifts up and does not tear down.

3. They help organizations to which they belong to adopt a servant role.

4. They are compassionate about weakness in others because they are conscious of their own.

5. They are generous at home as well as toward poor strangers.

6. They pay a fair wage and do their fair share of work.

7. They stand for their convictions against ridicule, scorn, or guilt by association.

Truth

Truth is the third effect divine Light has upon receptive persons. Ordinarily we consider a truthful person as one who won't lie to us. Our text suggests wider meanings about truthfulness. According to verse 17, *a truthful person understands God's will.* This implies several meanings: discerning right relationships with others, knowing when to speak and when to be silent, and gaining direction about important choices, (e.g., whom to marry, where to live, what career to follow). Truth also means understanding what God intends in the creation, how redemption restores humanity to its rightful nature, and how we should carry out our stewardship of the earth. Truth is the fruit of Light, opposed to deceit, which skulks in the dark.

Classical Christianity considered that God spoke through the word of creation as well as through the word of Scripture. The church is recovering the wholeness of that vision once again. No longer do we secularize the hard sciences. Nor do we subordinate religious knowledge to sociology and psychology. We recognize all ways of knowing as legitimate and all sciences as useful tools. We realize that describing reality isn't the same as explaining it, and that explaining it isn't the same as understanding it. Link both cognitive and affective knowledge with the will of God; this is understanding; this is wisdom. Then truth surrounds us with mystery, like a magnificent horizon that opens upon a universe incredibly grand and complex, with unimagined dimensions. We yearn for the unfolding of this mystery, senses quickened by Christ within, our hope of glory. Truthful persons speed the day of this cosmic awakening for they discern the will of God and live by it. They imitate God and love like Jesus did. ("Wake up, O sleeper," sang the early Christians as quoted in our text, verse 14, "...and Christ will shine on you.") We do well to heed their song.

All truth is ultimately God's truth, revealed to us in bits and parts, as we are able to comprehend it and most of all to live by it. Truth isn't shelved somewhere waiting for people to buy it. Truth is God's will, known and followed. I said earlier that we could interpret truth to mean understanding things, events, and people as they really are. "Reality" is no slippery state defined by quantum mechanics, but rather all the cosmic possibilities present in the will of God. Given the present misuse of the earth, and the nuclear cloud, it strikes me that scientists should consider research into the care of the earth a spiritual task, to be undertaken prayerfully like a minister leading a congregation, or a social worker helping abused children. God's will, not exploitive patronage, should determine priorities and financial support. Here truth serves public righteousness, as well as fairness within families and equity in commerce.

What are some cues about truthful people, those who demonstrate the effects of living in the Light? Here are some characteristics of truthful people. You may think of others.

1. They examine issues from all points of view before making judgments.

2. They aren't afraid to expose deceit and hypocrisy.

3. They understand the Holy Spirit as the spirit of truth; accordingly they honor God's activity in the ordinary as well as in the unusual events.

4. They would rather acknowledge honest questions about their faith than depend upon shoddy logic to sustain it.

5. For them truth compels obedience and not just discovery or intellectual theory.

6. These people treat all kinds of persons with integrity—children, strangers, friends, and enemies.

7. These people can accept criticism graciously, for they are more interested in truth than in their own feelings.

Conclusion

In our exposition of Ephesians 5:2-21, we have considered how God's light makes us whole persons—testaments of praise to our Creator—effecting within us goodness, righteousness, and truth. We noted these characteristics:

A good person finds out what pleases the Lord.

A righteous person makes the most of opportunities, overcoming evil.

A truthful person understands God's will.

We also inferred from the Ephesians passage several marks of good, righteous, and truthful persons. It remains to make some applications. This is Labor Day weekend, an American holiday that marks the resumption of serious work after summer holidays. For some of you it is merely a seasonal transition, for others, however—especially families—it marks new beginnings in school. Study is work, and so I challenge all of you who labor—whether in school, on the job, or in the home—to consider the place of your labor as holy ground where you offer, in love to others, the sacrifice of your energy to the Lord. Let your life be a fragrant offering to God.

As you learned the characteristics of goodness, righteousness, and truth, you may have identified role models who seemed to demonstrate these qualities of life. Will you now consider them as goals for your own life? Will you strive to be a good person in the home, at school, on the job, at play, striving to please the Lord? Will you take courage in hand and live righteously, overcoming evil with good? Will you be truthful, seeking God's will in respect to things, persons, and events, as revealed through Scripture and the creation? And will you support others who also seek to live as Children of the Light?

The late Rabbi Kook wrote about the fourfold song: the song of the self, the song of the covenant people, the song of humanity, and the song of the world. Put together they become the song of holiness, the song of God ("Lights of Holiness," Classics of Western Spirituality, Paulist Press, 1978, pp. 228ff). Put goodness, righteousness, and truth together and we hear the song of holiness sung by faithful people, on earth as well as in heaven.

Filioque, a Latin Commentary on the Meaning of Pentecost

Yachats Community Presbyterian Church, May 21, 1989

Introduction

I studied Latin in high school. So will you indulge me in using a Latin word to describe the meaning of Pentecost? The term is *filioque*. It means "and from the Son." The Holy Spirit proceeds from God the Father and from Jesus Christ, the Son. Why is this significant? Because it specifies a Christian doctrine of the Holy Spirit. It took several centuries for the church to get clear on this. They weren't just squabbling. The issue is important.

Why? Because the next great Christian celebration after Easter is Pentecost, literally fifty days after Passover. Today we celebrate Pentecost. Filioque helps us celebrate with understanding. St. Patrick used a shamrock to illustrate the trinity. I'll use a three-legged stool. Each leg needs the others. The inner Spirit depends upon God the Creator and Jesus Christ the Son. Without such three-point stability, faith is unstable. To use another analogy, our spirituality is like putting a camera on a tripod. We picture the world accurately when God the Father, Son, and Holy Spirit hold us steady. Today we focus on God the Spirit.

The word *Pentecost* may be a red flag to you. Whatever the spiritual glow of that historic

Scripture readings

Joel 2:28-31 (NIV here and in subsequent texts)

"And afterward, I will pour out my Spirit on all people. Your sons and daughters will prophesy, your old men will dream dreams, your young men will see visions.

"Even on my servants, both men and women, I will pour out my Spirit in those days.

"I will show wonders in the heavens and on the earth, blood and fire and billows of smoke.

"The sun will be turned to darkness and the moon to blood before the coming of the great and dreadful day of the Lord."

John 14:16-17

"And I will ask the Father, and he will give you another Counselor to be with you forever—the Spirit of truth. The world cannot accept him, because it neither sees him nor knows him. But you know him, for he lives with you and will be in you."

John 15:26

"When the Counselor comes, whom I will send to you from the Father, the Spirit of truth who goes out from the Father, he will testify about me."

John 16:13

"But when he, the Spirit of truth, comes, he will guide you into all truth."

Acts 2:1-4

When the day of Pentecost came, they were all together in one place. Suddenly a sound like the blowing of a violent wind came from heaven and filled the whole house where they were sitting. They saw what seemed to be tongues of fire that separated and came to rest on each of them. All of them were filled with the Holy Spirit and began to speak in other tongues as the Spirit enabled them.

ancient moment, it's been marred by people who make religion seem bizarre. It's like climbing a mountain to view the sunrise only to find junk littering the top. Zealots have spoiled the ecstasy they promote. Do you feel this way? If so, here's my word to you: Don't miss the main show because a few theater attendees are rude or snobbish. Jesus had us all in mind when, after the resurrection, he offered followers a spiritual presence more pervasive than his physical presence along Lake Galilee ever could be.

Put prejudice aside and consider Pentecost. For Israel, Pentecost provided an occasion to praise God with a feast of bread and lamb. It was a celebratory feast at the beginning of harvest. Families and strangers renewed their covenant with God. (Read Deuteronomy16 and Leviticus 23 for details.)

For Jesus' followers Pentecost celebrated the beginning of kingdom harvest. God's grace would gather people into righteousness worldwide. This powerful conviction launched the church. Jesus truly became the world's Messiah. The resurrection proved this outwardly, Pentecost inwardly. As Jesus said to his followers: "I tell you the truth, anyone who has faith in me will do what I have been doing. He will do even greater things than these, because I am going to the Father" (John 14:12).

People had difficulty understanding this kind of presence. It seemed less real than flesh and blood—inviting skepticism, magic, or psychological manipulation. But the Gospels present this inward filling as the point of Jesus' coming. John the Baptist introduced Jesus as the Messiah in this way: "...I baptize you with water. But one more powerful than I will come, the thongs of whose sandals I am not worthy to untie. He will baptize you with the Holy Spirit and with fire" (Luke 3:16).

Pentecost immersed believers into Jesus' grace and power. Even thick-headed Peter got the message. He had met with the others behind locked doors—scared, uncertain whether to pick up the old life or hang around for something more. Appearing on the beach one morning after the resurrection, Jesus inspired Peter to take the risks of faith. The experience recorded in Acts, with its symbolic tongues as of fire and burst linguistic limits, set his spirit aglow with divine presence. This experience of Christ's baptism loosened his own tongue, so that he could preach boldly: "...'Repent and be baptized, every one of you, in the name of Jesus Christ for the forgiveness of your sins. And you will receive the gift of the Holy Spirit'" (Acts 2:38).

After Pentecost Jesus' followers no longer questioned whether Jesus was the Messiah or whether his teachings were true. They knew it! Earthly memories of Jesus became subordinate to his continuing presence as they ate and worshiped together. In Pentecostal power they set out to evangelize the earth. Even to martyr's death they went, confident Jesus was with them.

Now you see why filioque is important. It reminds us to follow the Spirit in accordance with Jesus. Without this reminder, spirituality lacks stability. The stool won't stand, the tripod wobbles and the picture gets blurred. Consider filioque in relationship to three kinds of spirituality.

The first kind of spirituality is animism.
Animists believe that Spirit mysteriously and randomly permeates nature. Stuff houses deity. Animists have

no reference point in history, no covenant, no example of what God is like. They do feel a bonding with the earth and its creatures, but their spirituality is incomplete and often spooky. Its best side has been depicted by the film *The Gods Must Be Crazy*, in which a simple bushman indicts materialistic hypocrisies. Its worst side is illustrated by recent cultic human sacrifices.

Animists experience God as undependable, maybe as help, maybe as hindrance. We naively supposed that upon being civilized animistic people would no longer pay witch doctors to fob off spirits. We supposed such people would no longer subsist on roots and berries. Once educated these primitives would shuck superstition, quit sticking spears in each other, wear decent clothes, control nature by machines rather than incantations, use indoor plumbing, and invest in the stock market.

Obviously animists can't compete with modernity. Life is better for us now than for our primitive ancestors. And yet some benefits of technology are questionable. Technology hasn't eliminated fear but only altered its forms. Actually, some people look wistfully toward our animistic past. They yearn to be part of nature again, rather than her exploiter. So they explore reincarnation with movie stars, harass folks who wear fur coats, or steep themselves in fantasy literature. They want the privileges of modernity without the risks of primitivism. There is something of the animist in all of us, I think. Vacations prove it.

Actually, filioque reveals the mystery for which animists grope. Reason baptized by Jesus' Spirit offered animists (your ancestors and mine) a unified worldview. The words of our New Testament reading explain why: "The Spirit of truth will guide you into all truth." Scientific theory and applications became possible for them. God can be trusted as well as worshiped. Many Christians are actually converted animists, who find in Jesus' teaching about the Holy Spirit a better alternative to old religions and new secularisms. Converts from animism lose their fears. They discover a dependable creation, wherein they can improve living conditions with intelligence and good will. People can live responsibly on the earth when sin has been forgiven and the Holy Spirit energizes our common life.

In summary, the first kind of spirituality, animism, is long on intuition and sensory acuity but short on reason. Baptized with the Spirit of Jesus reason becomes increasingly coherent. In the life and sacrificial death of Jesus animists understand the universals of love and truth—and about moral accountability. The Spirit of Jesus is the Spirit of truth.

It has been popular to blame Christians for exploiting the earth. But it's a distorted Christianity. Grateful for God's grace and joyful at the Spirit's presence some Christians have forgotten the little connective "and" in the filioque doctrine. They forget that the Spirit proceeds from the Father *and* from the Son. The reasons for that neglect can be seen in a second kind of spirituality, pietism.

A second kind of spirituality is pietism.

By pietism I mean a spirituality that emphasizes disciplined personal devotion—systematic Bible study and Christian reading, prayer, public worship, personal virtue. A legacy of the Reformation, pietism offered all Christians devotional habits once cherished mainly by monks. Protestants located holiness in the home and on the job, not in the cloister. They viewed society as Christian families laboring according to their skills for mutual advantage. Jesus' gift of the Spirit is thus for everyone.

Pietists cope with secularism better than do animists. They do so, however, by separating life into compartments, protecting secular and sacred worlds from intruding upon each other. History is thus divided between holy and mundane. Separate spheres of ethics are set up for family, economic order, political order, and church. Science handles physical stuff (except for contested theories of origin) while the church handles spiritual stuff. Science claims the brain; church claims the soul.

Pressured by secular culture, pietists limited the spiritual realm to personal devotion and private morality. The Spirit's territory shrank considerably from the world Jesus died to save. So it happened that devout Christians, personally virtuous and well-mannered, could through public agencies such as corporations or states, act contrary to the Spirit of Jesus. Pietists forgot that the Spirit Jesus sent is the spirit of truth. For them Spirit became a means of privileged tranquility. Like the Stoic emperor, Marcus Aurelius, they could find inward peace in prayer after slaughtering barbarians outside the pale. Accepting Christ as Savior they unfortunately denied him as sovereign Lord of earth.

The nuclear age has made such divided loyalties difficult. *Pilgrim's Progress* doesn't play well in Peoria now. On a network of global communication, hungry children knock so hard at double-locked doors during devotions that pietists have begun to check economics and political science against biblical mandates for justice. Today, as in the early church, the question comes: Who is lord, Caesar or Christ? Strong words from the prophet Micah are pertinent.

> This is what the Lord says: "…The sun will set for the prophets, and the day will go dark for them. The seers will be ashamed and the diviners disgraced. They will all cover their faces because there is no answer from God."
>
> But as for me, I am filled with power, with the Spirit of the Lord, and with justice and might, to declare to Jacob his transgression, to Israel his sin. Hear this, you leaders of the house of Jacob, you rulers of the house of Israel, who despise justice and distort all that is right; who build Zion with bloodshed, and Jerusalem with wickedness. Her leaders judge for a bribe, her priests teach for a price, and her prophets tell fortunes for money. Yet they lean upon the Lord and say, "Is not the Lord among us? No disaster will come upon us." (Micah 3:5-11)

Despite such judgment for insensitivity, much can be said for pietistic faith, nurtured by prayer and other habits of the heart. I cherish my early training in such spirituality, including the discipline of tithing my income. Such spirituality is authentic to the extent that it resists legalism, gains prophetic power from Jesus' baptism with the Holy Spirit, and understands that this Spirit comes both from God the Creator and from Jesus Christ. Immersed in the Spirit of Jesus the senses perceive the world as it is, instead of blurred, or compartmentalized. In the life and sacrificial death of Jesus they understand the universal character of love and truth. They accept full moral accountability. With eyes newly opened they put their hands in the hands of Christ and reach out to the world in that name. The second way of spirituality, pietism, in sum, is long on reason and intuition, but short on letting the senses be God's messengers.

A third kind of spirituality is activism.
Activism is a twentieth-century term for certain Protestant and Roman Catholic Christians. Some of its leaders are called liberation theologians because they consider the Exodus a model for how Christ wants to liberate people in current political or economic bondage. Activists have broken down compartments secularists and pietists so carefully erected to keep out of each other's way. No iron curtain between the sacred and the secular for activists! Pietists may psychologize the beatitudes; not so activists! Jesus is on the side of the poor. With all the zeal of a Levi Coffin hiding slaves along the underground railroad, or a Martin Luther King, Jr. marching on Selma, they raise their voices for human rights.

As the name suggests, activists are impatient with speculation. They suspect that pietists use devotional exercises as avoidance technique. Activists apply Jesus' words about Pharisees to contemporary conservative Christians. In the 1960s the men wore their hair long, and the women wore flour sack dresses. They lived simply. Guitars were in, pipe organs out. They marched against the Vietnam War, participated in civil rights crusades in Alabama, and boycotted Nestlé for shoddy practices in third-world countries. Activists believe the Lord hates solemn assemblies and wants faithful action instead. Recently they marched in silent vigils along the Nicaragua border to protect villagers from the Contras. Pietists wish the whole movement would go away, like a bad dream, and the church could settle back to Isaac Watt hymns and quiet spirituality. In the 1980s this happened quite often—drugs and selective morality seduced the protest movement. It lost much of its prophetic power. But activism remains an option for many Christians, with the social agenda including now the right as well as the left. Rallies for women's rights or justice in Central America are paired with antiabortion marches. Activist prophets voice strong appeals for freedom and justice. Consider Alan Boesak, a South African black leader. This Cape Town pastor and president of the World Alliance of Reformed Churches spoke thus to American Presbyterians recently.

> My church has the Confession of Belhar...It is a beautiful document that says God is on the side of the poor. It says apartheid is heresy, and we thought we were prophetic when we said that. But we discovered that we became prophetic only when we were willing and able by God's grace to take courage and stand in the streets, and say, "This is the Confession"; and go to jail and say, "This is the Confession," and face the tear gas and the dogs and the guns and say, "This is the Confession of the Church." Then, and then only, are we prophetic. (*Presbyterian Survey*, March 1989)

Well, activists are long on sensing the world around them and trying to respond to it rationally. But they are short on the intuitive, on the mystical. Sadly, some of them lose their spirituality, and sometimes their Christian faith, while doing kingdom work. Zeal produces tunnel vision. Some activists become self-righteous moralists. Some fall into marital unfaithfulness while scolding the CIA or picketing porno shops. Curiously, activists tend to shift moral priorities from the private to the public realm, the reverse of what pietists do, but with the same selective morality, and a cheapening Christian faithfulness.

Activist spirituality is authentic to the extent that it resists legalism, gains power from Jesus' baptism with the Holy Spirit, and understands that this Spirit comes from Jesus Christ, the crucified Messiah. Baptized with the Spirit of Jesus, intuition becomes prayerful—activists now see God, and not just an ugly world or their own causes. They understand the sufferings of Calvary, yes, but also the resurrection, and the joy of Jesus' presence in the soul. Grace frames for them the universals of love and truth and hangs the pictures on the walls of their hearts. Thus chastened, they put their trust in the work of Christ and subordinate their efforts to his, finding patience in the power of the Spirit.

Conclusion

Activists and pietists and animists are now represented by Christian brothers and sisters in every land and every culture. Which describes you? Let me rephrase the question: How do you experience the Spirit's power? During times when senses are so loaded with wild mystery you can hardly contain the ecstasy? When the mind disciplines your devotion to God so that you experience a peace that exceeds understanding? When you so spend your energies in service to others that you carry the world's suffering in a heady mixture of sorrow and joy? How about all three ways? Thus you fully understand Pentecost. Thus you understand filioque. When the Spirit that God sends bears the authentic stamp of Jesus Christ, your faith rests firm. You perceive the world in true perspective. Then you are baptized with the Holy Spirit. Then you truly receive Jesus' promise: "When the Counselor comes, whom I will send to you from the Father, the Spirit of truth who goes out from the Father, he will testify about me" (John 15:26).

Reflections: Jack Willcuts Memorial

Jack Willcuts passed away September 23, 1989, and the memorial service was held at the Bauman Auditorium, George Fox College, September 27.

Hear the word of the Lord through the reading of Old Testament Scripture from Psalm 40:1-9 (NIV):

I waited patiently for the Lord; he turned to me and heard my cry. He lifted me out of the slimy pit, out of the mud and mire; he set my feet on a rock and gave me a firm place to stand. He put a new song in my mouth, a hymn of praise to our God. Many will see and fear and put their trust in the Lord.

Blessed is the man who makes the Lord his trust, who does not look to the proud, to those who turn aside to false gods. Many, O Lord my God, are the wonders you have done. The things you planned for us no one can recount to you; were I to speak and tell of them, they would be too many to declare.

Sacrifice and offering you did not desire, but my ears you have opened; burnt offerings and sin offerings you did not require. Then I said, "Here I am, I have come—it is written about me in the scroll. I desire to do your will, O my God; your law is within my heart."

I proclaim righteousness in the great assembly; I do not seal my lips, as you know, O Lord.

We pay tribute today to a dear friend and companion who lived so effectively among us. Like the psalmist, Jack waited patiently until God gave him a place to stand and had put a new song in his mouth. Then his ears were open to the Spirit and his heart to the warmth of divine love. And so this God-anointed messenger began a half-century ministry that reached around the world and touched thousands of persons for good. That world includes his family as well as the Quaker family. Through Jack's ministry many persons came to "see and fear and put their trust in the Lord."

Although he had begun deputation service while a student at Friends Bible College in Kansas, and continued it while living in Greenleaf, Idaho, Jack's ministry began with a small congregation in Rockaway Beach, Oregon. He was attending George Fox College (then known as Pacific College). Jack commuted each weekend to the coast and still participated in student affairs, attended to his studies, competed in intercollegiate speech contests (winning first place for the state of Oregon) and starred on the college basketball team. Recently Jack confided to daughter Jan that in this ministry he had overcome a poor self-image. Through this rigorous discipline he discovered the joy of Christian service. He learned early in life to channel energy efficiently, a trait that served him well, and those who benefited from such stewardship of mind, body, and soul. George Fox once urged followers to "prize your time." Jack demonstrated how to do this. We are grateful the church had the wisdom to record God's ordination of Jack Willcuts as a minister of the gospel, and to open channels for that ministry.

I said that Jack's first liberation came through a student pastorate at Rockaway. His marriage to

Geraldine Tharrington provided the second liberation. Love blossomed in that marriage, bore fruit, and spread in widening circles of extended family. The family unit became precious to him, and an apt biblical metaphor for the church. Significantly, he entitled one of his books *The Family of Friends.* That suggests a third liberating force in Jack's life, discovering the gift of writing. God gave him the gift but Jack worked hard to develop it.

These are Jack's personal characteristics as I observed them.

Discipline

For Jack, discipline brought freedom, not bondage. He accepted a logic of means and ends. He didn't try to "get by," or to substitute inspiration for effort. He worked at everything he did, including his sermons. And when that work had brought a sermon to readiness, he could hardly wait to preach! Unction came from having joined his labor with the Spirit's fire. No wonder we were blessed by his preaching! That same pattern of discipline prepared him for various positions of church leadership—pastor, missionary, executive, lecturer, writer, elder statesman. This discipline also gave him the wisdom to resist taking moral shortcuts for quick church gains. He distinguished between appropriate and inappropriate methods of gospel witness. He kept learning, read widely, and never coasted on past achievements.

Generosity

Jack set a pattern for generous giving, both of time and of money. His family exercised this responsibility quietly, both in respect to individuals in need and in respect to the church and its agencies. Almsgiving reflected compassion, not display.

Integrity

Son Stuart describes his father as: "the most consistent Christian I ever knew." Jack didn't talk behind people's backs, shaming some of us into better moral conduct. He took seriously Quaker advices about protecting the reputation of others.

Skill in listening

He counseled mostly by being a good listener, thus opening others to the Light within. Jack saw his task as doorkeeper for Christ, the true counselor of curious, questing, and troubled souls. He could listen to common people, said one grateful person, because he himself was a common man with common roots who in an uncommon way helped others. His gift for listening across cultural barriers enabled him to help the Aymara Quakers become indigenous, trusting them to let Christ teach appropriate cultural patterns for their Christian community of faith. This gift for listening brought him into leadership within the world community of Friends.

Affirmation

Family constituted the first circle of that affirmation. "He trusted us!" say his children in unison. They are especially grateful that God gave their father a few additional years following a serious illness of the sort that this time proved fatal. During this interim they moved spiritually as well as physically closer to their parents. They felt released to be themselves, unburdened by dependency upon a well-known father.

They are grateful to their parents for making them responsible—tied only by bonds of respect.

That gift for affirming others has been important to the grandchildren, also, whom he read to, and taught chess and other games, as he had his children. "Opa" listened to his grandchildren. One asked, "When I want to be by myself who will I go to now?" Another laments that "trips to OMSI just aren't going to be the same anymore." People in the churches where Jack and Geraldine served feel much the same way, regardless of age or station in life. Take, for example, the person who said to the family, "During my bankruptcy your father met with me every day." It isn't going to be the same anymore. We will have to follow Jack's example and become affirmers now.

Discernment

Jack learned how to guide without dominating. During a difficult time in her life Susan recalls finding a note on her pillow, with a reference to Psalm 40, the Old Testament Scripture that I read to you earlier. She then knew that the Lord had heard her cry and she could put her feet on the rock. Her father's discernment took shape practically, and in a timely fashion. This simple gesture encouraged her to let Christ Jesus sustain her faith, and helped her overcome negative feelings about herself. Quietly her father had offered a bridge of hope for a difficult crossing. Some of you know about Jack's bridges over troubled waters. One difficult day in Vietnam as youthful director of a relief program, Stuart turned to the Bible for help and discovered his father had underlined some verses in anticipation of trials. The admonition? Moses' words to Joshua, "Be strong, and of good courage!" Jack's discerning spirit had a practical bent.

Commitment

A convinced as well as a birthright Friend, Jack thought Quaker beliefs should be followed because they were true, not because they were Quaker. He never apologized or compromised Quaker distinctives, but rather gave them biblical focus. He held us to them firmly but not legalistically. His passionate convictions, affirmed with tenderness and good-humored recognition of human foibles, drew together at the cross persons concerned for social issues and those concerned for evangelical proclamation. Jack was an evangelical with liberal social concerns—like Jesus. This broad biblical commitment made his keynote addresses at Yearly Meeting—during the years he served as general superintendent—so memorable. With clarity of words and unction from the Holy Spirit he kept our eyes on our covenantal vision. He was a pastor's pastor. And he piqued our imagination with new ways to practice the kingdom—such as Youth Ambassadors, Friends Action Board, and ethnic ministries. He kept the yearly meeting on the cutting edge of Quakerism. Not just as superintendent, but as pastor of several of its churches—particularly at Reedwood—Jack helped us understand ourselves to be Christians belonging to the family of Friends. This commitment to Christian principles as understood by Friends earned him wide respect. Jack lectured or preached in many yearly meetings across the world, and was currently engaged with the Friends World Committee for Consultation in planning three regional conferences in 1991 for world Quakerdom. Jack gave imaginative guidance to boards on which he participated, including those of George Fox College and Friendsview Manor.

Joy

"Our parents never quarreled in our hearing," said the children. As his friend I never saw him angry. He saw the bright side of things, and had a handy store of jokes to use when things got gloomy or uptight. He liked to make ice cream, and had actually made enough to fill a freezer to celebrate Stu's birthday. The family ate the remainder while discussing arrangements for a public memorial. "A love feast" it was. To the last Jack served. I recall good times with Jack, as many of you do. One summer between college terms we worked in the woods cutting brush—a nasty task. Under Jack's encouragement we joined in singing at the tops of our voices some verses from Isaiah he had learned from an oratorio—"The valleys stand so thick with corn that they laugh and sing!" This young dust-bowl refugee—whose mother died when he was young and who had early experienced crushing economic loss—this young college student taught his friends about faith for all seasons. I cherish the memory of happy days when Fern and I met with Jack and Geraldine—sometimes in Tacoma, sometimes in Everett, Washington—to play golf, or ping-pong, or go hiking in the mountains. Such friendship helped us shrug off our inadequacies, laugh at our failures, and press on with renewed hope. Later there were home visits and occasional dinners. Then the pressure of busy schedules and distance stretched the bond, but did not break it. The ties remain, as they have to you, reinforced sometimes with brief conversations at Yearly Meeting, at lunches, or outings. Or by correspondence. I cherish the letters, don't you? Like the one which chided me for speaking disparagingly of an older church leader. Wrote Jack, "_____'s dour appearance is a mask to cover bashfulness. I've seen him a few times with it off and he's quite amiable." And another time, digging his egghead friend: "Sedulously avoid all polysyllabic profundity....Shun double entendres, prurient jocosity, and pestiferous profanity. That is naughty." This was in 1946, when we published the short-lived magazine, *Pacifica Theologica*. Later we enjoyed his observations of life on the altiplano among llamas, burros, and Aymara, finding in Christ a liberating gospel. Then his serious editorials in the *Evangelical Friend*, framed with humor and the joy of living. And then his books. Still later his epistles from England explaining language differences, e.g., "a child born of a British mother and an American father is 'hahlf' and 'half.'" And more seriously, "The spirit is present in both silence and speaking. I fear we dishonor the Lord in limiting Him to just one way or the other. God is bigger than all our Quaker boundaries in faith and practice....At this point, let us figuratively reach out to shake hands across the distances of sea and space, programmed and unprogrammed meetings, and live in peace."

Our New Testament Scripture comes from 1 Peter 3:8-12 (NIV). It formed the basis for a sermon Jack prepared for September 24, 1989, at Reedwood. He didn't get to preach it.

> Finally, all of you, live in harmony with one another; be sympathetic, love as brothers, be compassionate and humble. Do not repay evil with evil or insult with insult, but with blessing, because to this you were called so that you may inherit a blessing. For, "Whoever would love life and see good days must keep his tongue from evil and his lips from deceitful speech. He must turn from evil and do good; he must seek peace and pursue it. For the eyes of the Lord are on the righteous and his ears are attentive to their prayer, but the face of the Lord is against those who do evil."

From this Scripture Jack draws insights about Peter, the common man who became an uncommon disciple. Jack wrote of Simon: "He was genuinely human. He seemed always to be himself. Never struck a pose...Never tried to conceal his ignorance. He required correction, a good trait, too. There is found here a spontaneity of love that was natural, not put on like a salesman trying to close. Jesus, I think, noticed and liked this." Then, after relating Peter's failure in Gethsemane, Jack has these words about the power of Jesus Christ to change lives. "...This is the place to which we all must come before we can know the power of the Holy Spirit, that turned Peter from a deviating follower into more of a straight line follower. What you are is important, but what you are becoming is of greater importance...This is our hope...we are all people who know we are not good, but want to be better. That's why we put ourselves on the line and say, 'I need God's help.' ...One day the Lord wants to lay his hand on you and say, 'Your name is Simon, but it will become Peter.'"

Peter, the rock. That's our friend Jack, an ordinary person who became a rock, and an apostle of the Lord.

A Tribute to Our Friend Jack

We took him for granted,
like electricity.
A power outage
leaves the world darker,
its machinery silenced.
So, now, at his passing
we re-examine how things
human and divine connect.
We scramble to adjust—awed
by his energizing life.

Our friend seemed like a hub
from which our separate lives,
our various enterprises,
family, church, or otherwise,
like spokes radiate outward
to be joined at a common rim.
We've enjoyed a smooth journey,
and acknowledge now
the centering power
of his quiet spirit.

The storyteller steps off stage,
and the enraptured audience
folds newly discovered truths
between program notes
touched by tears and laughter.
God's messenger returns,
but the message remains:
good news for the home,
for the village, for the city,
Christ for the whole world!

Our friend Jack, suddenly,
like an autumn sun,
has slipped below our horizon.
But oh, the afterglow!

"How Can We Know the Way?"
A Sort of Conversation with Jesus

Reedwood Friends Church, July 29, 1990

A Sort of Conversation with Jesus

Narrator

Let's give Thomas credit, he wasn't afraid to say up front what some people thought then—and think now: "We don't know where you are going, Jesus, so how can we know the way?" In the following—Roberts's amplified, expanded, and greatly paraphrased version of the text—the dialogue reads like this.

Thomas

"We don't know what you are talking about,
going away, preparing a place, and taking us there.
Lord, could you be more specific?
With all due respect, Master, poetry is okay in its place,
but for getting directions we need straight prose.
These aren't easy times, people are edgy,
religion doesn't exactly have a good press right now,
and, as you've been hinting at not too subtly,
the powers are breathing down our necks.
I repeat: if we don't know where you're going
how on earth can we follow you?
Tell us what routes to take, draw us a map,
Line out the logistics, Lord. What's the game plan?
Where and what is this place you are preparing for us?
Is it a new Zion, another promised land to be reached
through a new Red Sea, and over more desert trails?
Will the Almighty give us again a cloud by day,
another pillar of fire by night?
And what's our organizational strategy?
Is each family on its own?
Or do we organize, collect funds, choose leaders?
We're confused. If, like Caleb and Joshua,
you're doing the advance work,
tell us how to prepare for what's coming,
how to handle the interval. Always, it seems,
God-followers have to live between times.
Do we wait here for Solomon's glory to float down
from on high, fiddling while Rome collects slum rent

Scripture reading

John 14:3-9 (NIV, emphasis mine)

"And if I go and prepare a place for you, I will come back and take you to be with me that you also may be where I am. You know the way to the place where I am going."

Thomas said to him, "Lord, we don't know where you are going, so how can we know the way?"

Jesus answered, "*I am the way and the truth and the life.* No one comes to the Father except through me. If you really knew me, you would know my Father as well. From now on, you do know him and have seen him."

Philip said, "Lord, show us the Father and that will be enough for us."

Jesus answered: "Don't you know me, Philip, even after I have been among you such a long time? Anyone who has seen me has seen the Father. How can you say, 'Show us the Father'?"

to finance gladiators, banquets of roast quail tongue, and orgies?
Or Phoenician-like should we abandon this land
of overgrazed soil, overfished lakes, and overpopulated cities
to sail beyond ocean's edge toward unexplored places?
Should we let stars beckon us from space?
And in some future Zion, whether here or there,
which we await with not so bated breath
will there be grape clusters so large
it takes two men to carry one on a pole?
Will there be lush gardens, and sturdy houses
with vine-covered porches where we can sit and watch
our children play, and our grandchildren, one generation
teaching another the Torah and enjoying divine shalom?
A land of milk and honey waiting for chosen people,
a verdant land yearning for the touch of human hands?
Or will it be inhabited by who knows what obstacles,
monsters maybe, or a place unlivable because of
drought, floods, storms, pestilence, or impossible weather?
Have you considered, Jesus, the common-sense
down-to-earth action for which the Zealots plead:
'let's drive out the Romans and stay here'?
Or is 'the way' just euphemistic talk about life after death,
about a heavenly kingdom beyond political realms,
removed from economic tangles and unfair taxation,
untouched by political intrigue and military occupation,
unimpacted by the death of Lebanese forests
and the desertification of farm lands?
Are your poetic words aimed to assure us of heaven's rest
after we finish our three score and ten?
Are you just shoring up the leaning side of our souls
so we can face our own mortality with quiet faith,
counting life here but prelude to the next?
By chance are you hinting at your own death?
And saying you will meet us in heaven?
Don't say it, Lord, we haven't the strength
to continue unless you lead us.
The way, Lord, how can we know the way
if we don't know where you are going?
So, Lord: show us destination point, give us goals.
And is the way immigration, exploration, revolution,
enduring the present evil world
in hope of a better life after death
...or what?"

Jesus

"I am the way…"

Thomas

"Well, that's straightforward enough, if rather terse.
But, knowing your penchant for paradox, Jesus,
characteristically bending our ears, always the teacher,
sliding meanings in edgewise and forcing us to ponder them,
okay, I'll play the game, dear friend, for I do love you,
in my thickheaded manner. Remembering these past three years
(is that all the longer it's been—it seems like a lifetime,
I mean, because so chuck full of things, exciting,
and yet it's like you just hailed us yesterday),
in any case picturing these past years
it appears we're to be sojourners, not at home here
but heading to new places, or at least to a new order of things.
I suppose you mean for us to be trusting as birds
for the Heavenly One's care, not worrying about tomorrow
(now that sounds a bit like pious resignation, doesn't it?),
and that you want us to attach more importance
to children than to social advancement, making money,
or to fine clothes and jewelry and fancy houses.
(These things don't seem likely on our budget, anyway.)
Whether our religious agenda will play in Beersheba isn't important.
And I suppose you want us to love tax collectors,
misfits, neurotics, and even Mary Magdalene, who hangs around
all the time, as well as those rich snobs who invite you
as a dinner guest when you're a celebrity
and snub you like a leper when you're labeled 'agitator.'
I suppose you want us to be more interested in justice
than in tithing vegetables we swap with neighbors.
Even though you scold them for hypocrisy,
it's obvious you want us to love the Pharisees,
and even Roman overlords who rob us blind and
may desecrate our temple again, Herod notwithstanding.
In short, you insist love is life's ethical foundation,
for public as well as personal relationships—the basic value.
You want us to see "the way" as the desired future lived now,
whether we emigrate to exotic foreign places
or just hang around the same old town all our lives.
I think you mean we should not only pray for the kingdom
to come on earth as in heaven but make it happen here
through bold actions and attitudes based on love.
So, your way has more to do with character than circumstance.
This sounds idealistic for these times and in this place,

even though that's how things will be in the afterlife.
I suppose 'the way' means neither toadying to power
nor lording it over others when we're in charge.
Such a middle ground is hard to stick to.
You may be able to throw the temple rascals out nonviolently,
but we lack your finesse, riots follow our efforts at reform.
We lack your spiritual discipline and power, Lord,
we lack your tough love, your courage, your faith.
Your way is costly, Lord, and before we pay the price
could we receive certain assurances, certain warranties,
as it were, that the plan works, that it's true? Athenian bookstores
were jammed to the roof with profound philosophies,
but did that stop Rome? No. People prefer good roads to good books.
If our covenant experience is any test—our Exodus trek—
those who love God unconditionally, without partisanship,
get enslaved by people who keep love's circle small—family, tribe—
and act from motives of greed or pride outside the circle
(a practice generally dubbed self-interest—and widely approved).
Is truth just PR to keep weak people submissive to the strong?
Oh, yes, I remember your story about the good Samaritan.
Ethnic loyalty certainly can blind us to who our neighbors are,
or more precisely, how to be neighborly. But really, Jesus,
do you expect the way of love to work on any large scale?
Is the kingdom actually true, or just religious talk?
And how do we know your way is better ethically than others,
and not just a temporary strategy for oppressed minorities?
Moral theories abound, and cynics think people
who claim one value system over other truths
are really bigots who would impose their notions
over other justifiable forms of social adjustment
to natural and social environment.
What is truth, anyway?"

Jesus

"I am the truth..."

Thomas

"Two aces, Lord! I should have expected it.
But, you smile as you speak, and your eyes nudge my mind,
so, if you'll not think me impertinent, I'll press on.
People take truth seriously. Socrates died for truth...
(be still, Simon, I'm talking: you may act first and then think;
well, I think first and then act, and, Philip, you wait your turn—
you want reassurance, I want truth). As I said,
before being so rudely interrupted, people die for truth.

If you are truth, Jesus, we ought to know the implications.
Truth is more than calculating numbers, miles, and money.
It's more than the using common language
to describe reality. It's more than universal ideas.
So, here we go again, round two of my assignment,
worthy teacher. On the basis of the last three years
sitting at your feet, what is truth? Essay-type question,
no multiple choice, no rote responses. Okay. Repeatedly,
you prefaced your pedagogical remarks at the table,
or walking along the roads, or resting by the lake,
with this line, "I tell you the truth." *Veritas, veritas, veritas—*
one could put that sign up everywhere
you gathered a crowd. It's how you are billed.
Teacher of truth, not like the scribes.
The Torah praises wisdom and damns folly.
But, I repeat, what is truth? Is truth knowing
all about plants and animals, the environment,
so we can enjoy good health and keep well?
Is truth understanding how to manage one's affairs?
To be socially at ease, and thus psychologically secure?
Is truth the mystique of empire, *Pax Romana*,
collecting all humanity under heaven, and in peace?
Is truth a heavenly repository for how history
unfolds along time's arrow and within infinite space?
Pondering your many homilies prefaced with
"I tell you the truth," I believe I know what truth is not.
It is not just whatever works. (The strongest few
always win that game.) It's not just universal ideas
lodged in a spiritual world (scholars and priests
thus rationalize privilege). Nor a super science textbook
(managers exploit this notion to manipulate others)
nor a set of blueprints for mastering the world
(politicians preempt technique to their purposes).
Let me try to state what truth is. It is explanation
set in the context of divine order. It is purpose
transcendent over cultural, social, and ethnic limits.
It is cause and effect moderated by divine mercy.
Truth is moral law established through love.
It is social community based on divine will.
Truth acknowledges that evil may diminish good for a while
but can never triumph over it. Truth means God's forgiveness
turns darkness into light, as may our forgiveness of others.
In your eyes, Jesus, and not just from hearing your voice,
I experience truth as passionate worship of the Almighty.

I see life whole, now, and values proportionate to purpose—
   the earth is the Lord's and its fullness. So I respect
as divinely created all creatures, and acknowledge
that people are even more important than things.
How awesome, Lord, to be co-heirs in creation,
to be not lords of creation but stewards on its behalf.
But, Lord, I must admit to nagging doubts.
Yours is a beautiful way, your perception of truth
is truly magnificent. Plato and Aristotle,
Seneca and Epicurus can't hold a candle
to the coherent vision of truth you present.
But I am haunted by an insidious question:
'Is it necessarily so?' Or do we humans
just impose ethereal notions on a silent world?
Do we just fuss about in our minds, like housekeepers
trying to keep ahead of clutter, and impose
or project our ideas of order on the rest of the stuff.
Maybe the world just exists without rhyme or reason,
rocks and spiders being as significant as humans
to the nature of reality. Maybe our notions
of meaning and truth are just that, notions.
Maybe the stars could just as well examine Aristotle,
as Aristotle the stars. Maybe Plato's ideas are no loftier
than the survival instincts of a fish in the Sea of Galilee.
Our values must relate to truth if they're to mean anything
other than prevailing social preferences.
But truth, also, must relate to reality if it's to mean anything
other than prevailing cultural preferences.
Otherwise humanity groans under endless cycles of violence
in which power struggles forever exact their toll
of cruelty, suffering, rebellion, cynicism, and death.
Yes, we do see in you the human face of truth,
we see that God isn't abstract, either, nor a super idea
nor a super thing, but personal, caring, loving;
and that we, male and female, bear God's image,
and in embodying this image should thus act out truth.
But, I repeat, what if this magnificent vision of truth
is just a human notion imposed on a reality that exists
without purpose, nature in the raw, mute, wild, uncaring?"

Jesus

"I am the Life."

Thomas

"Ah, yes, Jesus, I remember, part three.
I am the way, the truth, *and the life,* you said. Incidentally
is reality experienced three-dimensionally?
Do we experience God as outer source, the Spirit as inner force,
you, the Messiah, as the one setting history's course?
And do we share that reality in a threefold manner?
Entities in space and with inner force moving through time?
In any case, Adam and Eve's children are launched
by their Creator on an incredible journey
through time and space. We fear the worst but hope the best.
We are rebels against heaven who wistfully recall Eden's beauty.
Inexorably we are drawn along time's path toward eternity
by the Spirit's inner fire, toward an incredible future.
Yes, Jesus, you have shown us our past nestled in divine will.
You have hinted at a future similarly under divine purpose.
We've been slow to hear you. But we have! *Show us
how to live right now in the divine presence.*
Somehow the present scares me almost more than the future,
when I glimpse through your eyes what it means to live now.
Gift us, Lord, with the spiritual presence we need.
I remember what you repeated often, Jesus. You said
'I tell you the truth, whoever hears my word
and believes him who sent me has eternal life
and will not be condemned;
he has crossed over from death to life' (John 5:24).
What stuck in my mind is the present tense:
'whoever believes *has* eternal life.'
Sinners all, we *are* reprieved, aren't we, we *are* pardoned
from sin and death. Not were, not will be. Holiness surrounds us.
Death as despair or futility, death as the loss of selfhood,
death as the end of humanity, as the end of the cosmos.
Death isn't the final word in the cycles of reality.
It needn't distort and destroy us. Life shapes us, molds us.
If I understand rightly, the future of humanity
will be like what we experience with you being present
to teach us, to show us God's love, and to enjoy each other.
But only more so, the Spirit's dance has just begun.
So we stand at the portals of New Jerusalem.
Reality is neither inert stuff nor ethereal idea
but things and thoughts infused by divine purpose.
The heavens and the earth are being renewed.
Dimensions of time are being crafted into eternity.
I suppose we should take Isaiah seriously:

'the lion and the lamb shall lie down together
and no one shall be afraid in God's holy mountain.'
Listening to you, Lord, I interpret
Isaiah's words as more than wistful imagery, more like
an announcement what the outer world will be like
when enough people together demonstrate faith.
Then in God's own time you will gather the whole world
into the kingdom. You are king of creation, Lord of the earth,
and whoever listens to you—whether Jew or Greek,
man or woman, bond or free, smart or stupid, rich or poor—
all can live in the truth (John 18:37).
I see it now: where you are going is into the future.
And whatever happens to us you are preparing
that future and drawing us into your kingdom.
This gives us confidence. We now understand
reality is neither blind nor mute. Reality is no illusion.
Neither is it grinding necessity wherein people
must grub out existence in violence or despair.
Life is not something to escape from by drink,
hard work, conspicuous consumption, or fantasy.
I see rather that reality—both things and thoughts—
is the work of the Father who prepares us
to share the joy of bringing the cosmos into glory.
Thank you, Jesus, for announcing the kingdom.
You are the way. I will let love guide morality
rather than the letter of the law, which yields so easily
to self-righteous or selective application.
You are the truth. I will let such truth instruct knowledge
about the world rather than pragmatic judgments,
which so often rationalize self-interest. You are life.
I will bind my life to yours rather than to be shaped by the world.
Jesus, your way is wisdom. Your word is truth.
Your life is reality. I choose your kingdom,
come what may. Jesus, you are my Lord!"

Jesus

"Thomas, now you know me, and have seen the Father!"

Vocation

Yachats Community Presbyterian Church, October 21, 1990

Thoughts about work

In rural Idaho where I grew up folks were wary of persons (men, at least) without "visible means of support." On the farm everyone worked at tangible jobs, like pitching hay or milking cows, and in the city people offered supportive services, like cleaning seed, selling groceries, or fixing things. A person's status was measured by how one is (to use an another expression) "gainfully employed." This standard doesn't work very well in Yachats. Sure, some of us work regular hours for wages or salary, but others don't. I guess we are the "*un*gainfully employed," without visible means of financial support! We've done our time on the job or profession. We've sold the business or the family house. We've fled the city and abandoned the daily routine, including maybe a daily commute. Grateful for burdens lifted we now accept our invisible pensions, investment income, along with deposits of social capital, as our due. So we get up when we want and do as we like, our actions

Old Testament reading
Proverbs 24:27-34 (NIV)

Finish your outdoor work and get your fields ready; after that, build your house. Do not testify against your neighbor without cause, or use your lips to deceive. Do not say, "I'll do to him as he has done to me; I'll pay that man back for what he did."

I went past the field of the sluggard, past the vineyard of the man who lacks judgment; thorns had come up everywhere, the ground was covered with weeds, and the stone wall was in ruins. I applied my heart to what I observed and learned a lesson from what I saw: A little sleep, a little slumber, a little folding of the hands to rest—and poverty will come on you like a bandit and scarcity like an armed man.

New Testament reading
1 Peter 2:5, 9-12 (NIV)

You also, like living stones, are being built into a spiritual house to be a holy priesthood, offering spiritual sacrifices acceptable to God through Jesus Christ.

But you are a chosen people, a royal priesthood, a holy nation, a people belonging to God, that you may declare the praises of him who called you out of darkness into his wonderful light. Once you were not a people, but now you are the people of God; once you had not received mercy, but now you have received mercy.

Dear friends, I urge you, as aliens and strangers in the world, to abstain from sinful desires, which war against your soul. Live such good lives among the pagans that, though they accuse you of doing wrong, they may see your good deeds and glorify God on the day he visits us.

---

independent of financial reward. Our economic gains, if any, come mostly from investments secured through stored energy (ours mostly, but not always) converted to money. Earning a living isn't stressful now, although stretching fixed income through inflationary years may be for some. Living fairly well without regular work has a down side. The guiding routine is gone. Then, too, the social success structure is low key in Yachats. Books on "dressing for success" don't sell. It's hard to tell "ins" from "outs" on our laid-back Pacific coast. Shopping at the stores, or munching donuts and gossip at the bakery, it's hard to distinguish government pensioners from welfare or social security recipients. Blue jeans and windbreakers are great equalizers. We can't easily discern levels of success. Furthermore, there's little incentive to climb the professional ladder. We're camped at the top.

Such social leveling is commendable but takes getting used to by people subtly tuned to status recognitions based on "gainful employment." More than we acknowledge, we miss deferential treatment we used to get from employees, office staff, junior partners, or younger workers. For example, I'm no longer surrounded by students who sit respectfully at Dr. Roberts's feet and drink in wisdom. How can a long-time George Fox College guru get similar psychological feedback in Yachats? At city council meetings? No way! More likely dark looks or getting shouted at. I exaggerate, but you get the point. True, each of us is held in a network of reinforcing respect by relatives, former colleagues, correspondents, and fellow hobbyists. Previously the job mirrored our social self. Now we seek reflections in other mirrors. This isn't easy. Especially with change in home and routine.

I hope people who pump our gas, serve our sandwiches, and repair our roofs don't find us crabby and overbearing. If they do, perhaps it's because prima donnas perceptive enough to retire at the Gem of the Oregon Coast still grope for inward controls adequate to replace vocational ones. I wonder whether some people stick with professional routines into their nineties—not so much from altruism as from fear of finding themselves empty once the job is gone. Well, some of us have taken the risk that life isn't empty, but can be at least as full ungainfully as gainfully employed.

So this sermon is about vocation. About working in the world out of a sense of divine calling. I need it. What the Spirit teaches me may help you, whether you do or don't get paid for your activities within society in general, and in the Yachats community in particular.

This homily celebrates a Christian conviction given significance historically by Martin Luther. Next Sunday is Reformation Sunday, a major theme of which is salvation by faith. I chose a secondary theme of that Protestant awakening, however: Christian life as vocation. God's calling is to everyone, not just religious specialists, said Luther. He and other zealous Christians set out to reform a church that had crafted Jesus' gospel into a monopolistic religious machine for dispensing God's grace.

To use theological jargon, Luther taught the priesthood of all believers. The priesthood of all believers doesn't mean we each tailor-make our own religion, but rather, as Luther said, "every Christian serves as priest to his neighbor through the vocation by which he is called." Because faith should govern the conduct of all Christians, Luther reasoned, the distinction between clergy and laity is functional, not vocational. Prior to that time, ordinary Christians understood the term *vocation* or *calling* to refer to a divine summons for priestly or monastic life. People who responded this way—"the religious"—were expected to obey the counsels of perfection, to pray, study Scripture, be celibate, and live in communal poverty.

Luther considered such limits on holiness a perversion of the gospel. He set about to change it. Salvation comes by faith, not works, he said. The Christian must live in the world not opt out of it. Not the cloister but the hearth is the altar for holy sacrifice. Not monastic vow but marriage symbolizes the love of Christ for the church. The workplace, the mine, the factory, the university—here divine service occurs, prepared for by the Christian families who worship together. The work itself, whether a labor of mind or of hands, makes a way for God's grace and Christ's atoning power. A job isn't just a convenient way to earn money so one can attend to spiritual things after hours. It isn't just a strategy for lunch break evangelism. Work is being on-location for the kingdom.

This concept got shelved during decades of Protestant-Catholic bickering. Puritan groups picked it up again in the seventeenth century. Presbyterians thought good Christians ought to run government and business, so they appointed ruling elders and blessed capitalistic hustle. Baptists stripped away religious paraphernalia so that even "tinkers" could preach, and stoutly opposed state-enfranchised religion. Quaker convictions about Christ in daily life hastened fair market practices, a trustworthy banking system, and an end to economic injustice—slavery in particular.

These Puritan efforts languished. Sloth set in. The priesthood of believers being too demanding, the church relinquished its task to religious specialists. Capitalism shifted from stewardship to prudential greed. Free, lay religion succumbed to hucksterism. Barclay Bank cards lost the sweet Cadbury-chocolate Quaker flavor they once had. The Protestant term *vocational* got secularized. "Vocational education" came to mean shop training for kids who can't handle calculus or literature, or rehab programs for laid-off loggers and welfare mothers. Good programs, but still low on the social status scale. The grand concept of work as divine calling got pushed aside.

Oh yes, certain professions retained an aura of divine calling—medicine and science for conservatives, social work and education for liberals. And a professionalized ministry, of course. Denominational colleges spent extensive efforts preparing students for these professions while letting would-be welders fend for themselves at vocational schools or find a union apprentice program.

The word *vocation* itself needs rehabilitation. Our biblical texts help us do this. Furthermore, they convey to us Yachatsonians—gainfully or ungainfully employed—something about what God wants from us in our use of time and energy. Consider first textual implications, then some applications.

Implications of the text

1. Christians are "called" ones.
The word *vocation* derives from the Latin verb *voco, vocare*—to call. It means not just to summon but to select. Note the elitist phrases Paul employs: "a chosen people," "a royal priesthood," "a holy nation," "a people belonging to God"—all Jewish covenant words affirming special status. And engendering resentment. Claiming special status seems to contradict what Jesus taught about servanthood and God's universal kingdom.

What with Jews and Muslims fighting over Jerusalem's Temple Mount many of us might settle for a secular judgment that such religious claims merely illustrate a human penchant for ethnicity—for putting one's own kind at the social center. See how boldly Paul appropriates this language of belonging, and gives it new and transcendent meaning! Personal identity doesn't depend upon Jewish, German, or Irish bloodlines; or citizenship in the United States, Brazil, or Israel; or upon Presbyterian or Catholic or Quaker membership. Distinction comes from being called by Christ.

This is catholicity at its best. It's what Reformation doctrines of election implied before they got distorted to justify slaughtering Incas and Bantus and Senecas. Paul understood how the Jewish mission to be a "light to the Gentiles" had been fulfilled in Christ, according to Isaiah's prophecy. Israel typifies *all* kinds of human uniqueness. (Eskimos are one of the smallest ethnic groups in the world, but their word for others is *dog*.)

In a Venn diagram small circles find common meaning within an encompassing circle. Apples, gooseberries, kiwi, and pears are distinct, but they're all fruit. So family and government, and cultural, economic, and religious structures—although different—are all groups within God's human creation. The risen Christ has captured the "powers" that group people into circles and is bringing them under his command.

What makes "a people" special, according to our text, is being called out of the darkness of sin into the light of salvation, to this purpose: "That you may declare the praises of him who called you out of darkness into his wonderful light." What gives people stature is *active righteousness within all circles of endeavor,* according to divine love and truth. Forgiven, brought within the divine circle, Christians witness as best they can to God's mercy and purpose for the human community. God so loved the world that he sent the Son! The coming of Christ into time and space is unique, but not exclusive. This is the pattern for Christian witness.

2. All Christians are priests.
Some may be gifted for special, paid ministries, but all may serve as bridges for God's redeeming grace. The New Testament reading makes clear that God's house is not sacred buildings but the people who follow Christ's way, and that ordinary Christians (not just salaried ministers) are the holy priesthood. Christ is their high priest. The people, not the steeple, is the church. The text contains a beautiful phrase about making "spiritual sacrifices acceptable to God through Jesus Christ." What does this imply? We are responsible to use time and energy for the common good and God's glory whether or not we get paid for it. Look at it this way. A job, whether in the home, the school, or the commercial workplace, bends the shoulders and burdens the mind. Sacrifice is involved in commuting, studying, lifting, solving problems, cooperating with others. Strains are put upon family, upon friendships, upon the self. We don't always get our own way. Sacrifice can be grudging, as if every demand upon our time, energy, or compliance were an imposition. Or one can offer the self gladly, even if personal energy and will is nailed on a cross. If we hear Christ's call from Gethsemane as well as from the Emmaus road, then we make our sacrifices as priests, offering our dedicated

skills—those of the body, mind, and soul—and the opportunities afforded them, in joyous service to humanity.

When a career is over we hesitate to get involved as a volunteer—working harder and not even getting paid. Like students, maybe? We fear the burdens—the drudgery. But recall Jesus' promise: My yoke is easy and my burden light. We needn't measure all activity by its heaviest routine. Milton's poem about his blindness includes these lines: "Doth God exact day labor, light denied? No, they also serve who only stand and wait." Change that to: "Doth God exact day labor, *strength* denied?..." Family responsibilities continue whether members work at a paid job or not, at any age—nine or ninety. So it is in the human community, our larger family—our largest circle. Standing and waiting together also works for the common good. Christians never resign their priesthood. The common ventures of life can be Spirit anointed.

3. Ordinary circumstances offer means for effective Christian witness.
"Ordinary circumstances" means the workplace and school, home and community. Our Old Testament reading warns that laziness and poor judgment can bring financial ruin. In respect to our careers most of us retirees haven't been brought to economic ruin, but it takes tricky logic to make an obverse inference—that we were industrious and used good judgment. We may just have been lucky or had rich relatives. But if we consider our activities as Christian vocation then we should apply this warning to unpaid activities as well as to paid ones, to work as citizens and public officials. The proverb has more to say to us than to not be lazy; it speaks about priorities: "Finish your outdoor work and get your fields ready; after that, build your house." A further statement warns that injustice and vengeance breach social order. "Do not testify against your neighbor without cause, or use your lips to deceive. Do not say, 'I'll do to him as he has done to me; I'll pay that man back for what he did.'" It's easier to apply justice and priorities to personal than to social relationships. Jesus holds us to the goal and sustains us when we falter.

Christians in circumstances less favored than ours can teach us much. Impoverished or disenfranchised people, struggling for status and justice, identify more readily with Christ's call. Live such good lives, "among the pagans," Paul declares in the words of our New Testament text, "that, though they accuse you of doing wrong, they may see your good deeds and glorify God on the day he visits us." Russian Christians have seen this happen recently. After seven decades of economic oppression believers are worshiping now within the Kremlin walls. Their Constitution now grants religious freedom, including freedom to teach and evangelize.

Applications of the text
What does this Scripture about vocation have to do with us at Yachats, gainfully or otherwise employed? This: We have established a primary loyalty base. Not the company, not the university, not economic status, not the country, not the social club, not even the town, but the kingdom. We're identified not by what we do but by whose we are. We belong to Christ. Our times are his. As an old catechism states: "The chief end and duty of man is to honor and glorify God and to enjoy him forever." Dietrich Bonhoeffer urged Christians to live faithfully under what

he called divine mandates: labor, family, governance, religion. I add a fifth: culture (the arts). These represent activities in which we expend time and energy, whatever our age or skill. But today I make applications only to our divine calling to labor, and thus to serve as Christ's priests to our neighbors.

1. Let our labor have integrity.
Does our work honor the creation? Do our skills draw persons toward the kingdom of God? Are circumstances fair for all concerned? These questions apply to our investments as well as to the work that provided for them. Money is stored energy. Let it work for God's glory. Whether actively employed or not we are called to use this energy as good stewards of the earth. What about our spending and giving—do they accord with divine purpose? Avoiding legalistic hang-ups, covered by God's grace, and guided by the Spirit, we can avoid greed and a narrow spirit. Work needn't be drudgery, let it be an ode to joy!

2. Let work be honorably recompensed.
For those who depend upon money, given or received, is it adequate? Honest work for honest pay? For everyone, gratitude is recompense too—especially so for home-makers, children, students, and retired persons who don't get tangible rewards. Is their sacrifice of energy received gratefully and often acknowledged? This is important, especially for those who have no "visible means of support." I admire people in our community for how cheerfully they volunteer services, use professional skills part time, or do entry-level work at minimum pay. Consider the hours spent by the people on the fire department, the city council and its commissions, the chamber of commerce, the Lions Club and the Women's Club, the library, the churches, and other groups. Add informal actions such as providing healthcare, fixing a neighbor's water heater, mowing lawns. Calculate the dollar value of these contributions. It's enormous.

3. Let work become a context for reconciliation.
Like all small communities, Yachats citizens find themselves differing on difficult issues. Like purchasing the school grounds. Strident personalities polarize opinion. I ask members of this church to work as reconcilers. Break the cycles of recrimination. Reinforce the past public service stints provided by members of this congregation. Participation gives a platform for constructive criticism and is a better response than carping from the sidelines. Luther considered prayer a labor of priesthood, a task for all Christians, not just clergy (*Lectures on Romans*, Library of Christian Classics, Westminster, 1961, commenting on 12:12). Until election to the city council I didn't pray much for local authorities. Oh, sporadically I fulfilled the scriptural admonition by praying for our president—or in times of crisis, for other world leaders. But that admonition doesn't specify the level of authority. It includes leaders of all kinds. I could be more faithful in this labor of prayer. I expect you could be too.

4. Let work be the occasion for redemptive action.

This doesn't mean the gospel is only lived and not proclaimed, but rather that a lived faith makes people open to receive proclaimed faith. In January 1980, after the authorities had shut down his radio station—two months before he was murdered in the cathedral at San Salvador—Archbishop Oscar Romero wrote:

God's best microphone is Christ,
and Christ's best microphone is the church,
and the church is all of you.
Let each one of you, in your own job, in your own vocation—
nun, married person, bishop, priest,
high school or university student,
day laborer, wage earner, market woman—
each one in your own place live the faith intensely
and feel that in your surroundings
you are a true microphone of God our Lord.

What a fine irony! In our day of lazy, institutionalized religion a Roman Catholic priest—at the sacrifice of his own life—reminds Protestants about the priesthood of believers, about vocation, about living out our faith in ordinary circumstances. Those closer to poverty often learn about Christian vocation more quickly than others. Let's learn from them. "The church," as Romero said, "must always be the horizon of God's love" (*The Violence of Love*, complied by James R. Brockman, Harper, 1988, p. 161).

Toward the Third Millennium

George Fox College Baccalaureate, April 27, 1991

A sad old proverb reads, "Days go by and every vision fades." The prophet Ezekiel challenged it. Wrote he: "'The Lord Yahweh says this: I will put an end to this proverb, it will never be heard in Israel again.' Instead, tell them: 'The day is coming when every vision will come true. From now on there will be no empty vision, no deceitful prophecy'" (Ezekiel 12:21-24 JB).

I ask you, as people who celebrate the Spirit's power to stir youth to visions and old people to dreams, what are your visions for the next century? What are your dreams for the third millennium? Will you be guided by them? This is a decade for goal-setting; this is a time to take stock of things, to check out policies and plans for ourselves, for the church, for humanity. Certain words capture important dreams; they must be cherished and preserved.

Part of my professional task has been the repair of words—words abused in conversation, tortured in writing, bent by bad logic. The task resembles the process of restoring solid but damaged furniture. By day in the workshop of the mind the philosopher in me patiently restores words. I scrape off obfuscating paint, glue splintered reasoning, replace perceptual hardware, refinish connotative surfaces, and restore rhetorical luster. Thus words are conserved. By night, however, in the house of the Spirit, the poet in me arranges words within a special place of visions and dreams. In this furnished room I share my soul with family, friends, and passersby.

You may not refurbish words, but they guide your speech and your actions. How will you use them to furnish that hospitable room of visions and dreams in *your* house of the Spirit? In the workshop of my mind are three significant words: *tradition*, *community*, and *culture*. Let's restore them so they can function fittingly, into the next century, into the third millennium. Consider how these terms signify a divine offer and human response.

1. *Tradition*

Tradition contains the divine offer of truth. Not truth as abstract theory but as expressed in thought and action—in wisdom. *Tradition* is a name we give patterns of truth woven over time into the clothing of humanity. Jesus warned against traditions that burden rather than liberate; Paul warned against false philosophy derived from human tradition rather than from Christ (Mark 7:8-9; Colossians 2:6-10 NIV). So reject as "deceitful prophecy" manipulated aspirations and mythologies of ethnic supremacy or the warrior state. Like all good currency "tradition" gets counterfeited. And from "empty visions" cynicism sprouts. So don't junk good traditions; restore their wisdom. In the software of the mind tradition is a major folder enclosing many documents of truth.

Certain traditions are at special risk. Restore them for posterity. Civility is one; having good manners is more basic to civilization than correct clothing styles or dining rituals.

Care of the earth is a tradition under repair. Here talk is plentiful, and romanticized mystiques abound, but biblical stewardship is needed. Scientists, we need your dedicated efforts.

Intellectual treasures from the ancient world require restoration, especially systems of rational coherence, joining particular persons, things, and events in a harmonious network of the good, the true, and the beautiful.

Our traditions of equity, justice, and mercy have roots so deep they penetrate strata of religious covenants, down to Eden's primal dawn. Seeds from Sinai grow in jurisprudent soil everywhere, flowering profusely when nurtured by the moral law within. These plants are withering. Care for them.

Spiritual traditions are at risk. Religion has been emptied of glory. Scholars trade on its history. Entrepreneurs exploit religious nostalgia. Politicians milk votes from the faithful, and desperate clergy mortgage the gospel to keep up institutional appearances.

For millennia mystery has shrouded spiritual heights like clouds around a mountain. Now technological society threatens to displace that aura. Within smoggy cities the stadium becomes its temple, the computer its rosary, sex its only sacrament, the murder mystery its Golgotha, television its Bible, the weapons fair its feast of firstfruits, politics its priesthood, and science its salvation. Jewish, Christian, and Muslim zealots react in violence to this threat. Cults wax and wane. Ordinary people, however, yearn for justice and goodwill. They don't want bickering over Jerusalem; they want Zion in the heart and in the neighborhood. Those who hunger and thirst after righteousness are blessed and shall be filled, said Jesus. Will spiritual traditions regain their glory? Be faithful, and they will.

2. Community

Community is the divine offer of presence. Community means having unity with others. Through intertwined circles of affinity we respond to God's mandates: family, work, governance, religion, and culture. Certain circles require particular vigilance: the family needs stability and work dignity; governance and religion need accountability; and culture must enhance personal integrity as well as provide for social cohesion. What are your visions for community?

Dream "swords-to-plowshares" dreams with me! That technology—freed from addictive militarism—will rebuild geographic neighborhoods, feed the hungry and heal the sick, tend the earth and its creatures, and probe the cosmos. Dream that schools will teach children to become world citizens. That athletic competition will foster civility not violence, that ethnic and national priorities will blend with global ones. That commerce and governance may move toward justice not away from it. For the third millennium envision a United Nations honored and respected.

The Law of Moses states, "The alien living with you must be treated as one of your native-born. Love him as yourself, for you were aliens in Egypt. I am the Lord your God" (see Leviticus 19:34 NIV). Jesus extended the Law's admonition to love one's neighbor from a tribal to a global circle.

Aliens everywhere live among us now: the refugees, the dispossessed, the underclass, the homeless, the marginalized, the abused ones. Communities of faith minister to them internationally. In the next century, I predict, concern for justice will match heightened concern for compassion. God's light shines and won't be put out.

This will happen as the church is renewed. Communities of faith now languish, some from antiquarian irrelevancy, others from shallow theology. Restore these communities. Give the movements back their glow. The tercentenary of George Fox's death is 1991. This young English dissenter awakened the church from concern for status to concern for the prospering of Truth. Fox and a Baptist contemporary, Roger Williams, helped unshackle the church from bondage to the national state. "The prospering of Truth"—this suggests the Christian task. Not just for Quakers and Baptists (who could use a bit of regluing too!), but for Christians in various traditions: Orthodox, Roman Catholic, Episcopal, Anabaptist, Lutheran, Reformed, Moravian, Congregationalist, Wesleyan, Pentecostal. All communities of faith need refurbishing. This is a good decade to do it. What are your visions for renewing your Christian tradition for the next century, for the third millennium?

You nonchurch people, beneficiaries of the tradition that marks our common calendar, you could lend force to the church terrestrial if you would forego a fixation upon its institutional frailties. When Jesus Christ said the gates of hell will not prevail against the church (Matthew 16:18), he affirmed the power of faith to build and restore structures appropriate to the kingdom vision. Why not put your lives on line with Christ? Robotic spiders are coming, and space colonies, and genetic tinkering, and super weapons. The biblical community of faith, barely global, must soon go cosmic, or the four horsemen of the apocalypse—conquest, famine, war, and holocaust—will scourge the earth. Christ beckons you toward the third millennium. So set your course toward the face of the crucified and risen one, who has gone to prepare our place. Say "yes" to God's offer and find a faith community within which to witness Truth.

3. *Culture*

Tradition and *community* are good words, to be cherished and refurbished. So is *culture*. Culture is the name we give shared and enduring patterns of human endeavor. The divine offer through culture is creativity. We respond by tendering work as stewardship and art as praise. The pioneers who spread their homes and churches across this land embraced a work ethic, parochial, yes, but fired with democratic imagination. They also quested after beauty.

There was land to be possessed, but also a torch of culture, like precious fire, to be carried from ancient worlds to new, symbolized by Latin and Christian mottos on money and Greek colonnades on courthouses. You sons and daughters of pioneers stand at the edge of a westering dream two millennia in the making. Never lose its history nor its literature. On this trek, however, a bitter lesson has been learned: We can no longer trash one place, or its people, and move on. The lands have all been mapped. Penitence for ignorant and offending zeal is healthy, and in order, but not cynicism about the vision.

What use then for pioneering dreams? I tell you, the third millennium holds a hundred better ways to circumnavigate the globe. Find them! Mysteries scarcely have been probed. There are sequels to sod houses and cabins in the clearing. Find new ways to tend the earth and live in community. Maybe God is keeping us at home awhile to tidy up our rooms, and then, who knows what adventures he may offer us en route to New Jerusalem. Space colonization, new energy sources, justice rolling over nations like a mighty river, the poor raised up, the earth healed…Christ has triumphed over death! Kingdom ventures will be hindered if rude rituals of aggression mark social rites of passage. So education and the arts must truly liberate our imagination for the third millennium. Then God can reveal earth's mysteries—and our tasks.

Avoid pop art—it has been compromised. Nourish authentic folk art. Cleanse high art of snobbery and give patronage to gifted ones who demonstrate how the human spirit joins God in continuing the creation. Graham Greene and Leonard Bernstein died recently. Who will pick up the torch? Who will now portray the anguished human quest for God? When will "Ode to Joy" be played in Jerusalem to celebrate the reunion of Ishmael and Isaac?

As work loses drudgery, people must learn to play again. Find Christ in simple things that grow, or that someone makes—things that gladden the eye and the ear, that are good to touch and to taste and to smell. Nurture in yourself and others a love of books. They often provide fit frames for God's paintings. They pass from one generation to another the riches of tradition, community, and culture.

When this era began, the Christian vision was symbolized by a new magazine called the *Christian Century*. A shattered dream? In part, yes, but some of it remains. Although at terrible human cost, culture *is* becoming global, if not yet biblical. All traditions, communities, and cultures are drawn inexorably by the Light of Christ toward God's redemptive future. In the distance the seventh trumpet heralds the world's renewal. Can you hear it? "The kingdom of the world has become the kingdom of our Lord and of his Christ" (Revelation 11:15 NIV). If, a century ago, young people were tempted by an optimism too naive, youth now are tempted by a pessimism too cynical. A century ago college students aspired to win the world for Christ in one generation. What are student aspirations now? Nikos Kazantzakis wrote: "Train your heart to govern as spacious an arena as it can..." (*The Saviors of God: Spiritual Exercises*, Simon and Schuster, 1960, Third Step, #19). When you pray "Thy kingdom come, thy will be done, on earth as it is in heaven," ask God how you can be part of the answer in the next century, in the third millennium.

Does every vision fade? No. Visions and dreams come true. Tradition, community, and culture reveal divine truth, presence, and creativity. The apostle Paul wrote, "Hope does not disappoint us, because God has poured out his love into our hearts by the Holy Spirit, whom he has given us" (Romans 5:5 NIV).

Trek Toward the Third Millennium

"Travel light,"
seasoned travelers say.
Anticipating a major move
ask yourself forthrightly,
"Do we really need this stuff?"
Some things we need:
good furniture, family album,
prized books, tools, clothes,
cherished toys, paintings,
a car, friends' addresses,
genuine heirlooms.
Take these things with you.
But first, junk the junk
and share the rest.
"Travel light,"
wisdom whispers to us all,
on whatever diverse routes
we travel, *anno domini*,
toward the third millennium.
"Do you really need this stuff?"
Ask your neighbor, ask yourself.
Choose the basics: knowledge,
tradition, culture, community,
skills, faith, hope, and love
(and your God-stamped visa).
Take these things with you.
But first, junk the junk
and share the rest.
Trekking toward the century crest
make your mind strong for truth,
your hands gentle on the earth.
Set your will to use machinery
to good and humane purpose.
Be sure to pack your dreams
and visions, too! In deserts
clouds will cool and guide you.
At night the Spirit's beam
will draw you to new habitats.
A pioneer will greet you
in the third millennium,
humanity's Omega point,
Jesus, the Christ.

Silence

Yachats Community Presbyterian Church, November 10, 1991;
Waldport Presbyterian Church, May 25, 2005

Introduction

This message about silence draws upon the third of Zechariah's eight visions of hope for Judah during its captivity. This vision pictures people peacefully settled in the "holy land." The Zionism depicted—in contrast with contemporary forms—is inclusive, not exclusive. Jews are to be what Abraham envisioned, a people whose faith enables all nations to find God's blessing for themselves. The vision portrays God's presence in Jerusalem, and all nations reconciled and at peace. No need to survey Jerusalem's boundaries, the young man in Zechariah's vision is told, for the Lord will be "the wall of fire around it [and] its glory within." Here *is* something to shout about, certainly; but when the Holy One appears on the stage of the heart, as when he entered history at Bethlehem, silence is an appropriate human response.

New Testament reading
Luke 20:21-26 (NIV)

So the spies questioned him: "Teacher, we know that you speak and teach what is right, and that you do not show partiality but teach the way of God in accordance with the truth. Is it right for us to pay taxes to Caesar or not?"

He saw through their duplicity and said to them, "Show me a denarius. Whose portrait and inscription are on it?"

"Caesar's," they replied.

He said to them, "Then give to Caesar what is Caesar's, and to God what is God's."

They were unable to trap him in what he had said there in public. And astonished by his answer, they became silent.

Old Testament reading
Zechariah 2:1-5; 10-13 (NIV)

Then I looked up—and there before me was a man with a measuring line in his hand! I asked, "Where are you going?"

He answered me, "To measure Jerusalem, to find out how wide and how long it is."

Then the angel who was speaking to me left, and another angel came to meet him and said to him: "Run, tell that young man, 'Jerusalem will be a city without walls because of the great number of men and livestock in it. And I myself will be a wall of fire around it,' declares the Lord, 'and I will be its glory within.'

"Shout and be glad, O Daughter of Zion. For I am coming, and I will live among you," declares the Lord. "Many nations will be joined with the Lord in that day and will become my people. I will live among you and you will know that the Lord Almighty has sent me to you. The Lord will inherit Judah as his portion in the holy land and will again choose Jerusalem."

Verse 13 is our text:

"Be still before the Lord, all mankind, because he has roused himself from his holy dwelling."

Picture a ruler approaching an expectant people. Tiananmen Square, Red Square, or Central Park, come to mind, where recently large groups have gathered in hopes for new leadership. Or picture curtains being pulled before a concert begins. How expectantly the audience waits! This is how silence should be: a holy hush as the King of Glory walks on stage. How else should we respond but with awe, adoration, and worship? This we Christians know, but we become so easily preoccupied with mundane things that worship becomes routine, just a social event. The Quaker movement arose to recover to the church that holy hush as an expected experience for all. Quakers emphasize silence in worship. Whether alone or with others we should wait for Christ to stride on the stage of our hearts and share with us the drama of the kingdom.

I use speech to extol silence. I'm like a sign to be ignored once you get your bearings, or a like a stairway to be forgotten once the next floor is reached. Consider, then, some implications of the biblical text: "Be still before the Lord, all mankind, because he has roused himself from his holy dwelling."

Silence is freedom from noise and distraction.

First, observe that silence offers a retreat from too much artificial sound.

We require environmental serenity in order to achieve spiritual sensitivity. But machineried noise marks our culture. It can be oppressive not only for physical and emotional health but for our spirits as well. Add to such sound clutter the incessant chatter of advertising hype and program sounds on radio and television. Music, supposed to soothe the soul is, unfortunately, often a noisy and manipulative marketing tool. Without deprecating music's aesthetic and spiritual values, we must concede that people sometimes use music to insulate them against hearing the Lord's voice. Deep cries of the soul may be drowned out by wretched music, yes, and also by good music. Even hymn-singing can be seductive; we feel religious but our ears are closed to what God wants us to be and to do. Persons inexperienced at solitude are vulnerable to musical seduction. In a world overstuffed with noise even sermons and liturgies become like repetitive advertisements, clanging cymbals, signifying nothing.

Second, consider that silence signifies wonder at the world.

With sound damped, eyes can see, hands and bodies and things can touch and be touched. Food and aromas can be savored. Grass and trees and flowers, the sea and birds and animals manifest their presence. Physical silence forces us to remove the barriers of noise and face God, as it were, naked, no longer clothed by artifice, chatter, or machine comforts. Said Moses long ago,

> Yours, O Lord, is the greatness and the power and the glory and the majesty and the splendor, for everything in heaven and earth is yours. Yours, O Lord, is the kingdom; you are exalted as head over all. (1 Chronicles 29:11 NIV)

In the Arctic I have experienced a physical silence, which Barry Lopez describes so eloquently in *Arctic Dreams* (Scribners, 1986, p. 176):

> The silent arrival of caribou in an otherwise empty landscape....The long wait at a seal hole for prey to surface. Waiting for a lead to close. The Eskimo have a word for this kind of long waiting, prepared for a sudden event: *quinuituq*. Deep patience.

Silence provides solitude needful to the soul.

Silence teaches us to be at home with ourselves spiritually.

Maturity involves learning how to be comfortable alone as well as with others. No one can escape circumstances that lead to loneliness. Loneliness is not overcome, but only poorly masked by superficial socializing and entertainment. If in silence you invite God to the center of the self, then that silence blossoms into solitude, resplendent in all the colors of joy. We don't arrive at such joyous solitude without discipline, which most of us treat as something best left to monks. But contemplatives such as Thomas Merton encourage us to find solitude in our own way. "When we have really met and known the world in silence," Merton wrote, "words do not separate us from the world nor from other men, nor from God, nor from ourselves because we no longer trust entirely in language to contain reality... God rises up out of the sea like a treasure in the waves, and when language recedes His brightness remains on the shores of our own being" (*Thoughts in Solitude*, Farrar, 1976, p. 86).

Silence is crucial to meaningful prayer.

John Calvin likened prayer to conversation, but warned against abusing God's kindness through irreverence. He describes the discipline of prayer in this way: "We are to rid ourselves of all alien and outside cares, by which the mind, itself a wanderer, is borne about hither and thither, drawn away from heaven, and pressed down to earth. I mean that it ought...[not] hold itself within the limits of its own vanity, but rise to a purity worthy of God" (*Institutes*, Library of Christian Classics, vol. 2, chap. 20, book 3, Westminster, 1960, p. 4).

Silence opens the way to good relationships with others.

Richard Foster advocates occasional short retreats—three or four hours long—to gain perspective. "Like Jesus," he writes, "we must go away from people so that we can be truly present when we are with people....The fruit of solitude is increased sensitivity and compassion for others" (*Celebration of Discipline*, Harper, 1978, pp. 94-95).

As we stand before the mirror of God and see ourselves as we are, then we can more clearly see others as they are. Then we are better able to bring persons to reconciliation and peace. Where there is strife, wrote George Fox, "First learn the ministry of condemnation in yourselves...that the ministry in the Spirit be known, which preaches Peace by Jesus Christ, where there is no strife (Epistle 145)...Silence all flesh and see your ways be clean. As you grow therein, the Way of Peace will be more prized....All who are here established shall stand in strength, when others fall on the right hand and on the left." Thus baptized with the Holy Spirit we can more readily accept other people, without feeling threatened by their sins, envious of their successes, or arrogant about their failures. We can more easily love others unconditionally, without having to retaliate, or to vindicate ourselves.

Silence provides space for listening to the Lord.

Silence preserves a necessary distance between God and the self.

Hinduism can be criticized for blurring distinctions between God and creation. Our technological culture produced a similar attitude.

But the era that deified science is over. Everywhere now people look for a God who is more than the sum of events, more than the sweep of history, more than a mythic synonym for humanity, more than a master computer, more than a psychological projection. A seventeenth-century Indian peasant poet, Tukaram perceived the need for distance between God and humanity. He wrote:

> He who worships God must stand distinct from Him
>
> So only shall he know the joyful love of God;
>
> For if he say that God and he are one,
>
> That joy, that love, shall vanish instantly away.
>
> Where were the beauty if jewel and setting were one? (*Tukaram*, J. Hoyland, trans., Woodbrooke, 1932)

Scientists increasingly acknowledge transcendent mystery. Linear equations fail fully to explain. Theories of reality transmute into metaphors that shine dimly, like flashlights probing a cavernous cosmos.

In the past era people tried to turn the Lord of the universe into a useful social instrument. But God can't be tamed. It is we who must be tamed. God, not humanity, is sovereign. Through bloody wars and revolutions God awaits our response to his announced kingdom. We bow in silence to see the Sovereign Lord rousing himself from his holy temple. Once more we hear his voice calling us to faithful obedience.

Silence signifies submission to divine will.

Such submission is first judgment for our sins and then God's grace that restores us to the divine image. When Jesus caught the Pharisees in duplicity, as noted in our New Testament reading, they were reduced to silence. Guilt is appropriately acknowledged first by silent submission to divine judgment, then by restitution. God's good news is forgiveness, yes, but also a Spirit-gifted power to walk in righteousness. "Let all flesh be silent," says the Lord, do not usurp divine sovereignty.

Silence signifies Christ's presence in ordinary life as well as in worship.

Jesus is our pioneer now, not Moses. Singly and together Christ brings us through the wilderness to our Promised Land. We celebrate this deliverance in his name. Daily our table grace acknowledges Christ as Lord. Christ is present in the vocations we choose and in our homes. Christ is the head and we are the body, the church. This is our primary circle of belonging, encompassing circles of family, work, ethnic or political responsibility. On the Emmaus Road, Luke records, Christ was revealed in shared meal.

> When he was at the table with them, he took bread, gave thanks, broke it and began to give it to them. Then their eyes were opened and they recognized him, and he disappeared from their sight. They asked each other, "Were not our hearts burning within us while he talked with us on the road and opened the Scriptures to us?" (Luke 24:30-32 NIV)

Let Christ surprise you at the dinner table or church potluck, at work or school, at play, or when visiting neighbors. Such is the order of the burning heart, here is the new neighborhood created in Christ Jesus.

Silence signifies receptivity for God's word to us and through us.

One thinks of Moses abiding in desert stillness until God appeared to him on holy ground and commissioned him to be the liberator of his people. A classic case of effective social action arising from solitude is John Woolman. This sensitive young New Jersey tailor had cultivated habits of the heart that included Bible reading and silent waiting. And on the holy ground of his burning heart the Lord commissioned this youth a prophet to speak God's judgment against social wrongs, particularly violence to animals, economic injustices that led to drunkenness, and human slavery. This prophetic quickening began in the 1740s. In his *Journal*, Woolman wrote, "I...was early convinced in my mind that true religion consists in an inward life, wherein the heart doth love and reverence God the Creator and learn to exercise true justice and goodness, not only toward all men but also toward the brute creatures" (Moulton edition, Oxford University Press, *LPT*, 1971, p. 28). Because Woolman heeded as well as heard the Spirit, he quietly convinced Quakers and then other Christians to stop slaveholding. His humble but persistent witness quickened the conscience of the church, so it could truly leaven society to correct injustices hitherto overlooked or wrongly justified. What power came through silent waiting before the Lord!

Conclusion

Accept silence before the Lord not as a luxury, but as a necessity for effective Christian witness in the world. Mostly, Christianity is a quiet revolution, like the flowers and grain growing, like truth and love growing. I exhort you, find in silence a freedom from distractive noise; discipline yourself to turn lonely times into a solitude needful to your soul; discover within yourself a holy space for listening and obeying the word of the Lord. "Be still before the Lord, all mankind, because he has roused himself from his holy dwelling." Are you ready to listen to the Lord of Glory?

Egypt To and Fro

Yachats Community Presbyterian Church, January 12, 1992

What triggered Herod's wrath? The magi's remark about "the one born to be king of the Jews." Only by much maneuvering had Herod connived to get the senate to confer such a title on him, and to have it affirmed by Caesar Augustus. Herod had managed to survive for more than thirty years as "king of the Jews." Herod was the quintessential despot: He placated Rome by being a dutiful lackey for their imperial designs and building a harbor city ingratiatingly named Caesarea. He fostered Greek culture through art museums, statues in the streets of Jerusalem, and gymnasia for young men. He tried to placate the Jews by marrying into Jewish families (he had ten wives) and by building a grand new temple to replace the one rebuilt after the Bablyonian captivity. He used everyone, ruthlessly or beneficently, according to his own schemes. He put to death for conspiracy three of his sons and his favored wife, Mariamme. His boss, emperor Caesar Augustus, liked Herod's administrative skill but not his person!

Old Testament readings
Psalm 137:1-4 (NIV)
By the rivers of Babylon we sat and wept when we remembered Zion. There on the poplars we hung our harps, for there our captors asked us for songs, our tormentors demanded songs of joy; they said, "Sing us one of the songs of Zion!" How can we sing the songs of the Lord while in a foreign land?

Hosea 11:1-4
"When Israel was a child, I loved him, and out of Egypt I called my son. But the more I called Israel, the further they went from me. They sacrificed to the Baals and they burned incense to images. It was I who taught Ephraim to walk, taking them by the arms; but they did not realize it was I who healed them. I led them with cords of human kindness, with ties of love; I lifted the yoke from their neck and bent down to feed them."

New Testament reading
Matthew 2:12-18 (NIV)
And having been warned in a dream not to go back to Herod, they [the magi] returned to their country by another route. When they had gone, an angel of the Lord appeared to Joseph in a dream. "Get up," he said, "take the child and his mother and escape to Egypt. Stay there until I tell you, for Herod is going to search for the child to kill him." So he got up, took the child and his mother during the night and left for Egypt, where he stayed until the death of Herod. And so was fulfilled what the Lord had said through the prophet: "Out of Egypt I called my son." When Herod realized that he had been outwitted by the Magi, he was furious, and he gave orders to kill all the boys in Bethlehem and its vicinity who were two years old and under, in accordance with the time he had learned from the Magi. Then what was said through the prophet Jeremiah was fulfilled: "A voice is heard in Ramah, weeping and great mourning, Rachel weeping for her children and refusing to be comforted, because they are no more."

Like many rulers since that time, Herod felt threatened by Jesus. Augustus said of the one on whom he had bestowed the title "king of the Jews," "I had rather be Herod's pig than Herod's son." The historian Durant said that Herod got everything he wanted, except happiness. He died miserably, paranoid to the point of insanity, about two years after his murderous proclamation that sent Joseph scurrying in the night to the safety of Egypt.

What about the flight to Egypt? What was it like? Donkey travel went at the rate of about twenty miles per day. Depending where they stopped, the trip would have taken eight or ten days. Maybe they traveled a couple of nights and hid during the daytime, until they could join a caravan at Gaza. Who knows? At the bazaars Mary and Joseph may have bought foreign goods and enjoyed browsing about in a world trade center. Like young couples everywhere, I expect fear mingled with excitement. Egypt offered a haven with its large Jewish population, where Joseph and Mary hid in safety for a while (tradition says three years). I expect they were glad to return to their homeland, like all sojourners who have a chance to return to the place they call home.

Consider with me three themes from this flight of Mary, Joseph, and Jesus.

Flight from danger

The flight to Egypt symbolizes the faithful struggle of families to protect their children from danger. Young couples struggle to make a place for themselves and their small children in the face of dislocations caused, directly or indirectly, by economic or political despots or revolutionary upheavals. Sometimes they have to move to strange places. Haitians; Hmung people; boat people; Latin Americans; American workers looking for jobs, worrying over where to live, how to care for the baby. Homeless families. In our country many are without health insurance, and face predators on the streets, drug peddlers by the schools, television subversion of their children's virtue, ridicule for their morality and Christian faith. In this story of Joseph, Mary, and Jesus, God tells us he is in these struggles.

The grace of hospitality

The flight to Egypt shows the importance of havens, like that afforded Mary and Joseph and the baby in the community of dispersed Jews. We are admonished not to neglect hospitality. Young women in Nampa, Idaho, have founded a haven for sixty abused young children. God is present in such hospitality. Sometimes grandparents or other seniors provide temporary havens for the children of others. Sometimes aged persons themselves need comfortable havens. We need them in Yachats and sometimes supply them for each other, or bid our friends farewell as they seek secure living elsewhere. The homeless need shelters; the mentally ill need homes. In a democracy a priority of government is to provide havens. The Job Corps is an example of a local haven for youth who need both security and vocational direction.

Home returnings

The flight to Egypt shows us that life's journey is marked by transience. We live our lives in chapters—at one time in a hill village, another time in Bethlehem, then Egypt, then Nazareth, then Jerusalem. Sometimes there's really nowhere to lay your head. Even when we are more or less at home we remain always pilgrims, strangers in time if not in space. But for faithful persons most moves can become home returnings, chapters of life in which we do feel at ease, safe, cared for by others, loved and appreciated, with useful things to do and to enjoy. We find that security in Yachats. We are often journeying between Bethlehem and Egypt, and between Egypt and Nazareth. To and fro. Jesus' promise of many rooms in the resurrected life adds meaning to our sojourn. The New Jerusalem is both a garden and a city—Eden regained. Beyond a dread of the final journey is joy at the prospect of the dawning of the great day of the Lord. Rightly we speak of death as "home going."

Egypt To and Fro

Clip clop, clip clop,
Clip clop, clip clop,
clippity clip clip clop
plods the brown donkey
through the dark night.

Clip clop, clip clop,
Clip clop, clip clop,
clippity clip clip clop
plods the brown donkey
toward the dawn's light.

Tick tock, tick tock,
Tick tock, tick tock,
tickity tick tick tock
plod harried persons
through the dark night

Tick tock, tick tock,
Tick tock, tick tock,
tickity tick tick tock
God leads the faithful
toward the dawn's light.

(from *Look Closely at the Child: Christmas Poems*, Barclay Press, 1997)

The Leadership of Christ

George Fox College, Quaker Heritage Week, October 25-26, 1992
(also presented serially at Reedwood and Newberg Friends churches)

What is life's supreme mystery, hidden by or within art and culture, literature and history, societies and governments? In myriad nuanced stories of heroic struggle, of good and evil, will and circumstance, emotion and reason, failure and success, where, and what, is the plot? The mystery, I believe, is this:

> how humanity—cast in God's image—recovers its creation mandate,
>
> and people become faithful stewards of God's grace and glory.

Intimations of this re-creation were revealed in dreams and theophanies to ancient covenant peoples, and carried by the Hebrews tenaciously as promise. Typical are the visions of Isaiah and Daniel.

> Of the increase of his government and peace there will be no end. He will reign on David's throne and over his kingdom, establishing and upholding it with justice and righteousness from that time on and forever. The zeal of the Lord Almighty will accomplish this. (Isaiah 9:7)

Scripture reading
Colossians 1:25-28, NIV here and in subsequent texts

[Paul writes] I have become its [the church's] servant by the commission God gave me to present to you the word of God in its fullness—the mystery that has been kept hidden for ages and generations, but is now disclosed to the saints. To them God has chosen to make known among the Gentiles the glorious riches of this mystery, which is *Christ in you, the hope of glory.*

We proclaim him, admonishing and teaching everyone with all wisdom, so that we may present *everyone perfect in Christ.*

"In my vision at night I looked, and there before me was one like a son of man, coming with the clouds of heaven. He approached the Ancient of Days and was led into his presence. He was given authority, glory and sovereign power; all peoples, nations and men of every language worshiped him. His dominion is an everlasting dominion that will not pass away, and his kingdom is one that will never be destroyed." (Daniel 7:13-14)

The new covenant people saw in Jesus of Nazareth, crucified yet risen, messianic fulfillment of all these ancient hopes. The central event of history, they said, was God endorsing and modeling this vision in letters of human flesh. They restated this vision in terms of universal truth and in the ethics of love, as Jesus demonstrated and taught. The sacrificial death of Christ and the gift of the Holy Spirit provided empowering to live in God's kingdom. Through faith ideal became reality. The day of the Lord had dawned.

We call ourselves "Christians" because having received God's grace we affirm this vision. Our confidence to testify thus about Jesus and the kingdom arises because the mystery of divine/human interface has been revealed within and among us. Christ within confirms the mind about God's acts in the creation, in the cross of Jesus, and in the resurrection. Christ within confirms the heart about the mystery of God searching and finding faithful response, leaping over erected walls of race or tribe or tongue, triumphing over principalities and powers, pulling the fangs of death. Darkness cannot put out the Light. Periodically, the power of this vision of Christ within, the hope of glory, gets obscured by ritual or priestcraft or politics, and needs to be restated. It was powerfully restated in the seventeenth-century Quaker awakening. We are legatees of that vision, whether as Friends or others touched by that movement of Christian renewal. The vision needs once again to be restated.

In the midst of joys and sorrows, work and play, solitude and community, in situations of ease and struggle, growth and maturity—and finally death—humanity seeks a key to meaning. If you look closely, even in our television programs and print literature of frivolity, fantasy, and silliness you can spot despair hovering like a bankrupt director. If you have eyes to see and ears to hear you will agree that even in so-called secular society God is evoked in many ways, overtly or covertly, secretly or publicly, in profanity or prayer, in rage or penitence, with mixed, muddled, or sincere motives. We accept mystery, yes, but yearn for it to be mystery that reveals God's presence, rather than conceals it.

"The word of God in its fullness," to use Paul's phrase, is the mystery of this presence revealed. Not explained—this is more than the mind can grasp—but revealed. Revealed in such a way that all other revelations of God, through prophetic guidance, culture, moral law, and the unique biblical narrative, affirm divine indwelling. This God-dwelling binds my story to yours, and ours to all faith journeys throughout the ages—flawed though they may be by sin, diminishments, accretions, misrepresentations, exploitations, and hypocrisies. In the midst of human clutter caused by finitude and disobedience is a common, binding theme: God manifests love to us as we journey through time and space.

Consider then, thoughtfully, the meaning of Christ as the inward presence of God, for yourself, and for humanity. Because we are carried along the arrow of time, it will be helpful to ask what it means to be "in Christ," or to say "Christ within, the hope of glory" in respect to time—past, future, and present.

Our Quaker heritage offers certain insights about the presence of Christ through time. George Fox gathered many people to his message, in spite of heavy persecution, because he offered a renewed vision of the faith community that witnessed the kingdom through worship and work. His followers acknowledged that the existing institutional church had ritualized the past of Christ, often for priestly privilege, and in doing so had sacrificed the power of present, living faith. They acknowledged too that some zealous reformers were so preoccupied with millennium speculations they failed to honor Jesus Christ, present kingdom teacher, accepting only the promise and not the fulfillment. Like some current, but more secularized Christians, they substituted the arm of the flesh for the arm of the Lord.

In our day, media entertainment, hobbies, and travel are favorite ways to extend the present, to "broaden experience." Some seek help from exotic religious psychology or trendy Hindu thought. People's roots in current culture tend to be wide rather than deep. They lack continuity with the saints who surround us in eternity and cheer us on our race. This shallowness distorts the Quaker emphasis upon the presence of Christ, skewing it into a mere focus upon the psychological moment. Consequently, unfounded in real time, religious fuzziness characterizes both meditation and group consensus, both worship and service. There *are* good ways to find significance in past, future, and present. Quakers sought that in their emphasis upon the continuity of Christ over time.

A. Christ within reveals the mystery of where we have been.

In this sermon I focus upon how Christ within *gathers up the past* into significant memory and meaning. The past is Christ revealing the mystery of our journey thus far, holding us to a standard of truth posted at the center of history, a referent point to keep us on course. Personal and social memories become enriched by grace. Where we live can be located deeply, not shallowly, in time. We can live as neighbors with all the saints. Let me illustrate how the Christ within illumines the past.

In September of this year, 1992, Fern and I, joined by our son, Lloyd, and his wife, Cheryl, journeyed through Wales to locate our Quaker roots. The memory of Welsh Quaker ancestors, with names like Owen, Lloyd, Ellis, Robert, Sarah, Jane, and Bevan has been conveyed by scattered documents and by one generation telling and naming the next. Consider John Bevan, one of these ancestors. The story illustrates how the past is sustained by memory, and how the present leadership of Christ gives significance to such memories. Genealogy is but one way to enrich the temporary dimension to our lived-in space. There are other ways: archeology, history, literature, art—even photograph albums and family stories. Journals and church traditions trace the past. The Scriptures constitute our basic collective story. Any of these ways can be misused—avoidance techniques. But each also can become a means for knowing better where you've been and who you are. Thus your roots will wrap around the eternal rock and guard you from adverse contemporary winds. If you listen to the voice of Christ within your heart and within the church, mystery is revealed. Through memories sanctified, our experiences of Christ are melded with those of our faithful human forebears, whether physically related or not. As we are lifted godward in the community of faith, Christ shines more brightly as the hope of glory.

The Welsh people had responded enthusiastically when George Fox first preached among them in 1653. A clergyman named John ap John had been sent to investigate the movement, so it could be refuted. Instead he became convinced of the Quaker understanding of the gospel and was moved inwardly by its spiritual power.

John Bevan (John ap Evan; or *ab* Evan) in 1662 became convinced. He was a prosperous farmer with a new stone house, named Tref-y-Rhyg, in the Llantrisant district of Glamorgan, in southern Wales, a few miles north of Cardiff. At first his wife continued in the state church, but when her husband was excommunicated, she too joined Friends. During the 1670s persecution intensified. John, along with other Quakers, suffered imprisonment for refusing to take the oath, or to pay state-imposed church taxes. His cattle were taken by distraint to pay fines. But his faith in the present leadership of Christ increased through it all. He became an acknowledged minister to the thriving Welsh Quaker meetings. In 1683, after his aristocratic friend William Penn offered a Welsh settlement in the New World as a haven from oppression, John Bevan joined other Welsh Quakers (eventually to number four or five thousand) in migrating to Pennsylvania. One of the "first purchasers," he secured 2,750 acres of land in the Welsh tract near Philadelphia. There he and Hugh Roberts, of North Wales, became leading ministers.

At the beginning of the new century John Bevan returned to Wales with his wife and youngest daughter, and sought to rebuild the local Quaker meeting at his family farm, Tref-y-Rhyg, ministering to diminishing numbers of Quakers—those who had stayed behind to seek Christ's kingdom rather than immigrating. Bevan remained a vigorous preacher into his eighties. In 1720 he was imprisoned for refusing to pay tithes to the vicar of Llantrisant, from which church he had been excommunicated fifty-two years earlier. Bevan died soon thereafter, at the age of ninety, and was buried on his own land. Most of his family remained in America. One descendant was Stacy Bevan, who vigorously supported the revivals of the nineteenth century in Iowa. Another was my grandmother, Mary Bevan Roberts.

On our recent trip we drove out to the old Bevan farm house, Tref-y-Rhyg, whose current occupants, a family of Roberts, know of its seventeenth-century beginnings. The gravestone has been lost but not the legacy. As I stood on the driveway near the old wall that Bevan built I saw the green, rolling hills of Wales, with sheep grazing now as then, and thought: The past *is* part of the present. I am part of the past and the past is part of me. Christ within gives meaning along the arrow of time.

Your story differs from mine—God's house has many rooms—but each story contributes with cumulative force to the present and the future of the kingdom of God. Our journeys of the Spirit reach back to Paul, to Abraham and Sarah, and to patriarchs beyond the reach of history. Building upon their foundations we are cocreators with Christ. The hopes of generations past funnel through our choices. Nudged by Christ, we enter into their visions and dreams—faithfully, or unfaithfully—and the Spirit patiently weaves out of this network of sin, suffering, love and truth, grace and joy, a kingdom tapestry.

The apostle Paul, exasperated by the superficiality of the Galatian church, wondered, as sometimes we do, whether he had run his race in vain. Would he think this of us? The writer of Hebrews exhorts us "Therefore, since we are surrounded by such a great cloud of witnesses, let us throw off everything that hinders and the sin that so easily entangles, and let us run with perseverance the race marked out for us" (Hebrews 12:1). Are we listening to this cloud of witness?

What are the implications of Christ's presence with us?

First, we can more rightly interpret the acts of God in personal and general history.

Reading the past through the eyes of Christ lets us rest easily in the present, and gives perspectives for the future.

Second, we gain confidence in the power of love conjoined with truth.

The continuing presence of Christ, not just ancient words and deeds of Jesus, assures us that good overcomes evil and truth overcomes falsehood, although at the cost of redemptive suffering, Christ's and sometimes ours.

Third, we are stewards of a legacy to be shared.

Christ networks our shared memories of God's grace. These memories include a valiant Quaker witness to the real presence of Christ within the heart and within the community of faith.

How does this apply to Newberg Friends?

First, make sure that church and Quaker history is conveyed, one generation to the next in worship and education.

Let such an understanding of God acting in history guide personal, family, and church decisions. How wonderful that Newberg Friends, reading history through the eyes of Christ, sustains a Hispanic ministry, and in the Second Street Church is constrained to reach seekers, like George Fox did at Firbank Fell.

Second, don't let success deflect you from cross-bearing.

We are called, as Paul said, "to fill up what is still lacking in regard to Christ's afflictions" (Colossians 1:24). Holding John Woolman in memory will teach you humility and encourage a bold but loving witness for peace and justice, even when it may not be popular.

Third, cherish your unique responsibilities.

You are the historic Quaker center of Northwest Yearly Meeting. You have honored this trust in respect to the meetinghouse. Be equally eager to maintain the cemetery; count this heritage in your keeping as a joyous trust—not a burden. Here lie buried Friends who form our particular "cloud of witnesses." They testify to Christ within, the hope of glory. They cheer us on. Continue, also, to support George Fox College and Tilikum Conference Center and Friendsview Manor. Sustain yearly meeting and Barclay Press staff and facilities. Nurture those among you who, like Marie Haines did years ago, uphold the Quaker legacy in writing. Be faithful stewards.

In a beautiful reflection following the death of his wife, Helen, Lauren King wrote this poem, "Facing Backward" (*Verses for Helen*, published privately, 1992).

Facing Backward

Unable to turn head for forward look,

We travel through life facing backward,

Without sight of the hills, the valleys, the turns

Of the way ahead

We look instead at the road already traveled,

And never to be traveled again,

Grieving for ignorance and folly past,

Saddened at what might have been,

But hoping to gather from our backward gazing

Some wisdom for the road before us,

Longing never to have to say,

"Ah, had I only known."

To you God has chosen to make known in certain distinct ways the glorious riches of this mystery, which is Christ in you, the hope of glory. In this context proclaim Christ, admonishing and teaching everyone with all wisdom, in order to present everyone perfect in Christ.

B. Christ within reveals the mystery of where we are now.

When she was a young person, Edna St. Vincent Millay wrote one of her best-known poems, "Renascence." I quote from it to illustrate how the soul struggles for space against the pressures of past and future and the weight of the present. She wrote:

Renascence

The world stands out on either side

No wider than the heart is wide;

Above the world is stretched the sky—

No higher than the soul is high.

The heart can push the sea and land

Farther away on either hand;

The soul can split the sky in two,

And let the face of God shine through

But East and West will pinch the heart

That cannot keep them pushed apart;

And he whose soul is flat—the sky

Will cave in on him by and by.

(*Major American Poets*, Williams et al., ed. Mentor Books, 1962, p. 414)

I talk to you, George Fox students about Christ and time.

This is about how the present can be experienced meaningfully, joyfully—how the soul can "let the face of God shine through." My theme is that Christ within reveals the mystery of *where we are now*, as well as where we have been and where we are going. The apostle Paul spoke of that mystery in the Scripture reading chosen.

In the seventeenth century in what is called the Quaker Awakening, George Fox (after whom this college is named) along with other young associates and many disillusioned war veterans, recaptured the vitality of early Christianity. Christ is our present teacher, Fox said. Baptized by his Spirit we live in the kingdom. Christ is present as living Word. The Lamb of God who takes away sin is not stuck back in history, or in some future millennium, but present with us, enlisting us to spiritual warfare against the powers of sin and darkness. You students are legatees of that vision, whether as Quakers or as others touched by that movement of Christian renewal. The vision needs once again to be renewed. I invite you students to be part of that renewal.

Once in my childhood I was lost in a forest. I remember still the panic that came from not knowing where I was, from being literally lost in space. Fortunately I was found rather quickly. It is possible, also, to be lost in time. This is a contemporary condition for many young people around the world, not just in London, Amsterdam, Moscow, and Sao Paulo, but also in Los Angeles, New York, Seattle, and Portland. And in the smaller towns and villages, like Newberg, their wildly irrational behavior indicates that they are really lost in time. Like jaws of a closing vise, past and future seem silently to narrow the reality within which they must grasp at fleeting pleasures. The sky is caving in on them. And their cry, often expressed in music and graffiti, rises to a thin and shrill crescendo.

Maybe some of you are lost in time too, although rage or drugs haven't yet blown your mind. I offer you mystery revealed, Christ within you, the hope of glory. That divine presence is a power to keep you free from present, past, and future tyrannies. Christian faith is not a smug confidence that all's well, but a Spirit-informed way of seeing. Not only does Christly insight enables us to map the past and lay a compass to the future, but Christ present within the soul allows us to perceive the borders of the present. In *Arctic Dreams* (Scribners, 1986, p. 176), Barry Lopez writes: "The edges of any landscape—horizons, the lip of a valley, the bend of a river around a canyon wall—quicken an observer's expectations. That attraction to borders, to the earth's twilit places, is part of the shape of human curiosity."

I say to you that Christ within the soul, and among God's people, enables us to find the borders of the present. Apply this to the social landscape—the school, the workplace, the mall, the city, the countryside, the cultures of our political world, the cosmos. See people—ourselves included—and things through the eyes of Jesus. Now the sky is split, now the face of God shines through! Eternity frames the present. In a modern parable, *Joshua and the Children* (Macmillan, 1989, pp. 58-59), Joseph F. Girzone's protagonist, Joshua (Jesus), tells the Irish children, "Heaven is in a world beyond, just on the other side of a thin veil of time. If you could close your eyes and walk through that veil, you could be there. It is that close." The present is that close to eternity. It is precious; cherish it.

Daniel's vision has come to pass. Christ's dominion is everlasting, his kingdom will never be destroyed. Christ in you is the hope of glory. We too proclaim this, admonishing and teaching everyone with all wisdom, so that we may present everyone perfect in Christ.

What are some implications of Christ present with us?

First, the human struggle is infused with divine grace.

Despite terrible failures, finiteness, ignorance, and evil, God loves us and calls us to share the glory of creation. God's revelations in the past, and written in Scripture, are stamped indelibly on the heart. Although mere creatures on an outpost of a minor galaxy, we are important to God's purposes. The past is not "sound and fury signifying nothing"; the future is not random events and burned-out stars. The arrow of time reflects God's good purposes.

Second, personality receives a stabilizing center.

Christ bridges the chasm between human and divine. We need not try to make ourselves autonomous centers of the universe, little gods fighting for space in the sun. Nor need we yield our individuality to social or political orders. Neither need we become merely God's puppets. Christ within yields authentic personal identity in a context of love and truth.

Third, we find access to reality's true network.

The one present with us is the word spoken in creation and incarnated in history—the one gathering peoples to a renewed cosmos. Barricades separating the physical from immaterial are broken down. Spirituality infuses body and mind, things and thoughts, material and immaterial realities. The universe groans with Golgotha's pain but sings the resurrection song of the Lamb upon the throne.

What are some applications to the George Fox College community?

First, George Fox College is a place and time of God's visitation.

It's your "day of the Lord." Don't fret that you may be poorer than your parents, or that you are, or may become, a minority race, or that society is evil. Don't pine for the good old days or the second coming. Let Christ sanctify your imagination. Be at home in the present. Let history and literature open windows to the past so that God's sunlight can stream in. Let the sciences open doors to the world around you. Find the skills and the tools to take care of God's earth and its creatures. Let the arts penetrate the gloom and bring you joy. Be confident about the future. Nothing can separate you from God's love.

Second, trust Christ within to shape your personality.

Forget about posing, pretending, faking it, hogging center stage, pouting, gossiping, whining, blaming, conniving, and cheating. Don't wallow in abuses you may have suffered, real or imagined. Accept God's forgiveness for past sins and failures, and those of others, and say with Paul, "I have been crucified with Christ and I no longer live, but Christ lives in me. The life I live in the body, I live by faith in the Son of God, who loved me and gave himself for me" (Galatians 2:20). Your body is God's temple, don't litter it with mental or physical garbage. Sex is not a nighttime tennis match, but rather an integral part of the spiritual covenant of marriage. If you are single, stay chaste. Life is full of alternate excitements, popular culture notwithstanding.

Third, under the present leadership of Christ discover your basic vocation.

I said earlier that life's supreme mystery is this: how humanity—cast in God's image—recovers its creation mandate, and people become faithful stewards of God's grace and glory. If you listen you may hear Christ say words like this to you: "Let's be about the kingdom business, shall we? Proclaim God's forgiveness and the empowerment for truth and righteousness. Be peacemakers. Govern with justice. Care for the earth and its creatures."

In the kingdom business there are no sharp lines between so-called secular and church vocations. We serve others through all honest lines of work. To answer Christ's call you must study hard. Learning is your spiritual service now. Hone mind and spirit on the programs of the Peace Center and other cocurricular activities. On the May term abroad look at the world in Christ's light. In worship discover Christ as present teacher and learn how to heed inward promptings. Obey Christ in everything. Join the Lamb's war.

Offer your imagination to the Spirit's sanctifying power so that when you pray "thy kingdom come on earth as in heaven" you can put your energy where your prayer is.

It's an exciting time to be alive, isn't it? At the dawn of the third millennium A.D. John Le Carré wrote in *The Russia House* (Knopf, 1989, p. 286) that the old isms were dead, and "the contest between Communism and capitalism had ended in a wet whimper...[but] the grey old men...were still dancing away long after the music had ended." It's a new world. Now is the time for the gospel to work like leaven in the social order. Now is the time for Christ's light to expose sin and bring healing to humanity.

Ponder these poignant lines from Frederick Buechner's *The Sacred Journey* (HarperSanFrancisco, 1991, p. 107). "To journey for the sake of saving our own lives is little by little to cease to live in any sense that really matters, even to ourselves, because it is only by journeying for the world's sake—even when the world bores and sickens and scares you half to death—that little by little we start to come alive." The mystery is revealed. Christ within is the hope of glory!

C. Christ within reveals the mystery of where we are going.

Christ within *invests the future with significant direction and meaning.* The future is grasped by hope as Christ within reveals the mystery of where we are going. Let me illustrate how the presence of Christ guides into the future.

When George Fox came preaching to the Welsh communities, he gathered converts with the help of ministers such as Richard Davies, Robert Owen, Thomas Ellis, Hugh Roberts, and John Bevan. Rapid growth occurred. These Welsh Quaker families experienced persecution for their Christian faith. They were thrown into stinky prisons, their cattle were taken as fines, their daughters accused of being witches. Because they refused to take the loyalty oath, and to pay compulsory church taxes, Quakers were accused of being secret "papists." William Penn used his influence to try to achieve toleration, but when this failed he looked to the New World for a place where people could live in peace and religious freedom. His offer of a Welsh tract in America promised both a sanctuary from oppression and an opportunity to build a society patterned after Christ's kingdom.

Well, their hope for a tidy New Wales failed; their descendants lost the language and many of the contacts with the homeland. But their sense of Christ within guided their vision for the future, and they planted in the new land for all time certain freedoms as rightful human condition: to worship according to conscience, under free ministry, whether male or female, young or old, and the dignity of all persons, and their work, under God. The descendants of these immigrants carried that vision of a kingdom future as they spread out from Philadelphia to North Carolina, Ohio, Indiana, and Iowa. They formed rural economic colonies (mini-kingdoms) such as Damascus, Oskaloosa, Haviland, Greenleaf, Whittier, and Newberg. They carried with them aspirations to live their lives under the lordship of Christ, to live and see the increase of the peaceable kingdom.

Did they know where they were going? Yes, for Christ who entered history as God's word made flesh dwelt within them and among them as the Inward Light. They trusted their guide. And though outward circumstances moved them geographically, inner convictions, manifest in worship and strong fellowship, held them steady. It can be so with us, their spiritual and physical descendants. But we will need to listen more carefully to Jesus.

During the middle years of this twentieth century some Quakers lost or distorted the kingdom vision that marked the early movement. Like Thomas they got confused about where Jesus was leading them, and about the rooms in the Father's house. In envisioning the future they trusted too much in human wisdom to predict the course of things. Some relegated Christ to the sideline of history, or only to personal inner states. Others masked discouragement—a felt absence of Christ—by calculating the year of his physical return, forgetting that kingdom fulfillment is contingent upon believer faithfulness. In world-weariness they yearned for a millennial future but despaired of the world Christ came to redeem. They forgot that Christ's presence with them, and within the church, is the way into the future.

We can do better. God offers many rooms—in this life as well as in the next, in this country as well as another, in this culture as well as a different one.

What are the implications for grasping the future in the mystery of Christ within?

First, fears of diminishment are overcome.

Recently, in an interview, Larry King, popular show host, confessed the one thing he feared was death, particularly the loss of all adventure. Like Larry King, failures mix with successes in our lives. Nevertheless, we can say with Paul, "I consider everything a loss compared to the surpassing greatness of knowing Christ Jesus my Lord" (Philippians 3:8). The resurrection of Jesus Christ is a promise that we too shall live in dimensions exceeding those we now know, and that this new life beyond the curtain of death, will be as much greater than the present as flower to buried seed.

Second, partnership with Christ quickens creativity.

Christ holds title to the world's future but shares its formation with us. We are cocreators with Christ in our play and in our work. God opens the universe to our inquiry and to our participation as shapers of its future. The book of Revelation shows the kingdom of God as a garden-city. Take heart; human enterprise, with sin and ignorance removed, can enhance and not destroy the earth. The cosmos will be renewed. The Holy Spirit is earnest money that this is so. Such a hope makes getting up every morning a thrilling event! The adventure is exciting.

Third, we can more easily accept other people.

The principalities and powers will come under Christ's lordship. Tribes and tongues and nations will be gathered to God. Every knee shall bow and call Christ Lord. Such hope enables us to overcome the barriers that fear erects: caste, race, nationality, language.

What are some applications to the Reedwood community?

First, individual reassurance.

With such hope we need not be ashamed or fearful or discouraged by the all-too-evident marks of sin that characterize contemporary culture: greed, violence, cynicism, covenant-breaking, predation, injustice, exploitation, etc. Hope puts us on God's side. We have the insurance binder in our hearts against all the diminishments we face. The good, the true, the beautiful—these will prevail. Furthermore, our reassurance reaches beyond this life. Christ brings us through death's door into a greater glory. This is good news for all who are approaching heaven's porch.

Second, reassurance for the Reedwood church.

You are favored in many ways to prepare for the future. The Ong trust holds you to your stewardship in the future, for one thing. I know that you bear the burden of that trust. Make it a challenge rather than a crutch, a way to release ministry rather than to bind it. Quakerdom looks to Reedwood for exemplary and creative leadership. Reedwood Friends bears a particular burden to demonstrate in the twenty-first century what it means to express a Quaker witness to the world. Accept this leadership burden joyfully and humbly. It is not just our task; Christ is present with us, to lead us into truth, to teach us how to serve. I suggest that Reedwood Friends ponder what it means for Christ to lead us in respect to the three historic responsibilities of the church: the proclamation of truth, fellowship, and service. Early Friends ensured the continuity of this threefold task by Quaker education and by linking arms economically. An early elders' agenda included a discussion of apprenticeships, for example. In America this attention to work as sacramental service focused on agriculture, in England more largely through industry and the professions. Your own concern for the education of young people is admirable. In an economically stressed culture I look to Reedwood, as a progressive urban church, to provide leadership in respect to these problems and opportunities.

Third, we anticipate the future with confidence, not anxiety.

We are messengers of good news, announcing a mystery revealed—Christ within, the hope of glory! Therefore, as Paul wrote, "Let the peace of Christ rule in your hearts, since as members of one body you were called to peace. And be thankful. Let the word of Christ dwell in you richly as you teach and admonish one another with all wisdom, and as you sing psalms, hymns and spiritual songs with gratitude in your hearts to God. And whatever you do, whether in word or deed, do it all in the name of the Lord Jesus, giving thanks to God the Father through him" (Colossians 3:14-17).

To Give You Hope, and a Future

A centennial sermon, Reedwood Friends Church, June 6, 1993

Celebrating a church centennial is like six—actually, like *seven* exciting things:

1. finishing the first book of an exciting series

2. feeling through your feet a throbbing power as the odometer on your car turns 100,000 miles

3. marching down the aisle at graduation in solemn processional—a goal attained—and wondering what will happen next

4. gliding past Mount Hood on descent to Portland after a long and wearisome plane ride, reflecting upon what a beautiful and useful world God has provided

5. reaching a peak after an exhilarating climb, and anticipating the next one just ahead higher still, and those more distant whose glistening horizons beckon to greater effort, to greater glory

6. preparing reports carefully for a major company review, certain that your work testifies to skill and honest effort, but anxious lest impartial scrutiny reveals flawed stewardship

7. finding treasure hid in a field, right where you live, so rich a find you invest everything to secure it, renewed in spirit by discovering that God's realm is among us now, finding incredible joy in knowing that Jesus, the Christ, is present

"The kingdom of heaven," said Jesus, "is like treasure hidden in a field. When a man found it, he hid it again, and then in his joy went and sold all he had and bought that field" (Matthew 13:44, NIV here and in subsequent texts).

Today, as we celebrate the 100th anniversary of our congregation, I share thoughts about treasure found in the field and the joy of its possession. The centennial text is an appropriate word from the Lord to us as it was to Israel in an important time in their history. Jesus is good news about value to be found in the field of our own experience, in America, in our neighborhood, in our home, in our hearts. God's kingdom shines in an otherwise dark world. Jesus, the Messiah, has opened our eyes to a realm of reality where God's will is done on earth, as it will be in heaven. Excitedly, we claim this treasure. As the church, we celebrate its discovery. Hear again Reedwood's chosen centennial test. Be edified by it, in the year of our Lord, 1993.

Scripture reading
Jeremiah 29:11

"For I know the plans I have for you," declares the Lord, "plans to prosper you and not to harm you, plans to give you hope and a future."

Acknowledgment of exile

Shortly in the world's history one millennium will end and another begin. Today, for Reedwood, one century ends and another begins. It's a time to be retrospective, to ask where we go from here, to reflect on our covenant with God. Our Christian faith is being challenged by secular disbelief, ridicule, and hostility. It is being questioned religiously, as well, not just by other forms of historic religion—with whom dialogue is often fruitful—but more subtly by so-called "new age" religions that offer hungry (but often unwary) seekers spiritual solace at bargain rates. These religions lure people who want spirituality but on their own terms, without God's grace to spring sin's trap.

To all who follow Jesus, however, God's word in Scripture offers hope and a future. Even in hard circumstances. Our text assured an ancient, beleaguered people who 2,579 years ago were captured by Nebuchadrezzar. These assurances are reinforced by Jesus' words about treasure: We discover God's realm where we live, even when we are hauled against our will from Jerusalem to Babylon, whether journeys be geographic or cultural. What if we just acknowledge our "Babylonian exile" in America? What if Christians accept minority standing in a mostly pagan culture? Can we accept being strangers in a land where we once claimed spiritual title? As this bloody century concludes, America doesn't look much like God's site for the New Jerusalem. It looks increasingly like Bablyon.

To acknowledge this is hard. Religious crusades offer an alternative, as they did a millennium ago when Christian civilization likewise seemed threatened. "When 'Christian' Crusaders captured Jerusalem in 1099, they slaughtered seventy thousand Muslim inhabitants, snatched suckling babies from their mothers' breasts and threw them over the walls, herded surviving Jews into a synagogue and burned them alive" (Dale Aukerman, *Reckoning with Apocalypse.* New York: Crossroads, 1993, p. 73).

Today some believers use similarly extreme measures to protect their sacred turf—their Jerusalem—against captivity. Bosnian Christians slaughter Muslim families; Jews slaughter Arab children. Muslims slaughter Jews and Christians. Irish Christians kill each other. Governments slaughter religious deviants. Fundamentalists of the world fear captivity by godless culture, but they betray their own principles by the violence of their resistance, and by infighting against other people who believe in God.

The voices of people defending American "holy land" against secular captivity are becoming increasingly shrill, their tactics increasingly un-Christlike. This is the pattern: Troubled believers become zealots, zealots become fanatics, and fanatics become Satanic tools to destroy what believers originally wanted to save. It doesn't work; good ends get betrayed by evil means. We cannot burn down the house to save the children or destroy the infidel to save the faith. In ripping out the tares the wheat is destroyed. We have to acknowledge as reality a certain level of captivity before we can live faithfully, and constructively within the present world. "Those who refuse to recognize the enemy within," writes Aukerman, "are given enemies without" (*Reckoning*, p. 75).

Despite these circumstances, there is hope and a future for Reedwood folks, even in a violent world and in our own cultural captivity. The springing forth of Christian faith in the former Soviet republics encourages us. Our Christian brothers and sisters there have completed seventy years of exile in their own land. Spiritual hunger draws them to God. Easter services now occur at the

Kremlin. Billy Graham drew fifty thousand people to his 1992 Moscow meeting. President Yeltsin's mother received a public Christian burial. Madness had infected this modern Babylon, and its rulers, like Nebuchadrezzar, at last looked to godly people to interpret their visions. Russian deliverance from captivity is a sign that American Christians can successfully weather our own forms of tyranny—in our case cultural rather than political.

So we will treat Jeremiah as an optimist, not a traitor or even a pessimist. He helps us face adverse experience confident that divine light overcomes human darkness. Jeremiah sent a letter of hope to exilic elders after religious leaders, craftsmen, and artisans had been deported to Bablyon. He entrusted the letter to Elasah. I would be your Elasah, offering hope and God's treasure right where you live. You are captive in a world dominated by powerful Nebuchadrezzars, but you can live faithfully, vigilantly, prophetically, and hopefully in that world.

Live faithfully in Babylon

Acknowledging exilic status is the first word, then, but it is not the last. Wrote novelist David Brin: "To fall can be a gift...." What is diaspora, after all, except an opportunity, a second chance for a people to learn, to grow out of shallow self-involvement and become righteous, deep, and strong?" (*Earth,* Bantam, 1991, p. 491). A popular western song once expressed our sentiments, "Don't Fence Me In." Sadly, we can't escape external fences, but in God's mercy we can escape bondage to sin.

Hear the text of Jeremiah's letter. It is about living faithfully in Babylon and becoming righteous, deep, and strong.

> "Build houses and settle down; plant gardens and eat what they produce. Marry and have sons and daughters; find wives for your sons and give your daughters in marriage, so that they too may have sons and daughters. Increase in number there; do not decrease. Also, seek the peace and prosperity of the city to which I have carried you into exile. Pray to the Lord for it, because if it prospers, you too will prosper." (Jeremiah 29:5-7)

We are called to seek the prosperity and peace of the city. So we tolerate a plurality of viewpoints. We seek neither favored status nor special privilege. We consider government and culture as powers corrupted by sin but open, nonetheless, to God's redemptive purposes. Until that hour when the kingdoms of this world become the kingdoms of Christ, the leaven of the Spirit works within the human city. Despite its sin and rebellion, God loves this world. As God's children we too seek its good. Such counsel is better than brooding over conspiracy theories, calculating dates for the second coming, or damning the government. Jesus told us to occupy (not speculate or gripe) until he returns. Let the Almighty judge the nations and unfold the future. An ancient teacher, Jesus ben Sirach wrote: "Sovereignty passes from nation to nation on account of injustice and insolence and wealth" (Sirach 10:8 NRSV, Anglicized edition).

Sin within the soul gets imbedded in all social systems. So don't target Hillary Clinton or the United Nations as some new enemy to kick around (replacing communism or the pope, or the Jews, or the Masons, or the Trilateral Commission). Whatever the blend of ambition and altruism, public leadership isn't easy. So pray for persons in authority, work for justice, witness to Christ, and trust God for the future.

For captured Jews, working for the peace and prosperity of the city meant Babylon, an ancient city on the Euphrates river fifty miles from present day Bagdad, Iraq. The ancient empire, already fifteen hundred years old in Jeremiah's time, had developed mathematics, astronomy, medicine, and linguistics. Here were enacted the first great law codes to protect property and reduce oppression. Irrigation projects brought agricultural prosperity. Nebuchadrezzar restored this old empire to new glory during his half-century reign. He crowned the city's beauty with an enameled ziggurat 650 feet high, embossed with a golden shrine. This commercial center for half the world mixed the worst (labor exploitation, corrupt bureaucracy, immoral religion) with the best (material prosperity, high art, effective governance). Nebuchadrezzar had his name stamped on every baked brick, but he also prayed to Marduk: "Tis thou who art my creator, entrusting me with the rule of hosts…" (Durant, *Story of Civilization*, Simon and Schuster, 1939, vol. 1, p. 241). The conflict between ambition and ideals blew his mind.

We are called to seek the prosperity of our world, despite the dominating egoism of musicians, athletes, pundits, CEOs, scholars, and presidents. Our Babylon is a global empire interlinked by computerized commerce and enmeshed in a bewildering maze of beliefs. We cannot found a new Pennsylvania, we cannot erect Christian ghettos in the city. No fortresses can keep the world out. But God can keep us faithful in the city.

The global city can become a Babel once again—an ungovernable collage of miserable humanity, threatened by war and starvation—or it can live up to its name, Babylon, the gate of God. The city of humanity tacks between anarchy and tyranny. We seek its peace. But if power-mongers of our time, blinded by conceit, demand that we worship their images of gold we will refuse. We may lose status, position, power, or even life. But perhaps remorseful and frustrated rulers will summon us, like Shadrach, Meshach, and Abednego, from the infernos of their idolatry, and will reward our faithfulness to God by increased responsibilities. We may not rebuild temples in the homeland, but, like Mordecai and Esther, maybe we will ease the burdens of captivity, or like Daniel, open the gates of the city for the King of Glory to come in. We may become oracles of Christ, that stone cut from the mountain of history against which human kingdoms of iron, bronze, clay, silver, and gold grind themselves to dust. Christ's kingdom prevails; we have found the precious stone.

Live vigilantly in Babylon

We must live vigilantly, as well as faithfully, otherwise the faith we learn through adversity erodes into despair or nostalgia. Then our children will lose their heritage. Jesus will become a swear not a prayer word. As Paul wrote (Ephesians 6:12), "Our struggle is not against flesh and blood, but against the rulers, against the authorities, against the powers of this dark world and against the spiritual forces of evil...." We can acknowledge being sojourners without becoming enslaved. "Only when disciples recognize where and what Babylon is can they depart from it," writes Aukerman, "In any century disciples are to struggle for discernment of what constitutes Babylon, the beast, and the imperial image, lest they be drawn into that insurgency against God....Babylon should always be seen as occupying power" (*Reckoning*, p. 107).

We live vigilantly by being a gospel fellowship. As we settle in the secular city we strengthen our network of spiritual support. As Jack Willcuts said, we are the *family* of Friends. How will Reedwood be a Quaker family during its second century? Here are a few suggestions.

Keep the Quaker story alive, as a vital chapter in Christian history.

Sustain participatory worship so the Lord can minister through many persons.

Support and use the Quaker network: publications, summer camps, George Fox College, yearly meeting functions, and inter yearly meeting activities.

Accept responsibly your stewardship as a vital Quaker urban center.

Raise up and sustain Christ-touched missionaries to Babylon—persons who can provide political, economic, and cultural leadership locally, globally.

Honor the Christian mandates: proclaim the gospel, gather believers into fellowship, serve the needy and the brokenhearted.

Live prophetically in Babylon

Call the powers to account. Are they just, are they humble before God, are they kind to the earth (cf. Paul, Colossians 1:16)? For by him all things were created—things in heaven and on earth, visible and invisible, whether thrones or powers or rulers or authorities; all things were created by him and for him. Announce a worldview that affirms the creation to a society that fractures it, and testifies to redemption to a world that hungers for wholeness.

Part of our prophetic witness is to the church, which easily becomes too cozy in Babylon, often proffering prophetic silence to gain social acceptance. The church is then vulnerable to the voice of false religious prophets who confuse national interests with divine purpose. Pawns to militant power, they offer Jesus a Judas kiss.

Most of our prophetic witness, though, is to the world. The book of Revelation offered early Christians cryptic support in their witness. We too must challenge in Jesus' name the demons in society. Each tyrant, petty or powerful, is a little antichrist; lawlessness has apocalyptic implications; and every military frenzy (tribal or international) is an Armageddon.

The exilic people witnessed prophetically to Babylon. When the burdens of empire drove Nebuchadrezzar mad, God reached him by word and circumstance. These are the circumstances. Wealth became dissipated in luxuries and vice. As Durant observed: "A nation is born stoic, and dies epicurean" (*Story*, p. 259). Arrogance overcut the forests and depleted the soil. Rivers got polluted. The oppressed underclass revolted. All the high purposes of empire were shattered under the weight of accumulated sin. The empire tottered, and thirty years after Nebuchadrezzar's death, collapsed. Sovereignty shifted, and in such shifting the prophetic word gained entrance. Such is the lesson from ancient Israel in exile. Such is the lesson for us.

Vigilance requires prophetic voices today. Our own Dan Smith states that "Until such perspectives from the 'exiles' become a part of our Christian theology then we haven't understood the meaning of the Biblical Exile" (*Quaker Religious Thought* #79, 1992). In the article, "A Theology for Modern Babylonians," Northwest Yearly Meeting missionary Harold Thomas illustrates exilic insight into biblical faith by describing the vigilant faith of Aymara Quaker leader Pascual Quispe. As a boy Pascual saw his father publicly whipped by the owner of the hacienda to which his family belonged prior to the land reform of 1952-1954. Pascual himself, under the brutal military dictatorships of the late 1970s and early 1980s, dared openly to represent independent coffee-growers and publicly confronted a military commander whom he called to repent from enforcing an exploitive coffee-export monopoly. As a result, Pascual was forced into hiding to save his life until the dictatorship ended. This sounds like George Fox confronting Oliver Cromwell, doesn't it? Our Bolivian brothers and sisters can prepare us *norteamericanos* for living prophetically in Babylon during the next century. Their deliverance may precede ours.

Vigilance requires a Christ-like manner, putting truth in the context of love. Convincement begins with love's logic. A noted Quaker economist, Kenneth Boulding, died this spring. In memorial I cite from his 1942 lecture, "The Practice of the Love of God."

> There is no resting place for expanding love short of God and his whole kingdom. If our love ceases to expand, it will perish, as a tree planted in a narrow pot must perish if it does not break the vessel that confines it. But this is the mystery of love: that as it grows to wider and wider objects, the narrower loves are not made less, but are made more perfect. (p. 5)

> Let us not despair of the world. It is God's world....Is our peace, our comfort threatened? These things have come between us and His glory, and we shall find the true peace, the true comfort, the true security that lie in His riches, not in ours....Out of the utter defeat of Israel came the sweetest psalms and the noblest prophets; out of the collapse of Rome came Augustine and the City of God; after the fire and fury of the Thirty Years War came the divine cadences of Bach....God is always redeeming His world, in ways that we often do not recognize, and out of the very depth of the misery of our time there will come a reawakening of His love in the hearts of millions of His prodigal children, a new springtime to the weary earth. Let us press forward to that time; let us do more, let us anticipate it in our own lives...." (William Penn lecture, 1942 Philadelphia Yearly Meeting, subsequently published by Pendle Hill Press, 2000, p. 31)

Live hopefully in Babylon
We await the day of the Lord who sets the captives free, who regathers peoples to righteousness. We cannot plot the curve of the future but we can pledge our obedience to Christ, the Risen Lord, who will meet us in the next millennium. This hope is no narrow Zionism. It is no cheap rapture for the saints. "Such a 'rapture' is the religious counterpart of 'Star Wars,'" thinks Aukerman, "whereby church folk can evade the way of the cross by siding with militarist nationalism and can then evade the consequences when those come" (*Reckoning*, p. 63).

Hear again Jeremiah's word:

> This is what the Lord says: "When seventy years are completed for Babylon, I will come to you and fulfill my gracious promise to bring you back to this place. *For I know the plans I have for you," declares the Lord, "plans to prosper you and not to harm you, plans to give you hope and a future.* Then you will call upon me and come and pray to me, and I will listen to you. You will seek me and find me when you seek me with all your heart. I will be found by you," declares the Lord, "and will bring you back from captivity. I will gather you from all the nations and places where I have banished you," declares the Lord, "and will bring you back to the place from which I carried you into exile." (Jeremiah 29:10-14, emphasis mine)

Our hope in the near term is for the leaven of the gospel to permeate our society and bring a return to a more civil society, where justice, integrity, and reverence for God predominate. To a place where children are safe. Where the poor are raised up. Where old people do not need to double-bar their windows. Where the land is cherished. Where education leads to social good, not private gain. Where literature elevates the human spirit. Where music lifts body, soul, and spirit. Where invention makes the world more—not less—livable. Nebuchadrezzar stole the gold and silver vessels of the temple and put them in his temple to Marduk. In our Christian history cathedrals once commanded the highest place in cities, they were adorned with gold and silver. Rulers vied for churchly favor. Now insurance companies and sports arenas have stolen cathedral prominence and splendor. But Christianity is purified by these losses, as Israel was purified by its exile experience. One day the cultural treasures may once more bear the stamp of spirituality, and creativity will honor God, not the ego. But whether that day in history is soon or late, we claim Christ's kingdom as sufficient treasure now.

In the far term we hope for an ingathering of tribes and tongues and nations to a new heavens and a new earth, the New Jerusalem. At the name of Christ every knee shall bow. Beyond our own captivity and all others past and present, we await the final release that only God can bring. Jesus' resurrection assures victory, the Holy Spirit is our title to the land. We need not train guns against the city, as the Fifth Monarchy men tried in 1661, making life miserable for our Quaker forebears. Christians don't need garrisons stacked with machine guns. Although at every level society has been conned by the beast (Ellul thinks this is political propaganda) who usurps authority over every tribe, people, language, and nation (Revelation 13:7), Christ, the Lamb, conquers them. The eternal gospel sweeps the earth, gathering to Christ all who yearn for righteousness, from every nation, tribe, language, and people.

It takes courage to face exile. Jeremiah, the messenger of God, took abuse for it, anguished over it, and was stoned to death for it, prior to Israel's return. Jeremiah's hope was not easy. He lamented that "Nebuchadnezzar...has thrown us into confusion, he has made us an empty jar" (Jeremiah 51:34). But he also predicted that Babylon will be a heap of ruins, a haunt of jackals, an object of horror and scorn, a place where no one lives (Jeremiah 51:37). This came true. John the Revelator uses Babylon as symbol of human society seeking salvation apart from God, from Nimrod until the sixth century B.C., from Rome until the New Jerusalem (cf. Revelation 18:2).

In *Grapes of Wrath* (Viking, 1939, see chap. 14), an American classic about the

Great Depression, Steinbeck observes that when one man says "I lost my land" oppressors have nothing to fear. But when one dust-bowl refugee hunkers down with his neighbor on highway 66 somewhere west of Oklahoma, and shares food and misery by a campfire, then the lament is joined—"*we* lost our land," and oppressors should tremble.

I raise the ante: When Babylon's captives hunker down at the foot of the cross they hear God say, "I lost my land, too." The spirit of God among us is greater than the spirit of evil. The powers tremble: Christ has triumphed over them (Colossians 2:15). The harvesting angel begins to gather the grapes and throw them into the great winepress of God's wrath (Revelation 14:19). Babylon has fallen. This is our hope. This is our vision. The Holy Spirit whispers to us that it is so: Eden will be regained. God joins our efforts to divine providence.

Conclusion

Be faithful to Christ, senior citizens who hope to see the next century dawn with promise of deliverance from evils that wasted your spiritual heritage. Be prophetic, busy professional people who will bear well into the next century the burden of keeping goods and services flowing humanely in a time of turmoil. Be vigilant, young people just nesting your families in the city, searching for stability in a time when values are harder to manage than computers. Be hopeful for the kingdom, children and youth just learning history and how things work. Do not bow down, any of you, to the golden images of idolatry. Fasten your eyes on the God of Abraham and Sarah, the God of our Lord Jesus Christ, pioneer of the world's future. Human efforts cannot reform Babylon, you cannot return to a more comfortable past. But you can be God's instruments to convert the world to Christ. Frederick Buechner writes "No matter how swiftly the torrent tumbles, there come moments when, rounding a bend or where the streambed deepens, it flattens out suddenly to a surface so slow and smooth that you can almost see down to the bottom of it" (*The Sacred Journey*, p. 82). People of Reedwood, look at the stream, and renew your faith in Christ, see who you are, and where you are living.

"For I know the plans I have for you," declares the Lord, "plans to prosper you and not to harm you, plans to give you hope and a future."

A Voice Immeasurably Majestic

Yachats Community Presbyterian Church, August 22, 1993

Introduction

Taking visitors to Cape Perpetua, climbing a tree, hiking up a mountain—these are ways to enjoy perspective. Special occasions give us perspective too, like hearing again on PBS Peter, Paul, and Mary singing "Blowing in the Wind," or celebrating an anniversary. Whether the event is an actual mountain or special time, the ecstasy is inward, a picture projected by the software of the mind upon the monitor of the soul.

Implications of the mountaintop episodes narrated in the Scriptures

1. From a mountain (Sinai) God gave Moses perspectives on conduct necessary for the human terrain.

On this mountain Moses learned from God how certain moral boundaries establish the human community in peace and justice. Moses returned to the valley with God's universal moral law blazed on tablets of stone, and to a people who preferred selective, tribal righteousness. Ever since this mountaintop experience, the moral law—encapsulated in the Ten Commandments—has been humanity's glory but also its burden.

Old Testament reading
Exodus 24:12-18 (NIV)

The Lord said to Moses, "Come up to me on the mountain and stay here, and I will give you the tablets of stone, with the law and commands I have written for their instruction." Then Moses set out with Joshua his aide, and Moses went up on the mountain of God. He said to the elders, "Wait here for us until we come back to you. Aaron and Hur are with you, and anyone involved in a dispute can go to them." When Moses went up on the mountain, the cloud covered it, and the glory of the Lord settled on Mount Sinai. For six days the cloud covered the mountain, and on the seventh day the Lord called to Moses from within the cloud. To the Israelites the glory of the Lord looked like a consuming fire on top of the mountain. Then Moses entered the cloud as he went on up the mountain. And he stayed on the mountain forty days and forty nights.

New Testament reading
Mark 9:2-10 (NIV)

After six days Jesus took Peter, James and John with him and led them up a high mountain, where they were all alone. There he was transfigured before them. His clothes became dazzling white, whiter than anyone in the world could bleach them. And there appeared before them Elijah and Moses, who were talking with Jesus. Peter said to Jesus, "Rabbi, it is good for us to be here. Let us put up three shelters—one for you, one for Moses and one for Elijah." (He did not know what to say, they were so frightened.) Then a cloud appeared and enveloped them, and a voice came from the cloud: "This is my Son, whom I love. Listen to him!" Suddenly, when they looked around, they no longer saw anyone with them except Jesus. As they were coming down the mountain, Jesus gave them orders not to tell anyone what they had seen until the Son of Man had risen from the dead. They kept the matter to themselves, discussing what "rising from the dead" meant.

2. From a mountain (Carmel) God gave Elijah perspectives on authority.

From this mountain Elijah saw how idolatry corrupts governance, by substituting human will and ritual for divine sovereignty, true worship, and servant leadership. Elijah ran down the mountain to the valley a vindicated, if hunted, truth-teller, a prophet who demonstrated that God is not mocked by rulers who subvert religion into propaganda for evil public policy.

3. From a mountain (Hermon) God gave Jesus' disciples perspectives about how humanity is redeemed from transgressing the moral law and turning to idolatry.

On the mountain these disciples saw Christ glorified before their eyes, fulfilling and transforming the Law, embodying Truth and enunciating its principles. Peter, James, and John came down the mountain puzzled but partially prepared for Jesus' atoning death and redeeming resurrection. After Pentecost, baptized with the Holy Spirit, they would understand better the triumph of God's love in Jesus Christ, the pioneer of the world's future. We call this biblical event the transfiguration, because Jesus was exalted and glorified before his followers.

Applications of this episode of transfiguration

1. Special spiritual experiences enable us to gain truer perspective about Jesus.

We see flashes of insight about who Jesus is, in relationship to the past and the future in a mode of a mountaintop experience, like those that figured importantly for Moses and Elijah.

Moses was the lawgiver who showed boundaries for the moral life; Elijah, the prophet who challenged idolatry and tyranny; and Jesus, the new leader, prophet, priest, king. We see Jesus as at the center of history, as God's central word to humanity. We gain these insights in a highly personal way. Each meeting for worship is a miniature mountaintop experience with Christ. And some of our spiritual experiences bring us to an ecstasy wherein we enter into Christ's glory. Have you experienced this?

2. Spiritual visions inspire faithfulness, not memorials.

They come serendipitously; they cannot be preserved in stone or marble, scarcely even in memory. Although they arise out of daily faithfulness in prayer and obedience, and in terrain near where we live, they are transitory, like an extraordinary coastal sunset that catches you within the soul as well as within the mind. At the conclusion of a vision it is Jesus only whom we see, not the high moral law, not sublime truth, not human falsehood, not idolatry, but Jesus. Jesus only, confirmed inwardly by voice of God. Have you heard that voice?

3. Such visions prepare us for the future.

We get prepared for cross-bearing, losses, betrayals, cruelty, a hostile world, but also for success. We reenter the valley of ordinary affairs ready to be abased or to abound, able to handle sorrow and joy, to weather discouragements and setbacks to the kingdom, confident that the Lord whom we have seen exalted on the mountain will gather the peoples into God's kingdom. We return to the valley of ordinary living emboldened by the Holy Spirit, Christ's gift to God's family. Have you received Christ's gift?

Simon Peter's recollections were preserved by Mark in the Scripture reading. I have amplified them in a poem, "The Transfiguration" (from *Move Over, Elijah*, Barclay Press, 1967*).* By entering imaginatively into Peter's experiences, Christ may be transfigured for you, giving you new perspectives about Jesus, about your own faithfulness, and preparing you better for the future. May this be so!

The Transfiguration

We climbed way up Mount Hermon,
Higher even than where vineyards
Cling upon the southern slopes.
The olive trees below us
Lay like coiled ropes
Upon the fields.

He was a man possessed. Striding hard
Against the mountain, every muscle
Matching effort to his will,
He led us onward, upward, till
We'd gained a rock-walled plateau
Sheltered from the wind.
Here we stopped.

We could see far down
Into Jordan valley. Nearby
Snow-fed springs gave birth
To streams which joined the wind
In singing praises
To the earth.

Beautiful, indeed, and worth
The climb, I thought, basking
In the sun-warmed air.
While thus we mused and rested
Jesus spent the time in prayer,
As frequently he did. Suddenly
It happened.

I tell you, he was changed!
None could launder clothes as white
as Jesus' robe. So radiant his face
I could but stare, awe-stricken
At the sight.

We might have taken this in stride—
(With Jesus strange things happen)
But while we looked, bewildered,
Moses and Elijah stood beside
The Lord. Yes, I said Moses and Elijah;
Hear me out!

How did I recognize
Those ancient worthies? Well,
Jesus called to them by name,
And they recounted those deeds of fame
The scriptures tell about
Like it happened yesterday.

Anyway, they were present but
Not quite there, if you get
What I mean. Almost, you see,
They were here—and we
Gazed upon them from
An alien shore.

Moses grabbed up his staff
And gestured toward Mount Sinai.
Straight and tall he stood,
Hair blowing in the breeze. I
Can understand why Pharaoh
Failed to match his power.

The liberator spoke of how
God set a people free and
Made of slaves a nation.
A nation called of God and
Brought through forty years
Of wilderness to their salvation.

He told how Jehovah from the sky
Flung lightning bolts
From peak to peak
And creased the mountain
With the fury of His storm;
And how he'd come to seek
God's will in written form
To guide the people by,

Until God confirmed the covenant
And with His finger
Traced the ten commandments
Upon some slabs of stone.

Well, said Moses presently,
"The forms of law men write
With words, its burden
Haunts their hearts.
Law brings death to men.
I led Israel out of Egypt;
You bring Egypt out of them!"

Elijah spoke up then.
A lean and leathery man
Small wonder he outran
The horses down the
Crest of Carmel.
He told about that fiery test of faith
Through which he routed priests of Baal,
How God by fire from heaven consumed
The sodden sacrifice.

"Authenticating signs from God,"
He said, " alas were soon forgotten
And idolatry resumed;
Penitence affected
After oft-repeated sins induced
Religious stupor or bizarre piousity—
Not fear of God. Unblemished lambs
And ritual sacrifice do not atone
Carnality.

"To lay the axe upon the branches
Of man's sin will not suffice:
The roots must go.
The fire from heaven must start
Upon the altar of the heart."

The two quit talking then, and Jesus
Spoke to them in earnest tones.
His eyes swept over peaks and valleys
Stretching far below. He stayed his hand
Above Jerusalem. He wept—strong,
Anguished cries of yearning love
For Zion's beleaguered band.

I glanced at him to help him
In his need. Help him? Ah, no,
He stood shining like a tested sail
Upon a stormy sea.
Hanging on the very edge
Of ecstasy were we,
Lured by an awesome world
We could scarcely see.

And then he talked of death!
The Messiah die? It could not be.
We watched the scene unroll:
Jesus quoted servant prophecies
From Isaiah's scroll
And talked of sin-offerings, and death.
To this talk Moses and Elijah
Gave vigorous assent.

Incredible!
They looked full in the Master's face,
And without hesitation they said yes.
Yes to crucifixion for
The Lord's anointed one?
No, I thought, this cannot be.
Then I remembered prophecy.
In a quick burst of insight
It came to me:

Messiah's triumph was foretold
In connection with the feast of booths.
Of course! I saw it clearly.
Had they forgotten?
Our nation's greatness is not bound
By land and permanence of earthly rule.
Israel had marched in tents before.
Israel would march again! No mimicking
Of Maccabean revolt
No sad, contemplative retreat
To some communal desert home;
No tragedy ground out betwixt
Jerusalem and Rome.

Jesus shall reign!
The feast of booths comes this fall.
The Master must with patience deign
To bid his time. Then Moses' law
Will go forth in power,
His kingdom reach from sea to sea.
Jesus is God's strong deliverer.
Idols of the nations
He will grind to dust.

And so, forthwith, I turned
To Jesus with these words:
"Master, let us build three booths;
One for Moses, for Elijah one, and
One for you." (I hoped to jog
His memory, you see.)

Well...at that very moment
A cloud covered us—the Shekinah of God
I thought. God again will
Blaze the Law upon the rocks
And vindicate His covenant.

But from the cloud a voice came,
Softer than an evening breeze
Among the cedar trees,
Yet more embracing than the roaring tides,
A voice immeasurably majestic,
Caught up and echoed all around
That holy mount of God.

The rocks rang joyously,
Trees clapped their hands, the earth
Reverberated praise to God.
What could a stupid fisherman...
Babbling foolishly...
Prostrate I fell, covering my head,
As did the others.

And God spoke:
This is my beloved Son, hear him.

We felt again the sun upon our backs.
All earth had hushed...
Fears faded with the fading cloud.
And though still bowed,
The Master bid us rise,
And opening our eyes
We saw the ancient guests had gone.
Jesus only stood there
In our midst,

Etched upon our hearts forever
By the awe-full voice of God.
I knew then that Christ would die;
But only after Pentecost
Could I really tell you why.

The Thing with Feathers

Yachats Community Presbyterian Church, July 24, 1994

The Old Testament reading rejoices in deliverance from a "besieged city" and exults that one's hope is in the Lord. Faith in Christ is ground for a good hope. Poet Emily Dickinson wrote (*Collected Poems*, Courage Classics, 1991, p. 100):

> Hope is the thing with feathers
> That perches in the soul,
> And sings the tune without the words,
> and never stops at all,
>
> And sweetest in the gale is heard;
> And sore must be the storm
> That could abash the little bird
> That kept so many warm.
>
> I've heard it in the chillest land,
> And on the strangest sea;
> Yet, never, in extremity,
> It asked a crumb of me.

What is hope?

What is this thing with feathers, that perches in the soul?

1. Hope is a kind of prayer without words.

It is a yearning that spans the gap:

Scripture reading
Psalm 31:21-24 (NIV)
Praise be to the Lord, for he showed his wonderful love to me when I was in a besieged city. In my alarm I said, "I am cut off from your sight!" Yet you heard my cry for mercy when I called to you for help. Love the Lord, all his saints! The Lord preserves the faithful, but the proud he pays back in full. Be strong and take heart, all you who hope in the Lord.

2 Thessalonians 2:13-17 (NIV)
But we ought always to thank God for you...because from the beginning God chose you to be saved through the sanctifying work of the Spirit and through belief in the truth. He called you to this through our gospel, that you might share in the glory of our Lord Jesus Christ. So then.. . stand firm and hold to the teachings we passed on to you, whether by word of mouth or by letter. May our Lord Jesus Christ himself and God our Father, who loved us and by his grace gave us eternal encouragement and good hope, encourage your hearts and strengthen you in every good deed and word.

- between what we have now and what we may acquire,
- between what we know now and what we will learn,
- between what our circumstances are now and what they may become,
- between where we are now and where we will be,
- between who we are now and who we may become.

Paul writes: "Who hopes for what he already has? But if we hope for what we do not yet have, we wait for it patiently. In the same way, the Spirit helps us in our weakness. We do not know what we ought to pray for, but the Spirit himself intercedes for us with groans that words cannot express. And he who searches our hearts knows the mind of the Spirit, because the Spirit intercedes for the saints in accordance with God's will" (Romans 8:24b-27 NIV).

2. Hope is fear flipped over to catch God's Light.

Hope has a dark side, which is fear, just as love has its dark side, which is hate, and faith its dark side, which is doubt. When fear and hate and doubt prevail, the result is despair. When hope, love, and faith triumph the result is joy. Hope is breakfast time for the soul—the horizon of life spreads out ahead of us, luminous, full of excitement, danger, even, and risk, but mostly of promise. Hope believes the Light of Christ overcomes darkness.

3. Hope is trusting the power of God's Spirit to bring about the good.

Acknowledging ignorance, hope trusts the Spirit to teach truth. Admitting weakness, hope turns to God, and God's people, for help. Confessing sin, hope accepts God's forgiveness and God's sanctifying power. Hope believes God has a better way for people to live than in economic or psychological misery, and gives us the courage to find a better way. (The people who give relief to Rwandan sufferers demonstrate hope.) Hope gives us the courage to rise out of our own despondence, shake the blahs. Hope makes us eager to remedy the misery that ignorance, weakness, and sin inflict on others. Hope lets us see God's kingdom present now, as the divine milieu, in which we have our being.

What are your hopes?

General hopes:

Health, vitality, safety, food and shelter, pleasurable activities of work and recreation, adventure, knowledge and skills, mental lucidity. Reassurance that Christ is my Savior and Lord. Being kept from foolish decisions and from sinful thoughts and actions. Acceptance by others, recognition for who I am as well as for what I do; the courage to give and receive love, an acceptable level of interaction with family and neighbors. The ability to be alone and at peace with myself. Alan Arkin wrote a little book, *The Clearing* (HarperSanFrancisco, 1986, p. 179), about animals who display very human attributes. He creates this conversation between a wise bear and a discouraged lemming. The lemming, Bubber, says, "'Why do I ache so? There's a hole in me where the light leaks out. What's missing? What is it that I'm doing wrong?'

"'Something has not yet been completed,' [said bear].

"'Can you tell me what it is?' asked Bubber.

"'Look inside,' said the bear."

This is a good time to look inside, to examine where the light of hope has leaked out from your soul, to ask "what is missing?" To turn your fears over and expose them to God's light, to renew hope. Prayerfully consider several more kinds of hope: family hopes, social hopes, hopes for others, hopes for yourself.

Family hopes:

The home as a community of faith (Luther: home, not monastic cloister, the sacred place). Hope for young people, that the homes they set up will be holy places, not arenas of conflict. For us older ones that our children and grandchildren and great grandchildren will know Christ as Savior and Lord, that they will love each other, will handle adversity with fortitude and faith. That tragedy will not befall them, that they will cherish learning and shun prejudice, that they will become effective members of society and loyal members of the church. That they will accept themselves and others as children of God, that they will not succumb to greed, or to despair. That those who have turned away from active religious faith may return to the Lord. What are your family hopes? Pray that families will be secure, respectful of each other.

Social hopes:

For a just society in the United States, and everywhere in the world. That crime and cruelty will diminish. That leaders will demonstrate a high standard of morality. That morality will be public as well as private. That tribal and ethnic violence will cease. That nations may have a stable social structure (Russia, Haiti). That interdependence will be acknowledged as mutually beneficial (e.g., food, transport, shelter, literature). Ponder your social hopes, pray for Christ's peaceable kingdom.

Spiritual hopes for others:

That a spiritual awakening will occur as people in our country and the world repent from sin and turn to God.

That the churches may preach the gospel with integrity, that missionaries may preach Christ to the nations effectively, with respect for local culture. The world suffers from the effects of sin. It's time for a turning away from greed and human pride; it's time to fear the Lord, a time for contrition for sin, for acceptance of divine pardon and empowerment. What are your spiritual hopes for others? Pray for spiritual revival in our nation and around the world.

Personal spiritual hopes:

That the gospel is true, not a cruel hoax invented by well-meaning but duped people; that I can affirm my Christian faith against open or subtle ridicule, of being characterized as irrelevant. That I won't succumb to subtle sins that blindside me, won't blow it morally. That God is just, and I don't have to be final judge of anyone. That love works, that faith spans the unknown to reveal the mystery of life. That heaven is something more, not less, than the life we now know. That it isn't just a euphemism for quality of life, or for being remembered by those who come to the memorial. Pray about your personal spiritual hopes as you turn your fears toward the Light.

Conclusion

Hope walks hand-in-hand with God like a child who knows she belongs. Hope insists that Christian discipleship makes sense, that life is a good journey. Hope is the artistry of the human spirit that sustains personal faith and keeps society stable. When others would close the book on life, hope opens it to another chapter. Hope keeps love from becoming rigid and possessive. And, reciprocally, when the last enemy—death—approaches, faith keeps hope on course; and love gives hope the strength to walk through the dark valley into the Light of an eternal morning.

Circles

Berkeley Friends Church, April 13, 1996
(adapted from "Recovering the Church," Wilmington Yearly Meeting, 1995)

Consider Circles

A circle is an efficient enclosure, sturdier than squares. Wheels are wonderful applications. From ball bearings to baseballs, spheres reduce life's friction. The phrase, "I'm going around in circles" is a fact of cosmic life!

Language reflects social circularity. We say "this is my family." We cheer for our team. But belonging isn't easy. Feeling *unsure* we disparage other groups. Feeling *smug*, we denigrate "them." Feeling *fearful*, we demonize them. Feeling *paranoid,* we hate them. But hate is the calamitous resort of the fearful; and from its ruins love patiently rebuilds broken community. If we can't get along with others, even less can we get along without them.

Wrongly directed, circles imprison. Rightly directed, they liberate. We shape our circles and they shape us. Paul called these circles "the powers." They can be demonic, but Christ triumphs over their evil. The "cultural mandate" is Calvinist lingo for a Christian call to be active agents of God's redemption.

Scripture reading

1 Thessalonians 1:1-2 (NRSV, emphasis mine)

Paul, Silvanus, and Timothy, To the church of the Thessalonians in God the Father and the Lord Jesus Christ: Grace to you and peace. We always give thanks to God for all of you and mention you in our prayers, constantly remembering before our God and Father *your work of faith and labor of love and steadfastness of hope* in our Lord Jesus Christ.

In a strange vision, the prophet Ezekiel pictured a scene about the sapphire throne of God. The whole creation is there, symbolized by creatures with human, lion, ox, and eagle faces, bodies aflame with the Spirit, eyes everywhere, their natural grace enhanced by wings. Wheels of intricate design whirl within wheels. Jeweled beauty symbolizes rightly interacting circles of humanity (see Ezekiel 1 and 10).

Exekiel's vision depicts how lives intertwine. To be a creature of God is to coexist in intricate ways. The family is the foundational circle. Primary social circles involve work, governance, language, religion, and culture. Society is rich with subordinate circles: the school, the neighborhood, the sports team, the hobby group, the coffee klatch, the recovery group, the volunteer committee.

Government circles include towns, schools, states, trading alliances, the United Nations. The workplace and professional guilds constitute strong circles. Rightly ordered they offer space for the private and public good. A circle is democratic. When structure becomes too hierarchical or people too independent, then circles become distorted and finally broken. New affinities must then arise from the debris.

Joiners move casually among affinities. Loners don't. At times most of us have felt like misfits, no longer at home in a group. Often misfits huddle to protest alienation, and dissidents find affinity from what is opposed rather than affirmed. Fortunately, mutual human need pressures dissident groups to shift from destructive to constructive modes.

Each circle has a peripheral line that cannot be crossed without destruction. Both anarchy and tyranny tear circles apart—anarchy by resisting order, tyranny by restricting freedom. At the still point of every true circle, however, is a Center. The Center, the Logos, inexorably overcomes evil. In the end it encompasses the world. This is the word from Gethsemane and the empty tomb.

Pressed by enormous problems and exploited by an invasive media, our basic social spheres now lack strong rims. Superficial alliances are touted; they're ephemeral, like soap bubbles wafted on the wind. It is a task of the church to bring the circles of the world under the governance of Christ.

What about the church? The church is that circle of proclamation, fellowship, and service that demonstrates an encompassing social unity found in God's kingdom. The church affirms that humanity is of one blood, and proclaims that every tribe and tongue and nation will one day acknowledge this truth in Christ. The kingdom of God is the ultimate and enclosing circle. To it the church gives witness. But the church is finite. It can get bent out of shape by forces from within and without.

The Friends Church is a primary circle for us. We've suffered from disaffection, corrosion, and seduction. Our numbers have diminished. To use Ezekiel's imagery, the wheels no longer sparkle with iridescent light. Covenant is bent out of shape by factionalism, cultural confusion, fuzzy beliefs, and seductive ideologies. Alas, even Quaker circles can break. When this happens a nostalgic remnant memorializes the good old days when Quakers turned the world upside down.

That's gloomy, isn't it? It's not like Ezekiel's vision; it's not like Pendle Hill where George Fox saw a mighty people to be gathered to the Lord. So let's ask ourselves, and ask God, about our Quaker circles, why they have been damaged and how they can be restored? About functioning more smoothly among the other circles of the church, within the all-encompassing kingdom of God. As we approach Yearly Meeting time let's think about circles.

Paul commends the Thessalonian church as an "example to believers." Their "work of faith and labor of love and steadfastness of hope in our Lord Jesus Christ" was manifest "not in word only, but also in power and in the Holy Spirit and with full conviction" (see 1 Thessalonians 1). For us to receive such biblical commendation some recoveries to Quaker wholeness are needed. Consider these:

1. Recover the gospel as the proclamation of Jesus Christ.
We can be true to our historic calling and to the contemporary world by following Paul's example, to preach the word. It is time for Quakers once again to send a clear gospel word about Jesus Christ. Avoid theological ambiguity. Don't reduce theology to social science. Read the Bible to discern God's will, not to solve redaction puzzles or to prove apocalyptic theories. Don't dissipate Quaker strength through petty power struggles. The circle of Friends won't hold if the Christian center gives way. Accept liberal inclusiveness but avoid its shallowness. Accept fundamentalist tenacity of belief, but avoid

its intolerance. It's time to be forthrightly Christian.

Above all don't turn the gospel and Quaker tradition into a trade. Notional religion can be liberal or fundamentalist. The gospel witness is not just that religious experience occurs. It is about the sort of experience that unites the Christ historically revealed with the Christ discovered within. The "good news" is that our deepest inner experiences are validated by God's incarnation in time and space as Jesus the Messiah. Resist a pervasive subculture that thinks it has outgrown Jesus religiously. Resist the bad faith that enjoys the fruits of Christianity while whacking at its roots. Jesus Christ is both Savior and Lord. Not one or the other. Both. This is our message.

2. Recover the gospel as power to change lives.

Our hedonistic culture prefers to cover sin with a thin coating of Christianity rather than to repent from sinning and to live righteously. This culture prefers to be forgiven than to be cleansed, and to have guilt absolved rather than forgiven. We are called to be leaven and light in the world. To proclaim redemption from sin. To lift up the majesty of God and the divine call to holiness. To bask in historical greatness does not suffice, and neither does bashing (or trumpeting) received Christian tradition. Such responses are escape mechanisms from the more demanding tasks of Christian discipleship, from Jesus' call to live faithfully in our own time and in our own culture. Various forms of evangelistic outreach have characterized Quaker history, from Fox's open-air preaching to visitation ministry, to camp meetings, to revival meetings, to one-on-one counseling. Perhaps the method isn't as important as the willingness to share the good news of salvation with our neighbors. William Penn wrote about first having a sight of sin, then a sense of sin, then an amendment from sin. Both sin and holiness have become blurred in our time. Both seem odious to a lukewarm culture. Clarity about sin and righteousness, however, brings spiritual power. Within our churches may testimonies of salvation glow with the joy of those who have found treasure in a field, who have been lost but are now found, who were dead but are now alive.

3. Recover the gospel as love in action.

Be imitators of Jesus who loved people freely. The Quaker concern for social action is legendary—from antislavery efforts to soup kitchens for the poor. Social action includes education, peace witness, pacifist resistance to militarism, direct relief of poverty and hunger, aid to the dispossessed in wartime, local disaster relief, direct and indirect aid to persons discriminated against. Missionary efforts historically have included lots of social action, from establishing hospitals to teaching agriculture. The Friends Committee on National Legislation constitutes our lobby for influencing righteousness through political action. The American Friends Service Committee, historically a major channel for Quaker funds and energy into labors of love, has gotten so large, so professionalized, and so politicized, in the minds of some, that its relationship to Quaker yearly meetings, and its biblical foundation, needs to be rebuilt. Fortunately, it is listening to its critics. Some Friends opt for collective service opportunities ecumenically, in Christian agencies such as the Mennonite Central Committee, or World Concern, or World Vision. Do we bring a gospel witness to the evil in systems, or to the evil in persons? Can love redeem systems as well as persons?

To heal the person, to heal the structure? Both seem to be required if we believe Christ has triumphed over the powers of evil. Such are the tensions that face all who would heed Jesus' call to love neighbor as oneself.

Preoccupation with right doctrine can lead to a dogmatic legalism. So can preoccupation with political correctness. Even service caregivers can become Pharisaic, can forget that we are saved by grace, and that not of ourselves, it is the gift of God. Therefore we will not boast in our charity, but act for the good of others quietly, in the name and power of Christ. Service professionals must also beware of making the gospel a trade. An antidote to service burnout is to change the locus of benevolence. Look around you—opportunities for quiet social service may be right in your backyard. If we are always waiting for an ideal implementation of our testimonies by the general public we may become dour and pharisaic. Lighten up and experience the kingdom as a place of joy. This is my next point.

4. Recover the joy of the Holy Spirit.

The Holiness Movement swept across the Quaker landscape during the late nineteenth and early twentieth centuries. Many of our parents were reached by camp meeting revivals and zealous holiness preaching. Indeed some of us were caught up in this movement of spiritual discipline. By the time I was a young person, the Holiness Movement in our area had kind of petered out. In its heyday, however, it offered a strong antidote to the preaching of cheap grace, and a strong affirmation of Jesus' call for victory over sin. In some ways the movement reiterated the fervor of the seventeenth century Quaker awakening. This awakening shook Quakerdom to its core and introduced many changes—good, bad, and indifferent. Some of us remember the movement for its legalism, for reducing righteousness to easily manageable social constraints (like not wearing jewelry), and for avoiding the harder ethical issues like peace and justice.

It is not my point here to review this movement, but rather to highlight one of its *good* characteristics: fervent joy in believing. I know, some manifestations got reduced to silliness, like handkerchief waving and so on. But joy was reflected in the uninhibited expression of the experience of Christ. Have we modern Friends become dour? Maybe we are selective in our righteousness, choosing to focus upon social instead of personal issues, such as just wages for workers, rather than faithfulness to marriage vows. My point is to urge a recovery of fervency in belief. Charismatic Christians have been nudging us in this direction. We might accept their example on this point without necessarily adopting their theology or their trendy liturgies. Canby Jones has characterized Thomas Kelly's religious position as "mystical evangelicalism." Not a bad combination of deep and fervent spirituality.

There is a tendency for declining groups to become eccentric in order to gain attention. This is a demonic temptation. It is "creaturely activity," to use an old phrase. Quakers have been derailed by such temptations. There are better ways to affirm who we are. Recover joy in believing. Let repentance, humility, and intercessory prayer return us to the center of our faith. That center of our faith affirms the church in its wholeness, as the body of Christ.

5. Recover the fullness of the church.

This is a threefold task, for the church exists locally, covenantally, and globally. In each form it exists as the body of Christ. In the seventeenth century Robert Barclay warned against Ranterism, that elevation of individual over group claims of Spirit guidance. Barclay attributed the breakdown of Christian unity to persons who have departed from their first love and zeal for Truth but are ashamed to make open apostasy. So they become restless seekers of novelty, and cause divisions in the church. Are his insights apt? I think so. Barclay said that the church is a gathering of persons for whom Christ is rightly the head, who share with conviction certain doctrines and principles of Christian faith.

Church government should be viewed not as a tolerated bureaucracy but as a means for people to be moved by Christ into fruitful discipleship. It is not some bureaucratic tyranny that threatens us now, but rather a spirit of anarchy, in which Friends do what is right in their own eyes and the individual is the sole arbiter of truth. It is a false tolerance to consent to such an erosion of Christian unity. So how can we preserve the circle of the Friends Church so that it is indeed the body of Christ?

A. Be the whole church locally

Quakers are not a parachurch. In an effort to seem distinctive, Quakers sometimes minimize essential Christian teaching. This is a mistake. To be the whole church locally means that the whole Christian mandate occurs in the local community: proclamation, fellowship, and service. To be the whole church locally means that we accommodate to culture without compromising convictions. Obviously, certain cultural differences will mark Friends churches in different areas. The term "Society of Friends" has a strong tradition behind it, stemming from eighteenth century usage. The richness of the term "society" has faded over time and tends to connote a religious specialization. The Society of Jesus (Jesuits) is a specialized branch of Catholic service. This is not a model for Friends. The term "church" is an older and more definitive one in our tradition. This term conveys the truth that "the people not the steeple is the church," as George Fox said. Maybe it is time simply to call ourselves the "Friends Church." Or at least to refer to the local congregation as a church.

B. Be the whole church connectionally

Linked by a strong circle of covenanted belief and action, we constitute a series of regional circles of affinity. Our identity comes not just from a local community but from shared Christian beliefs and practices. Unfortunately, sometimes this connective circle reflects subcultural rather than covenanted Christian faith. Seekers are of all sorts, from disaffected fundamentalists to neo-pagans. In an effort to be as tolerant as possible (like talk shows), we have, unfortunately, bent over backward to accommodate the weird and the unusual. Sometimes eagerness to serve others has blurred our truth insights. This has resulted in widely divergent religious interpretation among Friends. Deference to difference has brought vagueness in witness. This ambiguity has been rationalized as a virtue—as if it is good that one can believe anything or nothing and still be a Quaker. How tragic! Judgment must begin at the house of God. Can two walk together unless they be agreed? At various times in history we have collectively sought the mind of Christ about the expression of our faith. One of these times was a century ago, when the conferences of 1887, 1892, 1897, and 1902 marked an earnest effort by several yearly meetings to restate their faith for greater clarity to the world and to build a structure for common ministry. This led to the Richmond Declaration of Faith and the Five Years Meeting (now Friends United Meeting). It may be time for the Friends Church to reaffirm its central beliefs. One occurrence that constitutes a marker for this renewal is the recent action by FUM to affirm its forthrightly Christian character. An event of potential significance is the forthcoming conference sponsored by *Quaker Religious Thought*. Scheduled for June 19-22, 1996, at George Fox College, in Newberg, Oregon, this international conference will deal with the relationship of Quakers to other Christians. Pray that this conference may be used of God to bring clarity to our corporate witness.

C. Be the church catholic

Link arms with Christians around the world as a witness to the kingdom. It is easier to affirm the church invisible than the church visible. But the body of Christ is made up of real persons, not just ideas. How to affirm the one universal church in practice not just in theory? Thinking about circles will help. Friends are one among the Christian family of churches. The word "sect" applies equally to these families, whether they be large or small. Thus Roman Catholics and Nazarenes and Presbyterians and Quakers are sects, sections of the church defined as all who name Jesus Christ as Savior and Lord. I know that in the first Quaker awakening people were being called back from the false to the true church. Some Quakers may still want to exclude others from the "true church." This zeal for restoration of a pure church has characterized other movements, of course. Church renewals never really doubt the continuity of the church over time, even in their diatribes against the false church. The early Quakers were as assiduous in quoting the church Fathers as were the Calvinists.

How can we be loyal Quakers and ecumenical Christians at the same time? I think a clue lies in accenting the covenantal character of our Quaker fellowship. The connectional church helps local churches take on a cultural coloring without compromise of convictions. The church universal is a concept hard to handle. But we can get a grasp of catholicity by empathy with churches under hardship and oppression, like the churches in China or in Sarajevo. Or with mission planted churches, such as the Quaker groups in Africa and Latin America. Our partnership in prayer and giving offers an important bonding with people outside accustomed ethnic and political circles. Our circles interlink when we receive as well as give within the larger circle of believers. One strong family strengthens other families. Acknowledging our covenant of faith fully affirms the church catholic *and* the church local. Think of how the church universal is affirmed on the local level. Ministerial associations, Bible study groups, service organizations, and ecumenical occasions such as the World Day of Prayer or Easter sunrise services are examples. There is so much unbelief in America today that Christians need to show what unites rather than what divides them. Circles can intertwine without losing their distinctive perimeters. Wheels move within wheels.

Because Quaker families no longer live in colonies, the ecumenical character of any local Friends meeting is often a given. People attend our meetings from many backgrounds, and for many reasons. Many Friends are nonresident, not regularly worshiping in a local Quaker meeting, but active in other ways—through mission and service, or through yearly meeting work, or in other denominations. In the face of such mixings how do we keep the Friends Church distinct? Obviously, deeply held convictions forthrightly witnessed is a major way. A second practical way is to preserve full membership for persons convinced of Quaker beliefs and to offer affiliate membership for attendees tentative in beliefs or residence. This procedure reserves to full members policy direction through office holding. Thus denominational covenant is preserved, catholicity is affirmed. A third important way to sustain the circle is to offer support wherever Friends live and minister. The covenant of faith, not residence, is the preeminent factor. That's why the Quaker network is so important. Local worship is a part of that network, but not the whole. The network takes various forms and priorities, books and magazines, summer camps, schools, visitation, correspondence, regional and area meetings, and world conferences, for example. Friends, locally and regionally, ought to give serious attention to how the Quaker network works.

Long before it was as convenient as it is now, Friends traveled widely in visitation ministry. I foresee a reemphasis upon that practice. Not just for well-known leaders, but for ordinary folk. Visitation can mean foreign countries, but it can also mean inter-visitation among regional Friends churches. In many places, quarterly meetings have become defunct or moribund. A vital network has been lost. Reemphasis upon the circle of covenant may make us more conscious of the value of sharing life in the Spirit with Friends beyond our local meeting.

These, then, are the five recoveries I hope for: 1) recovery of the gospel as proclamation, 2) recovery of the gospel as the power to change lives, 3) recovery of the gospel as love in action, 4) recovery of the gospel as joy in the Holy Spirit, and 5) recovery of the gospel as experiencing the fullness of the church. Then the wheels of the world will again glow like jewels, moving in all directions harmoniously, under the crystal dome, before the saffire throne of the Almighty.

Stories of Faithful Local Friends

Berkeley Friends Church, April 13, 1996

The person writing to the church of Thessalonica is Paul. His greeting graciously includes coworkers Silas and Timothy. The church was established about A.D. 49 on a missionary journey. This is described in Acts 17. The letter was written a year or so later. As was his custom, Paul first appeared in the Jewish synagogue, meeting for several Sabbaths with people and explaining from Scripture the logic of the Messianic coming and Jesus' resurrection. Jason's house served as headquarters for the young church, composed of both Jews and Greeks. The synagogue leaders stirred up opposition, and elicited official sympathy by claiming the Christian evangelists were insurrectionists who defied Caesar's decrees by proclaiming loyalty to Jesus. So Paul and Silas, nudged by the authorities, left town for Berea.

Thessalonica was a major city in Macedonia, situated at the junction of trade routes. Other than Jason we don't know the names of the people who formed the church, but we know the church succeeded. Paul was anxious about it of course; that's why he wrote these letters. He was like a mother forced to leave the children too soon. His letters dealt with matters theological, such as the meaning of the second coming, and matters practical, like how to handle persecution and exhortations to sexual responsibility. He headed off incipient priestcraft by reminding them how he labored without pay, and warned them about religious freeloaders. Most important, he showed them his love, and that he prayed for them. Maybe they didn't

Scripture reading
1 Thessalonians 1:1-7 (NRSV, emphasis mine)

Paul, Silvanus, and Timothy, To the church of the Thessalonians in God the Father and the Lord Jesus Christ: Grace to you and peace. We always give thanks to God for all of you and mention you in our prayers, constantly remembering before our God and Father *your work of faith and labor of love and steadfastness of hope* in our Lord Jesus Christ. For we know, brothers and sisters beloved by God, that he has chosen you, because our message of the gospel came to you not in *word* only, but also in *power* and in the *Holy Spirit* and with *full conviction*; just as you know what kind of persons we proved to be among you for your sake. And you became imitators of us and of the Lord, for in spite of persecution you received the word with *joy* inspired by the Holy Spirit, so that you became an *example* to all the believers in Macedonia and in Achaia.

all come up to the standard of spirituality noted in this greeting, but surely his expectation helped them do so. In any case, this introductory greeting is a model for us to follow in acknowledging the faithfulness of ordinary people (rich or poor, young or old, learned or unlearned) who keep churches going in the best or worst of times. I use Paul's standards of righteousness, then, as the basis for the stories that follow, stories of faithful Quaker people I have known, who are like some you have known.

"The work of faith"

"We always give thanks to God for all of you and mention you in our prayers, constantly remembering before our God and Father *your work of faith* ...in our Lord Jesus Christ."

So wrote Paul in our Scripture text. Tested by persecution or opposition, faith always constitutes work. It is more than a confident attitude that things will turn out well. It involved laying one's life on the line for gospel truth. Faith means convictions lived by, in all seasons. These stories illustrate such faithfulness.

Story 1
J. Allen Dunbar

J. Allen Dunbar was a grocery-store owner in the village of Greenleaf, Idaho. The town was named after the Quaker poet John Greenleaf Whittier. Iowa Quaker farmers had settled in this place when irrigation promised to make the desert bloom. My parents were among those pioneering Quaker farmers.

As a student at Greenleaf Friends Academy at first I considered Dunbar an old man crabbing at academy kids who loitered in his store. But I came to know him in a different light, as a wise and fair clerk of the monthly meeting and as a faithful delegate to the Yearly Meeting, concerned for missionary and evangelistic outreach. Dunbar was an elder able to discern the call of God upon young people. Jack Willcuts, Mahlon Macy, and I were among local kids whose call to ministry was fostered while he was clerk of the meeting. Some years later, when I was pastor of the Everett Friends Church, Dunbar rode with four of us younger people, and our baby son, to Colorado Springs, for the 1947 Conference of Evangelical Friends. He shared in that movement's vision for Quaker renewal. I think Paul, Silvanus, and Timothy had persons like J. Allen Dunbar in mind when they praised the saints and gave greetings of "grace and peace" to the church at Thessalonica.

How does J. Allen Dunbar illustrate the work of faith? It is a work of faith to acknowledge Christ as head of a thriving community of believers in a small farming community, and to offer one's talents as a human leader of that church. It is a work of faith to acknowledge that the kingdom of God has come to Greenleaf, Idaho, but that its fullness lies in the future in ways that elude our understanding.

Does my story remind you of a faithful local Friend like J. Allen Dunbar? A prayerful and wise clerk of the meeting, maybe? Voice your thanks to God for that person, and offer up a prayer for grace and peace.

Story 2
Paul and Gladys Strait

Paul and Gladys Strait are active members of North Valley Friends Church, near Newberg, attending regularly, giving generously to the local budget and to missions. Although retired now, Paul remains in many ways a curious boy. He has always tinkered with things. Out of his tinkering came several inventions. One invention was a portable key mill, which reduces down-time in industrial plants when adjustments to shafts are needed. This device received phenomenal reception worldwide, and gave rise to the Climax manufacturing firm in Newberg, now run by younger family members.

A few years ago, eager for new adventures, Paul tried to sail around the world. First he made trial runs up to Alaska with Gladys. Then with a young Friend, Steve Cathers, he sailed into the sunset hoping to circumnavigate the globe. Well, their boat was driven by a storm into a French nuclear-testing area somewhere in the South Pacific (in the area where the Greenpeace people recently have been arrested). Paul and Steve survived the ordeal, but their boat was confiscated by no-nonsense French gendarmes. So they didn't succeed, but at least they had fun trying.

Paul Strait reminds me of the eighteenth-century Quaker iron merchants, mechanics, and ship owners who relished the sacramental character of ordinary, earthy things, and espoused the dignity of hands-on work, spiced with adventure. Martin Luther said we are all priests to each other through the vocations to which we are called. Paul Strait was a faithful priest in the Reformation sense of that word. Whether in business or sailing the seas, Paul exhibits strong faith. Obstacles don't turn him gloomy. His faith enables him to see the world as it is, but also as it can become under God's redeeming grace.

How do the Straits illustrate the work of faith the apostle Paul wrote about in his letter to the Thessalonians? By confidently living in the world with Jesus Christ as Lord. I recall Paul arising in open worship to give a joyous testimony to Christ. The Straits's spiritual service has been neither dour nor dutiful, but adventuresome. It exudes confidence that the present joys of obedient Christian living are but a foretaste of what lies beyond the grave. Does my story of Paul and Gladys Strait remind you of adventuresome local Friends? Voice your thanks to God for them. Circle them with a prayerful halo of grace and peace. Rejoice in their faith.

Story 3
Ludlow and Ruth Corbin

For many years Ludlow and Ruth Corbin were pillars of Portland's Reedwood Friends Church. Ludlow taught science at Cascade in Portland. He had a way of making scientific inquiry exciting to students. For him the book of nature was God's other book, to be read as prayerfully as the written one, the Bible. Ludlow arranged annual field trips for Reedwood worshipers, taking them to a bird refuge and antelope range in eastern Oregon. Ruth served as a wise elder, often quietly discerning spiritual needs of others, often becoming an intercessory prayer partner with them. When she arose in meeting to speak everyone listened. Her words were powerful, discerning, pertinent, and to those who heeded the admonitions, comforting. Ludlow suffered a difficult bout with cancer before he died, but remained a radiant, uncomplaining Christian to the end. Ruth survived him for several years, continuing her intercessory ministry until God, too, called her home.

How do the Corbins illustrate the work of faith? Well, simply to be in the presence of the Corbins was like feeling an ocean breeze on a very hot day. Spirits were lifted. Doubts fell away. The natural and the supernatural meshed like hemispheres of a cosmic whole. The world made sense. Jesus made sense. Prayer made sense. The power of the gospel prevailed. Time kissed eternity. One felt resurrection power. The kingdom of God was among us. Faith triumphed.

I expect you know some Friends like Ruth and Ludlow. Praise God for them, and bless them with a benediction of grace and peace.

"Labor of love"

"We always give thanks to God for all of you and mention you in our prayers, constantly remembering before our God and Father *your...labor of love* in our Lord Jesus Christ." So wrote

Paul. Love is more than a passive attitude; it involves diligent actions. Actions that follow the example and teachings of Jesus. Love struggles upward to God, and outward to neighbor. Climbing upward is difficult, traveling widely is hard. Here are stories about persons who illustrate the labor of love.

Story 1
Albert and Lily Leakey

Albert and Lily Leakey lived in Everett, Washington. They had a thriving grocery business—a mom-and-pop store. Then the Great Depression struck and during these hard times in a mill town they generously extended credit to customers, to the extent that their business was ruined. Albert and Lily just couldn't get hard-nosed with needy neighbors. They absorbed debt until their own funds were gone. They sacrificed their own good cheerfully ("you can't let your neighbors go hungry!"). No bitterness, no complaint. They had learned the biblical secret of being content in all circumstances. They understood how the two great commandments fit together, like halves of a sphere. For them love was right action, not fuzzy feeling.

After the war big grocery chains moved in, and the Leakeys lacked capital to compete. They made do with Albert's odd jobs and a big garden; and the kids helped out. Financially, they never again rose much above the poverty level. They rarely, if ever attended Yearly Meeting, but they were faithful members in the Everett Meeting, and enjoyed fellowship with other Friends at quarterly meeting, and enjoyed the summer camp at Quaker Cove on the Puget Sound.

How do the Leakeys illustrate the labor of love? By taking Jesus' commandments seriously and making love the first principle of their lives. John Woolman would understand.

Do you know some people like the Leakeys? With memories hidden in family photograph albums? Remember them now, picture them in your mind. Thank God for them. These are kingdom people. Grace and peace rest upon them!

Story 2
Connard and Sarah Peterson

Connard and Sarah Peterson are apple growers from Entiat, Washington. They give leadership to a small Friends church in this farming community. They treat their workers and customers fairly. Mostly Hispanic, the seasonal laborers are eager to work each year on the Peterson farm. They know they will be treated fairly and paid well.

The Petersons have experienced ups and downs in this farming enterprise. Once the Alar scare shut down the market one whole year with devastating financial effect. Like others they were victimized because of the media penchant for sensationalizing one scare after another, even if allegations later proved unwarranted. In 1995 Japan removed the barriers to importing Washington apples, which now sell for the yen equivalent of several dollars apiece. That's good news to the Petersons. If you want to know about apples—not just apple marketing, but apple varieties and Quaker apple people from Johnny Appleseed on—ask Connard. He's been thinking about writing a book, but other things creep in...getting in the crop, fixing the packing sheds—you know how it is, one thing after another.

The Petersons are great yearly meeting people, their children, too. Connard has served as clerk of the representatives, and as an elder. When folks get too windy in discussions he has a way of bringing the issue back home, for clarity, for deliberation, and for resolution. Whether on a yearly meeting board or in the apple orchard, the Petersons are good workers, good stewards. Theirs is a labor of love. They ask not what they can get but how they can serve. And they serve with joy.

Are there people like the Petersons in your church? Be thankful for them. May grace and peace rest upon them.

Story 3
Laurence and Rosa Skene

Laurence and Rosa Skene were members of Newberg Friends Church for at least fifty years. For many of those years Laurence served on the cemetery committee, and as a trustee. He had good business sense, something churches often need—people who are levelheaded but not stingy. Laurence taught chemistry at George Fox College for about fifteen years. My wife, Fern, served as his assistant in the 1940s. Then Laurence became a building contractor and hazelnut farmer. Rosa cultivated African violets. Floral arrangements constituted her expression of art and her gift to others. Laurence built a house for us, and we appreciated firsthand his reputation for integrity as a builder.

The Skenes experienced the tragic side of life, and accepted the responsibility to bear one another's burdens and so fulfill the law of Christ. In 1946 Laurence assisted in Palestinian relief in Gaza under an AFSC program of food and housing. There he eased the pain of others. When their only daughter died as a young adult they experienced pain for themselves. About ten years ago Rosa developed a wasting disease, and Laurence patiently cared for her day and night until she died. Then a few months ago Laurence died, cheerful to the last, leaving to the college his modest estate, which was designated for three things: science education, a new maintenance building, and funds for the Peace Center. Laurence Skene taught us a lot about the labor of love, both for persons close to you and those far away. The Skenes understood themselves as members of the body of Christ, members one of another. Through hardships and pain they walked joyfully in the Light of Christ.

This poem expresses my appreciation for them. It may remind you of loving people you should thank God for and for whom you should offer a benediction of grace and peace.

Love in Sunday School

The Bible lesson is about Hosea,
whose efforts to restore
a fickle and unfaithful wife
constitute a parable of
God's unconditional love.
We discuss the implications
of covenant for Israel,
its meaning for the Church.

But the best commentary on love,
God's, and ours, that Sunday
is demonstrated convincingly
by a loving senior disciple
who continuously caresses his
faithful but incapacitated wife.

"Steadfastness of hope"

"We always give thanks to God for all of you and mention you in our prayers, constantly remembering before our God and Father *your...steadfastness of hope* in our Lord Jesus Christ." So wrote Paul. Hope is more than a cheerful attitude, although that's a good virtue! Optimists are fun to be with. It takes conscious purpose, good planning, and day-by-day efforts to be steadfast in hope.

As a prelude to these stories let me remind you we live in a cynical age, in which expressions of hope seem to be evidences of naiveté. In a recent cartoon strip, Calvin tells Hobbes, his tiger alter ego, "I'm writing a fund-raising letter. The secret of getting donations is to depict everyone who disagrees with you as the enemy. Then you explain how they're systematically working to destroy everything you hold dear. It's a war of values! Rational discussion is hopeless! Compromise is unthinkable! Our only hope is well-funded antagonism, so we need your money to keep us in the fight!" To this Hobbes replies "How cynically unconstructive," and Calvin offers this succinct retort: "enmity sells" (Eugene *Register-Guard*, July 1995).

Perhaps one reason cynicism is rampant is that hope is anchored only to personal desire, rather than to the will and purposes of God. These stories tell us about hope that is steadfast because it is anchored in Jesus Christ.

Story 1
Stan and Shirley Putman

Stan and Shirley Putman are members of Reedwood Friends Church, in Portland, Oregon. If you show up for worship some Sunday at 9:30, or considerably sooner, they'll be there in the foyer to greet you with warm smiles and firm handshakes. Their faces radiate their love of God and others. The Putmans make their living as graphic artists. They do very professional work. You may have noticed a brief credit line for their artwork on various books and publications of Barclay Press. Stan and Shirley also do watercolors for the joy of it, and to bless their friends. Through their artwork they help us see the world more clearly. Hanging on a wall of our house is one of Stan's seascapes. And although we live on the beach, and can watch the waves from our living room, the painting helps us to see it more clearly, and to praise the Creator more joyously for the world in which we live.

Artists are seers. The creativity of Christian artists reflects hope. The world is magic not mundane. Their artistry bursts with hope: that beauty will flower amid ugliness, that our perceptions can become avenues for the Spirit through the common things about us. These artists push aside dark cynicism to demonstrate the unity that comes when the human spirit joins the divine.

Maybe you know some artists like Stan and Shirley, people who get us out of the doldrums. People who are so steady that they prop us up on the leaning side. Friends who are steadfast in hope. Honor them. If they are artist types, buy a painting or a sculpture or a quilt from one whose talents join those of the Creator and call the creation good. The flowers of the artists, like the natural flowers, are meant to be enjoyed. Grace and peace be upon them!

Story 2
Bessie Tregelles

Bessie Tregelles somehow found her way from England to Kansas City, Missouri, where this London Quaker joined the local Friends meeting after World War II. I served at that meeting as pastor during my seminary years. Bessie was a plainly dressed, middle-aged, maiden lady who seldom talked about herself. Bessie faithfully attended all the meetings of the church, Sunday, midweek, and business meetings. I must confess wishing she would skip business meetings, for she questioned every proposed increase in expenditure. Once we were considering a new heating system for the meetinghouse. Everyone but Bessie favored the trustee proposal. She put her preferences aside, yielding to the will of others, not obstructing the unity of the group. Soon after that she invited us to dinner at her place. She sensed I considered her an obstruction to progress. It was pretty obvious, I guess! Her home was a tiny but tidy basement apartment, the meal simple but nourishing. In the conversation the reason for her reluctance to support added expenditures came out. So strongly did she feel her responsibility as a member that she could not conscientiously support with her voice what she could not support with her money. Her job was low paying and she simply couldn't add to her tithe. Well, we were able to convince her that new members could pick up the increased financial burden. I felt reproved of the Holy Spirit for a bad attitude toward her. I learned to appreciate the loyal opposition. She taught me that a group can't pay for anything, members of that group must. She had a firm expectation that the Spirit could make do with less as well as with more.

How does Bessie Tregelles illustrate the steadfastness of hope? Perhaps in this way: Her hope for the church wasn't based upon better heating systems or new carpets or advertising. It wasn't based upon being liked by people or disliked by them. Her hopes were not tied to social advantage. Her hope was in the yea and nay of truth-telling, upon the integrity of word and deed. She believed that people can disagree without being disagreeable, or without throwing roadblocks before others. She believed that it is not consensus we seek in business meeting but the mind of Christ. She taught me that a discerning spirit can anticipate breaches in friendship, and can prevent them from occurring by the breaking of bread together, along with honest conversation, and a mutual trust in the Holy Spirit.

Do you know people like Bessie Tregelles? Listen to them. Discern the difference between obstruction and loyal disagreement. Look for the anchors of their hope. Praise their steadfastness. May grace and peace be upon them!

Story 3
Ward and Marie Haines

Ward Haines took early retirement from being a mail carrier in Portland and moved with his wife, Marie, to Newberg, Oregon, where they faithfully attended the Friends church. Ward wanted something to do with his time so he went to work for George Fox College as a groundskeeper. He loved plants of all kinds and delighted in making living floral arrangements on the campus. He had, as they say, a green thumb. A nice thing about this job, from Ward's standpoint, was being around young people, listening to their laughter, observing their blossoming friendships. He was an outdoors sort of person, not particularly gifted with words, although he was a fair singer. As a conscientious objector who served in reconstruction service in France after World War I, he served on the Yearly Meeting Peace and Service Committee. And he served as quarterly meeting superintendent for a time. But he was more at ease putting hands to the soil and producing horticultural artistry than doing indoor things.

Marie, on the other hand, loved words, and she was good with them. She had a clear and mellow voice. When she spoke people could hear. She did not need a microphone. She had studied elocution long before electronic amplification came about. Once each year she loved to dress up in traditional Quaker garb, grey bonnet and all, and tell stories to the church about

George Fox and the early Quakers. She wasn't just a history buff. She could rise in meeting and pray, or call for a song, or exhort. Whether literally or not, she quaked before she spoke. And her words were powerful. Some of her stories were put in print for the benefit of children, in a book called *Lion Hearted Quakers.* Our children read them, I know, and probably learned much about their Quaker heritage through them.

How do the Haineses illustrate the steadfastness of hope? Well, for one thing they understood that a covenant people require the reinforcement of tradition to sustain their calling, and that a bit of pageantry perks up tradition and keeps hope alive. For another thing, Ward and Marie were always cheerful. The believed the Scriptures that all things work together for good for those who put their trust in Christ. Christ spoke to their conditions as fully as to George Fox. They were experiential Christians and convinced Friends.

Do you know some people like Ward and Marie Haines? If so, be grateful for them. They help one generation to praise God to the next. Grace and peace be upon them!

Story 4
The Russell Baker family

The Russell Baker family owned a dairy farm not far from Newberg, faithfully attended West Chehalem Friends Church, and took part in yearly meeting activities. Above the valley floor that served as pasture for their cattle was a pleasant hillside that Russell and his father had reforested many years before. They had built a new house there. One day a disastrous storm made him ponder the meaning of life and work. Then the Lord came to Russell and said, some things are more important than others. You've worked hard all your life, and made a good living, raised your children, supported your church. You are getting up in years. Why don't you turn that property into a ministry? You've dealt with cows long enough, why not enjoy people for a while? So Russell did. He sold the dairy farm and stock, but retained the forested upland. With his bulldozer he widened the creek, built a dam, and created a lake. He stocked the lake with fish. He cleared out berry vines and made trails and roads through the eighty-acre forest. Then he gave the land to George Fox College with the proviso that it be used for a retreat center. Their house became the first building to house activities. Then the Bakers moved to Friendsview Manor.

And so Tilikum was established. It is a beautiful forested place. A veritable Eden. Every day of the year, almost, some group is there. In the summer children flock to day camp. They paddle canoes and fish and swim in the lake. They explore the flora and fauna and learn about the Creator and the Christian story. They pet the donkeys and sheep in the old barn. In the fall and spring Elderhostel groups hold their sessions there. Various church groups hold retreats. It is an ongoing enterprise, self-supporting, with a competent staff; Tilikum's first director, Gary Fawver, served for a time as president of Christian Camping International, U.S.A. The old Baker farm is one of the nation's finest retreat centers. The Bakers died happy in the realization that their dreams and hopes had been realized. The labor of ordinary hands can be consecrated to divine purpose. Their hopes weren't based upon economic or political circumstances, or personal advantage, but upon Jesus Christ. They understood the force of the old gospel song, "My hope is built on nothing less than Jesus' blood and righteousness/ I dare not trust the sweetest frame but wholly lean on Jesus name."

I expect you know people like the Bakers who turn worldly possessions into kingdom goods. Praise God for such folk. Grace and peace rest upon them all, these brothers and sisters of the Christian Way. Remembering them makes us want to sing together that old gospel song, "My Hope is Built."

Today we have told stories about real-life applications of the exhortations Paul gave to the Thessalonian Christians long ago. We have illustrated the work of faith, the labor of love, and the steadfastness of hope. May you receive these words of Scripture and their applications in the power of the Holy Spirit, with full conviction, accompanied by joy, so that you become examples to others of what it means to be Christian in all the seasons of life.

Receiving an Inheritance

Yachats Community Presbyterian Church, October 13, 1996

Three times I have inherited money. The first inheritance was from my Aunt Mae. This occurred when I was thirty-two, barely into my teaching career at George Fox College, and quite poor. The portion allotted me was under a thousand dollars. I had anticipated that it might be more. But my aunt, you see, had spent most of her carefully earned fortune philanthropically while she was alive. She enjoyed helping others. And I had been a benefactor. When I went to Boston to study for my doctorate, she deposited to my account three thousand dollars in the Seaman's bank of New York. It covered all tuition and fees. Wonder how much it would take now? Well, I used the last hundred dollars of that account to buy an academic robe upon graduation. I still wear that robe each commencement at George Fox. Fittingly enough for a zealous Quaker happily married in midlife to a staunch Presbyterian, Aunt Mae died on Easter Sunday, 1955. She left a wonderful legacy of stewardship. She had the gift of helps. I was but one of several recipients who, to use the words of our text, "shared in the inheritance of the saints in the light." Christ's light. Aunt Mae was a saint who consecrated her worldly goods for kingdom purposes, and who enjoyed immensely sharing it with others.

Scripture reading
Colossians 1:11-12 (NRSV)
May you be made strong with all the strength that comes from his glorious power, and may you be prepared to endure everything with patience, while joyfully giving thanks to the Father, who has enabled you to share in the inheritance of the saints in the light.

A few years later I received a surprise bequest from an aunt and uncle I barely knew, Harry and Henrietta Ulfers. Childless, they had fought harsh North Dakota winters, years of drought, and lean years of the Depression to emerge shortly before death with land that had increased in value greatly after World War II. At their death the land was sold and their estate divided mostly among sixty-four nieces and nephews. By the time all heirs were searched out and probate ended the estate was considerably reduced in value. Each niece and nephew received a few hundred dollars. This was appreciated, but I wondered at the time if it would not have been better if the couple had bequeathed their estate to missions, to a school, or to some compassionate ministry, where the money would have made a significant impact.

The third time I received a financial inheritance was when my mother died in 1964. Because my parents had been prudent before and debt-free during the Depression, this legacy was ample to provide each of us adult children with investment income that helped bring financial security.

For some of you, like for my wife, Fern, the death of parents has come later, and often the cost of caregiving has equaled or exceeded the legacy received. Many of us here this morning are now the givers and not the receivers.

I tell these stories to show how interconnected generationally we are, that money is only a part of inheritance, and that one generation's faithfulness carries down to the next. In reading the Old Testament one is struck by the importance of inheritance to the Israelite people. Some has to do with land, which equals sustenance, but more concerns a spiritual legacy, with being a people chosen of God for witness to the world.

When Paul wrote from prison to the fledgling Christian community at Colossae about an incredible inheritance, he wasn't talking land or bonds but about the gospel of Jesus Christ. Maybe Paul recalled Jesus' parable about the worth of the kingdom being like a connoisseur of jewelry who finds the perfect pearl and sells all he has to possess it.

We share that glorious inheritance. Let's consider what that means.

1. First, this inheritance is acknowledged by conversion.

Christ redeems us from sin and we gratefully accept the conditions. This experience is called *conversion*. By conversion we are included in what God wills for the world. We don't qualify for that inheritance except by the grace of God and our thankful acceptance of that redemption. Conversion is the answer of a good conscience toward a gracious God. For some persons, conversion occurred long ago. For others it is a recent event. Some persons are just opening the door to let Jesus come in. For all of us, conversion marks the surrender of our wills to the will of God. We give thanks to God for enabling us to be legatees of the kingdom.

2. Second, this inheritance is witnessed by the Spirit.

The Holy Spirit documents our inclusion in God's family. When we listen inwardly, God the Spirit witnesses to our spirits that we are children of God and heirs with Jesus Christ. When people enter into a contract—a land purchase, for example—a deposit constitutes a performance bond. The Holy Spirit is God's performance bond. God has given us his word. In Ephesians 1:14 (NIV) Paul writes that the Spirit is "a deposit guaranteeing our inheritance until the redemption of those who are God's possession—to the praise of his glory."

Is it the case with you, as it is with me, that sometimes the heart must jog the mind that this is so? Because we are busy with many things, we need to listen to that inward voice of God. Such good listening involves several disciplines. Prayer, meditative retreats during the day, Bible and other devotional reading, the setting of priorities of time and material possessions. When I was sixteen I began the practice of tithing to the church and Christian causes. Although it was difficult at first, I have found this discipline to be richly rewarding. All spiritual disciplines make us active participant in God's kingdom. They check against drifting into self-centeredness. Surely you have discovered this about spiritual disciplines.

3. Third, this inheritance is threatened by sin.

Sin can cut us off from the kingdom. We have been delivered from darkness, let's not fall back into it. Paul warns, "For of this you can be sure: No immoral, impure or greedy person—such a man is an idolater—has any inheritance in the kingdom of Christ and of God" (Ephesians 5:5 NIV). The writer of the book of Hebrews warns us not to sell our birthright. "See that no one is sexually immoral, or is godless like Esau, who for a single meal sold his inheritance rights..." (Hebrews 12:16 NIV).

The warning against sexual immorality and godlessness is forthright, isn't it? If this warning is for you, heed it. But did you also hear the warning against greed? Let me share a sorry little story about greed. Once I fell for a Ponzi scheme. A well-recommended person met individually with a number of us, urging an investment plan that would enable each investor to make lots of money—so we could support missions more fully. "I could give my money directly to missions," Mr. Jones said, "but think how much more mission outreach can be supported if I help you all make money." Jones's business was producing and distributing 3-D postcards. Remember them? He had great plans for expansion, involving Japanese production and worldwide distribution. The first cards carried Disney and Holy Land motifs, and sold for a dollar each. I didn't particularly think I would buy one, but people have different tastes, don't they? Flush with extra funds from my mother's legacy, the venture sounded good to me. Who could knock the cause—get rich and support missions at the same time. So I invested several thousand dollars. At first, checks arrived bearing high interest, but soon they got behind schedule. It took a bit of prodding to get them. Then checks quit coming altogether; finally phone calls were not answered.

You can guess the rest of the story. The pyramid collapsed leaving recent investors devastated and all of us financially battered. Some people lost retirement savings; others, like myself, inheritance money. W.C. Jones lost his life, a suicide. When the legal dust settled and the warehouse of cutesy overpriced 3-D cards was liquidated, we received ten cents on the dollar. You see, my outward motivation was serving the Lord but my inner motivation was greed. Greed isn't good news for the kingdom. Whatever its form, sin dissipates our inheritance. "For this reason," wrote an early Jewish believer, "Christ is the mediator of a new covenant, that those who are called may receive the promised eternal inheritance—now that he has died as a ransom to set them free from the sins committed under the first covenant" (Hebrews 9:15 NIV). Christ not only forgives our sins but also delivers us from them. No more ritual offerings. Christ is the eternal offering that takes away the sins of the world. Praise God for this!

4. Fourth, this glorious inheritance yields life eternal.

Although cultural conditioning makes it seem noble to view death as a sacrificial clearing out to make room for others, the gospel declares better news about eternal life. The word *eternal* is not just a euphemism for quality life in the present biological mode of existence. The early believers understood the legacy in this way: "An inheritance that can never perish, spoil or fade— kept in heaven for you" (1 Peter 1:4). Our legacy certainly broadens and deepens life now, but it also continues after death. This is why we celebrate Easter.

I understand *eternal* to mean self-conscious existence after death, not just having our memory placed in the storage vaults of human history. Do you puzzle about where to put all the resurrected people? Ponder, then, the size of cosmos, and the power of God the Creator.

When I was a boy, talk about the second coming and the windup of earthly affairs disturbed me. I was just beginning to live, thrilling with adventures such as riding my horse Eagle across the desert, learning how to shoot baskets with either hand, practicing my tennis serves, getting a driver's license, taking girls on dates and eating banana splits. Nearly six decades later I sort of feel the same way! I am still in love with life here on earth, although my experience is greatly broadened, and I have a rich treasure of memories. But now I can glimpse distant horizons. The metronome of time beats differently. The kingdom has come, yes, in part; it is among us. But the kingdom is also coming for each of us, and for all of us together, in the near or far future, bringing a realm of reality in which personal identity continues, unshackled from sin. A renewed cosmos is promised. Knowing what faith in Christ brings in love and truth, how can the resurrected life be less joyous in heaven than on earth? Won't it be rather infinitely richer, like flowers sprung from seed sown in the ground? If we listen carefully, the Holy Spirit within tells us this is so. Our inheritance won't fade away, but grow, like all good investments. Let's take a few moments for silent prayer.

Lord, we ask your Spirit to testify to our spirits that we are children of God. We acknowledge our conversion, our turning to you. Break the grip of besetting sins. Forgive us; but also cleanse us from those sins, lest foolishly we bargain away our true inheritance. We are assured that the kingdoms of this world will one day become the kingdom of our God that every knee shall bow before the Lord. Reassure us also, Lord, about our personal place, and that of our loved ones, in the next life. About our rooms in heaven. We can wait to learn the mysteries of the new Jerusalem, but we do want your assurance that Jesus and all faithful souls will be there. In Jesus' name, amen.

I conclude with this prayer of Paul: "I pray also that the eyes of your heart may be enlightened in order that you may know the hope to which he has called you, the riches of his glorious inheritance in the saints" (Ephesians 1:18 NIV).

The Burdens of Discovery

Reedwood Friends Church, November 17, 1996

Introduction

"Bear one another's burdens and in this way you will fulfill the law of Christ." The words of our text seem paradoxical: to be humble yet have pride, to carry one's own load yet let others bear its burden, to restore those who sin while resisting temptation. The verses teach that although each person is responsible for right conduct, temptations abound, and people sin. The gist of the matter is this: Being too *independent* or too *dependent* can lead to sin. *Interdependence* guards against such entrapment. The people of God act as an interdependent community. Their loving care may prevent the more difficult task of spiritual restoration, or it may sustain restoration.

What are the burdens we bear for each other? Many could be listed, including help during accidents and bereavement. Today we consider just one: *the burden of discovery*. How we discover the world varies with life stages, from childhood through old age. Emotional burdens accompany discoveries. At each stage temptations assail. At each stage faithful people may fulfill the law of Christ. To modify a slogan, "It takes a church to bear each other's burdens."

Scripture reading
Galatians 6:1-5 (NRSV, emphasis mine)

My friends, if anyone is detected in a transgression, you who have received the Spirit should restore such a one in a spirit of gentleness. Take care that you yourselves are not tempted. *Bear one another's burdens, and in this way you will fulfill the law of Christ.* For if those who are nothing think they are something, they deceive themselves. All must test their own work; then that work, rather than their neighbor's work, will become a cause for pride. For all must carry their own loads.

A burden of a child is finding out about the world

A baby grasps a father's finger, sees and returns a smile. A baby's cry brings reassuring sounds from Mother. Baby begins to crawl, so parents put harmful things out of reach and teach acceptable limits to grasping. A small child starts to dart across the street and is grabbed, fortunately, by an older sibling, and taught that the world is not only fascinating but also dangerous. Right touch is taught daily by family members, and also by a patient dog and a not-so-patient cat. A child arranges pretty stones, or molds clay, or turns somersaults, thus learning balance, proportion, rhythm, and design along newly opened sensory gateways to God's world.

From older generations a child learns to articulate in words what is tacitly sensed of God's creation. A baseline is established for discerning through life which things are to be respected for their own sakes and which things can be shaped to one's own purposes.

Good homes achieve this. Some do not. Consider this scenario: A woman seeks counsel from the pastor. The current husband is an alcoholic. The woman's face is drawn and anxious as she pours out a litany of troubles. The woman's small daughter, meanwhile, hugs the legs of the pastor, trying to move herself from periphery to center of attention. Her needs are as urgent as mother's, but she lacks words to express them. She finds the world frightening and craves loving, reassuring, touch.

There is so much of worth in the world for a child to discover! So many wonders to see, to hear, to taste, to smell, to touch, it's difficult to organize them. Unfortunately the Trickster beguiles impressionable minds into adding sinful ends and means to categories of understanding, namely, greed to accumulate and violence to secure. Wars, alas, start in childhood. A faithful generation understands that children can transgress, and corrects them gently, helping them discover Jesus the Savior, whose Spirit becomes the guide through life. Education only provides skills in selfishness unless put in a context of love for God and love for others.

To find love—human and divine—is a child's most important discovery, and a major responsibility for the covenant community of faith. We bear this burden in several ways:

- we protect against danger
- we sharpen sensory acuity and dexterity
- we give knowledge to interpret what is sensed
- we provide worship rooted in awe before the Creator
- we provide opportunity to witness what has been found

A burden of a youth is finding a niche in the world

A short story in four parts:

Story One
A young lad enters high school one morning wearing olive green twill jodhpurs bought at a fire sale, and field boots with steel plates affixed. Tramping across study hall he gets grinning attention from students, but frowns from the teacher.

Story Two
On a fall evening a young lad and a friend take a basket of rotten apples and fling them on a neighbor's neatly landscaped lawn, racing away from the irate owner, ahead of an imagined shotgun blast.

Story Three
A young lad kneels in the sawdust at a summer camp service and accepts the divine offer of salvation. In the joy of discovery he sings, "I have decided to follow Jesus." The lad discovers in Christ a more satisfying niche in life than showing off or vandalizing property.

Story Four
A young lad is approached by church elders and asked to help lead gospel services in an unchurched community. He agrees, and not long afterward feels a call to ministry. He has never turned back from that discovery.

This story is about one lad. I am that lad.

Doors of discovery open wide to young persons in our society. Our youth have computers, good schools, trips abroad, athletics, movies, skiing, beautiful clothes, straight teeth, comfortable homes, cars to drive, pizza to eat, peers to hang around with. Alas, the Trickster exploits that adventuresome spirit, distorting curiosity into lust, or drugs, or lascivious literature. By extravagant purchases they are fleeced of their funds by celebrity hawkers in the employ of rich CEOs.

It's hard to find your place in society when you are young. So many beckoning paths! And conflicting voices. So much to explore in physical and social worlds.

"What if I miss out on something?" is a youthful lament. Resisting constraints of those who care for them, they fall into the clutches of those who don't. Do thirteen-year-olds *freely* smoke Camels or Virginia Slims or are they *programmed* to do so? In confusion they ask, "Whose directions shall I follow into this wilderness called life: parents', peers', celebrities', teachers', ministers', the media's?" Sadly, pied pipers often supplant true guides. Sin seems more alluring than godly obedience. The church has a responsibility to young people. Here are some ways to bear their burdens of discovery:

- we protect against exploitation
- we supply rational boundaries to freedom
- we foster supportive peer relationships
- we provide worship centered in following Jesus
- we provide opportunity to witness what has been found

A burden of a young adult is finding a constructive vocation

To discover one's right calling is hard for young adults in a rapidly changing world. Its terrain can turn rough, as these stories illustrate. The first is made up, the others actual accounts.

Story One

A newly married couple sits on the living room floor of their apartment going over bills. Rent is the largest at $700, then payment on college loans, utility bills, and credit card accounts for gasoline, groceries, new running shoes, etc. There isn't enough money this month so they decide to pay the minimum on the major credit card. The young husband works full time at a computer store; the young wife holds down a thirty-hour entry-level sales job. He has finished college, she hasn't. She wants to secure a teaching certificate. He hopes to get into programming, but it hasn't worked out yet. They want to start a family soon....Well, it's frustrating, but they figure things will work out, so leaving the ledger on the floor, they don sweats and go to the gym for a game of racquetball. Picture them a year later, this time sitting on chairs in the office of a credit counselor. They are badly in debt, she is pregnant. No racquetball. Life, they discover, is no bed of roses. Maybe they'll move to Oregon and get a new start!

Story Two

Dave works at a factory that assembles mobile homes. A unit has been returned because of structural defects. The boss tells Dave just to put filler in the cracks, and sand and repaint the panel. Dave has a degree in materials engineering. He knows the difference between repair and cover-up. What should he do? He likes his work and hopes to advance in the company. He gets a good salary, plus benefits. Acting prudently he can support his wife, a three-year-old son, and a new baby daughter. The Trickster says it's the boss's call. As a Christian, though, he doesn't feel right being party to deceit. So he says to the boss, "I can't conscientiously do it" and suggests alternate, more expensive repairs. The boss rejects the suggestion and assigns the job to someone else. The next week Dave is laid off. He discovers what Jesus said about in the world having tribulations. He discovers cross-bearing.

Story Three

The year is 1656; the place, Balby, England; the occasion, a meeting of Quaker elders; an agenda item, concern for the right apprenticing of young Friends.

Story Four

It is a century earlier. A miner's son, Martin Luther, discerns that church leadership isn't the only spiritual vocation. "We are all called to be priests to one another," he declares, "through the work we do." We label this Reformation insight "the priesthood of all believers." The community of Christ must bear the burdens of young adults seeking faithfulness in whatever honest work they do, not just on spare-time tasks at the church. Here are some ways we bear their burdens:

- we guard against ethical compromise
- we provide guidance and funds for vocational preparation
- we recognize and honor the giftedness of each
- we offer the continuity of the church during mobile years
- we provide opportunity to witness what has been found

A burden of a mature adult is finding right uses of power

Mature adults have found that competence and accountability are satisfying forms of power. They find joy in good work amply rewarded, in home ownership, in economic stability, in knowledge and skills acquired. They no longer worry about a niche in the world. They ride waves of social change like experienced windsurfers. They test products by reason, not by celebrity endorsement. They know their strengths. They carry their own load. But the Trickster can deceive them, too. What are some of their burdens? Consider these hypothetical scenarios.

Story One
After thirty years of marriage, Jane and John get a divorce. She is an executive in a brokerage firm, he a sales representative for a tool company. Each is professionally successful, and strong-willed. Their marriage had been an arena for contending egos, with affection negotiated, not freely given. They have cheated on each other. With grown children gone they considered their marriage contract completed. But the divorce hasn't been as liberating as expected. They are discovering hidden and tragic costs to egoistic power. Humbled by failure, each seeks a new beginning. Each has returned to church. They've learned how power corrupts. It's a heavy load. Fortunately, they have found God's grace.

Story Two
Dr. John Doe is a successful physician, with three assistants. He holds responsible positions on the hospital board, in professional groups, as elder in the church. Recently his liability insurance has doubled; an HMO is trying to take over his clinic; a rebellious daughter has been arrested for shoplifting; his own health suffers from stress and overwork; he and his loving wife hardly see each other; and worship is mostly a time to worry. Dr. Doe feels driven by circumstances beyond his control. He's trying to find the meaning of servant leadership.

Story Three
Terry is a scientist doing genetic research. Over the years Terry has kept science and religion separate. Scientific training has been thorough, but not biblical education. Recent publicity in news magazines questioning what Jesus really said, and controversy in local schools over creationism vs. evolutionism have shattered those neat compartments. For the first time since adolescence, disturbing doubts fog the mind. Is religion just an unscientific way to cope with the unknown? Can the conflict between faith and reason be resolved? Terry is experiencing the "dark night of the soul." To discover unifying faith in Christ is a heavy load. How does the church share the burdens of Terry, of Jane and John, of Dr. Doe?

- we guard against the corruption of power
- we provide appropriate channels for service

- we offer support during times of stress
- we challenge the mind to greater Christian discipleship
- we provide opportunity to witness what has been found

A burden of an older adult is finding the best use of time

Older adults in our society generally have more discretionary time than at any other stage in life. Retired people don't have to hurry off to school or work each morning. They aren't shoved here or there, like children. What do older adults do all day? Well, one fishes, another watches television. One reads, another putters in the shop. One golfs, another knits. They write admonishing letters to their grandchildren. Some work at McDonald's out of necessity, others because they're bored at home. Some couples follow pleasant weather in their motor homes, and chat with other nomads at RV parks. Curious folk attend Elderhostel conferences at places like Tilikum or the Ozarks. Others trek to ancestral sites in Europe. Some join Volunteers on Wheels to repair churches or build houses for the poor, like Jimmy and Rosalyn Carter did. Others grumble that so many volunteer tasks have been fobbed off on them by church and service clubs that they might as well go back to work for money. Aggressive tycoons hang on to routines; they commute daily to the city and totter to executive offices, refusing, like Senator Thurman, to give up power. But most in this group, whether by necessity or by choice, have stepped aside for others.

So what's burdensome about that? The burden comes from feeling we aren't needed anymore. That we are on the shelf. Having stepped aside we find professional skills eroding. How to cope? First, we must rediscover what has been hidden since childhood: a capacity to identify oneself by who we are, not by job or status. Second, we must acknowledge that our labor carries an impact long after the retirement party. Third, we must guard against becoming contentious critics. Fourth, we must find new paths for Christian vocation (Dealous Cox illustrates this with his leadership at George Fox University and in the yearly meeting). Fifth, we must engage more fully in Bible reading and intercessory prayer. Finding the best use of time is a part of discipleship at every stage of life, including this one. The church can bear the burden of this discovery. Here are some ways:

- we guard against both sloth and cynicism
- we offer opportunities for avocational service to others
- we offer a supportive context for making decisions
- we offer worship that restores biblical perspectives
- we provide opportunity to witness what has been found

A burden of a very old adult is finding joy in ordinary things

It is said that old people dwell in the past. Why not? They have accumulated a lot of it and can enrich the present with good memories. Restricted in movement, these adults also rediscover the joy of ordinary things. This is childlike, but not childish. Consider these true stories.

Story One

Amrel Headley is a long-time widow with no children. She recently celebrated her 97th birthday. The people in the foster-care home made it a festive occasion, and her niece and family came. When we visit her she extols the beautiful garden, and says how she enjoys the patio on sunny days. She displays scrapbook pictures of her husband, and cards received. Her caregivers, immigrants from Romania, are Christians. They treat her with respect. Feeble, and with failing eyesight, Amrel struggles to read her Bible and to walk a bit each day. Her life is narrowly circumscribed now, but she is content and awaits with serenity her summons Home.

Story Two
Lauren King is a literature professor retired from Malone College. He is in his early nineties. A few years ago he and his wife moved to Friendsview Manor. Sadly, Helen died shortly thereafter, so Lauren moved back to his Ohio home. Lauren has discovered that an aged body can have a sharp mind. Why shouldn't a professor continue to use his? So, encouraged by his friends, five years ago he wrote a book about faith, *The Way You Believe*, and dedicated it to two deceased Quaker leaders—Everett Cattell and Jack Willcuts. On the flyleaf of my autographed copy Lauren wrote: "in gratitude for your encouragement." Last year *Quaker Religious Thought* featured Lauren's carefully researched "New Testament Account of the resurrection," which elicited good responses.

Trickster efforts to turn Amrel into a bitter old woman and Lauren King into a grumpy old man clearly have failed.

Not every very old person is able to find such zest for living as have these two. Perhaps if the church shared their burdens more thoughtfully more would be able to do so. How do we bear the burdens of discovery for very old people? Here are some ways:

- we protect against poverty, loneliness, and exploitation
- through activities we challenge faultfinding and pettiness
- we draw out accumulated wisdom for the guidance of others
- we offer worship that sustains faith during declining years
- we provide opportunity to witness what has been found.

Conclusion

Bearing burdens is about love in action, whether for children discovering the world, youth finding a niche in it, young adults finding a vocation, mature adults finding a right use of power, older adults finding the best use of time, or very old adults recovering joy in ordinary things. Dorothy Day, that valiant friend of the poor, wrote many years ago: "When you love people, you see all the good in them, all the Christ in them. God sees Christ, His Son, in us. And so we should see Christ in others, and nothing else, and love them..." (*Fritz Eichenberg: Works of Mercy*, Robert Ellsberg, ed., Orbis, 1992. See text accompanying the Day woodcut.).

Caesar or God?

Yachats Community Presbyterian Church, October 12, 1997;
Friendsview Manor, November 4, 2004

Mark Twain said that it wasn't the parts of the Bible he couldn't understand that bothered him, but the parts he could understand. This passage from Romans 13 is one of those. Let's put it in context by recounting an episode in the life of Jesus. Matthew reports the event this way.

> Then the Pharisees went out and laid plans to trap him in his words. They sent their disciples to him along with the Herodians. "Teacher," they said, "we know you are a man of integrity and that you teach the way of God in accordance with the truth. You aren't swayed by men, because you pay no attention to who they are. Tell us then, what is your opinion? Is it right to pay taxes to Caesar or not?" But Jesus, knowing their evil intent, said, "You hypocrites, why are you trying to trap me? Show me the coin used for paying the tax." They brought him a denarius, and he asked them, "Whose portrait is this? And whose inscription?" "Caesar's," they replied. Then he said to them, "Give to Caesar what is Caesar's, and to God what is God's."
> (Matthew 22:15-21 NIV)

Scripture reading
Romans 13:1-10 (NIV)

Everyone must submit himself to the governing authorities, for there is no authority except that which God has established. The authorities that exist have been established by God. Consequently, he who rebels against the authority is rebelling against what God has instituted, and those who do so will bring judgment on themselves. For rulers hold no terror for those who do right, but for those who do wrong. Do you want to be free from fear of the one in authority? Then do what is right and he will commend you. For he is God's servant to do you good. But if you do wrong, be afraid, for he does not bear the sword for nothing. He is God's servant, an agent of wrath to bring punishment on the wrongdoer. Therefore, it is necessary to submit to the authorities, not only because of possible punishment but also because of conscience. This is also why you pay taxes, for the authorities are God's servants, who give their full time to governing. Give everyone what you owe him: If you owe taxes, pay taxes; if revenue, then revenue; if respect, then respect; if honor, then honor.

Let no debt remain outstanding, except the continuing debt to love one another, for he who loves his fellowman has fulfilled the law. The commandments, "Do not commit adultery," "Do not murder," "Do not steal," "Do not covet," and whatever other commandment there may be, are summed up in this one rule: "Love your neighbor as yourself." Love does no harm to its neighbor. Therefore love is the fulfillment of the law.

Tax talk gets attention, especially when taxes seem unfair. Currently the IRS has been on the hot seat before Congress for rough collection tactics. Recently Waldport homeowners successfully resisted the imposition of a surtax aimed at remedying a utilities shortfall. When Yachats raised sewer and water rates to cover system repair a few months ago, people groused a bit. We like what certain taxes provide, but generally resist them. We assume a tendency for government to spend more and more, until stopped. People in Jesus' time were just as concerned about where their money went as we are. So the incident narrated in the Scripture lesson caught the ear of listeners. It was, after all, a politically staged event, and as such probably drew a crowd.

The context of the event

If you've had someone try to trap you in your words you know the pressure Jesus was under, and admire how adroitly he avoided being snared. (Most of us could use help in avoiding verbal traps.) The issue at stake in this event, and in the events of our lives, however, is an old one: conflict over authorities—human and divine.

This was one of several efforts to entrap Jesus. On another occasion the Sadducees had tried to make his belief about heaven look ridiculous. This time, however, opposing groups—the Pharisees and the Herodians—ganged up on him. Their tricky question involved a Roman poll tax, which was imposed upon the Jewish client state and under protest for twenty-five years. The Zealots had unsuccessfully revolted against it. Some were crucified for their resistance. To support this tax would make Jesus look like an unpatriotic Jew, to oppose it was politically dangerous. The conservative Pharisees were vexed by restrictions imposed by an empire they considered idolatrous. In contrast the liberal Herodian party favored accommodation with Rome, even at the expense of certain religious preferences.

Whose picture was on the coin? The emperor Tiberius. He had been a popular general under the powerful Augustus (his stepfather), who forced him to divorce a beloved pregnant wife to marry a philandering aristocrat, Julia. When badly used Tiberius finally became Caesar at fifty-five he was convinced "Rome could be saved from a vulgar degeneration only by an aristocracy stoic in conduct and refined in taste" (Will Durant, *Christ and Caesar*, Simon and Schuster, 1980, p. 260). To accomplish this goal he tried to reestablish the senate, but they demurred, instead conferring upon him the dictatorial powers Augustus had assumed. Tiberius was prudent, not extravagant. He didn't want to be worshiped, despite the subscription stamped on a coin in his honor—"son of God." About taxation he wrote, "It was the part of a good shepherd to shear his flock, not fleece it."

Increasingly during his reign, political management defaulted to the Praetorian Guard. Melancholy, poetic, and philosophical, by the time of this episode in Jesus' life Tiberius had retired to the Isle of Capri, lamenting the moral rot and political corruption he could not root out. Governance is never easy, and is almost impossible without a basic moral consensus. A plot to assassinate him failed. But when the old man fainted on a trip, a turncoat smothered him with a pillow. He was, said one historian, "the ablest ruler the Empire ever had."

Did Tiberius, leader of one of the world's greatest empires, ponder what belonged to God and what to Caesar? From a Stoic context I think he did. In a pagan society the ruler is supposed to be God's bridge to humanity—*pontifex maximus*. Tiberius didn't buy this cult of empire garbage. But certain successors did, and consequently followers of Jesus were killed because they wouldn't burn a pinch of incense and declare "Caesar is Lord." One of these was a young Christian mother thrown into an arena in the year 203, where she was gored by bulls and finished off by the knife of a reluctant gladiator. Her memorial is a spectacular ocean headland—in our backyard—named by Captain Cook in 1778, Perpetua.

So when Jesus asked to see the coin with Tiberius's picture on it, the Pharisees were caught in hypocrisy. They benefited economically from a stable currency while protesting its idolatry. Even the worldly Herodians were forced by Jesus' answer to ponder how God is sovereign in a mixed society. Jesus sagely tossed this question about authority back to his questioners, and people have puzzled for centuries about how to answer it. We too are forced to sort out what belongs to Caesar and what belongs to God. History suggests some responses.

Responses to the question

1. One response is for the church to defy Caesar.

Its ultimate cost is martyrdom. This occurred in early Christian centuries when ego-driven emperors fancied themselves God and demanded worship, unquestioned obedience, and not just respect and civic responsibility. Christian martyrdom by rulers who claim ultimate authority has occurred recently in Africa and China. We rightly call such rulers tyrants. Christ against Caesar is one stance of the faithful church. Sometimes it's the only response. The thirteenth chapter of Revelation, written by a Christian working the salt mines of lonely Patmos, depicts the state at its idolatrous worst—Babylon is a beast, but Christ will prevail over it. Remember Russia under Stalin, Germany under Hitler? Currently Burundi has the dubious distinction of leading the world in atrocities, including the slaughter of Christians who include both Hutu and Tutsi in their fellowship. We do well to keep in mind such ancient, recent, and contemporary witness so we don't slip slowly into idolatry.

2. A second response is to replace a pagan state with a godly one—Christ over Caesar.

The gospel has a way of patching up broken societies, and this can lead to institutions of religion asserting authority over government. This was the medieval solution, which salvaged classical culture, offered compassionate care to the needy, and triggered scientific thought. But it left a bitter legacy of persecution when benign force became malign forces. Like a virus, the cruelty of Rome infects any church-state and destroys the leavening power of the gospel.

3. A third response is for the church to receive favored status from the state.

Christ in league with Caesar. This was the Reformation answer. "*Ejus regio, ejus religio*"—"whose the rule, his the religion." The state confers favored status and in turn receives the blessing but not prophetic criticism from the church. Its legacy is Catholic Spain and Protestant England, Catholic France and Protestant Sweden. The intertwining of church and monarchy is evident in England. One of the longest words in the English language reflects a historic struggle over power: *disestablishmentarianism*.

Having witnessed the drowning of their members by church-state Lutherans, the Mennonites weren't happy with this favored status approach, nor were Quakers, driven from Wales to America by persecution (three were hanged on Boston Common). The Baptists as well as the Quakers tried to have their own colonies, but sin seeped into Rhode Island and Pennsylvania, as well as into the persecuting commonwealth of Massachusetts. Russia, sickened by atheistic communism, has now reconferred favored status upon Russian Orthodoxy. Freedom is again being tested. Christian dissent historically has challenged any favored status approach, however, and makes the case for religious freedom through a fourth position.

4. A fourth response to what belongs to God and what to Caesar is to separate religion and government.

Christ and Caesar are paired off. One sphere deals with religious matters, the other sphere with worldly matters—secular vs. sacred. Keep politics out of religion, religion out of politics. So we curtain off the authorities symbolically: American flag at the post office, the cross in the sanctuary. "Amazing Grace" sung in worship, "Star Spangled Banner" at ball games. This approach has merit. It keeps the church from becoming a government bureau. It prevents religious monopoly. It resists secular suppression of faith.

But it doesn't fully answer what belongs to Caesar and what belongs to God. Check out the media. Which sphere dominates? Only exotic religion gets big coverage. Proponents for separation of church and state say "the state can have my body but the church has my soul." Can you really separate your body from your soul? Can the Ten Commandments be divvied up? The state grounds its laws on certain ones: no stealing, no false witness, no murder. The church underscores those about no idolatry, no adultery, and honoring father and mother. Some groups assert the Sermon on the Mount applies only to a future millennium. That's quite appealing to me as mayor of Yachats; but my mind says its a cop out. So is assigning the Old Testament to the state and the New Testament to the church. If I'm to answer Jesus' call to love the Lord God with my whole body, mind, and soul, and my neighbor as myself, I must heed that call to the limit of my strength, nonselectively. That's not easy. Only by God's grace can it be approached. Conscience isn't easily compartmentalized. You can't turn God on and off.

So, we struggle to achieve parity. Prayers are offered in the Senate but not in public schools. Legislators look to the church to uphold virtues that make governance possible. Churches lobby the state on behalf of their principles of righteousness. Both church and state educate. Both offer care for the homeless and the hungry. Through laws to ensure justice the state prevents churches from getting corrupt and ripping off people. Through its proclamation of biblical truth the church keeps the state from usurping divine prerogatives. Actually both church and state give ear to God, the one overtly (and sometimes loudly) the other covertly (and often quietly). Institutions are composed of whole persons, not split selves. In frustration, abetted by a cynical culture, people often lash out at both institutions—church and state. The most imperious institution of our times, however, is neither. The Babylon of our times is not the United Nations nor the World Council of Churches but rather a worldwide commercial empire made possible by high technology. We profit from the coin of this empire; can we avoid its idolatry? The authority of both church and state are challenged by a pantheon of celebrity gods, hyped worldwide by an advertising priesthood. George Washington's face appears on a quarter, with the inscription "In God We Trust." I don't want one with Elvis Presley's face on it. Given the anarchist mood, this could happen!

Thoughts about this fourth response

We are less sure, therefore, that this two-sphere scheme is as good as we thought. Partly because there is no way faith and politics can be neatly divided. Our allegiance to the state is subordinate to our allegiance to the one God Almighty, maker of heaven and earth. "We ought to obey God and not men," said our spiritual forebears in the first century. So say we. Our aim is to obey God *through* governance, ordained for our good. In a time of cynicism about government we may need to be more prayerful and discerning about what this involves of our time and energy. Otherwise anarchy threatens governance and a host of petty tyrants disrupt human society. When the chips are down our allegiance is to God. What Paul calls "the powers" must bow to God. These powers are all our cultural institutions—family, commerce, culture, religion, and the state. We live our lives within this world. Our movements are subject to its restraints, but should be guided by God's will as revealed in Jesus Christ, our Lord.

It is hard to be in the world but not of it. Jesus calls us to be leaven and light in a sinful society. Jesus asks us to be Christian within the circumstances of our lives. We are all captives to a social situation that is not ideal. If you are tempted to become critical of these powers in America or Yachats you might consider places where social order has really crumbled. With the guidance of the Scriptures, the covenant of faith, and the leadership of the Holy Spirit we must figure out for ourselves what is right and wrong. God is our authority. All human authority is derivative. What belongs to Caesar? What God allows or delegates. Having caught us with society's coin in our hand Jesus makes us acknowledge we are part of a society, not standing apart from it. We are in the world. But we don't have to be worldly.

A thoughtful Jew in the crowd, listening to the dialogue with Jesus, would answer the question about what belongs to God by recalling the Sinai tablets, the covenant promises, rituals preserving awe before the Almighty, a history of sins and deliverance, a rich literature of devotion, a legacy of prophets who feared neither religious nor secular hierarchies in calling people to obedience to the Almighty. Today, as thoughtful Christians, to answer the question about what belongs to God we recall also the teachings of Jesus and the New Testament exhortations about love and truth and justice and mercy. These belong to human life and cannot really be pigeonholed within institutional forms. It is too simple to say that the state administers justice and the church love. Persons are whole and must be ministered to in whole ways. Service to others is service, under whatever agency.

Applications of our Scripture text

If you feel trapped by irksome government, consider Jeremiah's counsel when he exhorted Jewish captives: "Seek the peace and prosperity of the city to which I have carried you into exile. Pray to the Lord for it, because if it prospers, you too will prosper" (Jeremiah 29:7 NIV). Would it be apt to say all people of godly faith live in exile? That we are strangers in a strange land? That we are never quite "at home"? Like Joseph of old, we may feel that we've been sold to foreigners. So, do we gripe and complain? Of course, but mostly we work for good where circumstances have placed us. And when we do so we may find—especially in America, in Oregon, in Yachats—that much government is good despite bureaucratic excesses and political scandals. Paul, writing to Christians living in Rome, in less than ideal political circumstances, offers these suggestions about honoring God through government. These are the words of our Scripture.

Ponder them again. [See Romans 13:1-10 on page 191.]

It's helpful to consider submission in personal not institutional terms. Did you catch the implication of that last verse? Taxpaying and governance are ways to love your neighbor as yourself. At all levels, government means—or should mean—neighbors helping neighbors share the good life. As always, criticism is better when constructive.

I have been wondering: At the time these Pharisees and Herodians were trying to trap Jesus in order to bring him down, was a local city council in session, maybe trying to figure out how to keep the wells full and the aqueducts clean? Did the agenda include justly settling a property dispute? I wonder who attended. I wonder who engineered plans to increase the water supply, and who struggled during a fierce storm to repair the water lines?

Conclusion

What do I render to God?

- I worship God with awe, fear, love, and joy.
- I obey the moral law: God defines what is right and what is wrong.
- I express gratitude for God's forgiveness, grace, for salvation from sin.
- I show proper love for myself and my neighbor, as created in God's image.
- I demonstrate good stewardship of God's creation.

What do I render to Caesar?

- I honor those who govern as agents of God.
- I promote and accept laws supporting the common good, including taxation.
- I require those who govern to provide justice for myself and for others.
- I serve in government when it is needed and I am able.
- I pray for those in authority.

Let's close this worship by praying for elected officials. We will offer a time of silent prayer for each group of officials. If you feel led to offer vocal prayer, please stand and do so. Pray that officials may be granted wisdom, be kept from greed and from temptation, and from a lust for power. Pray that they will serve conscientiously. Pray that through their efforts local neighborhoods, regions, and the world will become better and safer places to live. Pray that justice may prevail forthrightly and not become bogged down in bureaucratic or partisan bickering. May our leaders do what is right and not what is expedient.

First we pray for our national leaders, for President Clinton, for members of Congress—especially those from Oregon: Ron Wyden, Gordon Smith, Darlene Hooley, Earl Blumenauer, Bob Smith, Elizabeth Furse, and Peter Defazio. We pray for the Supreme Court, and for ambassadors, and for the United Nations, and for international organizations that clothe and feed refugees, and work for peace.

Second we pray for our state leaders, for governor Kitzhaber, and for the legislators from our districts—Terry Thompson and Gary George. And for members of boards and courts and commissions [silent congregational prayer, followed by pastoral prayer].

Third, we pray for our county commissioners, Don Lindly, Nancy Leonard, and Jean Cowen and for the various agencies, courts, and staff who maintain records and keep things orderly [silent congregational prayer, followed by pastoral prayer].

Finally we pray for Yachats councilors, Don McDonald, Martha Dillen, Paul Plunk, and Joel Evans, and for city workers, and for other persons who volunteer to work on commissions or at the library and the Log Church Museum [silent prayer, followed by pastoral prayer].

And pray for me, as mayor, that I might have strength for the task—and wisdom [out of the silence a worshiper, Martha Beck, rose and prayed for me]. Amen.

The prayer of confession (in unison)

Lord, we sense your presence here. Show us how to be followers of Jesus in our daily life. Guide us by your Holy Spirit. We find it easier to criticize than to help. We grumble about the church. We complain about schools. We gripe about government. We grouse at neighbors, and sometimes at family members. Maybe we have good reasons, maybe we don't. But our attitude leaves something to be desired. We have received so much and ought to be more grateful. Forgive us. Teach us patience. Show us constructive ways to be involved in our town, in our state, in our nation, and in the world. May Christ use our witness as godly leaven in a troubled world. May our words and actions bring light to those who grope in the darkness.

Assurance of God's grace

Leader: Be of good cheer. God forgives and heals us. The Holy Spirit abides within us and among us. We can be renewed in righteousness.

People: Thank you, Lord, for mercy and for grace. Amen.

Justice and Mercy

Yachats Community Presbyterian Church, April 26, 1998

The Prayer of confession (in unison)

Lord, sometimes we don't hear your voice very clearly. Speak to us today through Scripture, song, litany, and sermon. Teach us through the example of persons with whom we worship. Touch us through hands that grasp our hands. Reach us through eyes that seek and meet our eyes. Most of all, Lord Jesus, preach to us in the inner sanctuary of our souls! Here we listen for your voice. Forgive our sins, mend our torn emotions, heal our hurts, calm our fears. Speak your words of peace, Lord, into our hearts.

Introduction

Last fall I preached a sermon about what belongs to Caesar and what belongs to God. Today we consider another pair of words: *justice* and *mercy*. A few weeks ago in Arkansas, two boys waylaid and shot classmates and a teacher. In the aftermath the public poured out compassion on the victims and pondered how judgment and mercy apply to the child perpetrators—and we cast about for who else might share the blame—family, television, whatever. To be "tough-minded but tenderhearted" is an admirable attitude, but to be both just and merciful isn't easy.

Does justice belong to the state and mercy to the church? No, both are moral principles basic to public and private life. Justice and mercy are required for social order. Both are divine commands. Laws support equity and the honoring of covenants. Mercy goes beyond minimal legality in order to demonstrate the compassion of God through "random acts of kindness" and through social structures such as families, health care, and education.

These two terms, or equivalents such as *judgment* or *kindness*, often appear linked together in the Bible. Listen for that linkage in the following Scripture verses (NIV):

Scripture reading
Micah 6:8 (NIV)

He has showed you, O man, what is good. And what does the Lord require of you? To act justly and to love mercy and to walk humbly with your God.

Amos 5:15

Hate evil, love good; maintain justice in the courts. Perhaps the Lord God Almighty will have mercy on the remnant of Joseph.

Zechariah 7:9

"This is what the Lord Almighty says: 'Administer true justice; show mercy and compassion to one another.'"

Psalm 43:1

Vindicate me, O God, and plead my cause against an ungodly nation; rescue me from deceitful and wicked men.

Isaiah 42:3

[speaking of the gentle strength of Messiah] A bruised reed he will not break, and a smoldering wick he will not snuff out. In faithfulness he will bring forth justice.

Matthew 23:23
"Woe to you, teachers of the law and Pharisees, you hypocrites! You give a tenth of your spices—mint, dill and cummin. But you have neglected the more important matters of the law—justice, mercy and faithfulness. You should have practiced the latter, without neglecting the former."

Consider justice

Justice comes in three forms: attributive, retributive, and distributive.

1. Attributive justice means offering a tribute for being a good person—made in God's likeness.

The horror of the Jonesboro tragedy was offset by a wide tribute to the courageous teacher who gave her life for a student. Attributive justice is offered through good wages, praise, memorials, and medals of honor. Even a thank-you card qualifies as a tribute—sometimes even just a parental smile or a good hug. In this place of worship, the McGuire Room and the Emma Adams Fellowship Hall commemorate two special persons. Senator Mark Hatfield's name appears on various Oregon buildings, a tribute to his legislative efforts. Recently members of this congregation joined with other family and friends to commemorate Bill Adams for his efforts in securing the 804 Smelt Sands trail. They prepared a large stone with a plaque as a tribute to Bill. These are examples of attributive justice. People deserve to be honored.

The danger, of course, is that certain attributions become selective commercial trade-offs, or ego-laden celebrity hype. In the media, ordinary folk who make the world a better place through being fair in their dealings don't get the recognition they often deserve. The church is a place where such worth ought to be, and generally is, quietly affirmed.

2. Retributive justice means imposing punishment for evil deeds.

Murder, theft, rape, financial scams, and other such crimes affront the Almighty. There is good reason to be outraged at acts of evil. God and humanity made in God's image are offended. In colonial America Jonathan Edwards once preached a sermon entitled "Sinners in the Hands of an Angry God." Curiously, this rather ponderously read sermon triggered a remarkable wave of penitence. Is our over-indulgent society ready for another great awakening based upon contrition for sin as an affront to God? Perhaps. Right now society mostly reacts harshly *against its own hurt* by building more prisons separating selected bad guys from us good guys. We have become harsh on crime but tolerant of a culture that spawns sophisticated theft and unsophisticated violence. Recently in Texas a woman was executed for murder. Her repentance seemed so genuine that thoughtful people are again asking whether capital punishment doesn't presume prerogatives of vengeance that belong only to God.

A culture that reduces principles to preferences finds it increasingly difficult to deal with evil. So it spawns a legal labyrinth to adjudicate conflicting preferences, driving society toward tyranny or anarchy. Either way, freedom suffers, and so do people.

3. Distributive justice means seeing that people are afforded equity in respect to goods, services, and opportunities—"life, liberty, and the pursuit of happiness."

Being fair is easier when we know people as neighbors rather than strangers. People who covenant together to be governed by constitutions and laws do so in order to achieve a balance of personal and corporate justice. But dividing the pie of goods and services, so to speak, isn't easy. If we are governed by principle not by preference, justice will come closer to God's will. This is true also if we put people ahead of rules. Secular as well as religious Pharisees use legal maneuvers that hurt people. Allowing fire district rescuers beach access at the Yachats River bay is more important than protecting a few square yards of broken shells. "Do unto others as you would have them do unto you" is a solid foundation for law.

Politically, conservatives espouse the rights of persons in particular, liberals the rights of people in general. Greed and avarice can be found in both groups. Recently as mayor I received a letter from a citizen suggesting that huge water bills, arising from homeowners' absence and neglect, should be forgiven. Ordinances don't fall from Mount Sinai, he said. He has a point; mercy sometimes is extended by local government in various ways. The dilemma is knowing when and whom to forgive, and whether mercy extended for one will become exploited for selfish gain by others. Which brings us to the topic of mercy.

Consider mercy

1. Mercy means acting compassionately to victims of misfortune.

A community shows mercy to persons who suffer from catastrophes such as fires or floods, or sick children. Our Yachats bulletin boards show how our townspeople are raising funds to help Matthew Schuster. Circumstances often bring burdens greater than can be borne by a family alone. Thursday the crew of the ship *Daio Azalea* plucked a shipwrecked yachtsman from the ocean off Coos Bay. International law requires mariners to assist others in distress. God asks us to love mercy whether it is legally mandated or not. All such actions reflect Jesus Christ, the supreme rescuer.

2. Mercy means acting compassionately to victims of injustice.

You remember the classic story Jesus told about an "outsider" Samaritan who showed mercy to the man who fell among thieves. What a powerful and apt parable! Because in some manner we have all been victims of injustice, and like the scribes, for one reason or another we have all passed by on the other side of victims of violence.

More than fifty years ago I sent off for a wrench set advertised in the Sunday supplement in glowing terms and at a low price. Well, it turned out to be a worthless miniature. Much later we were conned into a Ponzi scheme—an expensive lesson in not letting greed for gain cloud judgment, even when the scheme is couched in altruistic terms. I'll bet some of you have been ripped off too! It isn't pleasant! Fortunately I have never been physically assaulted, although once I thought a hitchhiker was going to do me in and take the car. How desperately I prayed!

Currently many Yachats homeowners feel like siege victims, wondering whether our homes and property will be taken or our entitlements justly upheld. [Reference is to a ten-year controversy in which certain activists asserted public right to an old right-of-way covered with beachfront homes, claiming that road realignment many decades previously had not officially "vacated" the never-built-upon right-of-way. After much legal wrangling, and enormous financial and emotional costs, a settlement was reached that guaranteed clear title to the homeowners. I was one of the effected property owners, and for much of the time a city council member.]

To act on behalf of victims requires compassionate use of time, energy, and money. Acts of mercy can be public as well as private. Bankruptcy laws give losers a new start. Courts award compensatory damages to people who have been hurt by others physically, financially, or emotionally. Pardons are given to guilty but penitent persons. Relatives and neighbors rally round victims of violence and threats of injustice just as they do around victims of a house fire or tornado. Mercy fulfills the law.

3. Mercy means acting compassionately toward perpetrators of injustice.

On the cross Jesus forgave a penitent thief hanging beside him. I wonder what the victims of that robber thought. My heart knows about forgiving those who despitefully use me, but my mind finds it easier to show mercy to victims of violence than to its perpetrators. It's front-page news when a Christian family follows Jesus' example by forgiving a drunk driver whose actions have taken the life of a child. What a powerful witness to Jesus' call for mercy.

Mercy doesn't mean giving in to wrong, however. Jesus spared the life of a woman taken in adultery but told her to sin no more. Zaccheus, a white-collar thief, promised Jesus to make a fourfold restitution for what he had extorted. It's no good saying everyone is a victim—of bad genes, environment, whatever. Mercy means honoring a person made in the image of God, however marred, by holding that one accountable for conduct. The term *penitentiary* comes from a view that incarcerating someone for a while might lead to penitence and an amendment of ways. It is an effort to blend justice with mercy. Sometimes it works, sometimes it doesn't. I know persons for whom it worked, who now lead constructive lives. Work camps and therapy are forms of mercy aimed at rehabilitation. They are redemptive alternatives to vengeance.

Within the Christian community to elder offenders is a way to call persons to account with the hope of restoring them to faithful discipleship. Some Mennonites have a practice of shunning people who sin against their community. Such tough love hopes penitence will arise when a conscience is cleared of self-deception by the censure of persons who love them and want their best. A sage from long ago, Catherine of Siena, used Jesus' parable of the good shepherd to depict the staff as justice, the sheepdog as conscience. If a person has the staff of justice then conscience will work: "Conscience barks like a dog, excitedly, until it rouses reason." Whoever has a conscience, said Catherine, has a capacity for justice (*The Dialogue*, Classics of Western Spirituality, Paulist Press, 1980, p. 257).

How to hear the barking dog is the problem! Maybe leg shackles and stocks and shunning would provide a shamed silence out of which conscience as the voice of God could be more distinctly heard. "With what judgment you judge, you shall be judged," said Jesus. This caution can lead us to extend no moral discipline, or it can prompt us to do so prayerfully, lest having preached to others we ourselves fall into sin. This thought leads to considering mercy in a fourth way.

4. Mercy means responding to others as God has responded to us.

Our cry for vengeance is muted in the face of God's overwhelming grace. The chorus from one of the songs in the musical *Jonah ben Amittai* (David Miller and Arthur O. Roberts, 1986) demonstrates this understandable cry for vengeance. Said Jonah:

> You are too tenderhearted, Lord,
>
> forgiving wicked folks who weep.
>
> That's why I tried to run to Spain.
>
> You have embarrassed me, me your trusted seer.

> And you yourself, whom they now fear
> will be forgotten in a year or two.
> You are too tenderhearted, Lord.
> Forgiving wicked folks who weep.

The old prophet needed to understand divine compassion, the kind demonstrated preeminently by Jesus' atoning death on the cross. And so must we. Every Sunday we pray the Lord's Prayer, which includes forgiving others as God has forgiven us. Jesus' tears at Golgotha were for all of us. Our compassion toward another—whether victim or perpetrator—is enhanced when we acknowledge that "all have sinned and come short of the glory of God." By this prayer we acknowledge that inescapably we are caught up in a maze of structural or personal evil that results in victims and victimizers. We acknowledge, also, that though we do not steal we sometimes covet; although we do no murder we sometimes hate. And that silently we may let others act unjustly to our advantage. Or be just legally but not morally, outwardly but not inwardly. Sometimes we have been unmerciful when we ought to have been kind.

We are all saved by grace. This doesn't license us to sin, at Christ's cost, but rather forces us to acknowledge that sin laces the human community in ways that make us—even against our best intentions—participants in injustice, persons ourselves in need of mercy, and needing courage and wisdom to extend mercy to others.

It is a mercy that God in Christ sets captives free, whether our chains are those of the oppressed or the oppressor. It is a mercy to check and correct the evildoer as well as to aid the victims of the evildoer. It is a mercy to overcome evil with good. Prayer is an act of mercy, for it triggers a turning from evil whether by the victim or the victimizer. Mercy shares the pain and burden sin imposes on others. Mercy does not indulge evil, but forgives and restores those who succumb to its power. Mercy does not deny the need for restitution or punishment, but it reaches beyond such requirements. Some things can never be made right again. Only divine forgiveness overcomes tragedies and makes us whole. Death yields to resurrection. Easter always reminds us of this truth.

Justice brings spiritual renewal to individuals, to families, nations. Of the Messiah, Isaiah wrote (42:1 NIV) "Here is my servant, whom I uphold, my chosen one in whom I delight; I will put my Spirit on him and he will bring justice to the nations." Justice and mercy signify the presence of God's kingdom. We are witnesses of that kingdom, come and coming among the nations.

Walk humbly

Our text from Micah includes a third exhortation; to walk humbly with our God. To act justly and to love mercy unerringly lead to humility. Justice is difficult to determine as well as to do. Mercy desensitizes us in its multiple requests. What can we do but humbly rest in God's amazing grace—grace that redeems, that cleanses from sin, and that restores us individually and as a people, in God's righteousness? Consider the words of the hymn "Amazing Grace."

A Job Well Done

Angell Job Corps Commencement, Waldport, Oregon, August 13, 1998

Do you know what's special about you graduates of Angell Job Corps? It's that you give dignity to the word *job*. You've been at the job corps and now you are ready to be employed in a full-time position. No word that is used to describe how one person serves others should be put down, like saying, "it's just a job," or "it's just a menial job." To hold a job is important. A medieval reformer, Martin Luther, whose father was a blacksmith, said we are all priests to our neighbors through the work we do. Through ordinary work we become God's messengers. Actually, the biblical word *messenger* is about the same as the word *angel*. So, shall we say you are angels from Angell Job Corps?

What I'm getting at is, there are no unimportant jobs, but rather various tasks requiring different kinds of muscular and mental skills. Honest work fulfills the divine call to love our neighbors as ourselves. Good work lets society function effectively, like a well-maintained machine. And it takes many kinds of skills to do this.

Recently you have been learning skills that make the world function rightly. You have learned crafts of carpentry, masonry, auto mechanics, clerical, plumbing, painting, forestry, culinary arts, and others. Furthermore, you have learned to apply these skills by jobs done for your neighbors in the area. As mayor of Yachats I speak on behalf of our citizens in saying, "We appreciate your work!" We appreciate you for work performed at the commons and the library, for building benches around town, and for serving dinners on many occasions. Yes, we are proud of you, proud of Angell Job Corps! We wish the best for you as you leave. We believe your polite, professional service will be appreciated in new neighborhoods where soon you will live and employ your skills.

During your stay at Angell Job Corps here on the beautiful Oregon coast you have acquired and sharpened special skills. You have discovered a vocation, a calling. You have also made friends with staff and students. Their support has been important. You are now ready to use these talents on behalf of new neighbors in new places. Your minds and your muscles have been trained to serve, and you anticipate opportunities to do so. It's an exciting time! I congratulate you on your achievements. I feel, and share, the excitement that comes from entering the next stage in your life. Part of that excitement is wanting to prove to others and to yourself that you can do a good job. You are eager to demonstrate this in new circumstances. But circumstances aren't always ideal, so I encourage you to persevere. Keep your wits when things are frustrating. People can be greedy, selfish, prejudiced, or lazy. Companies can be sold or go bankrupt, and workers get laid off. But many people are unselfish and most companies care for their employees. Be patient during hard times and humble during good times. Above all, keep on learning, always keep on learning! There is so much more to learn, not just about your craft, but about life itself. Keep your eye on these goals and you will find lasting satisfaction in the work that you do.

Great satisfaction comes from a job well done. Working competently lets us feel good about ourselves—whatever the job, whether or not we get praised, wherever we live. In the long run, pride of craft means more than financial success. Good work carries its own rewards. There's a lot of satisfaction when mind and muscle work smoothly together. To be a skilled worker means that a job is a central part of life and not just a forty-hour interlude to be endured for the sake of pleasant weekends.

When I toured this campus a few years ago a student proudly showed me a table she had designed and crafted. "I've hand rubbed it with forty coats of linseed oil," she said. The piece was truly beautiful to see and marvelous to touch. This Job Corps graduate may not be able to be that thorough with every cabinet she installs. But she had achieved competence in a craft. Competence brings satisfaction, and satisfaction brings inward peace. And inward peace helps us get along with family and friends and neighbors.

So, my young friends, take pride in knowing that when you have completed a task in a shop or in a field or in an office, your greatest satisfaction will come from putting your hands upon your work and saying to yourself: "I did a good job!"

A Job Well Done

Satisfaction comes in many ways,
in sports, good food, vacation days,
time spent with friends, or books,
by enhancing our, or others', looks.
Such pleasures come and go.

Most fun provides an afterglow
of joy, but some can leave a trail
of tears. One pleasure never fails
to satisfy: a job well done,
a job well done!

"Blessed Are the Peacemakers"

George Fox University, November 4, 1998

My friends at George Fox, I ask you to follow Jesus and be peacemakers. It's not easy to be Christlike. But it's worth it! My best counsel is to listen to what Jesus said to his first disciples, and to what by his Spirit he speaks to us today. I'll read the familiar lines from Matthew 5.

It's clear Jesus wants us to make the world a better place, to be like salt to preserve life, to make it palatable; to be like light, showing the way to the good life. I live on the shore of the Pacific Ocean. *Pacific* in Latin means peaceful. Storms that toss logs upon our shore make us wonder how appropriate the name is! A Latin term *paci ficari* literally means to make peace. A *pacifist* is one who makes peace. Does this word throw up a red flag? Do you think pacifism only refers to refusing military service? If so, this illustrates how meanings get rearranged when words are clear but their implications difficult to handle.

Consider a more inclusive approach. If you reconcile

Scripture reading
Matthew 5:3-16, emphasis mine (NIV here and in subsequent texts)

"Blessed are the poor in spirit, for theirs is the kingdom of heaven.

"Blessed are those who mourn, for they will be comforted.

"Blessed are the meek, for they will inherit the earth.

"Blessed are those who hunger and thirst for righteousness, for they will be filled.

"Blessed are the merciful, for they will be shown mercy.

"Blessed are the pure in heart, for they will see God.

"Blessed are the **peacemakers**, for they will be called children of God.

"Blessed are those who are persecuted because of righteousness, for theirs is the kingdom of heaven.

"Blessed are you when people insult you, persecute you and falsely say all kinds of evil against you because of me. Rejoice and be glad, because great is your reward in heaven, for in the same way they persecuted the prophets who were before you.

"You are the salt of the earth. But if the salt loses its saltiness, how can it be made salty again? It is no longer good for anything, except to be thrown out and trampled by men.

"You are the light of the world. A city on a hill cannot be hidden. Neither do people light a lamp and put it under a bowl. Instead they put it on its stand, and it gives light to everyone in the house. In the same way, let your light shine before men, that they may see your good deeds and praise your Father in heaven."

---

quarreling people, aren't you a peacemaker—a pacifist? Sure. If you legislate to provide justice, isn't that pacifism? Why not? And if you proclaim God's grace in such a way that a penitent sinner finds forgiveness, aren't you making peace? Of course. If you help a hurting neighbor, aren't you a peacemaker? Or negotiate a settlement between Israel and Palestine? Yes. But consider more complex scenarios. Bonhoeffer tried to assassinate Hitler in order to stop the genocide of the Jews and the gypsies. Was he a pacifist? What about the efforts to "pacify" Vietnam villages by spreading napalm, or—more recently—by bombing Bagdad? How about air strikes to stop Milosovic from driving ethnic Albanians out of Kosovo? Is this peacemaking? Hmm, well...the ambassador's mediation, perhaps, but bombs that kill people...?

It's easier to apply Jesus' words to interpersonal rather than to international relationships, but Jesus doesn't draw the line between private and public peacemaking. In every sphere of life how and when does peacemaking stay consistent with the spirit of Christ? That's the tough question! Jesus didn't make peacemaking easy for us. He didn't say, "Oh, well, my teachings don't apply until the millennium." He didn't limit neighbors to folk in our city or nation. Fortunately, Jesus did offer us his Spirit—to be with us forever.

My talk is part of the John Woolman series, named after an eighteenth-century New Jersey tailor whose quiet but tenacious faith in Jesus stirred Quaker and then Christian consciences a long way toward ending slavery. Why is Woolman a sort of Quaker saint? Because he just followed Jesus' list of the beatitudes from start to finish, and that's why he became such an exemplary peacemaker. Consider his "ladder of spiritual assent."

- He was certainly poor in spirit, humble, self-effacing.
- He demonstrated empathy, mourning over the pain of others.
- So meekly did he assert his convictions that even slave owners knew it was God's spirit rather than Woolman's that touched their consciences.
- A hunger for righteousness led him to act on principles, not just talk about them.
- He was merciful and compassionate to everyone, and to God's creatures.
- In purity of heart he saw God, and the kingdom God wants, on earth as in heaven.

So he became a peacemaker and suffered for it. But he served as salt in a tasteless culture and light to a dark world. The jewels in his heavenly crown are thousands of persons lifted from bondage, thousands of persons made sensitive to how justice fosters peace. You don't have to be a New Jersey tailor to be a peacemaker, You can be a George Fox University student letting Jesus Christ direct your life now, vocationally and avocationally, personally and publicly. You can take seriously Jesus' teaching: "Blessed are the peacemakers."

Let three principles guide your response: follow Jesus, bear the cross, and wear the crown.

First, to be a peacemaker means following Jesus.
This doesn't means wearing sandals and a robe, or being a carpenter in Nazareth. It does mean sharing widely the good news of God's grace to those you work with and live amongst. It does mean making Jesus' prayer to God your own: "Thy kingdom come, thy will be done, in earth as in heaven." Following Jesus means justice to the oppressed. It means loving God with heart, soul, mind, and strength, and your neighbor as yourself. It means holding to a single standard of truth ("let your yes be yes and your no, no"). Following Jesus means demonstrating compassion—clothing and feeding the destitute and the damaged. It means cherishing children and protecting them from exploitation. Following Jesus means acknowledging in deed that God has made of one blood all persons—we are all kinfolk, whatever our skin color, gender, physical shape, nationality, or language. Following Jesus is what peacemaking is all

about. Quite a challenge, isn't it? William Penn lamented that some folks want Jesus as Savior but not as Lord—a securer way of sinning, he added, because it comes at Christ's cost. Must Jesus bear the cross, alone? No, there's a cross for you and me.

Second, to be a peacemaker means bearing the cross.
Bearing the cross doesn't mean having to put up with rude customers, or breaking a leg during basketball season, or getting the flu during test week. It doesn't even mean coping with a family divorce or death in the family, although these are certainly burdens to be borne with prayer and the help of caring people. Bearing the cross does mean suffering loss because of your commitment to Jesus Christ. It hurts to be ridiculed, criticized, or smugly patronized for being a Christian. To bear the cross means to endure subtle and often cynical cultural pressure to scrap your faith and get on with "the real world." Cross-bearing may even mean coping with unbelief or compartmentalized belief within the church itself.

More importantly, to bear the cross means sweating out your own Golgotha, anguishing about how to confront evil in the world without using evil means to do so. How to avoid a loveless idealism, or a dishonest pragmatism. To be a peacemaker on campus, on the job, with the boss, with the coworkers. To build community, not destroy it. To bind up broken bodies and broken hearts and broken families and broken towns and broken nations and not get burned out doing so. Cross-bearing involves scheduling some of your time for peacemaking, like the medical teams who annually tithe their skills to bring compassionate healing to impoverished people. Cross-bearing means being bold for peace without becoming self-righteous and censorious, retaining compassion for victim and perpetrator, combining a burning zeal for truth with an intense love for persons.

And finally, cross-bearing means losing, if not your life, at least some of your dreams for God's kingdom where you live. If you are not betrayed by a kiss, you may be abandoned by friends in whom the cares of this world gradually choke out the seeds of truth. You may see only halting steps toward peace in complex situations like the entrenched tribalism in Ruanda or the Balkans, or the social chaos that fosters killings in schools, or drug entrapment, or economic oppression. Darkness at noon may mark your home or community. Or your own soul. Times will come when strength almost fails and you wonder whether, having preached to others, you yourself will be cast away. And you question whether God has forsaken you. Evil taunts; you feel its thorns in your mind, its spear in your heart. Drained of self you cling only to God and cry out with the words of Paul, "I have been crucified with Christ and I no longer live, but Christ lives in me. The life I live in the body, I live by faith in the Son of God, who loved me and gave himself for me" (Galatians 2:20).

This is cross-bearing. If you follow Jesus you bear the cross. Fortunately, Jesus has not left us alone. The risen Lord strengthens us. The Spirit Jesus sends enables us to bear the cross. The cross isn't God's final word, resurrection is. Thus my third point.

Third, to be a peacemaker means wearing the crown.
Paul wrote to young Timothy: "Now there is in store for me the crown of righteousness, which the Lord, the righteous Judge, will award to me on that day—and not only to me,

but also to all who have longed for his appearing" (2 Timothy 4:8).

Doing right is its own reward, of course. To have a clear conscience takes a heavy burden off our minds, doesn't it? Doing right even if we suffer for it brings joyous unity with our Lord Jesus Christ and with all who have longed for his appearing, the saints past and present.

Beauty marks the road of holiness all the way, from poverty of spirit to peacemaking. The creation itself seems to glow when we express love toward God, toward neighbors, and to earth's creatures. The universe, as Paul said, groans under the burden of human sin, awaiting redemption. And then comes awards day, graduation—when God says to us, "Well done, good and faithful servants, enter into my joy!" Having glimpsed the garden city, the New Jerusalem, our excitement can only increase with the promise of a cosmos renewed in righteousness—unmarred by sin—and our continued presence in it. No more tears, no more sorrow. Such is the resurrection promise. This is our guiding light. Do you wish to be a peacemaker? Do so in the strength and wisdom of God's Spirit, valiant for Truth. Follow Jesus. Bear the cross. Wear the crown.

Marking Time

Yachats Community Presbyterian Church, December 1995; Berkeley Friends Church, February 14, 1996; Twin Rocks Friends Camp, September, 1999

I like to watch odometers turn from nines to zeros and flip to a higher set of numbers. Turning the first thousand (1,000) miles on a new car is fun to watch! Subsequent ones quicken the pulse, too: watching four zeros pop up to mark ten thousand, reaching fifty thousand. To watch the odometer roll up five zeros at one hundred thousand miles calls for celebration (and arranging a major tune-up). By adroit planning (such as circling the block a few times) one arrives at one's garage at just the right time, thus savoring the magic moment! Do you share my pleasure in such markings in time and space?

If this seems silly consider more meritorious events: birthdays and anniversaries, national holidays, inaugurals, the dawning of a new year. Daily devotions and weekly worship are mini-celebrations of the work of the Spirit within time and space.

We now approach a major marker—the coming of the third millennium. Not just a new decade or a new century. A new millennium dawns, two thousand years of Christian faith. Three zeros turning up on history's most important odometer. Actually the year 2000 is the last one of the second millennium, and January 1, 2001, begins the third; but in our fascination with zeroes we fudge a bit. Oh, there are other calendars—Jewish, Islamic, Chinese, for example—and any numbering system is arbitrary, but our calendar is a significant way to mark time. Let's invest the year 2000-2001 with special significance.

Separating hype from hope

This turning time has been advanced as a date for the second coming, because it

Scripture reading
Psalm 90:1-12 (NRSV)

A Prayer of Moses, the man of God.

Lord, you have been our dwelling-place in all generations.

Before the mountains were brought forth, or ever you had formed the earth and the world, from everlasting to everlasting you are God.

You turn us back to dust, and say, "Turn back, you mortals."

For a thousand years in your sight are like yesterday when it is past, or like a watch in the night.

You sweep them away; they are like a dream, like grass that is renewed in the morning;

in the morning it flourishes and is renewed; in the evening it fades and withers.

For we are consumed by your anger; by your wrath we are overwhelmed.

You have set our iniquities before you, our secret sins in the light of your countenance.

For all our days pass away under your wrath; our years come to an end like a sigh.

The days of our life are seventy years, or perhaps eighty, if we are strong; even then their span is only toil and trouble; they are soon gone, and we fly away.

Who considers the power of your anger? Your wrath is as great as the fear that is due to you.

So teach us to count our days that we may gain a wise heart.

fits an old scheme, influenced by Ussher's chronology (2,000 years to Abraham, 2,000 to Jesus, 2,000 to the return of Jesus). The scheme is arbitrary and contrived, but at least this major calendar turn-over prompts us to consider things in a context of God's purposes. In the depression-ridden 1930s, speculation about the second coming was rife. Prophecy charts showed the end of the church age, how Russia was Gog, and suggested the armies of Armageddon. That apocalyptic fervor returned twenty years later when nuclear war seemed ominous, and it has been renewed at century's end.

Millennial fervor received impetus in America from colonial scholars Jonathan Edwards and Timothy Dwight. The latter predicted the Jews would get Palestine as their Caanan and North America would become the new Caanan for gentiles. This variant to British Israelism offered a catchy combination of patriotism and kingdom talk, an odd amalgam that continues to characterize prophetic pronouncements. In *Reckoning with Apocalypse: Terminal Politics and Christian Hope* (New York: Crossroads, 1993, p. 63), Dale Aukerman warns against this unholy marriage of nationalistic and apocalyptic aims. He thinks pretribulation rapture talk "is the religious counterpart of 'Star Wars.' In such a scenario church folk can evade the way of the cross by siding with militarist nationalism and can then evade the consequences when those come."

With the year 2000 looming (or some thirty some years later if dated from the resurrection), prophetic popularizers busily hyped their conjectures in books and cassettes in the 1990s. John Walvoord's *Armageddon, Oil, and the Middle East Crisis* sold a million copies. "Is Saddam the Antichrist?" reflects a typical sermonic shift from the Russian bear to newly demonized Arabic groups. A predicted date of September 1994 came and went without any unusual divine appearance; but speculation continued. Conspiracy theories were rife. *The McAlvany Intelligence Advisor*, a monthly journal out of Phoenix, Arizona, indicts various persons alleged to be fostering America's plunge into an awful New World Order. Prominent among groups indicted by these alarmists are the generic "Liberal Eastern Establishment" and specific ones such as the Council on Foreign Relations, and the Trilateral Commission. McAlvany hints that the year 2000 could witness the rise of the antichrist, whom he associates with world government. His clients and magazine readers are advised to get rid of stocks and bonds and property, sell their city houses, store dried food, and head for the hills. And invest in gold or silver. McAlvany just happens to be a broker of these metals.

At the end of the decade speculation took on a new dimension. Because IBM mainframes twenty years ago lacked the versatility of the MacIntosh computer platforms, the "Y2K problem" has heaped fuel on fires of speculation. Cities and corporations are spending huge sums to correct this, and predictions range from "no problem" to disaster. Historian Gary North opts for the latter. He thinks the chaos occurring on December 31 of this year will be like the tower of Babel, "the biggest problem that the modern world has ever faced." He and others foresee the computer failure as a trigger mechanism sending civilization into a tailspin not experienced since the fall of Rome. How they tie it in with the second coming isn't so clear, but *they* see it as God bringing judgment upon the earth. (See, for example, *Y2K Tidal Wave*, Armageddon

Books, 1999, also McAlvany's Web site and that of others, on the Internet. See also a critique by Susan Bauer "Y2Krazy" in Sept.-Oct. *Books and Culture*.) Hal Lindsey, Michael Hyatt, Steve Farrar, and Grant Jeffrey are among evangelical scholars whose alarmist books urge survivalist techniques, and often offer the entrepreneurship that profits from it—a situation at odds with prophetic integrity.

This and other such movements feed on fear of the unknown, apprehensions about the pace and significance of technology, and a generic distrust of government. Of course there's evil in the world, but trying to encircle it within one group or another only obscures the subtle powers of evil. Conspiracy theories deny the triumph of Christ over Satan. Their theories blind people to real demonic power. As Aukerman says (*Reckoning*, p. 107): "Only when disciples recognize where and what Babylon is can they depart from it. In any century disciples are to struggle for discernment of what constitutes Babylon, the beast, and the imperial image, lest they be drawn into that insurgency against God....Babylon should always be seen as occupying power."

To keep hope from degenerating into hype, recall the words of Jesus: "No one knows about that day or hour, not even the angels in heaven, nor the Son, but only the Father" (Mark 13:32 NIV). Even after the resurrection the disciples confused Christ's vision of cosmic renewal with nationalistic interests. "Lord," they asked him, "are you at this time going to restore the kingdom to Israel?" Jesus replied, "It is not for you to know the times or dates the Father has set by his own authority. But you will receive power when the Holy Spirit comes on you; and you will be my witnesses in Jerusalem, and in all Judea and Samaria, and to the ends of the earth" (Acts 1:6-8 NIV).

Our Lord's words are clear, aren't they? God's gift is the Holy Spirit, not privileged foreknowledge. Jesus' words are a command to witness the good news to all humanity, not a license for political leverage. The future is contingent upon human responses to divine initiatives. Don't get trapped by prophecy hype. We are called to faithful discipleship not to speculation about the future. Our summons at millennial turning is to bright hope in Jesus Christ, not to dark paranoia or triumphalist judgment.

Approaching the new millennium constructively

Some of us will just be glad *to reach* the third millennium, to watch that row of nines on the calendar turn to zeroes, and the one to flip up heralding the new era. There are other personal and social goals worth deeper pondering. I'll suggest a few.

1. Use this millennial turning to look back, to examine our historic journey through time and space. We are twentieth-century folks. And our century has been a violent one. At its beginning the slogan "the world for Christ in our generation" quickened college youth to volunteer for missionary and educational service around the world. At its end idealism has waned and cynicism waxed. Civility has crumbled. What binds society together is a volatile mix of violence, self-interest, and commercial exploitation. Or so it seems.

Acknowledging divine judgment over sin is one way to accept this tarnished century. Humbly we accept God's mercy and forgiveness. We can use these transitional years to reflect upon our country's heritage, and, more importantly, to consider how the church has moved through the centuries. How has the leaven of the gospel permeated culture? How has Christ's light drawn people to God's kingdom?

At the end of the second millennium, old inter-church rivalries have subsided. Protestants no longer treat Catholics as pagan; Catholics no longer anathematize Protestants. In many countries of the world, ordinary people—as well as their leaders—reach across denominational boundaries to affirm a common Christian homeland. In China the gospel leaven worked after missionaries were expelled. In Russia the churches offered light during dark decades, and now provide the moral ground for rebuilding social order. In Africa and Latin America the gospel became strong, to the tearing down of strongholds of sin and the building up of the kingdom.

Gazing backward a thousand years we must acknowledge the power of the gospel to transform lives and to mold society. Only pockets of religious people now justify crusades. Those who do are generally labeled terrorists, not heroes. Nobody *justifies* slavery. Women have achieved greater equality. Christian compassion has built hospitals, stimulated medical advances, and provided care homes and hospices. Confidence in God as Creator has overcome animistic fears. This enabled science to arise, based upon reliability of the created order. Yes, looking back we can see, like the wake of a ship, a path from worse to better. Not because of the passage of time, but because of the faithful witness of people like you and me. Not for every ship, but for the ones driven by the wind of the Spirit.

So let's look at what was going on in the world at the end of the first millennium of the Christian era. Was there apocalyptic fervor when the odometer of European chariot wheels clocked 999 years since Christ? Yes, some, but no more than other dates such as 1660. Scholars argue over this. For our purposes it is more important to see this era in context.

For Europe, recovery from the collapse of Rome provided contextual boundaries. This collapse came about for various reasons that you studied in history of civilization several decades ago! Here's one historian's assessment and his summary. Thomas Cahill writes: "Changing character of the native population brought about through unmarked pressures on porous borders; the creation of an increasingly unwieldy and rigid bureaucracy, whose own survival becomes its overriding goal; the despising of the military and the avoidance of its service by established families...lip service paid to values long dead; the pretense that we still are what we once were; [polarity] into richer and poorer..." (*How the Irish Saved Civilization*, Doubleday, 1995, pp. 29-30).

Pax Romana had been broken centuries before, but the dream of unified society lingered in the development of imperial authority and in the preservation of literature. Charlemagne's coronation in A.D. 800, and more pointedly the crowning of Otto I—a German (Saxon)—in 962 witnessed to the quest for imperial authority. At the time of his death in 1002, the fiction of the Holy Roman Empire was established. It was built upon the merged dreams of world religion and world monarchy—the king as the Lord's anointed. The unity of the church has survived the collapse of Rome, but not the unity of governance. The pope was the vicar of Christ on spiritual order, the emperor God's agent on behalf of temporal order. A fiction it was, because it only comprised a portion of Europe—Germany was fragmented, and France quite independent. And it ignored the cultural unity of the Byzantine empire to the east. And, of course, the rest of the world. (*Great Events*, vol. 3, Frank Magill, ed., Salem Press, 1973, offers useful historical data.)

Creative movements distill, preserve, and expand value in the face of cultural disintegration. It's the phenomenon of the saving remnant. Irish monasticism was one such movement, leaven working during the dark ages between the collapse of Rome and the dawning of the second millennium. The Irish *peregrini* preserved the manuscripts of the ancient world, but they did more. They were missionaries, and they recovered a theology of creation (Cahill, *How the Irish*). Cahill notes that Patrick was the first true missionary to persons outside the pale—that is, to the barbarians, the Ecumene. (Even Thomas went to Hellenized India.) "What is remarkable," he writes, "is not that Patrick should have felt an overwhelming sense of mission but that in the four centuries between Paul and Patrick there are no missionaries [of this sort]." Despite the superstitious Irish warriors, terrorized by fear assuaged by nightly getting drunk, "Patrick's peace was no sham: it issued from his person like a fragrance."

Irish Christianity contributed much to a recovery of a biblical doctrine of creation—of nature. These earthy folk reaffirmed the Hebrew awe that the earth is the Lord's. As Cahill writes, with understandable overstatement (*How the Irish*, p. 133): "This sense of the world as holy, as the Book of God—as a healing mystery, fraught with divine messages—could never have risen out of Greco-Roman civilization, threaded with the profound pessimism of the ancients and their Platonic suspicion of the body as unholy and the world as devoid of meaning." (But what about the Greek gymnasia, and their sculptures?)

"In this tradition, there is a trust in the objects of sensory perception, which are seen as signposts from God. But there is also a sensuous reveling in the splendors of the created world which would have made Roman Christians exceedingly uncomfortable."

What was going on in and around the year 1000 that shaped the modern world?

Peak of Byzantine power. From the fifth to the fifteenth centuries, Constantinople was the greatest market center in the world. Under Justinian, Nestorian monks had ventured to China, and trade flowed. Silk became a major manufacturing item. Art and architecture were well done. For several centuries the economy was strong, medicine advanced, culture was sophisticated. Code Justinian offered a system of justice. Women had rights, universities flourished. Hypatia, a woman philosopher and a major intellectual force, as a pagan was so influential the monks battered her to death and dismembered her corpse. Simeon the Theologian sought to encourage mystical, experiential faith. (See "Vision of the Light," *Discourses*, Classics of Western Spirituality, Paulist Press, 1980, pp. 245ff.) At millennium, Basil II was a strong warrior, but more Spartan than Athenian. Culture declined until in 1071 the eastern empire was decimated by Normans and Turks, until in 1453 Constantinople fell to Islam.

The rise of Islam. Turkey, Mesopotamia, Syria, Afghanistan, all of Persia, Armenia, and much of India were brought under Muslim dominance, especially under Mahmud (998-1030). Cultural centers and universities merged Turkish and Arabic peoples under one strong ideology. Wealth piled up from subjugation and colonization. In 1005-1015 Avicenna completed his *Canons of Medicine*, dealing with diseases, drugs, psychological problems. His views held authority for centuries. Muslim invasion of India occurred in 1000.

Reunification of China. Under the Song dynasty, a neo-Confucian, rigidly ordered, holistic social order lasted until the nineteenth century. It exhibited cultural creativity and literature (block printing was invented two centuries before during the Tang dynasty).

Emergence of Christian leadership in Europe beyond Britain, France, and Italy. A thousand years ago the gospel came to Russia under Vladimir, to Norway under Olaf Tryggvason, to Austria under missionaries invited by king Boleslav II, to Poland under Boleslav the Brave. Bernard of Menthon established a monastery on an Alpine pass as a haven for travelers at risk by storms and bandits. His dogs helped rescue lost travelers. In the year 1000 the prince of the Keraits, a Turkish people, accepted Christianity. Culture took shape through Christian leavening. Not only through cathedrals, as the dominant architectural symbols, but schools as well, and medieval drama. Songs and litanies such as *Te Deum Laudamus* and "the peace of God," and "rules of war" may have been triggered by apocalyptic hopes. Ruling kings were: Canute of Denmark/England/Norway, Christian king 1019-1035; Olaf Tryggvason, king of Norway 995-1000. Conversion of Hungary occurred under Stephen (Vajk), king 997-1000. Stephen sought from Pope Sylvester recognition as king and the authority to organize the church. Crowned in 1000, Stephen founded a unified Hungarian state, with monetary system, codification of law, organized defense. He was canonized in 1083. Pagan uprising took place in 1046 with massacre of Christians; restoration occurred under Ladislas I, and Croatia and Dalmatia were added to the realm.

The Conversion of Russia to Christianity. Vladimir of Kiev, 980-1015, induced the civilizing force of Byzantium upon Slavic people. The patient missionary work of Cyril and Methodius in the eighth century had produced an alphabet and literacy, turning the vernacular into written language. Legend has it that Vladimir sent envoys to investigate Islam, but he liked pork and wine. He rejected Roman Catholicism ("fasting is too dour"). He liked the beauty of the Greek liturgy and the splendor of Constantinople. This gave Russian religion a strong inter-tie between aesthetics and belief. *Orthodoxy* came to mean not just correct theology but also "true glory." Theodosius, founder of Russian monasticism, showed Christian social concern by working with serfs. Orthodoxy developed a mystique known as the "Third Rome" after the fall of Constantinople.

What were the constants in human understanding at the year 1000? An order to things, the arrow of time, a mystery beyond order, fear of God, and a hope for a better future. The disciplines of spirituality—although often in monastic forms of withdrawal from the world—were already fecund. Consider a passage from the *Discourses* of Symeon, an abbot of Eastern Orthodoxy. Symeon was referred to as "the new theologian." He represented the continuity of experiential, mystical Christianity against which more pragmatic religious institutions were measured for their faithfulness to God. In one of his morning discourses to the monks, Symeon writes (*Discourses*,

Classics of Western Spirituality, 24, no. 7, pp. 248-249):

> When God brings His hidden saints to light it is in order that some may emulate them and others be without excuse. Those who wish to remain amid distractions as well as those who live a worthy life in communities, in mountains, and in caverns (Hebrews 11:38) are saved, and God bestows on them great blessings solely because they have faith in Him....He who has promised to save by faith alone does not lie, my brethren! So show mercy to yourselves and to us, who love you and often lament and shed tears over you—for God, who is compassionate and merciful, commands us to be such! Believe in the Lord with all your soul....Draw near to Him....Without Him there is no place to stand, no limit, nothing to hold back sinners as they fall.

Without God, there's no place to stand. In 1969 D. Elton Trueblood, a Quaker philosopher, wrote a book with the title *A Place to Stand*, showing that both intellectual and spiritual integrity require such a basic premise. Coming closer to our time, let's consider the interval between 1000 and 2000. What was permanent, what changed? What produced disintegration of society, what produced unity? Consider what has forced a world unity of sorts: demographic expansion by Columbus, Balboa, Magellan, Cook, the arctic explorers. Ponder the impact on old societies—by discovery and colonization, by the Black Plague, an import that nearly destroyed Europe. What happened to the indigenous peoples during expansion? Compare Tasmanians with Inuit. Slavery within Africa and exported for colonization heightened a tension between empire and tribe and facilitated the emergence of dominant languages.

Think of the major discoveries and inventions since 1000: calendar, moveable type, combustion engine, table of the elements, electricity, vaccines, atomic/nuclear energy, moveable sound, computer technology, and looming on the horizon—genetic manipulation and artificial intelligence.

The thirteenth century was a high point in the medieval fusion of religion and governance, followed by industrial and then technical revolutions, the Reformation and religious awakenings, the Renaissance and the Enlightenment, the rise of national state system, the development of free churches, parliamentary governance, and democracy. But note also violence on a scale not experienced before—from Ghengis Khan to Stalin, from the Hundred Years' War to the Thirty Years' War to the terrible wars of the 1900s.

Jacques Ellul, in *The Betrayal of the West* (Seabury Press, 1978, pp. 197-199), offers a pessimistic assessment: three movements—blind negation, "frenzied pleasure in destroying"; movement without direction, "we are rushing nowhere at an ever-increasing speed"; and repetitiveness within acceleration, a world of limitless repetitions, "a thousand books on a novel idea"—"end of reason," "end of self-awareness," "end of self-criticism," "end of freedom." Barely masked fear marks our age, even in affluent societies. Film has been able to hype the anxiety of the affluent at the end of our age. As Amanda Loos writes, "Hollywood has... [produced] explosive blockbusters which prey upon, hype up and commodify millennial fervor and end-of-the-world anxiety" (see "Visioning the Apocalypse" from Internet, Millennium Web site).

2. Use this millennial turning to look around, to assess the circumstances of our lives now.
Looking around can make us depressed and sad. Is the

world better or worse than it used to be? The answer depends upon what our experiences have been, what standards we apply, and how to sample society. On the one hand it looks like the world has become worse. Ponder the callous killing of civilians in recent wars, tribal violence, political corruption, scam artists who victimize vulnerable people, senseless inner-city shootings, and drug abuse. The news parades moral degeneration—mothers killing their children, children killing their parents and siblings. Marriages fall apart more easily than they did, and people who grew up with unlocked doors now bolt them securely. More optimistically: better health and living conditions for the first world; struggles upward for the developing countries. Space exploration, with prospect to escape the pollution of the planet Earth.

What is permanent, what changes? Examine the matrix of change:

Cultural: music, arts, social interaction, exponential electronic access to art. Consider crossword puzzles as cultural indicators: Celebrity names (twenty on one), require television or movie viewing—not books—for one to know the answer. What is permanent? The tension between the urge to build and the urge to destroy. In the quest for beauty, the persistence of that triad of the human spirit: faith, hope, love. What is changing? Styles, technology, cultural models.

Political: democracy in conflict with various tyrannical or anarchic powers. What is permanent? The desire to belong—a tension between the individual and the group, the one and the many. What is changing: the size of the "neighborhood"—it's become global.

Scientific: significant advancements in medicine, transportation, restructured consciousness and social organization; ways of learning; communication.

Economic: market-driven now, with material goods the sign of prosperity.

Religious: a tension between the particular and the universal. Christian claims for unique events in tension with a quest for tolerance of all systems of belief and thought. The particular and the universal are in high and uneasy tension.

Demographic factors: Reflect upon changes in population, climate, environment.

Constructively, consider how the leaven of the gospel is calling Protestants and Catholics to peace in North Ireland. Think of all the people who work to educate children, to aid the unfortunate, to make the lives of others better, to bring joy through the arts, to use technology to relieve poverty and sickness. There are many unheralded heroes. Beneath surface cynicism is a deep hunger for God and latent faith despite loud and secular skepticism. Although the world's weather is harsh, love prevails inside communities of faith, hurt people find healing, children learn Bible truths, sinning people find forgiveness. Inquiring, awe-stricken minds find order and beauty in the universe and have ears open to hear the voice of God. Across the globe millions of people profess faith in Christ.

How might we witness to the power of God's grace and the beauty of God's truth? How might we light candles in the darkness of our own community? This is a good time to look around prayerfully for kingdom work to do.

3. Use this millennial turning to look ahead.

We can do this by feeding on apocalyptic fears. Y2K disruption triggering nuclear disaster, Muslim fanatics instigating a reign of terror through bombings, nerve gas, biological agents. Climate-induced disasters, including tidal waves destroying coastal cities (Bangladesh nearly wiped out). Plague from mutated viruses. Artificial intelligence goes amok. A comet strikes the earth and destroys the human population—or large segments of it. Space invasion by superior races eager to prevent the human virus from contaminating the universe. Clarke's monolith and its shadowy super lord. Or we can feed on religious scenarios, for example, Jesus' return in year 2000. We could parse Daniel's prophecy to demonize some nation, and spot the Antichrist arising from within Islam; or see Saddam Hussein, for example, as being in league with religious liberalism that embraces pluralism. Or see world government in league with ecumenical religion. Or the Trilateral Commission and corporate domination of the world by IBM or Bill Gates.

We could become obsessed with such apocalyptic scenarios; or, more positively, we can face up to life changes in the next century and beyond as friends of Jesus, willing to occupy until he comes. To contextualize without compromise is a current missionary slogan. So what will be the context? What computer technology will do to civilization is almost beyond imagination. Genetic manipulation is scary. We can forecast an increased blurring between natural and virtual reality. Some biblical passages imply that when things get too terrible, the second coming is assured. On the basis of that view some Christians object to social reform or new technologies, for fear of hindering God's plan. They seem to welcome social tragedy as a sign of Jesus' coming. Others, however, cite the parables of Jesus about leaven in the loaf and tiny mustard seeds growing to large bushes. And they recall Jesus' words telling us to occupy until he comes. These Christians believe the work of the Spirit will make things better and prepare the way for Jesus to bring the kingdom to fruition.

Is the future more promising or less so? Will evil flourish, or the good? *Both*. Evil increases in resistance to God's will, and greater intelligence enhances the capacity for evil doing, as we have learned to our sorrow. Technology doesn't automatically advance the good. But evil is self-defeating. Goodness is never self-defeating. It beats swords into plowshares at every level of technology. People love darkness because their deeds are evil, but light diminishes darkness. Judges it. Dispels it. Darkness can't put out light. The good gleams brighter as the world gets darker. This is God's world. One day history as we know it will wind to a close. Before the Prince of Peace every knee shall bow, in heaven and on earth. Then the Lord of Glory will gather tribes and tongues and nations and we shall be one flock and one people. The new heavens and a new earth will be marked by the righteousness so joyously acclaimed during Advent season. The whole cosmos will be renewed according to God's purposes. It's good to take the long view at this time of millennial turning. As Nilos Kazantzakis wrote in *The Saviors of God* (Simon and Schuster, 1960)

> Train your heart to govern as spacious an arena as it can. Encompass through one century, then through two centuries, through three, through ten, through as many centuries as you can bear, the onward march of mankind. Train your eye to gaze on people moving in great stretches of time.

We share in humanity's march toward the Promised Land. Jesus' resurrection is the victory that assures our own participation, now and in heaven. Baptism by the Holy Spirit is our down payment on humanity's future home. The kingdom is here like leaven in the loaf, and the dough is rising. The kingdom comes, personally and cosmically. Not some Darwinian survival of the fittest, not some cosmic accident a million years away marks our personal and corporate destiny, but the kingdom, coming in God's own time and way. The Lord of creation is also the Lord of redemption. Isaiah's vision of the peaceable kingdom sustains this hope: "They will not hurt or destroy on all my holy mountain; for the earth will be full of the knowledge of the Lord as the waters cover the sea" (Isaiah 11:9 NRSV).

4. Celebrate the third millennium.

One thing we can do together, after looking back, looking around, and looking ahead: We can celebrate the third millennium. The ancient Israelites provided for a special jubilee every forty-ninth year. This was a time to redress inequities and make new beginnings. We can do the same. We can forgive grudges, quit grumbling, spruce up our personalities, worship God instead of things—or instead of the self. Together we can rejoice that Light shines in the darkness. Why not have a real party to celebrate the work of the Spirit in the world during the past two thousand years? To celebrate is a sign of wisdom. As Frederick Buechner wrote:

> No matter how swiftly the torrent tumbles, there come moments when, rounding a bend or where the streambed deepens, it flattens out suddenly to a surface so slow and smooth that you can almost see down to the bottom of it. (*The Sacred Journey*, Harper, 1991, p. 212)

This is a time when we can almost see to the bottom of things. A time to get intoxicated with the Holy Spirit. Because of our secular society, I don't suppose schools can celebrate, but families and churches can. It's time to plan the millennial year celebration (2000-2001) by writing plays and stories, composing songs and poems, scheduling festivities, inviting friends and neighbors from around the world to join us. We can celebrate right where we live.

It's a time, too, for making pilgrimages of the spirit, forsaking dull and perfunctory discipleship for an exciting trek to an inner holy place where God and the soul unite in ecstasy. Let new perspectives enter center stage the drama of your salvation. These are jubilee years! As celebrants we wait, lamps trimmed and hopes bright, for the entrance of the heavenly Bridegroom. Wrote one old saint, Abraham Isaac Kook:

> Each time that the heart feels a truly spiritual stirring, each time that a new and noble thought is born, we are as though listening to the voice of an angel of God who is knocking, pressing on the doors of our soul, asking that we open our door to him that he might appear before us in his full majesty. ("Lights of Holiness," Classics of Western Spirituality, 1978, p. 212)

The Crisis of Faith

Reedwood Friends Church, June 27, 1999

That God's word in our hearts should flourish and bear fruit is the point of this parable. In other parables Jesus left closure to the hearer. In this case he provides the interpretation. The parable shows three instances of failure: first, the seed didn't properly germinate; second, the sprouted seed was shallow-rooted and withered; and third, the plants that did grow got crowded out and bore no fruit. In contrast, seed received by well-tended soil grew and multiplied at various exponential levels. This parable teaches us something about the crisis of faith in our times.

Consider the seed on the path. Here intellectual difficulties precipitate loss of godly faith.

What is sown in the heart is snatched away by unbelief. Some of us have been so trampled by truckloads of information that the divine word can't sink in. We hear but don't understand. In a culture of unbelief, minds that should be God's garden spots become trampled human thoroughfares. So

Scripture reading
Jesus' parable of the seed and soil (from Matthew 13:3-9, 18-23 NRSV)

And he told them many things in parables, saying: "Listen! A sower went out to sow. And as he sowed, some seeds fell on the path, and the birds came and ate them up. Other seeds fell on rocky ground, where they did not have much soil, and they sprang up quickly, since they had no depth of soil. But when the sun rose, they were scorched; and since they had no root, they withered away. Other seeds fell among thorns, and the thorns grew up and choked them. Other seeds fell on good soil and brought forth grain, some a hundredfold, some sixty, some thirty. Let anyone with ears listen!"

"Hear then the parable of the sower. When anyone hears the word of the kingdom and does not understand it, the evil one comes and snatches away what is sown in the heart; this is what was sown on the path. As for what was sown on rocky ground, this is the one who hears the word and immediately receives it with joy; yet such a person has no root, but endures only for a while, and when trouble or persecution arises on account of the word, that person immediately falls away. As for what was sown among thorns, this is the one who hears the word, but the cares of the world and the lure of wealth choke the word, and it yields nothing. But as for what was sown on good soil, this is the one who hears the word and understands it, who indeed bears fruit and yields, in one case a hundredfold, in another sixty, and in another thirty."

God's seed doesn't receive sufficient moisture and nutrients to germinate. Is it the hearer's fault, or the fault of others? Either, or both, perhaps. In any case, a mind that ought to be receptive to God's revealed truth has become hardened against wonder, mystery, revelation. If understanding is beaten down by huckstered data, then the soul becomes impervious to God. Skepticism erodes first belief, then values. It's not hard to discern such scenarios in our society, is it? Maybe even in those we love? Or in ourselves? People are concerned about paving over prime farmland. How much more ought we be concerned about paving over the soul. It's trendy now to tout intellectual superiority over previous ages, to discount Bible history, to portray New Testament miracles as so much PR spin, to deconstruct what Jesus said, to deny central Christian teachings about the atonement and the resurrection of Christ. John Updike shakes a prophetic finger against such snatching away of God's seeds of truth in the world and in the heart. In a poem "Seven Stanzas at Easter" (*Telephone Poles*, Knopf, 1979) he writes:

Seven Stanzas at Easter

Make no mistake: if He rose at all
it was as His body;
if the cells' dissolution did not reverse, the molecules
reknit, the animo acids rekindle,
the Church will fall.

It was not as the flowers,
each soft Spring recurrent;
it was not as His Spirit in the mouths and fuddled
eyes of the eleven apostles;
It was as His flesh: ours.

The same hinged thumbs and toes,
the same valved heart
that—pierced—died, withered, paused, and then
regathered out of enduring Might
new strength to enclose.

Let us not mock God with metaphor,
analogy, sidestepping transcendence;
making of the event a parable, a sign painted in the
faded credulity of earlier ages:
let us walk through the door.

The stone is rolled back, not papier-mâché,
not a stone in a story,
but the vast rock of materiality that in the slow
grinding of time will eclipse for each of us
the wide light of day.

And if we will have an angel at the tomb,
make it a real angel,
weighty with Max Planck's quanta, vivid with hair,
opaque in the dawn light, robed in real linen
spun on a definite loom.

Let us not seek to make it less monstrous,
for our own convenience, our own sense of beauty,
lest, awakened in one unthinkable hour, we are
embarrassed by the miracle,
and crushed by remonstrance.

Quaker philosopher Elton Trueblood perceived a looming crisis of faith back in 1969, and wrote that to overcome this crisis "the Christian intellectual provides our best hope because he has access to both the reasons of the heart and the reasons of the head...and knows how to combine them" (*A Place to Stand*, Harper & Row, 1969, p. 31). Some scholars heeded his insight. A few years later the Society of Christian Philosophers was organized. It has become a major intellectual force in America. George Fox professors belong, and recently hosted a conference. Let this same concern for strong intellectual support for God's seed in the soul be present for all of us, especially for our children, at all educational levels. The loam of fertile minds should not be pounded into hardpan by entrepreneurs, whether they are peddling merchandise or sociobiological theories. If you find it difficult intellectually to believe in Christianity, wait silently. Look within. Listen. Let God's Spirit unpack your trampled soil. Be a temple of the Holy Spirit—body, mind, and soul. Receive the joyous proclamation of the gospel of Jesus Christ, as seed in rich soil needing for growth only sun and rain. You might pray like a skeptic whom Jesus healed: "I believe, Lord, help my unbelief."

Consider seed on rocky ground: Here social difficulties precipitate loss of godly faith.

If one's life is beset with troubles, especially a new believer's, despair threatens to hinder faith. Troubles from within or from without make developing deep roots difficult. Dysfunctional families, poverty, illness, accidents, divorce, death of loved ones, fratricidal wars—these make for rocky ground. So do personal vices, from pettiness to crippling addictions. Rocky soil may take the form of oppressive social circumstances. Recently Quakers in Rwanda have suffered from the tribal strife in their country. Nearly half of the churches were closed for different lengths of time last year. Nonetheless the number of members this year has risen nearly 30 percent (to nearly 3,000), and the school program expanded to serve nearly 4,000 primary and secondary schools, and Friends have modeled intertribal peacemaking in a violent world. I wonder about the faith of oppressed people in the chaos in the Balkans. Will faith in God prevail, here as in Burundi? Or will despair and cynicism prevent God's seed from getting deep roots? The words of Archbishop Oscar Romero in *Violence of Love* (Harper, 1988, p. 161) twenty years ago are reminders of how God suffers with us and for us:

> It is a black night that we are living.
> But Christianity discerns that beyond the night
> The dawn already glows.
> The hope that does not fail is carried in the heart.
> Christ goes with us!

The resurrection *follows* Gethsemane and crucifixion, and Pentecost *follows* resurrection—God's Holy Spirit is with us, even in the darkest times.

In New England and elsewhere in the world, neighborly farmers get together to remove rocks from their fields. They use these hard stones to build walls. The walls they build protect young plants from the wind, from predators, from trampling, and from disputes over turf. After the rocks are removed, mulching adds tilth, and the plants flourish, even where the climate is severe and conditions harsh. Is this what gospel fellowship is about? Clearing stony impediments from our hearts and from our neighborhoods near and far, so God's Spirit can bring spiritual growth? Turning adversity into gain? Converting rocky times into blessed times? Converting hard circumstances into heroic triumph? Yes! In our deepest suffering, God is present; resurrection, not crucifixion is God's final word. Isn't it especially important that the church get out the stone boats to clear the rocky fields of the young and the young in faith? I think so.

If your faith in God has withered, if you have lost the joy you had when first you believed, because hard things have happened to or around you, silence yourself before the Lord. Look within. Listen. Let God's love flow through the hands of others. Let them help remove the rocks in your field and make them into boundaries defining who you are.

You are a temple of the Holy Spirit—body, mind, and soul. Hear this word: God's seed in the soil will not only sprout up joyfully, but grow deep roots. Having overcome hardship, having experienced suffering, you too will become strong to help when despair threatens to drive out faith in others' fields of the soul. Such mutual care demonstrates that we are the body of Christ.

Consider seed growing among thorns: here social ease precipitates loss of godly faith.

When life is relatively serene, fairly free of troubles, and one is sustained by a good and godly education, in good health, then the social and personal soil is rich. But this wealth invites subtle competitors to faith. Weeds grow in good ground too. How does this happen? When things are going well we tend to credit ourselves and forget God. We forget that civil order rests upon spiritual wealth produced by religious faith, and is augmented from time to time by spiritual awakenings, and by moral reforms. In spiritually leavened culture, all truth is understood as God's truth, and compassionate caring people handle their hardships with godly faith. They reduce these hardships; they make life easier, safer, healthier. People consider themselves stewards of God's earth and colaborers with Christ in the kingdom.

Under such benign circumstances, persons attuned devoutly to God's will become cocreators, using gifted imagination to produce incredibly practical and aesthetic order and beauty in the world—joining God's creation with our own, making it possible for people to live peaceably, to be well-fed, well-housed, healthy, and happy. A strong public morality makes such social community possible and pleasurable. True spiritual awakenings increase the public trust and moral integrity basic to such cultural creativity.

But culture can turn idolatrous. *This idolatry starts with pride and is fed by self-gratification.* Soon worship of the creation—whether natural or artificial, whether God's creation or our own—ensues. This is idolatry. Satan comes as an angel of light, clothed in a dazzling cloak of prosperity. Almost imperceptibly pride of life begins to diminish our holy awe before the Almighty—that fear of the Lord that is the beginning of wisdom. Subtly self-gratification supplants worship of the almighty God. Maybe it's weekend skiing, or running a business, or making shrewd investments, or becoming a connoisseur of cuisine, or raising horses, or building houses, or being mayor of Yachats! Or even doing church. If pride and self-gratification replace consecrated, humble service as markers of our culture, then the kingdom faith Jesus taught will get crowded out. And without the leaven and the light of the gospel, our culture will increasingly succumb to disintegration and decay.

Both high art and folk art will degenerate; literature will titillate instead of inspire; music will collapse into noise; entertainment will pander to gratuitous violence; and education will struggle to teach any values at all (even tolerance) and simply program information into our children's minds, controlled by the highest media bidder. Kingdom plants don't flourish in a thicket of Scotch broom, with seedpods popping and taking root everywhere.

In thinking about this parable, the wonder is that it has taken so long for God's gardeners in America to discover that once-fertile fields have become choked with brambles. The answer is not the shrill rhetoric of the radical right, but penitence, and renewed Christian discipleship, so that once more we hear God's call to be faithful stewards of the kingdom. Service to others is a primary task of the body of Christ, the church. Do you know what gladdens my heart during this crisis of faith? Professionals like those in Northwest Medical Teams, who offer themselves to the service of distressed people, and ordinary people who quietly serve others on the job or volunteer compassionate service in many unheralded ways.

Our task, then, as another parable teaches, is not to root out the weeds by religious inquisitions, but to let the Spirit cleanse our hearts of pride and self-indulgence, and to do this with the prayerful help of our brothers and sisters. If you have been so busy with the cares of this world and so preoccupied with the burden of its abundance that God-talk seems almost irrelevant—quaint, even—maybe it is time to silence your mind, to look within, to listen, to bow contritely before the Almighty, to hear again Jesus' words to busy leaders hooked by the hubris of pride and self-gratification, "Repent and believe the gospel!" Then, in the garden of your soul God's good seed will flourish and not be overrun by weeds. Let Jesus cleanse your temple—body, mind, and soul. Let worship lead you to a disciplined service to others, on and off the job. Recover your calling to be a steward of the earth and a good neighbor to all creatures, including your fellow human beings!

Consider the good soil.

Because we all experience threats to faith from being trampled on, beset with troubles, or hemmed in by worldly cares, the good soil of faith arises from fields restored to productivity. It isn't just the luck of the draw. Whenever in a penitent and contrite spirit we accept God's forgiving grace, and let the Spirit of Christ empower us in company with other believers, faith is restored. Doubt yields to belief. Despair gives way to hope. Indifference is replaced by a passionate love for God and a concern for others. This is the Christian answer to the crisis of faith in our times. That answer is about affirming Christ in history and in the heart, about affirming Christ in word and in deed.

That the atoning act of God in Christ effectively changes lives was a basic tenet of the seventeenth-century Quaker awakening of the church. Robert Barclay insisted that Quaker teaching in no way lessens or detracts from the atonement and sacrifice of Jesus Christ, "but on the contrary magnifies and exalts it." Barclay declared that the outward event of Christ's death *for us* and the inward birth *in us* produce fruits of righteousness and peace. Joseph John Gurney captured in verse the Quaker insistence upon Christ crucified and risen as the reality toward which ancient religious sacrifices pointed:

> Pictures of truth with various art combined,
> Their end and substance in *one* Saviour, find.
> Saviour, incarnate, glorified, enthroned,
> Whose precious blood for all our race atoned,
> Well versed in death, familiar with the grave—
> A man to sympathise, and God to save—
> Thy prospect spreads interminably bright,
> Thy boundless retrospect is filled with light.
> (*Sabbatical Verses*, London: Arch, 1837, p. 22)

Turn to God like good soil welcoming good seed! Let God sow that seed through the word of creation. Let the word revealed in Scripture and lived out in the community of faith nourish that soil, sensuously, rationally, intuitively—at the center of your being. Let God's Spirit wash over you like sun and rain in a fertile garden. Let Jesus Christ truly become God's word within and through you. Whatever happens then, as the old poet said, your future is "interminably bright." My friends, believe the gospel! Christ is present with us, here, now! Amen.

On Being Christ-Centered: Jesus as Lord

Reedwood Friends Church, October 10, 1999

In bucolic Idaho, shortly after my parents helped me memorize the ABCs of the Bible, darkness descended on Europe, and soon the world. Adolf Hitler had seized power in Germany and begun to "aryanize" the church. He expelled Jewish Christians from the church and forced the church to adopt Nazi principles of organization. The churches mostly succumbed to these pressures, and some Christians embraced them. The pro-Nazi "German Christian" movement became a cultural force. People glorified Adolf Hitler as a "German prophet" and preached racial consciousness as another source of revelation. Commenting on this initial enthusiasm for Hitler, Helmut Thielicke commented "The worship of success is generally the form of idol worship which the devil cultivates most assiduously."

Scripture reading
2 Corinthians 5:17-20 (NRSV, in this and subsequent texts)
So if anyone is in Christ, there is a new creation: everything old has passed away; see, everything has become new! All this is from God, who reconciled us to himself through Christ, and has given us the ministry of reconciliation; that is, in Christ God was reconciling the world to himself, not counting their trespasses against them, and entrusting the message of reconciliation to us. So we are ambassadors for Christ, since God is making his appeal through us; we entreat you on behalf of Christ, be reconciled to God.

Looking back upon the century we see the holocaust of Jews, Gypsies, and Poles; the slaughter of civilians in eastern Europe, the Soviet Union, China, Vietnam; enormous military casualties of two world wars; Korea, Vietnam, the Middle East; fratricidal strife in Ireland, Africa, and Europe; tyranny and terrorism around the world. What violence!

Last Sunday we considered what it means for Christ to be our Savior, today we ask, what does it mean to follow Jesus Christ as Lord? The German Christians who opposed Nazi ideology and resisted Hitler's perversion of Christian discipleship can help us avoid a "Babylonish captivity" of the church in our times. At Barmen in 1934, a resistance movement—the "Confessing Church"—adopted a declaration drafted by Reformed theologian Karl Barth and Lutheran theologian Hans Asmussen (see the Global Library, http://www.global.org/Pub/Barman.asp). This document forthrightly repudiated the claim that other powers apart from Christ could be sources of God's revelation. Not all Christians courageously resisted the regime, but some who did—such as the Protestant pastor Dietrich Bonhoeffer and the Roman Catholic priest Bernhard Lichtenberg—were arrested and executed in concentration camps.

A key statement in this declaration is this one about authority: "Jesus Christ, as he is attested for us in Holy Scripture, is the one Word of God which we have to hear... trust and obey in life and death." Like early Christians, these believers resisted "emperor worship." Christ, not Hitler, is our Lord, they said. The Barmen declaration links redemption and discipleship—believing and following. It cites the words of Jesus: "I am the way and the truth and the life. No one comes to the Father except through me" (John 14:6 NIV). "Very truly, I tell you, anyone who does not enter the sheepfold through the gate but climbs in by another way is a thief and a bandit. I am the gate. Whoever enters by me will be saved" (John 10:1, 9 NRSV). To these German Christians, Hitler was a bandit, trying to usurp God's kingdom, which they would not subordinate to the German Reich. The Barmen declaration properly labels these verses "evangelical truths." To be evangelical is not only to experience Jesus Christ as Savior, but also to follow Christ as Lord. (William Penn lamented over halfway Christians, who want Jesus as Savior but not as Lord, the crown but not the cross.)

This historic struggle over lordship has counterparts today. Scripture texts that sustained our brave German brothers and sisters can sustain us in America today. Who are the thieves who would destroy communities of faith in our time? Are they political figures? Super nationalists? Revolutionists? No, such tyrants have mainly stiffened the backs of the faithful, as in Burundi, or China, or Ireland, or Indonesia. Rather the bandits are leaders of world culture who offer ersatz salvation: self-indulgence instead of self-denial, social order without moral order, the good life without godliness. The worship of success. Os Guinness uses the term "modernity" to denote a world culture that substitutes material splendor for the glory of God and caters to sin instead of overcoming it (*Dining with the Devil*, Baker, 1993).

What does it mean to accept Jesus Christ as Lord? It means acknowledging our primary allegiance to the kingdom of God; it means serving under divine authority; and it means entering joyously into God's glory.

Belonging to God's kingdom

Jesus spoke about the kingdom of God in parables about mustard seeds that grow phenomenally, about rescuing lost sheep and rebellious sons. To follow Christ as Lord is to belong to a realm in time yet in eternity. Paul puts it in terms of citizenship. "But our citizenship is in heaven. And we eagerly await a Savior from there, the Lord Jesus Christ, who, by the power that enables him to bring everything under his control, will transform our lowly bodies so that they will be like his glorious body" (Philippians 3:20-21 NIV).

We hold multiple citizenship. Consider all our affinities: family, neighborhood, professional, ethnic, religious, recreational, national, cultural. The kingdom of God is the enclosing circle. Humanity, though shattered, is of one blood. These circles of belonging aren't sovereign, but they often try, leading to strife and misery. Christians belong to an eternal realm— not some ethereal idea, but people actually being gathered into the "Peaceable Kingdom." This is what God is doing through the death and resurrection of Jesus Christ. Sometimes these subordinate circles, these "powers" stay within, or partly within, the circle of God's realm, leavened by God-fearing people, and judged, reproved, and instructed by God's Light. So law is based upon divine commandments, courts rule justly, families love and nourish their members, commerce produces needed goods and services at fair prices, workers are trustworthy and well paid, ball players show sportsmanship, art ennobles, and neighbors help each other. In short, the social contract works.

Sometimes, however, these powers—ordained to hold life together—spin out of the circle of God's sovereignty. Sin infects with greed, dishonesty, or violence, and affinity circles are breached. Power corrupts. Loyalty is betrayed. Systems flounder between tyranny and anarchy, then fail, sometimes several at a time: the family dysfunctional, governance corrupt, culture depraved, economy destroyed, religion idolatrous. People seeking the dignity of their own person feel abandoned, alienated. Then the citizens of heaven, who obey God on earth as in heaven, stand against these earthly powers gone demonic. In doing so they often suffer—they bear Christ's cross, sometimes to the death. If our contemporary world culture becomes a Tower of Babel, it too will fall, and the citizens of heaven will patiently rebuild the world, until Christ—the conquering Lamb—brings about the final cosmic restoration. When orchestral variations fade into silence, theme notes ring out again. Hear it! God still reigns. And slowly, with the persistence of truth and the passion of love, God's people prevail. They feed the starving, shelter the homeless, bind up the broken in body and spirit, educate the ignorant and the misled, lift artistic creativity from the ashes of depravity, bring civil order out of chaos, purge religion of idolatry, and rejoice with penitent sinners in God's gracious redemption. The gates of hell can't prevail against the church when it is thus truly the body of Christ. As citizens of God's kingdom, Christians restore the circles of human belonging within the sphere of God's kingdom.

Serving under God's authority

The citizens of heaven serve on this earth under God's authority. In an age that prizes individuality and a plurality of options, such submission poses a challenge. If Christ is the good shepherd, then are we sheep? Milling about? Having to be herded by dogs? Let's swallow pride for a moment and look at what is happening. Children (and sometimes adults) are led like lemmings to the sea by clever advertising agents and style setters who tell them what to want and to buy—from pants to celebrity cards to cigarettes— what music to hear, what values to have, what leaders to follow. A few days ago Fern and I watched a grandson play football in a high school game. I noticed how the coach sent in plays, encouraged the players to do their best to follow. And I note that even professional players, much more skilled than high school youth, rely upon good coaching. Even golf pros who make millions of dollars look to instructors. So I guess it is not demeaning but uplifting for the self to be under the direction of Jesus Christ. Remember what he said, "My yoke is easy and my burden is light." He's a good player-coach, no matter how experienced we are. That Jesus, the good shepherd, was willing to lay down his life for us certainly encourages our trust. Jesus Christ is a trustworthy Lord. We submit ourselves to others, and honor them, in the allegiance circles of our lives. Children submit to parents, spouses to each other, employees and employers, merchants and consumers, voters and elected officials. But we will never call a spouse "Lord," nor will we give that name to a boss, or a CEO, or a pastor, or a government official. Such would be false sovereignty. Jesus Christ is Lord.

How do we know what God wants us to be and to do? One way is to read what God reveals in the Bible. Learn how God has patiently prepared a people. Hear what Jesus taught the first followers, and what Christ teaches us today. Listen to the Holy Spirit within the heart, within the church, in the world. To follow Christ as Lord requires a special kind of serving. Jesus defined it this way: "You know that the rulers of the Gentiles lord it over them, and their great ones are tyrants over them. It will not be so among you; but whoever wishes to have authority over you must be your servant" (Matthew 20:25-26 NRSV). God isn't a tyrant, nor should we be.

Reedwood calls itself a community of ministers. What does this mean? It means exhorting in worship, pastoral visitation of the sick and lonely, committee tasks, Sunday school teaching, evangelism, counseling, mediating differences, sheltering the homeless, offering fellowship, sending young people to summer camp, articulating the Christian faith orally and in writing. But ministry is more. Ministry includes all that we do, vocationally, avocationally, as a witness to God's kingdom. Quaker youth who help build homes in Mexico are engaged in ministry. The physicians whom Reedwood sends abroad to offer free medical service are engaged in ministry. They are also ministers in their home clinics.

Ministry is imbedded in all honest vocations, in education, commerce, research, engineering, science, technology, service industry, building and repairing things. And in the arts by which we become cocreators with Christ. We seek the good of others in serving them. No task is too lowly for those who have seen Christ wearing the towel, washing the disciples' feet. This priesthood of believers Luther talked about, Quakers put in practice.

Through special and ordinary ministry we serve as ambassadors for Christ. Ours is the ministry of reconciliation. Hear again words from our text:

2 Corinthians 5:17-20
So if anyone is in Christ, there is a new creation: everything old has passed away; see, everything has become new! All this is from God, who reconciled us to himself through Christ, and has given us the ministry of reconciliation; that is, in Christ God was reconciling the world to himself, not counting their trespasses against them, and entrusting the message of reconciliation to us. So we are ambassadors for Christ, since God is making his appeal through us; we entreat you on behalf of Christ, be reconciled to God.

Entering God's glory

There's another aspect of acknowledging Christ as Lord: finding the presence of Christ gloriously exhilarating. More thrilling than climbing a mountain peak, or watching a sunset splash color across the sky. No grumpy reluctance at having turned away from sinful fun. No grumbling, plodding service in an unpopular cause. Nothing so dull and doleful. To say "Jesus is Lord" depicts joyous fellowship with the Word who spoke the world into being, and is gathering people to the kingdom. Eyes uplifted, not cast down, we stride buoyantly, no longer burdened by a load of sin. Not discouraged by lingering darkness, for in Jesus Christ we see the coming dawn. No longer having to stuff days and nights full of diversions in order to dull the pain of estrangement. At home with oneself. At home with God. At home with humanity. At home with creation. Confident that the kingdom of God is within us, among us, and one day will bring this sin-cursed world into righteous and cosmic harmony. Paul calls this union with Christ an "eternal weight of glory" (2 Corinthians 4:17 NRSV). Ecstasy comes and goes, but the glory never fades! In God's grace servanthood turns into friendship for those who have demonstrated obedience to God's will. Be patient. It will come. This is what Jesus said:

> "Greater love has no one than this, that he lay down his life for his friends. You are my friends if you do what I command. I no longer call you servants, because a servant does not know his master's business. Instead, I have called you friends, for everything that I learned from my Father I have made known to you." (John 15:13-15 NIV)

At the outset of this message I cited the pledge of the Christians who rose up against Nazi idolatry: "Jesus Christ, as attested for us in Holy Scripture, is the one Word of God which we have to hear...trust and obey in life and death." So I pose three questions, drawn from that confession, for you to consider prayerfully, and in the light of our Scripture reading:

1. Will you hear what Christ, as God's Word, speaks to you through Scripture, the discernment of the Church, and the prompting of the Spirit?

2. Will you trust God's will as thus revealed in Christ, the Word?

3. Will you, singly, and in company with other Christians, obey God's will as revealed in Christ, the Word? In life and death?

Adventure in Contentment

Yachats Community Presbyterian Church, October 15, 2000

Last year I preached a sermon to myself about patience, and invited you to listen in. In that sermon I mentioned frustration with city water problems and the 804 South issue. Well, some of the water problems have been resolved. New water lines have been installed and this summer a 500,000-gallon raw-water tank replaced the Reedy Creek weir washed out in 1996. During recent dry months we've needed that storage capacity! The 1890s right-of-way issue continues to plague us and our neighbors, but hope for justice guides us like a beacon from above.

Today my sermon is about contentment. A book on the shelf of my childhood home was entitled *Adventures in Contentment*. I don't remember much about it, but I thought the title seemed odd. [A family member later found a used copy and sent it to me. It was written by David Grayson and published by Grosset & Dunlop in 1907.] How could a contented person be adventurous? But then, I was a child, and this was an adult book (*adult* in the truest sense of the word: a book written to enlighten mature persons, not pander to depravity).

For some reason that title haunts me, *Adventures in Contentment*. Increasingly I find it an apt term, not an oxymoron. *Adventure* denotes well what occurs when we find inner peace, when we wake up in the morning and acknowledge, "Yes, I'm content." Contentment doesn't connote passivity, but being joyfully centered upon what God is doing in me and in the world. Peace of mind is neither an album of past blessing nor a wish list for future serenity; its a present gift from God. Paul's words to young coworker Timothy constitutes our text:

Scripture reading
1 Timothy 6:6 (NRSV)

"...There is great gain in godliness combined with contentment."

The apostle Paul experienced enough trouble to give authenticity to this maxim, so let's ponder adventures in contentment. We usually associate *discontent* with ungodliness. Secular culture loves discontent. It's the stuff of drama, from movies to soaps to opera. But Paul's exhortation implies that some people try to exhibit *godliness* without being contented, thus marring kingdom witness. To use a colloquial expression, they become "crabby complainers." A story from a past era illustrates this. After the town's interdenominational revival had concluded, the three participating pastors met for coffee, and compared results. The Baptist minister said, "The revival worked out great for us! We gained four new families." The Pentecostal preacher said, "We did even better than that! We gained six new families!" "Well," said the Presbyterian preacher, "we profited even more: we got rid of ten cantankerous families!"

First, look for adventurous contentment with material things.

Does contentment mark our use of possessions? God has given us a creation richly to explore and to use. We are cocreators with God. Our wills shape the material world to intelligent purpose. Sometimes for good, sometimes for ill. A Proverb (30:8 NIV) reads: "give me neither poverty nor riches, but give me only my daily bread." Most of us are somewhere within a broad middle ground economically, burdened neither by poverty nor by wealth. Paul wrote young Timothy (1 Timothy 6:8 NIV), "If we have food and clothing, we will be content," and told early Christians of his own experience: "I have learned to be content with whatever I have" (Philippians 4:11 NRSV).

What about my own possessions? Well, I have one good suit, which I'm wearing today, a dozen shirts, various trousers including the two pair of jeans I usually wear on alternate days, various shoes and boots, several nice sweaters, and in general more clothes than I need. We own debt-free a comfortable house overlooking the ocean. We have a dependable car, plenty of food, and can afford to eat out, travel, and play golf. We pay our bills and have financial resources stashed away for our "declining years," whenever that comes. We could have invested more shrewdly, if we had known the stock market was going to rebound so bullishly from its 1987 plunge just before we retired, but...why worry? It's just money. In her novel *Damage* Josephine Hart warns about becoming "smug people with a soft protective cloak of wealth wrapped around them" (Knopf, 1991, p. 139). As the Russian author Yevgeny Yevtushenko wrote in *Wild Berries* (Holt, 1984, p. 57), "The only bank where you can deposit all your savings is your memory. That bank will never go bankrupt." I expect he was too young to worry about Alzheimer's. These novelists echo biblical counsel. So maybe I should spend more time in relationships that build great memories, and in cherishing them, than in finagling investments and calculating my net worth. In any case it's good to be free from a compulsion to buy stuff just because we have more disposable income now than when we were Depression kids, or when we were a struggling young couple burdened by family responsibilities.

Hear the advice of Barnabas, Apollos, Pricilla, or whoever wrote the book of Hebrews (13:5 NRSV): "Keep your lives free from the love of money, and be content with what you have; for he [Jesus] has said, 'I will never leave you or forsake you.'" Let's heed that advice. It's a matter of priorities, isn't it? As always, Jesus' words challenge us. We are challenged by the words from Matthew, "'Do not store up...treasures on earth...but store up...treasures in heaven....'"

So, let's covenant with God that material things will be our servants and not our masters. *How* do we store up heavenly treasure? I can't supply a checklist. But I daresay if we pray we'll find ways to invest our time, energy, and money for the good of others and for the good of our souls. Certain Northwest Native Americans used to have a ceremonial practice called "potlatch," in which a person's status was determined by how much he could destroy. Burning one's fur coats, canoes, and houses conferred status. In more subtle ways extravagant waste is a social marker in many societies. In the kingdom of God the marker is stewardship. Conspicuous consumption aggravates social inequity, fosters strife, and dulls the soul. In contrast, adventurous contentment puts feet to the phrase in the Lord's Prayer, "thy will be done in earth, as it is in heaven." Don't get me wrong, I'm not for asceticism. God declared the creation good. He created the universe with material stuff, not just ideas. We are part of that creation he dubbed "good"! We belong here, a fact some environmentalist zealots overlook. The earth is the Lord's. The universe is a feast of good things, abundantly available so long as we shun greed and superfluity, so long as we remain God's loyal servants, so long as we love our neighbor as ourselves, and so long as creativity stays within the boundaries of divine will. Good adventuring always involves joining mind, body, and spirit in godly activities. It doesn't take much intelligence to destroy, but it takes wisdom to build constructively within boundaries of truth and love. Contentment arises when we play life's game by God's rules.

Second, find adventurous contentment under difficult circumstances.

How might we find contentment under trying circumstances? A basic approach is to accept difficulty as part of life's course. Some difficulties relate to family matters. Others to our jobs, or to unexpected events such as floods, or fires, or bad tires, or defective house siding, or accidents—or bad luck. We all struggle to keep body and mind healthy and to handle aggravating circumstances. Many difficulties are of our own making. They arise from poor choices, bad judgment, from sins. Like the game of golf, life has its hazards. Contentment results not from escaping troubles but from overcoming them. Think about it: Life in Yachats is Edenic compared to situations elsewhere in the world. Territorial strife in Israel, persecution of Christians in Indonesia, plague in Africa, floods in Bangladesh—as Solomon said, it's "the little foxes that ruin the vineyards" (Song of Solomon 2:15 NIV). Some obstacles to contentment are so petty they irritate rather than elicit our heroic responses.

In whatever form, trying circumstances wake us at night, they frame our days with worry in spite of Jesus' words. But whether circumstances are difficult or petty, don't let them destroy your peace of mind! Caught in any storm, cling to the cross and feel the strength of heavenly arms holding you steady, and hear the voice of Jesus saying, "I am with you always!"

How can I become less problem-conscious and more kingdom-conscious? Perhaps by being a more joyous and straightforward witness to God's saving grace through Jesus Christ. By showing love more effectively to children and grandchildren, to parents, to neighbors. By returning good for evil. To act in accordance with both truth and love is easier to talk about than to do. Sometimes truth-speaking comes across as autocratic and uncivil (tolerating every idea and everybody—except firm Christian believers—seems to be the philosophy of the day). How can one be both honest and winsome? I don't know about you, but I need help on this. Some well-intended words and deeds are misconstrued as manipulation. Susan Howatch says it well in *Glittering Images* (Knopf, 1987, p. 233): "We're very much at the mercy of those we love, and never more so than when those we love don't love us quite as we would wish in return."

Oh, Lord, help me here! Am I self-deceived; are my motives muddled? I don't think I charge for love, I don't think I exact reciprocity, but I do yearn for acknowledgment of love lavished upon family and community. You know my heart, Lord. May appropriate actions flow from good intentions. Help me be content to love without keeping score, knowing that all things are measured against your extravagant love.

The apostle Paul experienced hardship—and eventually martyrdom. He wrote: "I am content with weaknesses, insults, hardships, persecutions, and calamities for the sake of Christ; for whenever I am weak, then I am strong" (2 Corinthians 12:10 NRSV). The key phrase in that verse seems to be: "for the sake of Christ." Not for ego, not public acclaim, but for the sake of our leader, Christ, who as leaven and light is making things new and right in this sin-blasted world. And despite all the headlined evil, there are many wonderful people who daily exemplify goodness, who find a serene divine center to their lives. This ranks high in God's newscast.

Third, find adventurous contentment in each chapter of life.

As you know I will conclude my mayoral stint at the end of this year. In thinking about the past decade of service on the council, I read the Old Testament account of David's reflections upon his tenure. Forty years instead of nine, and far more historically significant. Fortunately, Yachats hasn't been as bloody as these olden days when people were slaughtered for opposing the king! As recently as a couple centuries ago dueling settled quarrels quickly and sometimes fatally! Now people just sue. But at least we aren't physically assaulting each other. Surely God's patience was tried in olden times, and is tried now. Jesus brought humanity a new understanding of God's covenant—it's a covenant of peace, not of strife, of truth and love conjoined. I wish that could be understood better in Jerusalem, and in Yachats.

I'm glad our town has been leavened by the gospel. Think of all the service freely given by our citizens through churches and other organizations, through neighborliness. The city staff has exemplified cheerful stewardship. Council and commission members have been civil and caring. Citizens understand that we public servants are human too. We don't always get it straight, but we do our best. Some criticism is par for the course, whether or not deserved. Novelist Harry Kemelman wrote: "People are always happy to hear of anything reprehensible of someone in authority. It makes them feel good about themselves. It doesn't have to be anything specific, you understand. Just a suggestion of something" (*One Fine Day the Rabbi Bought a Cross*, Fawcett, 1989, p. 196).

An Old Testament seer wrote: "...One who rules over people justly, ruling in the fear of God, is like the light of morning, like the sun rising on a cloudless morning, gleaming from the rain on the grassy land" (2 Samuel 23:3-4 NRSV). What a challenging epitaph for political service that is! Time has dimensions of both constancy and change. Such is the rhythm of life. Each day offers an eternal present, but each day introduces an exciting new page in life, and sometimes a whole new chapter. Accept each opening page or chapter with joy and not regret. Surf the cresting waves of time! In his novel *Three Cities* (Carrol and Graf, 1983, p. 515), Sholem Asch wrote: "Your future tasks are ripening for you in invisible fields that God has sowed for you, and God has chosen you as His servant that you may carry out your tasks, which are His also. That is why it does not matter whether the things you have to do are small or great; they all come from *one* source, they all have *one* purpose: to accomplish God's work on earth." I like that.

Getting older is one sobering change. The birth of a great grandchild underscores that change for us. At this hilltop it's easier to foresee diminishment rather than enhancement. But consider this divine paradox: The body weakens, but the Spirit strengthens! And even when the mortal book of life ends its final chapter, an immortal and more glorious one opens. Paul wrote the following words, which sustain me, and I hope they sustain you.

2 Corinthians 4:6-11, 14, 16-18; 5:1-5 (NIV)

For God, who said, "Let light shine out of darkness," made his light shine in our hearts to give us the light of the knowledge of the glory of God in the face of Christ.

But we have this treasure in jars of clay to show that this all-surpassing power is from God and not from us. We are hard pressed on every side, but not crushed; perplexed, but not in despair; persecuted, but not abandoned; struck down, but not destroyed. We always carry around in our body the death of Jesus, so that the life of Jesus may also be revealed in our body. For we who are alive are always being given over to death for Jesus' sake, so that his life may be revealed in our mortal body.

...We know that the one who raised the Lord Jesus from the dead will also raise us with Jesus and present us with you in his presence.

...Though outwardly we are wasting away, yet inwardly we are being renewed day by day. For our light and momentary troubles are achieving for us an eternal glory that far outweighs them all. So we fix our eyes not on what is seen, but on what is unseen. For what is seen is temporary, but what is unseen is eternal.

Now we know that if the earthly tent we live in is destroyed, we have a building from God, an eternal house in heaven, not built by human hands. Meanwhile we groan, longing to be clothed with our heavenly dwelling, because when we are clothed, we will not be found naked. For while we are in this tent, we groan and are burdened, because we do not wish to be unclothed but to be clothed with our heavenly dwelling, so that what is mortal may be swallowed up by life. Now it is God who has made us for this very purpose and has given us the Spirit as a deposit, guaranteeing what is to come.

I conclude with a poem my friend Elton Trueblood wrote, at the age of ninety-three:

Adventures

Over the next new hilltop,
Or through the garden gate
Or just around the bend of the road,
The great adventures wait,
And when my mind leaps not,
And when my heart is cold
To the call of the road and the gate and the hill,
I shall know that I am old.

The prayer of confession (in unison)

Lord, in humility we confess anew our faith. We honor Jesus Christ as both Savior and Lord. Sometimes we cherish saving grace but we avoid the costly discipleship. Teach us contentment during hard circumstances. May we cope with adversity and infirmity as people joyously following your light. Sometimes we find it easier to complain than to rejoice. Forgive us, Lord. We have so much to be thankful for: life, family, neighbors, civil order, and the Holy Spirit within and among us.

The Day of the Lord

Yachats Community Presbyterian Church, June 23, 2002

Three years ago I preached a sermon to myself about patience, and invited you to listen in. Two years ago I preached about contentment. Today my sermon is about heeding God in troubled times. When a ship's in trouble it signals "Mayday!" Today a ship is icebound off Antarctica, with a hundred men wondering whether they'll be rescued today or tomorrow—or ever. Our Scripture text revealed how the disciples were anxious about the future, about the day of the Lord. "When's the big day for your kingdom, Jesus?" "What's next?" Instead of assuring them of quick success, Jesus predicted chaos, persecution, apostasy, false religion, catastrophe, and lawlessness. But he also told them that the good news of the kingdom would be proclaimed throughout the world before the end. His violent death on the cross underscored his words. So did the subsequent destruction of the temple, and the scattering of Israel, and two thousand years of troubles of the sort Jesus predicted.

Is our world, like that trapped ship—buffeted by howling, frigid winds—in danger of sinking? Sure; in the last few years, scores of ministers have been assassinated in Colombia, thousands of Christians have been slaughtered in Africa, Asia, and Middle East countries. Although the Christian church learned the hard way that inquisitions and crusades don't advance the kingdom, many Muslim leaders haven't yet, and would use the power of the sword to purge apostates or persecute persons of other religions. Hindu India and Muslim Pakistan are poised to nuke each other. The Enron and pharmaceutical scandals take second place only to terrorism for "lawlessness prize of the year." Famine and plague (AIDS) scourge many countries. Hundreds of persons starve to death daily; a tenth of the world's population is underfed and dependent on handouts. Apostasy prevails in some churches as leaders scuttle fundamental Christian teachings in an effort to accommodate ego-centered culture. Clerical sexual sins scandalize the faithful and fuel unbelief. But—and this is important: *The gospel is reaching the ends of the earth by proclamation and through compassionate service by agencies leavened by the gospel.* Help is on the way for the stranded ship of humanity.

What do we mean by "the day of the Lord"? Sunday is, of course, "the Lord's day" on the calendar, a time for worship. But "day of the Lord" has a larger meaning and it is this: *In the course of life—individually and corporately—some times are especially momentous.* The Greek term *kairos* signifies divine visitation, testing times, ominous times, exciting times. In such "days of reckoning" God says to us "listen up, discern what's going on, find the right path." Biblical passages about the day of the Lord paint word pictures about times of judgment and—for those who listen to the Lord—clarified vision and new opportunities. Consider these biblical passages.

In this first passage, the prophet Joel speaks. From locusts devastating a drought-stricken land he draws lessons about divine visitation.

Old Testament reading

Joel 2:1-3, 12-13 (NRSV)

Blow the trumpet in Zion; sound the alarm on my holy mountain! Let all the inhabitants of the land tremble, for the day of the Lord is coming, it is near—a day of darkness and gloom, a day of clouds and thick darkness! Like blackness spread upon the mountains a great and powerful army comes; their like has never been from of old, nor will be again after them in ages to come.

Fire devours in front of them, and behind them a flame burns. Before them the land is like the garden of Eden, but after them a desolate wilderness, and nothing escapes them.

Yet even now, says the Lord, return to me with all your heart, with fasting, with weeping, and with mourning; rend your hearts and not your clothing. Return to the Lord, your God, for he is gracious and merciful, slow to anger, and abounding in steadfast love, and relents from punishing.

Here's what Peter wrote about end times.

New Testament reading

2 Peter 3:10-14 (NRSV)

But the day of the Lord will come like a thief, and then the heavens will pass away with a loud noise, and the elements will be dissolved with fire, and the earth and everything that is done on it will be disclosed.

Since all these things are to be dissolved in this way, what sort of people ought you to be in leading lives of holiness and godliness, waiting for and hastening the coming of the day of God, because of which the heavens will be set ablaze and dissolved, and the elements will melt with fire? But, in accordance with his promise, we wait for new heavens and a new earth, where righteousness is at home.

Therefore, beloved, while you are waiting for these things, strive to be found by him at peace, without spot or blemish.

Peter asks the key question—"What sort of people ought you to be?"—and indicates that by living lives of holiness during crises in our lives we actually hasten the coming of that final day, when the whole cosmos will be restored for a redeemed people. So let's look at the day of the Lord from different angles. *First as judgment upon nations, then as judgment upon individuals, then as spiritual awakening, and finally as the windup of earthly affairs at the return of Jesus as the triumphant Lamb of God.* Whether we're looking at the day of the Lord as personal crisis, a crossroads for decision, a national time of troubles, or the end of the world, let's keep ever before us Peter's admonition to be found by the Lord at peace, "without spot or blemish."

The day of the Lord as judgment upon nations

The prophet Amos wrote (5:20 NRSV): "Is not the day of the Lord darkness, not light, and gloom with no brightness in it?" And Ezekiel proclaimed (30:3 NRSV): "...The day of the Lord is near; it will be a day of clouds, a time of doom for the nations." Earlier I spelled out a doomsday scenario. Our world teeters on the brink of disaster, but let's not wallow in gloom. It's been this way for thousands of years. And, of course—although less newsworthy—lots of good things happen. The question is: *What can we learn from the darkness?* Here is how Thomas Merton reads the signs of our times:

> We are living in the greatest revolution in history—a huge spontaneous upheaval of the entire human race...a deep elemental boiling over of all the inner contradictions that have ever been in man, a revelation of the chaotic forces inside everybody. This is not something we have chosen, nor is it something we are free to avoid....All the inner force of man is boiling and bursting out, the good together with the evil, the good poisoned by evil and fighting it, the evil pretending to be good and revealing itself in the most dreadful crimes, justified and rationalized by the purest and

most innocent intentions....And so we fear to recognize our *kairos* and accept it.
(*Conjectures of a Guilty Bystander*, Doubleday Image Books, 1968, p. 67)

So, with Merton, *first* let us acknowledge our day of the Lord, and seek to be faithful in our times. No pretending it isn't here. *Second,* in facing a national or cultural or personal day of visitation we pray for guidance, not favor. Singing "God bless America" isn't enough. This contemporary prayer expresses a need to ask God what's up. Maybe you've felt the same way.

On Your Agenda?

Lord, it scares me what scientists are up to.
Like tinkering with DNA.
Are they going to make artificial people soon, designed for social slots? Super athletes,
super warriors,
super nerds? Clever devils?
Ruthless rulers?
Powerless peons?
Your will is supposed to be done
on earth as in heaven.
Is this stuff on your agenda?
Seems to me it could be hell on earth.
Or am I missing something?
(This poem and others following are included in my *Prayers at Twilight*, Barclay Press, 2003)

Third, we ask God how we might more faithfully witness God's kingdom where we live, in our community, among family and friends, in our country, in our world. We are citizens of that whole world God so loved he sent his Son to redeem. Sometimes we feel overwhelmed and powerless to influence the principalities and powers that govern. But God will show us ways to be light in a dark world and to be leaven in a tasteless society.

The day of the Lord as judgment upon individuals

During any momentous era such as we are now living in we find our own lives checked at the bar of judgment. External troubles force us to check our own addictions, our pretenses, our evasions, our complicity in the heavy, icy sea of sin that puts our own soul in peril. It may mean admitting we need to be rescued. The old Southern spiritual says, "It's not my brother nor my sister but it's me, O Lord, standing in the need of prayer." When God's voice calls through the clouds of doubt and distress it is time to repent for sins, including sins of the disposition and, above all, the subtle sins of pride. Our personal day of the Lord will expose and burn away the fog of self-deception, enabling us to see ourselves as God sees us, and maybe as others do. The day of the Lord is a time to prostrate ourselves before the Lord, as Joel said, and plead his grace, being open to a fresh baptism with the Holy Spirit. It's a time to let belief in Christ become a conviction of the heart, not just a notion in the head. These prayers express such contrition:

Either Way

In parochial school we learned about purgatory,
a kind of penalty box to make one obey the rules.
Later my Calvinist husband scoffed at this.
The elect are perfected in "the article of death," he said.
Crabby as I've been, either way would suit me fine.
Yes, I know, I should start being Christ-like now.
Guess I've been locked inside my own purgatory
and at my age should start acting more heavenly.
Will you forgive me, Lord? Clean me up now, and outside heaven's gate, if necessary.

Especially My Arrogance

Oh Divine Creator, for years I've doubted
your existence, or ignored it.
Now the future seems bleak.
Not just mine but humanity's as well.
Grade school kids kill each other,
Aids has become pandemic in Africa,
mad cow disease has hit Europe.
Fanatics terrorize us.
Politics is corrupt everywhere.
Our culture's getting gross.
Drugs are abused. Gene therapy
won't guarantee the good life, either
So if you are there, God, or here—
whichever—please let me know.
I'm old, lonely and crabby; so heaven
interests me. My sins are obvious,
especially my arrogance
at cutting you out of my life.
Can you forgive me?

The day of the Lord as visitation—an awakening for individuals

In the aftermath of America's awful civil war in the nineteenth century, widespread penitence occurred, followed by spiritual reform and social righteousness. Christian colleges proliferated. Missionary zeal flourished, service agencies got going. Truth and love were conjoined in Christian caring. Such renewal is going on in Burundi now, after its horrible civil war. September 11 provided a wake-up call for comfortable nations, with a response of camaraderie and appreciation for those who risked their lives amid the tragedy. Each Sunday we pray, "thy will be done in earth, as it is in heaven." As Christians we need to focus our sights on heaven so that our lives will be guided by eternal perspectives. That's important in a day of darkness, when it becomes evident that moral standards can't be sustained apart from heavenly principles. We are especially concerned that our children and grandchildren recover awe before the Almighty and bow in contrition before him, and follow Jesus as Lord. This poem expresses that yearning:

I Wish They Would Learn

When I was young we kids were afraid of hell.
Now, it seems, young folks are afraid of
    heaven.
They can't imagine anything more exciting
than their affluent lifestyle. Skiing every
    Sunday.
Shopping at the mall. TV celebrity shows.
Making scads of money, getting stock
    options.
They don't fear you, Lord, they ignore you.
Maybe a depression would do them good.
Or a service stint in Somalia. I know, Lord,
when you're young heaven talk is taboo,
too gloomy, too threatening. Was for me
    once.
But I wish they would learn soon that fear
of the Lord is the beginning of wisdom.

The day of the Lord signifies the end of earthly time and the onset of eternity.

Today's Scripture readings envision the wrap-up of earthly existence and a creation renewed in righteousness. For individuals, death marks that transition from earthly to heavenly time. So any present visitation of the Lord can help us live more faithfully and acknowledge the eternal significance of life with Christ. Sometimes loss, tragedy, trials, and death of others make us conscious of that fact. The paired prayers in the following poem illustrate this.

Has George Found Billy?

Lord, there's this waitress at the diner
where I eat. Bonnie is big and brassy,
doesn't take any guff. She dyes her hair red
and her lips are puckered up from smoking,
but she has a good heart. Has coffee with me
when things are slow. Lonesome. Her hubby
beat her up and fled to Mexico years ago
and left her with this retarded son to raise.
Well, Billy drowned in the river last week.
Sad. So I hugged her today and said, honey,
in heaven Jesus will make Billy whole
in his mind as well as in his body.
She needs you, now, Lord.

God, there's this old guy who shuffles in most days
about four. George wears high pocket pants,
an old plaid shirt and red suspenders. He orders
a hot dinner sandwich and coffee. Drools a bit.
Had a stroke I imagine. Lonesome. Used to play
catch with Billy sometimes out behind the diner.
After Billy drowned, the guy said he'd pray for me.
Never had anyone talk to me like that before;
so I kissed the old codger on the forehead
and said, well dearie it can't hurt me none.
And now I learn the old guy is dead. So here I am,
praying best I know how. Mostly I want to know,
Lord, has George found Billy yet?

The day of the Lord signifies cosmic reconstruction.

The great day of the Lord signals the renewal of the earth itself, indeed, recreation of the cosmos. A Jesuit anthropologist, Teilhard de Chardin, pictured how things build up to climax in cosmic history (*The Divine Milieu*, New York: Harper & Row, 1960, pp. 152-153):

> One day, the Gospel tells us, the tension gradually accumulating between humanity and God will touch the limits prescribed by the possibilities of the world. And then will come the end. Then the presence of Christ, which has been silently accruing in things, will suddenly be revealed—like a flash of light from pole to pole....Like lightning, like a conflagration, like a flood, the attraction exerted by the Son of Man will lay hold of all the whirling elements in the universe so as to reunite them or subject them to his body.

Jesus' resurrection gives us assurance of this new creation, and that we will have a part in it. This assurance steadies us to live by Jesus' kingdom teaching on earth. We've seen the blueprint of the future, and it's great!

Conclusion

Any visitation of the Lord produces awe. And it should. We put our hands to our mouths, like Job of old, and listen to what God has to say. The prophet Zephaniah put it pointedly: "Be silent before the Lord God! For the day of the Lord is at hand; the Lord has prepared a sacrifice, he has consecrated his guests" (Zephaniah 1:7 NRSV). Ah, I like that! The day of the Lord is more than judgment. You and I are invited to be among God's guests! To sit at his table, to sleep in his house. Out of the ashes of disaster comes new growth. Out of chaos comes order. From failure, success; from death, life. In Christ we triumph over adversity.

Nothing can separate us from the love and care of God. Could this be your day of visitation? As an early Christian wrote: "'Today, if you hear his voice, do not harden your hearts" (Hebrews 3:15 NRSV). Don't brush the Spirit aside, but pray, rather, "speak, Lord, for I'm listening. Renew a right spirit within me." Maybe you can resonate with this prayer.

Touch Would Help

Lord, many years ago you came to me
in a conversion experience so vivid
it's recalled now with tears of joy.
"I have decided to follow Jesus," I sang,
"no turning back, no turning back!"
It's still the song of my soul.
But I don't feel very spiritual now.
Concerns about property and health
nag at me. Is there some vision
of heaven, some touch of your Spirit
to bless these twilight years?
A heavenly touch would help, Lord.

These are my sentiments! I hope they're yours. Let's conclude this worship with a bit of silence before the Lord. God's visits are sometimes serendipitous. Like C.S. Lewis said, we are "surprised by joy." So if today the Lord has surprised you with a special inward visitation, accept the gift with tears of joy, and witness your renewed faith publicly, out of the silence, if you wish, or after worship to someone you love.

Exploring Heaven

Waldport Presbyterian Church, May 18, 2003
(adapted from Exploring Heaven *and* Prayers at Twilight*)*

Confronting the mystery of heaven

Heaven is our inheritance, according to our text, but it isn't something we think about regularly. But it does come to mind, especially when life-destroying events occur among us, like the murdered Longo children being dumped into the slough not far from here. Tragic death reminds us we're *all* on life's journey toward an uncertain location. This much *is* certain: That journey will take us *through the valley of the shadow of death*. What lies beyond? Let's confront the mystery of heaven forthrightly.

Have you observed a bit of fuzziness when people speak of heaven? Often they treat heaven in a cheery but vague manner, equivalent to saying, "things are tough now, but don't worry, they will get better; God is with us, and death isn't the last word." What an evocative final phrase! If death isn't the last word, what is?

As children we resist generalities about heaven, craving specifics, such as, Will our kitty be there?

Scripture reading

1 Corinthians 15:12-26 (NRSV)

Now if Christ is proclaimed as raised from the dead, how can some of you say there is no resurrection of the dead? If there is no resurrection of the dead, then Christ has not been raised; and if Christ has not been raised, then our proclamation has been in vain and your faith has been in vain. We are even found to be misrepresenting God, because we testified of God that he raised Christ—whom he did not raise if it is true that the dead are not raised. For if the dead are not raised, then Christ has not been raised. If Christ has not been raised, your faith is futile and you are still in your sins. Then those also who have died in Christ have perished. If for this life only we have hoped in Christ, we are of all people most to be pitied.

But in fact Christ has been raised from the dead, the first fruits of those who have died. For since death came through a human being, the resurrection of the dead has also come through a human being; for as all die in Adam, so all will be made alive in Christ. But each in his own order: Christ the first fruits, then at his coming those who belong to Christ. Then comes the end, when he hands over the kingdom to God the Father, after he has destroyed every ruler and every authority and power. For he must reign until he has put all his enemies under his feet. The last enemy to be destroyed is death.

1 Peter 1:3-4 (NRSV)

Blessed be the God and Father of our Lord Jesus Christ! By his great mercy he has given us a new birth into a living hope through the resurrection of Jesus Christ from the dead, and into an inheritance that is imperishable, undefiled, and unfading, kept in heaven for you.

During childhood the present seems to stretch endlessly before us, so we shrug off puzzling questions about an afterlife until teen years, when tragedy flings into our faces queries about mortality.

A middle-school girl is raped and murdered by a neighbor, and friends weeping at the crime scene wonder about heaven—and hell. A buddy and his girl friend take a curve too fast and wrap

Dad's pickup and themselves around a tree—arriving at the morgue instead of at the schoolyard. High school pals at the cemetery stare wide-eyed at the grave and try to fathom the nature of the afterlife the preacher talks about.

When we're older and face the death of loved ones, questions shoved aside during busy career years, return to plague us. A poem expresses an inner dialogue:

Circumstances force us to face our finitude. They compel us to admit that death will come, inevitably, in spite of exercise routines, healthy diet, inoculations, routine mammograms or prostate probes, cataract surgery, hip transplants, by-pass surgery, gene therapy, and stem cell treatments. In quiet moments we admit to ourselves, death is scary to contemplate. It *is* the final enemy. So the ultimate question haunts us: what follows death?

As we begin to explore heaven, questions arise, such as: What sort of reality is it? Who will be there? What will we be like? What will people do all the time? Where is the universe going? Let's consider these questions.

Affirming the reality of heaven

People have different ideas about heaven's location. Here are some of them:

- Heaven is an illusion; it's not located anywhere.
- Heaven is a reality located in the mind.
- Heaven is a reality located in culture.
- Heaven is a spiritual realm, coexistent with natural reality.
- Heaven is a reality located in the mind of God.
- Heaven is a reality congruent with creation. Let's affirm this position.

Putting it Together

I've kept my life as a scientist and as a believer
separate for years. But my wife died last month
and now I'm trying to put the compartments together.
My head says she is just ashes strewn at sea.
But my heart tells me Martha lives, somewhere.
Help me sort it out, Lord.

Heaven is in synch with creation; it's not just a noble notion. Exploring heaven is difficult because our minds aren't yet geared to all dimensions of reality. But clues lie scattered about. Look in history, in the human mind, in culture, in the revelations of God, and in the physical universe itself. Intimations are found in God's word spoken through nature, in history, in the stories of humankind, and preeminently in Scripture. These clues suggest that heaven is as much a part of reality as cats and dogs, microbes and moose, whales and wrens, mountains and oceans, quarks and black holes and a hundred billion whirling galaxies—as real as people, as eternal as God. What evidences are there for heaven as an actual place for personal life after death? They are diverse but they demonstrate a pattern of coherence that sustains our hope. Picture that pattern as an arch. An arch is an effective engineering design, whether used in cathedrals or highway bridges. In its simplicity of design an arch is both beautiful and useful. Now picture the resurrection of Christ as the keystone in that arch and other evidences as lower or higher tiers of stone resting on a foundation of *purposeful intelligence.* (The universal nature of intelligence indicates that everlasting life is a reasonable and viable implication.) Rising from that base on one side at a lower level, the evidence consists of *persistent and diverse cultural intuitions.* ("Homesickness for heaven" pervades stories and rituals of all human cultures.) At a higher level *scriptural revelations affirm an afterlife.* Rising from the base on the other side at a lower level, the evidence consists of *personal otherworldly experiences* (such as near-death experiences) and at a higher level *the testimony of the witnesses to Jesus' resurrection.* Finally, picture *corroborative personal spiritual experience* as the superstructure dependent upon and affirming the integrity of the arch. This superstructure is a "cathedral of the spirit," or, to change the figure—a bridge across an abyss of death and despair.

Jesus told his followers: "In my Father's house are many rooms; if it were not so, I would have told you. I am going there to prepare a place for you. And if I go and prepare a place for you, I will come back and take you to be with me that you also may be where I am" (John 14:2-3 NIV).

In the light of Jesus' life, his atoning death, and especially his resurrection, it doesn't seem credible that Jesus was speaking euphemistically about followers joining him in a sacrificial death honored by posterity. No, Jesus' words signify a gathering of real people at a real eternal place. I trust his word. Angela of Foligno, friend of Francis of Assisi, in a dream heard Jesus say, "My love for you has not been a hoax" (*Complete Works*, Classics of Western Spirituality, 1993, pp. 309-310). Amen! Why did the Spirit-baptized disciples fan out from Jerusalem so boldly to proclaim the gospel? Because they had witnessed the resurrection! So had Paul, and so have all of us who find Christ as Savior and Lord.

This is foundational Christian doctrine: In raising Jesus from the dead, God demonstrated a power sufficient to resurrect our bodies too. In his resurrected body Jesus talked with the disciples and shared food with them, and yet he disappeared from their sight. Jesus could accommodate to earthly dimensions and also transcend them. The ascension that followed several weeks of appearances signified that such transcendence was the norm—at least until, as he said, "I will not leave you orphaned; I am coming to you" (John 14:18 NRSV). He left our dimensions of reality so the Spirit could extend divine presence more fully. Christian worshipers pray together as Jesus taught the first disciples: "Thy will be done in earth, as it is in heaven." Surely this means that heaven exists in a more definitive way than what we now experience on earth.

Who will be there?

Forgiven and redeemed people from all times and from every tongue and tribe and people and nation will be there, along with angels, and who knows what other orders of creation. The resurrection of Jesus is the confirming sign of our own resurrection. In resurrecting Jesus, God answers our question "is there an afterlife?" with a resounding "yes!" Accepting God's redemptive offer of grace, our heavenly heritage is assured.

As the apostle Peter put it, "...God shows no partiality, but in every nation anyone who fears him and does what is right is acceptable to him" (Acts 10:34-35 NRSV).

Peter's affirmation should ease our minds; we're not on the selection committee to determine who gains heaven and who doesn't, and neither are other folks. Human judgments are fallible and often biased, consequently innumerable victims cry out for a redress of wrongs only God can provide. Penitent sinners find God more forgiving than their social peers, from whom they may bear a lifelong stigma of moral failure. Heaven is needed to set things right, as the following poem notes:

A Reasonable Requirement

My friend says one should be content
with this life, make the most of it,
and not whine for second chances.
I pondered this, and then I thought
about this guy wrongly imprisoned,
locked up twenty years, on death row
part of the time. I think of children
blown to bits by terrorists, people
starved in gulags, gassed by Nazis,
people gunned down by drug dealers,
innocent and helpless civilians sacrificed
as "collateral damage" in political wars,
and it struck me that hope for heaven
is a reasonable requirement for justice,
as well as a gift of your love, Lord.

Violence imbedded in cycles of tyranny and anarchy, and fostered by depraved culture, has provided a pattern for society. That pattern will end. The throne of God is the final and determinative court of appeal, to which all are brought, rich or poor, favored or scorned, innocent or guilty. The biblical picture of God holding court on a golden throne symbolizes a powerful check against usurpation of divine sovereignty by persons or by clans, tribes, states, cliques, pressure groups, or corporations. Justice is owed many persons, and God will not let them down. Right will prevail, not wrong. Heaven—and hell—exhibit divine judgment as well as mercy.

The incarnation signifies the embodiment of God's saving Word. The prologue to John's Gospel puts it succinctly: "The Word became flesh and lived among us." God's truth shines within each person to impart knowledge of and judgment about right and wrong. People can penitently accept and obediently follow that Light, or they can reject it, sear conscience, and become alienated from God—forever if they wish.

Heaven completes human redemption. People are to be cleansed from sin, not just forgiven. The Bible pictures the redeemed wearing white robes. In heaven the poorest peon sports a toga. In language from the old sacrificial system we are "washed in the blood of the Lamb." Holiness is our destiny. "Pursue peace with everyone, and the holiness without which no one will see the Lord" (Hebrews 12:14 NRSV). Redemption transforms us individually and socially—and prepares us for now for the heavenly kingdom.

What will we be like in heaven?

Jesus' triumph over death heralds ours. He is the pioneer, the first one through the mountain pass! As Paul said, "If for this life only we have hoped in Christ, we are of all people most to be pitied" (1 Corinthians 15:19 NRSV). Life is the final word; and that word means personal, conscious eternal life. Like Jesus we will have spiritual bodies adapted to cosmic dimensions. In past decades people have been reticent to affirm a resurrected body. Our culture struck a deal: science handles physical things, religion handles souls. *How misguided!* Rightly understood science is an effort to read God's word in creation, compatible with God's word in Scripture and in Jesus Christ.

By "becoming flesh" God affirms the worth of physical existence, including bodies. Being a spiritual body *increases* physicality—sin free. God pronounced each step of creation "good" and that of humanity "very good." So heaven is for whole healthy persons. No divine harvesting of our ideas or memories, no stripping us bare of bodies to extract souls. Heaven glorifies personhood by endowing our bodies with enhanced powers, minds with greater comprehension, and with spirits tuned to God's whole creation.

Resurrection bodies retain self-conscious identity and recognizable configuration. On earth we move within three spatial dimensions—*length*, *width*, and *depth*. Physical mobility occurs linearly within the fourth, time. Our technology has greatly increased dimensional mobility. We go farther, range wider, and probe deeper than did our ancestors, but still within four dimensions. It seems credible that resurrection bodies will achieve incredible mobility within many additional dimensions. Real space travel awaits us!

Spirit and body are not contradictories. A plant is greater than the seed from which it springs. From the death of a seed comes the life of a plant. As Paul said: "What is sown is perishable, what is raised is imperishable...it is raised in glory!" (1 Corinthians 15:42-43 NRSV). For us older folks some resurrection glory is captured in lines from the poem:

A Comfortable Lap

I don't want to be an
  antique displayed
in some celestial museum, I
  plan
on having a strong new
  body,
good friends, and exciting
  adventures.
Am I on target, Jesus?

What will people do all the time?

Empowered by God's Spirit (and freed from sinful hindrances) in heaven we'll have increased abilities. But if our persons change (as from seed to stalk), so will the size of God's garden. It's reasonable to expect that our mandate for Eden's stewardship will continue, with the renovated cosmos—and a renewed earth—as our workplace. We'll have things to do, the will and skill to do them, and the wisdom to do so in God's way.

Heaven will include that uniquely human contribution to life on earth—the city. By "the city" I mean not just a place of urban living but *civilization*, with its languages, its technologies, its governance, and its culture. On earth the physical city has often degenerated into a cesspool of iniquity marked by poverty at the center and greed at the periphery. Nature has suffered, too, from human sin and ignorance. God's city, however, has come to earth to a degree. Nurtured by righteousness, the human city hints of a coming splendor. Civilization has brought health and safety, release from misery, and creative enjoyment to millions of people: working, playing, socializing, learning, and creating. Already the earthly city explores its galaxy and probes outer space. It has catalogued the human genome. Scientific discoveries promise healthier and extended living for earth's inhabitants, or at least for some. With the curse of sin destroyed in a final apocalypse, surely human beings in heaven will become good stewards, completing and extending God's cosmos. Civilization is not old; it has barely begun!

So look for heaven to offer incredibly wonderful things to do in a society based upon love and truth. This is good news for ordinary folk, like the one in this poem:

I Feel Spiritual

When I told my friend I wanted to golf
in heaven, he said don't be stupid,
you got to focus on joys of the soul,
not pleasures of the body. So I said, okay,
I'll sing a hymn and polish
a pearly gate first, and then go golfing.
Al, he said, you must learn to think spiritual.
Well, I find it hard to separate physical
from spiritual. I feel spiritual nailing siding
on a Habitat for Humanity house
and fishing with my grandson. Lord,
I hope heaven will be even more rewarding.

Where is the universe going?

We should expect no diminishment of the earth that has nurtured and sustained us, but its renewal within a cosmos newly opened to us. God's cosmic re-creation awaits human redemption. The universe is an enormous place (expanding at an accelerating rate) with mysteries untapped. According to some scientists, ordinary matter makes up only five percent of cosmic reality, and we're in contact with only ten percent. There's a lot to the cosmos we have neither eyes nor instruments to perceive, nor brainpower to fathom. Yet.

Our covenant of stewardship remains in force today, even though sin has diminished its effectiveness. In spite of terrible misapplication of God's principles, human intelligence has harnessed energies for creative enterprises that bring health to the body, delight to the mind, and joy to the spirit. Our restless creativity evidences a God-implanted curiosity. We yearn to be cocreators with the Divine. Purified in heaven from the curse of sin (and adapted physically to multiple planetary systems), humanity will join the Master Architect in cosmic reconstruction.

I see heaven as blending the natural and artificial according to a divine blueprint. Gone will be the coarse brutality of primitive eons. Gone the grinding poverty of failing subsistence systems. Gone the sophisticated brutality of technological society. Present will be the glories of the great forests, the pure streams, the stillness of Arctic night, the sonorous cadence of crickets on a summer evening, the beauty of sunsets over the sea. Present will be human-built structures more magnificent than medieval cathedrals or modern corporate towers or sports stadiums. Heaven is depicted in Revelation as the city of God, with verdant, healing trees along streets of brilliant beauty.

What the cosmos restored in righteousness will look like materially, and how it will incorporate our earth, our solar system, our galaxy (and the billions of others we know of and hypothesize), angels, other creatures, and human artifacts, we cannot say. We *can* infer that it will embody the classic longings of the heart: the good, the true, and the beautiful; and that humanity will share in shaping God's own dreams—dreams for the peaceable kingdom.

Conclusion

Exploring heaven is exciting. We've already begun that adventure. Our leader is more than a heroic prophet, more than a renowned teacher. Jesus is a *present*—not a distant—Savior. Joyfully we proclaim "What a friend we have in Jesus!" We have found Jesus to be right about things pertaining to life on earth, and we're confident he is right about life in heaven too. General evidences for eternal life offer plausibility. Our friend Jesus Christ offers promise. Christ's presence in the heart and in the community of faith confirms that promise. That presence quickens expectations and removes fears. Christ within and among us is, indeed, our hope of glory! In worship, fellowship, and service we now experience aspects of God's eternal kingdom, righteousness, peace, joy—and we long for more! Supremely, we anticipate exploring heaven because Christ beckons us there! He summons humanity into the renewed world. Jesus the Messiah leads humanity across its multiple and sundry deserts and over barrier rivers into the cosmic and eternal Promised Land.

The church celestial is linked with the church terrestrial. Your friends and loved ones now in heaven aren't in some sort of limbo waiting for termination of earthly affairs. Given the relativity of time, in relation to us they are already enjoying Jerusalem the Golden. They are ahead of us in understanding, too, and their presence is less circumscribed than ours. Sometimes we shiver with intimations of them hovering around us. The book of Hebrews refers to them as "a cloud of witnesses." They watch how we do our laps in the relay race of life. When I become discouraged I like to picture my deceased friends cheering me on! Or when I wake up in the night with a solution for some nagging problem, it occurs to me that one of them has been kibitzing over my shoulder, empathetically nudging me with hints on the subject. They are with us, mind touching mind, spirit touching spirit, and one day, thank God, hand touching hand!

Biblical doctrine teaches that God created humanity for the sake of companionship. What a beautiful thought: God creates us with special mental, physical, and spiritual endowments so heaven won't be lonely! How incredible to learn that God not only loves me but needs me and wants me around! And that he needs and wants my neighbors, known and unknown to me, as well as the cosmos with all its things and its creatures great and small.

The hope of heaven is a beacon guiding us on our earthly journey. We see a Light ahead, beyond the vale of death, and we follow that Light. Intimations of heaven are imprinted in our minds and engraved upon our cultures. These dreams and visions mold the psyche and offer opportunities to seek and find the good, the true, and the beautiful. Our hopes for an afterlife are expressed in stories etched on cave walls and enshrined in art and literature. The resurrection of Jesus Christ assures us that such ancient and enduring visions, even if crudely articulated, derive from our Creator and Redeemer.

A concluding prudent word is appropriate, however. If our hopes for heaven were too lucid we would shirk our responsibility on earth, neglecting to learn how to live as persons created in God's image. If our hopes were too opaque we would despair, crushed by tragedy, beaten in a losing duel with death. In either case, we would fail to live faithfully in God's kingdom. *It is in our earthly home that we must freely respond to the divine initiative. It is here and now that we must let God overcome the sin in our lives and in our communities. It is on earth that God redeems and sanctifies us in preparation to live in eternity according to the divine image stamped on our hearts.*

Lord, on that great day may we, along with Job, hear the morning stars sing together and all the heavenly beings shout for joy! Praise your holy name!

Be Strong in the Lord

Northwest Yearly Meeting of Friends Church, July 23, 2003

How to be strong in the Lord

Our text offers four word pictures about being strong in the Lord: a young associate, a soldier, an athlete, and a farmer. In original context, an older apostolic leader, Paul, counsels a young minister—Timothy. In a contemporary context, an older leader, Arthur Roberts, urges younger folks to be strong in the Lord. Let's look at each picture.

Be strong like an eager young associate. At a job corps located near our coastal home, young people learn trades. At the annual public picnic these youth proudly tell visitors "I'm a carpenter," or "I'm an electrician," or "I'm a bookkeeper," or "I'm a cook." Actually, they're apprentices—learners—much like students at George Fox University training to be engineers or teachers or doctors or ministers. At this picnic director Holmes speeds about campus in his wheelchair, cheering on the kids, affirming the staff, and letting us taxpayers know the public is well served by this federal program.

Northwest Yearly Meeting of Friends is a kind of kingdom "job corps" where persons once floundering through life have experienced God's redeeming grace and now gratefully help each other do effective kingdom work. Samuel School is one example of how in Northwest Yearly Meeting, older folks help younger ones. Have you participated in this program as students, teachers, or mentoring elders? If so, please stand. How many youth and leaders have done service stints abroad; or built a house for Habitat for Humanity? Please stand. If you've been my student, please stand. Now, can you spot someone who in a special way has been your kingdom job corps leader, teaching you how to be an effective kingdom worker? If so, please stand. Thank you all, you may be seated. Truly we are the body of Christ!

So, kingdom job corps members—contemporary Pauls and Timothys—heed God's word of Scripture: *Be strong in the Lord.* In your homes and churches be as conscientious as a UPS driver delivering an important package. Be as attentive as a novice learning to drive a semi. Be as alert as an apprentice electrician. Be as diligent as a pre-med student doing lab assignments. Be as serious as a novice teacher

Scripture reading
2 Timothy 2:1-7 (NRSV here and in subsequent texts)

You then, my child, be strong in the grace that is in Christ Jesus; and what you have heard from me through many witnesses entrust to faithful people who will be able to teach others as well. Share in suffering like a good soldier of Christ Jesus. No one serving in the army gets entangled in everyday affairs; the soldier's aim is to please the enlisting officer. And in the case of an athlete, no one is crowned without competing according to the rules. It is the farmer who does the work who ought to have the first share of the crops. Think over what I say, for the Lord will give you understanding in all things.

hearing the principal explain educational objectives. One generation teaches the next how to read a book, how to frame a house, how to service a car, how to heal a body, how to instruct a mind, how to discipline the spirit. Like the child Samuel, we learn from older persons how to listen to God—through a parent, an aunt or uncle, a Sunday school teacher, a pastor. We older folks teach younger ones, then step aside and watch you assume responsibility. For a few decades, you'll do the job and then hand the torch to others, in turn watching prayerfully and with joy, as they do their job well too. And in heaven a "great cloud of witnesses"—from the apostle Paul to recently deceased friends or grandparents—kibitz over our shoulders and cheer us on.

In the business of life who is our journeyman carpenter? Who is our head mechanic? Who is our skilled surgical instructor? Who is the master teacher? Who conducts the final exam? Jesus. Will you be Jesus' trusted assistant? Will you keep the faith by diligent study and effective work? Reformer Martin Luther said we're all priests to one another through our vocations. Luther's father was a blacksmith, the son a professor. So whether God calls you to weld metal, teach, build houses, run a store, heal bodies and minds, or pastor a church, through whatever calling, *be strong for the Lord!* My friends, the twenty-first century is ours to witness God's kingdom.

Young people, you are fifteen or twenty, your parents and teachers are forty or fifty. I'm eighty years old. Walter Lee and Beryl Woodward are pushing one hundred. Several generations are in this auditorium tonight. So let's all heed the admonition from the psalm (Psalm 145:4, 11-13):

> One generation shall laud your works to another, and shall declare your mighty acts....They shall speak of the glory of your kingdom, and tell of your power, to make known to all people your mighty deeds, and the glorious splendor of your kingdom. Your kingdom is an everlasting kingdom, and your dominion endures throughout all generations.

Be strong like a soldier. News clips from Iraq showed soldiers lugging around lots of gear—and sometimes an injured companion. Soldiers have to be strong to tote heavy loads over rugged terrain under harrowing circumstances. If soldiers must be strong for carnal warfare, how much more should we be strong as soldiers of the cross. Don't get so entangled in culture you become lazy or not alert to orders. Keep in shape physically, mentally, spiritually! Be willing to suffer hardship. Don't be a couch potato, lazing around while the world burns. Life isn't soft; it's hard. Jobs get lost, accidents happen, houses are burned, people are raped and murdered; schools close, companies go bankrupt, hard times come, crime plagues our cities, hunger and disease ravage whole populations of the world. Like molten volcanoes, wars spew hot destruction across the landscape. Things are tough in a sinful world. They threaten body, mind, and spirit. So, my friends, whether you're thirteen or thirty, sixty or ninety, be strong like a soldier. Keep your body fit. Don't stuff it with fat and sugar, nourish it with good food. Keep your mind fit. Don't stuff it with celebrity chit chat and chaffy cinema. Fill it with useful knowledge and sanctified sensing. Keep your spirit fit. Don't stuff it with religious play-acting; infuse it rather with spiritual discipline and demonstrated love. What army commands your allegiance? God's army. Who is your commanding officer? Jesus. If you've been AWOL, get back to base, pronto!

"In the world you face persecution," said Jesus, "but take courage; I have conquered the world!" (John 16:33). Our Scripture text warns us not to get so trapped in worldly culture we can't respond to Christ's orders. How does culture entangle us? Both by forces inside and outside us. Especially when one is young there's a strong inner yearning to be affirmed as an individual, a need to belong, to know who you are and to be acknowledged by others.

As a sophomore I transferred to Greenleaf Friends Academy from Caldwell high school. My problem was how to get attention, how to get my worth acknowledged. So I devised a scheme. A local store was having a distress sale, unloading stuff that doesn't sell. In one bin I spotted olive green jodhpurs—just my size! Do you know what jodhpurs are? They're flared twill trousers that lace down the ankles and are tucked into field boots. Upscale Brits wear them on fox hunts. Well, nobody in cowboy Idaho ever wore them—until I came along! So on a Saturday I bought the jodhpurs for 25 cents; then I nailed metal protectors on my boot heels. On Monday I went to school and clomped triumphantly across the study hall! Did I get noticed? You better believe it! But the novelty soon wore off and I joined the other guys wearing the subculturally mandated kid apparel—dirty cords.

At *every* stage in life we use symbolic clothing or adornment to be affirmed. We might even use modes of behavior—the class clown, the eccentric professor. I want people to know I'm a unique individual and not a number. So do you. The ego craves a niche. Conversely, we seek symbolic ways to fulfill a yearning to belong. We love ourselves and want our uniqueness noted; we also love others and want to be like them. Inner conflict ensues—the individual self in tension with the social self. Merchants know this, of course, so they use celebrities to hype clothing and adornments to make us feel unique, "outside the box"—just like the other sheep they've shorn by clever ads!

Well, ordinary love dictates that we affirm others by accommodating to social conventions; so we decide whether to wear suits or jeans, beards or three-day stubble, crew cuts or spiky hair, high-rise pants or hip huggers, whether to drive a sleek sedan or a boxy SUV. Given this tension in our lives it's hard to discern whether choices are really ours or are merchandized implants. The same tension occurs in intellectual matters. Do we really believe this political or economic or religious theory, this latest academic fad; or are we caught up in an affinity cult? Sometimes we must stand against culture on behalf of truth and justice, like sentries guarding God's valuables. In any case let's take our cues about who we are and how we belong from our commander—from Jesus Christ. Jesus demonstrated both how to stand alone and with others. As our present leader, Christ speaks through our covenants of faith; through trusted elders. That voice is clarified through worship and discerned by private prayer. Satan sometimes comes as an angel of light, seeking to deceive even the elect; therefore we remain always on the alert, seeking rightly to discern which words and actions are appropriate for soldiers of the cross.

Consider biblical examples: Jesus spots a rascally official who yearns for recognition but faces isolating scorn by the folks he cleverly conned. Jesus calls, "C'mon, Nicodemus, let's have lunch at your house!" Jesus calls quiet Andrew and enlists him as a soldier in God's kingdom. Jesus confronts Simon Peter one-on-one after the brash fisherman had fled Golgotha, and leads him back into kingdom service. The risen Christ calls Mary by name and deputizes her to rally the bewildered troops. A Nicodemus is in this auditorium tonight. So is a Simon and a Mary. Are you listening to Jesus?

Christ calls us into a transgenerational community of faith. Together we support and sustain each other; we live and die for each other under orders from our commander, Jesus. The stories of our faith community fortify us. Many valiant young seventeenth-century Quakers came out of Cromwell's army. Disillusioned with carnal warfare they left the Puritan "new model army" and enlisted in what one dubbed "the Lamb's war." Currently, soldiers in Iraq, for whom "collateral damage" is defined by a graphic imprint of a child with arms blown off, are candidates for the Lamb's war. Like Christian service groups now ministering in many troubled places, young people in our century have also been nudged by the Holy Spirit to witness God's covenant of peace in a world of violence. Through hardships and suffering our spiritual ancestors found ways to do it; as their spiritual descendants, let's be faithful to Christ in *our* century.

Recently I received a letter from Fred Gregory, formerly with Mercy Corps, and now director of the Peace Corps in Uzbekistan. He reopened that country to aid workers after 9/11, and now has more than a hundred volunteers teaching English and health education. Fred notes the service ministry in this same country by Ron Hayes, of Northwest Medical Teams, and that of Stuart Willcuts, president of AirServ International, conveying service workers to Iraq. Fred wrote: "I believe that I am in a strategic place at a strategic time in history. My call to serve continues, in this new and important place and mode."

Fred's letter reminds me of a convocation talk I gave at George Fox thirty-seven years ago, in which I challenged students to go beyond negative protest and make a *constructive* response to the Vietnam war. Three students heard God's voice through that speech and they volunteered to go to Vietnam to provide healing service. Another joined later. Who were these Quaker students from GFC and the Northwest? Jon Newkirk, Jerry Sandoz, Dorlan Bales, and—you guessed it—Fred Gregory. Often dodging bullets, Fred operated a feeding program six miles from Mai Lai, where the infamous massacre occurred. Fred Gregory demonstrates what it's like to be a strong soldier for Jesus Christ. Some of you young people will follow in his steps.

Be strong like an athlete who contends valiantly for the prize, and does so playing by God's rules. If rules aren't followed athletic contests turn into brawls. Even Sosa can't get away with using a cork-filled bat. So it is with life. Don't try to play the game of life outside moral boundaries; don't cheat yourself, don't cheat your friends and loved ones, your neighbors, your Lord. "Moral failure" is all around us: cheating on tests, buying term papers, lying to get ahead, slandering folks, sexual cheating. Jesus summarized the rules in the game of life: love God with heart, mind and spirit; love your neighbor as yourself. A weakling can trip an opponent. It takes strength, discipline, and courage to play by the rules of life. You don't take steroids to win an athletic contest. You don't bypass morality to serve the kingdom. Listen to what the Bible says in 1 Corinthians 9:25-27:

> Athletes exercise self-control in all things; they do it to receive a perishable garland, but we an imperishable one. So I do not run aimlessly, nor do I box as though beating the air; but I punish my body and enslave it, so that after proclaiming to others I myself should not be disqualified.

Whose team are you on? God's team. Who is your coach? Jesus. Are you going to play hard and play by the rules? Yes. Be strong like an athlete!

Be strong like a good farmer. Ralph Beebe's history of Quakers in the Northwest is aptly titled *Garden of the Lord*. Many Quakers who came to the Northwest over a century ago to plant churches were engaged in agriculture, and some were orchardists—planting apples, plums, walnuts, and hazelnuts. Do you remember the story of Johnny Appleseed? Here's what I found about him on the Internet (The Processed Apples Institute, 2002, site designed and maintained by HQ CyberServices).

> Johnny Appleseed spent 49 years of his life in the American wilderness planting apple seeds. His real name was John Chapman and he was born September 26, 1774, in Massachusetts. He created apple orchards in Illinois, Indiana, Kentucky, Pennsylvania and Ohio. After 200 years, some of those trees still bear apples.
>
> Johnny Appleseed's dream was for a land where blossoming apple trees were everywhere and no one was hungry. A gentle and kind man, he slept outdoors and walked barefoot around the country planting apple seeds.
>
> Johnny was a friend to everyone he met. Indians and settlers—even the animals—liked Johnny Appleseed. His clothes were made from sacks and his hat was a tin pot. He also used his hat for cooking. His favorite book was the Bible. Johnny Appleseed died in 1845. It was the only time he had been sick—in over 70 years!

I also learned from an apple growers network that "Each year the people of Fort Wayne, Indiana, invite visitors from throughout the nation to celebrate the pioneer spirit of "Johnny Appleseed." His gravesite in Archer Park is a national historic landmark.

Like John Chapman, we're in the world to make it a good place, for others and for ourselves. On the third day of creation God planted apples and other trees. We gardeners flubbed our task and were driven east of Eden. But we are still called to care for the earth responsibly, not sinfully. Baptized with the Spirit's fire we go back through the flaming sword, to care for Eden right this time.

Being good farmers means tending the earth that nourishes others, and enjoying its fruit ourselves. This means we shouldn't demean the physical world in which we live and work, but rather tend it as the very garden of the Lord, and enjoy its bounty. Enjoy the apples we provide for others. We're not all orchardists like the Petersons of Entiat, but we all honor God and serve our neighbors through our earthly tasks.

Paul's picture has a deeper meaning. He exhorts Timothy to husband resources of the human spirit. The orchard is a metaphor for God's kingdom. Through Christ we have been grafted onto Abrahamic rootstock. From this orchard, from the sovereign Lord's kingdom, as Paul states (Galatians 5:22), the world receives its bounty. What is that fruit? Paul tells us: "the fruit of the Spirit is love, joy, peace, patience, kindness, generosity, faithfulness." The writer of Hebrews sums up the rewards for being good farmers of God's seed: "Now, discipline always seems painful rather than pleasant at the time, but later it yields the peaceful fruit of righteousness to those who have been trained by it" (Hebrews 12:11).

Around the globe are many kingdom orchards with a variety of apples. Our brand is called Quaker. It was well grafted onto sturdy rootstock. Our particular kingdom orchard is Northwest Yearly Meeting of Friends Church. Our orchard has fifty some established rows and fifteen newly planted ones. God has other good varieties of apples, but this is our orchard. We enjoy its fruit; we work so others may enjoy it too.

It's folly for a farmer to not have food in the house. It's folly for those who have ministered God's nourishing truths to fail to be nourished by those same fruits of the spirit. Paul warns of leadership temptations, "lest having preached to others I myself become a castaway." It's possible for a pastor to preach love to others and not partake of fruit of the spirit in the family. It's possible for an elder to admonish youth in the ways of righteousness but succumb to sexual immorality. It's possible for a philosopher like myself to affirm the logic of Christian belief and then be lured into dark doubt. It's possible for scholars to teach students God's word through Scripture or through the book of nature, and yet themselves be spiritually underfed. The book of Revelation sustains our kingdom hope for holiness by a vision of trees in a garden city freed from sin—trees that provide healing for the nations.

Can it be said of Northwest Yearly Meeting, as Paul said of the Colossians?

For we have heard of your faith in Christ Jesus and of the love that you have for all the saints, because of the hope laid up for you in heaven. You have heard of this hope before in the word of the truth, the gospel that has come to you. *Just as it is bearing fruit and growing in the whole world, so it has been bearing fruit among yourselves from the day you heard it and truly comprehended the grace of God.... so that you may lead lives worthy of the Lord, fully pleasing to him, as you bear fruit in every good work and as you grow in the knowledge of God.* (Colossians 1:4-6, 10, emphasis mine)

Whether material, mental, or spiritual, it's God's world; don't mess it up.

Whose orchard do we tend? God's. Where is this orchard? Among all tribes and tongues and peoples and nations of the world. Where is our orchard located? Northwest Yearly Meeting. Who teaches us to tend our orchard? Jesus. What do we receive from our work? To share and to enjoy the peaceable kingdom. Together, in Christ we savor the fruit of righteousness: love, joy, peace.

Conclusion

Hear our text again.

2 Timothy 2:1-7

You then, my child, be strong in the grace that is in Christ Jesus; and what you have heard from me through many witnesses entrust to faithful people who will be able to teach others as well. Share in suffering like a good soldier of Christ Jesus. No one serving in the army gets entangled in everyday affairs; the soldier's aim is to please the enlisting officer. And in the case of an athlete, no one is crowned without competing according to the rules. It is the farmer who does the work who ought to have the first share of the crops. Think over what I say, for the Lord will give you understanding in all things.

Invitation

Paul asked Timothy to think about what he wrote, and to let the Lord give understanding. I ask this of you, my friends. Let's settle into a short silence so we can better listen to the Lord. If the Lord points out sin in your life, whatever your age, repent and accept divine forgiveness. If the Lord asks you to be a more faithful apprentice, a more dedicated soldier of the cross, a more conscientious athlete for Jesus, a better farmer of God's created order, then from the bottom of your heart say "yes"! If the Lord is calling you to special ministry, say "yes" and report this to an elder in your church. Let's join in silent prayer.

Please stand and sing a chorus through which the Lord spoke to me sixty-five years ago: "I have decided to follow Jesus." For some of you singing these words in 2003 may be a major step in your own conversion. If you would like publicly to witness this decision for Jesus, please walk down to the front of this auditorium and kneel before God at the altar as an outward sign of that inward response to the Spirit; then receive my concluding prayer as a blessing by this community of faith.

Halloween

Yachats Community Presbyterian Church, October 26, 2003

Why celebrate Halloween? Many centuries ago Christians began setting aside days to celebrate their spiritual heritage by honoring valiant followers of Jesus. One such heroic Christian was an African woman, Vibia Perpetua. One thousand eight hundred years ago she was martyred for her Christian testimony. On her "holy day," March 7, 1778, Captain James Cook sailed past a rocky headland near where we live, and appropriately, gave it her name. Four years ago I helped celebrate a project at this beautiful spot, reading this poem.

Scripture reading
Ephesians 2:8-10
(NRSV here and in subsequent texts)
For by grace you have been saved through faith, and this is not your own doing; it is the gift of God—not the result of works, so that no one may boast. For we are what he has made us, created in Christ Jesus for good works, which God prepared beforehand to be our way of life.

Perpetua

We celebrate a reconstructed road
winding up a coastal headland
to the overlook at Cape Perpetua,
a point for viewing ships at sea,
soaring birds, and spouting whales.

This tranquil place gives us space
to tune our ears and focus eyes
upon the artistry of breakers
cresting blue-white on the shore.
We've time here to smell the flora
and to touch the trunks of trees
shaped by vicissitudes of storm
and adverse circumstance.

Receive the wind upon your face
as God's kiss of peace to you,
and to your friends, and to visitors
from everywhere. Renew your bonds
with humanity and with all creation
here, where earth and sea blend
with the sky in perpetuity.

Scan time's horizon carefully, too.
Generations past have climbed
this mountain, or camped a while.
Visualize Depression era workers
and lonely war time sentinels.
Observe Captain Cook and his sailors
Tacking offshore in a March storm.

See a young mother in Carthage,
Vibia Perpetua, rock firm in faith
as tyrants threw her to the beasts
eighteen centuries ago. Perpetua,
an apt name for this rocky cape.

How does Perpetua relate to Halloween? Well, there got to be so many saints over the centuries and so many "holy days," that Odilo of Cluny, a French church leader, international peacemaker, and friend to the poor, started the practice of setting aside one special day each year—November 1—to honor them all at the same time. First it was a special day to honor martyrs and other saintly folk, and prayerfully to consider improving one's own Christian discipleship. Later it became a holiday to honor all friends and loved ones who've crossed the dark valley into heaven, like our Memorial Day. All Saints' Day became "All Souls' Day." The word *hallow* is like our word *holy*, so the evening before this special day is "Hallow evening"—Halloween.

What about all the weird stuff: "trick-or-treat" masks, witches on broomsticks, impish mischief, and scary costumes? Well, Odilo wisely chose a day celebrated by Celtic and other pagan people as the end of harvest and the beginning of a new year. In a bold stroke of cultural transformation, the sagacious abbot transformed an ancient pagan festival filled with fear of the underworld into a celebration of Christ's triumph over malicious powers—real and imagined. (Once people know that "things that go bump in the night" don't exist or at least are harmless, they can poke fun at them.) So over time rituals were developed to dramatize how Christ overcomes the darkness that plagued superstitious pagans. In playful drama the demons symbolically run wild in the darkening night; but in the morning we celebrate how Jesus Christ's sacrificial death and life-giving resurrection triumphs over everything that is evil, false, and ugly, and celebrates everything that is good and true and beautiful.

Symbolically, in Halloween rituals Satan's tricks are foiled by Jesus' treats. Threats of violence are met and overcome by generous acts of love. On Halloween we say "good riddance!" to evil and we honor those people who have triumphed over death, hell, and the grave. At this special time we say "hello" and "goodbye" to them, and look forward to meeting them and all the saints on heaven's shore.

All Souls' Day has gotten so secularized recently that the significant and triumphant part of the holiday has been neglected. Witches and weird costumes are more easily merchandized, I guess, than white robes and halos. The evening is celebrated more than the morning. We won't let Wiccans repaganize Odilo's day, nor merchants preempt its message! Today as Christians we remember with gratitude all those folks who have successfully "fought the good fight" against Lucifer, the Destroyer, and who now with all the saints sing "glory to the Lamb!" Let's examine our own lives for evils lurking—not as imaginary creatures of the night hiding in haunted houses—but as Satan's minions lurking in the dark side of the ego and in corrupted society; and then let's ask God to lavish upon us healing grace, to deliver us from all our fears, whether from without or from within, to show us the triumph of the cross and the resurrection.

In a way the church is to blame for this perversion of All Souls' Day. Honoring the dead became such a big thing in the medieval church that bishops, exercising more entrepreneurial skill than Christian wisdom, devised a money-raising scheme based upon heroes of faith. They sold indulgences. You see, people knew that their departed dead weren't nearly as saintly as Perpetua and the other heroes of the faith. They were also taught by medieval theology that most folks faced heavy-handed purgatorial cleansing—years of it, perhaps—before they could enter heaven. So on All Souls' Day one might visualize one's dear departed uncle being whipped by the angels month after month in a celestial woodshed to punish him for rascally attitudes and deeds earthside. It was a way to beat the hell out of him. But priests had a solution for distraught families: Why grieve over such harsh and extended punishment when you can purchase an indulgence to shorten the purgatorial sentence and speed your errant uncle through the pearly gates? How better show charity than digging into your pockets to assist some poor soul, sobbing on the brink of hell, to enter heaven with no more purgatorial delay? Such indulgences were possible, people were assured, because over the centuries the saints had left such an enormous legacy of holiness that clergy could dole out surplus merit to morally challenged folks. One top traveling salesman was Tetzel, who unctuously intoned this little advertising jingle: "Soon as the coin in the coffer springs, so soon does a soul from purgatory spring." Such a purchase was called an indulgence, and indulgences were sold to raise money for church building projects.

Well, this money-raising scheme outraged a thoughtful monk, Martin Luther, and Tetzel's jingle really ticked him off. In holy fury Luther penned and nailed on the church door at Wittenberg, Germany, ninety-five reasons why selling indulgences was an abomination in the sight of God. Number 86 reads:

> Why does not the Pope, whose riches are at this day more ample than those of the wealthiest of the wealthy, build the Basilica of St. Peter with his own money, rather than with that of poor believers?
> ("The Ninety-five Theses," The Christian Classics Ethereal Library, www.ccel.org op. cit.)

The Reformation was born.

So, on Halloween let's remember Perpetua and Odilo, and Luther, yes, and unctuous "telemarketer" Tetzel, and rejoice that we are saved by grace, and that not of ourselves but it is the gift of God to all who come in faith. When on October 31 the kids come to our doors in kooky costumes calling "trick or treat," let's just stuff goodies in their plastic bags and rejoice with them that God sets us free from Satan's tricks, whether cloaked in pagan darkness or foisted upon us by misguided servants of the Light.

Hear again our Scripture text:

Ephesians 2:8-10
> For by grace you have been saved through faith, and this is not your own doing; it is the gift of God—not the result of works, so that no one may boast. For we are what he has made us, created in Christ Jesus for good works, which God prepared beforehand to be our way of life.

To Luther we owe a debt of thanks this Halloween for recovering to the church a clear doctrine of God's grace.

Implications of the text

First, we are saved by grace through faith.

Salvation is a gift. We can't earn it. There is no such thing as surplus merit available for anyone to dispense: minister, counselor, parent, spouse. Not even early church martyrs like Paul and Perpetua or the two thousand Christians around the world who lost their lives last year to persecution have extra holiness to be purchased or donated to bail out less spiritual folks. Saintly souls do inspire us; on occasion they may even kibitz over our shoulders and urge us to be strong soldiers for Christ; but we can't borrow from their banked goodness, either in this life or the next.

Second, we're all called to good works.

I said earlier we can't earn salvation; but we can, and must, follow the way of life God has prepared, a life of moral integrity and faithful witness. Christ leads all of us. There is no spiritual elite authorized and empowered to do kingdom work so the rest of us can goof off. Martin Luther rightly called for a priesthood of believers, by which he meant that each person is a priest—a servant—to one's neighbor through the vocation with which he is called. His father was a blacksmith, Martin a professor. Whatever our vocation and avocation, we are called through our lives to love God and others. Luther insisted the home is the hallowed place, and celebrated it himself by marrying a nun, Catherine. The egghead theologian marveled at the beauty of physical love. When their first child was born he joyously washed and hung the diapers on the clothesline. When neighbors chuckled at this the former monk said, "Let them laugh, the angels in heaven rejoice."

What we celebrate on All Souls' Day is the wonder that God's grace infuses ordinary life: work, play, marriage, socializing. The home is the sanctuary for the Spirit—the place where God dwells with us, works with us, plays with us, loves with us, suffers with us, yes, dies with us, and shares resurrection with us.

Third, through grace we recover the divine image stamped upon us in creation.

That image is to be spiritual beings, creative and holy in body and mind, loving God and neighbor and caring for the cosmos. The kingdom life God has prepared for us pertains both to this life and to the next. The Lord's Prayer includes this phrase: "Thy will be done in earth, as it is in heaven." Did you notice where the comma went? Let's do it again: "Thy will be done in earth, as it is in heaven."

The apostle Paul, soon to lose his life for the gospel and to become one of the first of the honored saints, wrote young Timothy (2 Timothy 4:1-8):

> In the presence of God and of Christ Jesus, who is to judge the living and the dead, and in view of his appearing and his kingdom, I solemnly urge you: proclaim the message; be persistent whether the time is favorable or unfavorable; convince, rebuke, and encourage, with the utmost patience in teaching. For the time is coming when people will not put up with sound doctrine, but having itching ears, they will accumulate for themselves teachers to suit their own desires, and will turn away from listening to the truth and wander away to myths. As for you, always be sober, endure suffering, do the work of an evangelist, carry out your ministry fully.
>
> As for me, I am already being poured out as a libation, and the time of my departure has come. I have fought the good fight, I have finished the race, I have kept the faith. From now on there is reserved for me the crown of righteousness, which the Lord, the righteous judge, will give me on that day, and not only to me but also to all who have longed for his appearing.

The first Sunday in November is fittingly called "Reformation Sunday," honoring that momentous time when the church recovered its balance and affirmed the triumph of Christ over all the devils on earth or in hell. It is said that in anguished spiritual struggle, Martin Luther the monk once threw an ink bottle at the devil who was taunting him. Did he hit or miss? I don't know about *that* occasion, but I know that Luther found, and trusted One, Christ Jesus, who didn't miss triumphing over evil in Luther's time, and doesn't miss now in Yachats on Halloween 2003.

We conclude worship today singing one of Luther's hymns: "A Mighty Fortress Is Our God." Note especially verses three and four:

> And though this world,
>   with devils filled,
> should threaten to undo us,
> we will not fear, for God
>   hath willed
> His truth to triumph
>   through us.
> The Prince of Darkness
>   grim,
> we tremble not for him;
> his rage we can endure,
> for lo, his doom is sure;
> one little word shall fell
>   him.
>
> That word above all earthly
>   powers,
> no thanks to them, abideth;
> the Spirit and the gifts are
>   ours
> through him who with us
>   sideth.
> Let goods and kindred go,
> this mortal life also;
> the body they may kill,
> God's truth abideth still,
> His kingdom is forever.

Have a good Halloween and a better All Souls' Day!

Patience

Friendsview Retirement Community, July 7, 2004;
Waldport Presbyterian Church, July 25, 2004

Introduction

A doctor's client is well named: a "patient"—one who waits in the waiting room, dutifully filling out forms, waits to meet the doctor, endures sundry painful procedures, lines up at the pharmacy to fill the prescription, waits for the bills to get paid, and most importantly, waits for healing to occur.

I struggle to be patient, particularly when a process takes longer than what I think it should, or could, and I can't speed it up. What the Spirit speaks to me may be helpful to you.

Patience is a spiritual virtue. The Bible is filled with godly exhortations to be patient, whatever happens. The "whatever" bothers me. Like other virtues, patience is sharpened by adversity. It's not difficult to be patient if nothing or nobody riles you. But through adversity, patience is developed. Where do we find adversity? Everywhere—in circumstances and in people, including those we love, and in ourselves.

In a Bible search on the words *patience*, and *patient*, I found many verses. Most New Testament references are from the apostle Paul. Now this guy was a type-A personality if there ever was one! Although he didn't feel sorry for himself, Paul did on occasion list all sorts of aggravating and life-threatening circumstances, such as shipwrecks, stoning, escaping over a wall, people who left him in the lurch, opponents who perverted the gospel and impugned his motives, and imprisonment. His list makes mine seem petty, although I've learned that little things often irritate more than big things. A toothache may challenge faith more than a windstorm. As a proverb states, it's "the little foxes that ruin the vineyards" (Song of Solomon 2:15 NIV). So consider with me some scriptural exhortations about patience.

Wisdom increases our capacity for patience.

Proverbs 19:11 (NIV) says, "A man's wisdom gives him patience; it is to his glory to overlook an offense." It's good to be magnanimous although easier in some circumstances and with some people than otherwise. We're supposed to get wiser as we get older, and if we handle our experiences well, we do. But retired folks have to help each other not to become crabby, complaining about this and that to compensate for not being actively engaged in the workaday world.

Ecclesiastes 7:8 (NRSV) says, "…The patient in spirit are better than the proud in spirit." Hmm. I guess our egos sometimes make patience difficult—for others as well as for ourselves. I have to sort out whether I'm being stalwart for truth or just stubborn, whether principle is at stake or vanity. Whether ego or Deo has the keys to my mind. How about you? Can we accept with grace what happens even when it hurts, even when we are humbled? Sirach 2:4 (NRSV, Anglicized edition) reads "Accept whatever befalls you, and in times of humiliation be patient."

God's patience instructs us in righteousness.

Isaiah the prophet-statesman became exasperated with Israel and figured God must be even more so. He wrote "Is it not enough to try the patience of men? Will you try the patience of my God also?" (Isaiah 7:13 NIV). Patience isn't just rolling over and being crushed by evil, or putting up with every sort of nonsense. Patience is about holding fast to truth without wavering, but not using ungodly methods in doing so.

If Jesus can throw the rascals out of the temple, I surely can cheer the effort. But then I recall Isaiah kneeling awestricken before the Almighty, and hand to my mouth I want to make sure I'm hearing the divine voice correctly before I judge others. I recall Calvary and wonder about my capacity for cross-bearing. Suffering, it seems, comes with kingdom territory, but vengeance belongs to God. I'm not the Almighty's sheriff, but I am part of the church, and prophetic speaking is included in the gospel mandate.

James, the brother of our Lord, commended the prophets (James 5:10 NIV): "Brothers, as an example of patience in the face of suffering, take the prophets who spoke in the name of the Lord." One who would be God's voice for truth and justice must be patient—take the long view, and not be arrogant. Patience includes tenacity for truth, not indulgence of evil.

As beneficiaries of patience we should reciprocate.

Paul uses himself as an example (1 Timothy 1:16 NIV): "…I was shown mercy so that in me, the worst of sinners, Christ Jesus might display his unlimited patience as an example for those who would believe on him and receive eternal life." God is patient with misguided idealists and zealots of every stripe in the hopes that they, like hard-headed Saul, will be converted and turn their energy in the right direction. Most of us have suffered from hard-headedness in one way or another, and upon receiving God's mercy we're ready to make patience a virtue. The late Charles Beals once reproved me for a stubborn impatience: "Arthur, has it ever occurred to you that you might be wrong?" Paul wrote young Timothy, "You, however, know all about my teaching, my way of life, my purpose, faith, *patience*, love, endurance" (2 Timothy 3:10 NIV, emphasis mine). Like Paul, we can urge younger folks to be prepared in season and out of season to correct, rebuke, and encourage—with great patience and careful instruction (see 2 Timothy 4:2).

Jesus prayed, "Forgive them, for they don't know what they are doing" and suffered at the hands of those who reviled and abused him. Jesus' disciples should expect some flack from evil folk, and have patience with them. At least we're not suffering persecution like some of our Christian brothers and sisters in many parts of the world.

Paul teaches us that patience is a fruit of the Spirit. We need several kinds of fruit for physical health. For spiritual health we are offered nine kinds, according to Galatians 5:22-25 (NIV):

> But the fruit of the Spirit is love, joy, peace, patience, kindness, goodness, faithfulness, gentleness and self-control. Against such things there is no law. Those who belong to Christ Jesus have crucified the sinful nature with its passions and desires. Since we live by the Spirit, let us keep in step with the Spirit.

The writer of Hebrews links patience to active faith and declares that laziness fosters impatience. "We do not want you to become lazy, but to imitate those who through faith and patience inherit what has been promised" (Hebrews 6:12 NIV).

Understanding God's purposes helps us be patient.

This means God's purposes in the trials that we experience, and also God's purposes for the cosmos itself. The resurrection is the bond that holds together "what's in life for me?" and "where is the universe going?" Job asked (6:11 NRSV) "...What is my end, that I should be patient?" It was mostly God's presence, not God's answers to the problem of pain, that satisfied Job. And will satisfy us.

James and Peter admonish us similarly, James writes (5:7-8 NRSV), "Be patient, therefore, beloved, until the coming of the Lord. The farmer waits for the precious crop from the earth, being patient with it until it receives the early and the late rains. You also must be patient. Strengthen your hearts, for the coming of the Lord is near." Patience lets us know that the Lord is already near and that, whatever our future in a cosmos with billions of galaxies, the new heavens and new earth have already begun in our hearts and in our communities of faith.

Tempestuous Peter, who ought to know from experience, writes (2 Peter 3:9 NRSV) "The Lord is not slow about his promise, as some think of slowness, but is patient with you, not wanting any to perish, but all to come to repentance."

Patience under adversity is a common scriptural theme.

"Patient endurance" is a frequent expression. In the parable of the soils Jesus said that even when God's seed is sown in good soil it bears fruit only through patient endurance (Luke 8:15). Paul added that patience in suffering brings spiritual triumph when framed by joyful hope and prayer (Romans 12:12). Joyful hope and prayer—now there's a recipe for dealing with adversity! It's a bit of a stretch for us, isn't it?

Patience is the first characteristic of love.

In that beautiful tribute to love, 1 Corinthians 13, the first characteristic is patience. "Love is patient; love is kind; love is not envious or boastful or arrogant." Surely if we are to love others as ourselves, then we must be patient with ourselves as well. If God waits, so may we. This chapter is often read at weddings, a reminder that marriages are strengthened when a man and woman are patient with each other, and homes become secure when patience is the context for the family. I think this is true of extended families as well.

Patience sustains good relationships with others.

Scripture counsels us to be patient with lazy folks, students, the timid ("fainthearted"), the weak (1 Thessalonians 5:14), the poor who ask our help (Sirach 29:8) and those whose minds fail them (Sirach 3:13). Wrote Paul, "The Lord's servant must not be quarrelsome but kindly to everyone, an apt teacher, patient" (2 Timothy 2:24 NRSV).

Conclusion

So, let us demonstrate patience in all circumstances and in respect to others. Let us also be patient with God, and with ourselves. The resurrection of Christ is God's pledge to us that truth and love will triumph. In this life. In the next. Keeping in step with the Holy Spirit is what I want to do, and if patience is part of the rhythm, that's what I will strive for. Will you?

Metaphors of the Atonement

Reedwood Friends Church, August 1, 2004

It may be a while since you've reflected upon the atonement, about how Jesus Christ is "the procuring cause" of salvation, about *how* Jesus' death saves. As Paul wrote, "...Just as sin reigned in death, so also grace might reign through righteousness to bring eternal life through Jesus Christ our Lord" (Romans 5:21, NIV here and throughout). Grace means God's help is needed; and that it is freely offered—and gratefully received. *How* does Jesus' death bring us to righteousness and eternal life? Certain classic word pictures help us understand this mystery.

The first picture:
Christ ransoms us from the devil.

The theory goes beyond an apparent religious primitivism. This social metaphor—ransom—(more current than we'd like to acknowledge) powerfully hints at how Jesus' death saves. Think of hostages for whom ransom can't be paid lest more hostages get taken. What a moral dilemma for nations! Recently Iraqi insurgents have beheaded unredeemed captives and threaten more. This theory of the atonement pictures people trapped by evils from which Christ rescues them. Early Christians said Jesus was the price God paid Satan to release us hostages. Jesus is held in hell's stockade for our freedom. (Remember the children's game "steal sticks"?) But hell couldn't hold Jesus, as the resurrection demonstrated. Jesus gave his life *as a ransom*. This is how biblical writers phrased it (Mark 10:45, 1 Timothy 2:6). Sin is conquered, evil is defeated. So each Easter gladly we sing "Up from the grave he arose, victory o'er his foes."

When God delivers the poor from want or provides the homeless a habitat, we rejoice that he finds human instruments for these beneficent purposes. We rejoice when God sets prisoners free, whether from political bondage or from personal addictions, such as gambling, pornography, gluttony, greed, power trips, drug abuse, phobias, a vengeful spirit, and (basically) from pride.

People delivered from bondage generally rejoice, although, like the ancient Israelites, some still pine for Egypt after deliverance from its slavery. People delivered from traps set by others or by themselves, however, usually neither wallow in neurosis nor quibble about modes of deliverance. Hearing Jesus' voice they take up their confining bed and walk! Free at last! That's what ransomed people shout when shackles fall.

Consider a second theory:
Christ satisfies divine honor.

Nearly a thousand years ago an English theologian wrote a pamphlet entitled *Cur Deus Homo,* "Why Did God Become Man?" Anselm used a metaphor of royalty insulted to explain the atonement. Privately, this monk reasoned, a ruler may wish to forgive an insult, but the state's honor is at stake, so he can't. What's the application? Sin so grossly insults God it requires more than humanity can muster to satisfy. Accordingly, God accepts Jesus' sacrifice, who as human being (one of us) takes the rap representatively and as Divine satisfies the insult. Thus God's honor is preserved.

Anselm's picture is puzzling. Superficially, God seems to resemble a petty dictator bothered by sassy serfs. But, like parables, metaphors point to realities beyond them, not to logical equivalences. Look at the realm of human experience for which this theory provides a relief map: sin *is* an enormous and costly affront to the universe God created. Ponder historical situations of social insult: jousts between jilted lords, eighteenth-century dueling (e.g., Hamilton vs. Burr), or gunfights in the nineteenth-century West—the mystique for which continues in pop culture.

In the old city of Prague, in 1618, a group of Protestant nobles threw a Hapsburg prince from a window. The noble wasn't hurt—a circumstance Catholics attributed to angels and Protestants to luck in landing on a haystack. The insult, however, precipitated a war that lasted thirty years. Violence in Europe, America, Asia, and Africa illustrates the vicious cycle of ethnic insult and retaliation. Nazi genocide of Jews and Gypsies outraged the world. The Nuremberg trials labeled them "crimes against humanity." Sadly, the Holocaust corrupted some of its victims—like abused children who themselves become abusers. Consequently Muslim and Christian Arabs are insulted by Israeli actions such as leveling olive orchards and erecting walls.

Think of the insult to humanity when parents drop progeny over cliffs, or set them afire, or chain them up, or lock tots in the house for a night on the town. Or when berserk persons spray a playground with gunfire, or boys murder a toddler for the fun of it, or rapists chop up victims, or corporate schemers victimize retirees who trusted them with life savings. In such cases the public, not only the family, is outraged. Like Abel's blood, such insults cry for retribution. Such acts insult humanity made in the image of God. They insult God.

In the atoning life, death, resurrection, and continued lordship of Jesus Christ, God satisfies the insult of sin in ways both just and loving. Jesus saves by becoming the servant—by enduring suffering, not inflicting it. This is grace greater than our sins. Jesus' death suffices. God's honor is satisfied and so is ours. We don't need to slaughter neighbors or sacrifice children to propitiate Deity. God provides the sacrificial lamb.

Consider a third theory:
Christ substitutes for us.

Christ takes the punishment we deserve. He bore the curse laid on us for having broken moral principles, which in our minds we accept. This view isn't about paying extortion money to the Devil or salvaging divine honor. It's about breaking divine law. Again, the point of this picture isn't to compare God to a harsh judge, but to signify the meaning of Jesus' crucifixion. Persons of conscience, having with shame and sorrow acknowledged sin, are instructed in the meaning of Christ's atonement.

When George Fox languished in gaol for religious freedom, a young friend offered to take his place. Oliver Cromwell, hearing of this, asked his councilors, "Which of you would do the same for me?" No one volunteered to be a substitute. When God asked who would take the rap for the worst of us, Jesus replied, "I will." He chose to bear our punishment, even to death.

This substitutionary view is popular among Christians, which means we should be wary lest it be distorted by what Bonhoeffer called "cheap grace"—we walk away from the consequences of our sins because a heavenly granddaddy pays the fine. We crucify Christ afresh by such presumptions on God's grace. "Sinning at Christ's cost" is William Penn's indictment.

A good feature of the substitutionary view is that Christ identifies with humanity. Jesus is tempted like we are, yet without sin. He sweats out fears of what happens to good people in a bad world. Gethsemane is watered with real tears. Jesus is one of us. By his stripes we are healed, as the movie *The Passion of the Christ* depicts with terrifying emotional force. A person who bails out an errant person receives more than cheery thanks. Bonding occurs between benefactor and benefited. Recipients of grace follow the Lord by taking up the cross. They become empathetic agents of reconciliation, as coheirs with Christ in the kingdom. Following the lead of their Savior, Jesus Christ, they too demonstrate substituted love.

A fourth way to explain how Christ's death procures human righteousness is:

The moral influence theory

For a twelfth-century monk, Peter Abelard, the theory goes like this. For grace to be really free and unmerited, a loving God must bear the burden of human sin without attaching conditions such as having to pay off the devil, assuage insults, or exact fines for breaking divine law. God's unconditional love is so powerfully revealed in the life and death of Jesus that it awakens within us sinners a reciprocal response: "We love him because he first loved us." This metaphor draws upon social experience. A smile earns a smile; those who respect others themselves receive respect. Love is reciprocal.

There are questions about this theory. How can the death of Jesus effect human moral transformation if it just depends on our attitudes? Do people dispassionately decide for good or evil? Like choosing fish instead of fowl on a menu? If people are *that* free, then what difference does Jesus' death make? Carnality seems insufficiently accounted for. Another objection: It appears to put Jesus in series with other charismatic martyrs whose death is influential.

Looking deeper, however, we can find merit in this social analogy. What more powerfully motivates than unconditional love? Why should love be demeaned as causally ineffective to account for God's transformation of our sinful nature? Especially when one recognizes that the church is Christ's body. The one in whose name we conclude our prayers is not only Lord of the church, but also Lord of history and Lord of the cosmos. Is there a better hero to follow? Love energizes, suffering love especially. The writer of Hebrews says: "In bringing many sons to glory, it was fitting that God, for whom and through whom everything exists, should make the author of their salvation perfect through suffering" (Hebrews 2:10-11).

A George Fox colleague, Phil Smith, adds to these traditional views of the atonement a fifth metaphor:

The reconciling peacemaker

Picture a battlefield, with God as the righteous king and humanity as rebels against his legitimate rule. Much like Augustine's account of the Fall, sinners are united only in their rebellion against God. Human "community" is fractured by all sorts of selfishness. God fights to defeat the rebels in the most surprising way, by becoming the defenseless Lamb of God. "Do not weep! See, the Lion of the tribe of Judah, the Root of David, has triumphed" (Revelation 5:5). A Lion/Lamb is at the center of God's throne.

Paul depicts it thus in Romans 5:10-11:

> For if, when we were God's enemies, we were reconciled to him through the death of his Son, how much more, having been reconciled, shall we be saved through his life! Not only is this so, but we also rejoice in God through our Lord Jesus Christ, through whom we have now received reconciliation.

The peacemaking picture resembles Abelard's moral-influence picture in that God reaches out to rebels; but it explains more forcefully why God's efforts at reconciliation led to the cross. As in Jesus' parable, the death of the Son is the rebels' idea, not God's, and represents their most determined attempt to thwart God's rule. He had one left to send, a beloved son. As Mark 12:6-8 reports:

> He sent [the son] last of all, saying, "They will respect my son." But the tenants said to one another, "This is the heir. Come, let's kill him, and the inheritance will be ours." So they took him and killed him, and threw him out of the vineyard.

In the peacemaking picture, God allows sinners to expend the full energy of their rebellion. They have rejected his law, rejected his prophets, and now they reject him. In killing the Son and heir, sinners have carried their rebellion to its greatest possible extent; they may even think they have conquered God. That's how rebellious humanism thinks: Get rid of God and we will really be free to enjoy the earth; it'll all be ours. None of this religious stuff. But the slaughtered Son rises from the dead, and his patient but authoritative entreaty to us rebels is not silenced. "Here I am! I stand at the door and knock. If anyone hears my voice and opens the door, I will come in and eat with him, and he with me" (Revelation 3:20).

It wasn't just Pilate, his soldiers, the religious establishment of Jerusalem, and Judas who killed Jesus. All of us—rebels against the sovereign God—crucified the Savior, but, wondrously, the reconciliation he offers extends to all of us! Our part is to admit we've exhausted all powers of self-direction (we've used up our ammunition, as it were) and submit finally to the rule and fellowship of God. We surrender to the conquering Lamb of God. And in that surrender—initially so difficult for the ego—comes joy at finding our true selves. We recover from egoistic tunnel vision. Having been caught in God's powerful net of grace, we are surprised to discover we've arrived at our true home. Rejoice with me again in these words from the apostle Paul:

> But God proves his love for us in that while we still were sinners Christ died for us. Much more surely then, now that we have been justified by his blood, will we be saved through him from the wrath of God. For if while we were enemies, we were reconciled to God through the death of his Son, much more surely, having been reconciled, will we be saved by his life. (Romans 5:8-10 NRSV)

Jesus is the peace child, both symbol and agent of reconciliation. Governance has been placed upon this child's shoulders, as Isaiah foresaw. Pagans lord it over each other, but that's not God's way, taught Jesus. Whoever would lead must serve, first God, then self and others. Jesus invites us to be citizens of God's kingdom. We are, indeed, saved *by his life* as well as by his death.

Conclusion

We'll never remove all mystery from the atonement. But these social metaphors help us realize how Jesus' death effects salvation—how Jesus saves. We become better Christians when the mind is sharpened on the lodestone of this mystery. The ransom theory of atonement shows salvation as release from bondage. The satisfaction theory pictures Jesus restoring honor to God and God's whole creation. The substitutionary theory shows the cross regenerating goodness. The moral influence theory highlights the power of love. The peacemaker theory shows *how* God subdues and reconciles rebellious humanity. The atonement may not easily be explained, but in penitence it may be received readily; it can be *experienced*. This I witness with profound gratitude to God and with great joy! Let this be your witness too! Lines from an old Johnson/Towner hymn read:

> Marvelous, infinite,
>   matchless grace,
> freely bestowed
>   on all who believe!
> You that are longing
>   to see his face,
> will you this moment
>   his grace receive?

> Grace, grace, God's grace,
> Grace that will pardon
>   and cleanse within;
> Grace, grace, God's grace,
> Grace that is greater
>   than all our sin.

Gratitude

*Friendsview Retirement Community, midweek meeting,
November 3, 2004
(Using poems from* Let the Spirit Soar, *published by the city of Yachats, 2000)*

We express gratitude for people of the past who have contributed to our lives

- For those founders of our country with a yearning for freedom of life, liberty, and happiness
- For our parents, grandparents, siblings who nourished us, physically and spiritually
- For the apostolic witness to Christ and successive witnesses through the Christian centuries
- For people at Friendsview and in various local churches who strengthened our faith

We Remember

This month America proclaims
a holiday to celebrate gratitude.
Thanksgiving is a time when family
and friends happily stuff themselves
on turkey, cranberries, and pumpkin pie,
casting a ritual backward glance
at pilgrim ancestors. Like them
we have gleaned earth's bounty,
but in more comfortable circumstances—
and have survived another year.

Each November we remember,
as did migrants to our shores,
a faith imprinted now on dollar bills,
and on fives and tens and twenties,
fifties, and on that crisp new issue
with Ben Franklin's picture on it,
slightly (and fittingly) off-center.
What's written on larger bills

Scripture reading
Colossians 3:12-17
(NRSV here and in subsequent texts)

As God's chosen ones, holy and beloved, clothe yourselves with compassion, kindness, humility, meekness, and patience. Bear with one another and, if anyone has a complaint against another, forgive each other; just as the Lord has forgiven you, so you also must forgive. Above all, clothe yourselves with love, which binds everything together in perfect harmony. And let the peace of Christ rule in your hearts, to which indeed you were called in the one body. *And be thankful.* Let the word of Christ dwell in you richly; teach and admonish one another in all wisdom; and with *gratitude in your hearts* sing psalms, hymns, and spiritual songs to God. And whatever you do, in word or deed, do everything in the name of the Lord Jesus, *giving thanks* to God the Father through him.

I wouldn't know but I imagine
they all say it: "in God we trust."
If, as cynics say, this be pious cant,
then what final authority endows
us with those unalienable rights
that government is set up to sustain—
life, liberty, the pursuit of happiness?
The motto has it right: trust in God,
however named, however worshipped,
is foundational to civic order,
offers moral context to our laws,
and guidance to our social goals.
Each November, we remember.

Psalm 145:4 (NRSV) reads, "One generation shall laud your works to another, and shall declare your mighty acts."

We express gratitude for the joy of intergenerational sharing.
- Gratitude for young folks at George Fox who enrich our lives as we enrich theirs
- Gratitude for children, grandchildren, great grandchildren whose love is reciprocal
- Gratitude for people who serve us here at Friendsview, and whom we serve, too
- Gratitude for persons around the world to whom we share our stored energy—money—for their—and our—spiritual and physical good
- Gratitude for small favors to and from ordinary folks with whom we share each day

Foliage Isn't Everything

Why alders strip their leaves each fall
and stand around stiff and bare
through cold and rainy months
while conifers proudly flaunt
their lovely coats all year long
is something a botanist could
elucidate at some length,
patiently ignoring my poetic
anthropomorphism.

Maybe it's all about symbiosis
in a healthy biosphere.

It looks as though some things,
and some people, apparently,
sacrifice more to common good
or just have more to give,
than do others. Or does social
inequity fashion them
into givers and takers?

But maybe there is more
to giving and receiving
than meets the eye: perhaps
a nexus of needs and goods
reciprocally exchanged?
Or losses that redemptively
mulch the soil for growth?

In folks as well as forests
foliage isn't everything.

These passages of Scripture remind us about love, the basis of gratitude:

John 13:34 (NRSV): "I give you a new commandment, that you love one another. Just as I have loved you, you also should love one another."

John 15:12 (NRSV): "This is my commandment, that you love one another as I have loved you."

John 15:17 (NRSV): "I am giving you these commands so that you may love one another."

Romans 12:10 (NRSV): "Love one another with mutual affection; outdo one another in showing honor."

We show gratitude for God's grace

- Gratitude to God for forgiveness of sins
- Gratitude to God for quickened consciences
- Gratitude to God for healing bad memories
- Gratitude to God for making every path taken a road to heaven
- Gratitude to God for the gift of eternal life through Jesus Christ, our Lord.

Ephesians 2:5, 7-8 (NRSV) reads: "Even when we were dead through our trespasses, [God] made us alive together with Christ—by grace you have been saved...so that in the ages to come he might show the immeasurable riches of his grace in kindness toward us in Christ Jesus. For by grace you have been saved through faith, and this is not your own doing; it is the gift of God."

Blows the Fog Away

Some days regret like cold fog
whirls about nooks and crannies
of the soul, warping memory
within a gray miasmic mist.
We grope for familiar landmarks.
Our way forward becomes clouded.
What could or should have been
floods the mind, distorts the view.
We crave clear light, and warmth.

Fortunately, gratitude blows
away the gloom, A conscience
quickened by remorse is something
to be thankful for. Also memories
of roads well chosen and followed,
of the helping hands of friends
and family, of opportunities
to begin again, of forgiveness,
divine and human. Gratitude!

The Kingdom of Light

North Valley Friends Church, January 9, 2005
(previously presented at George Fox College, chapel, May 14, 1980)

The theme of this message is found in the phrase "the kingdom of light." Notice how light contrasts with "domain of darkness" in depicting Paul's prayer for us to share in the inheritance of the saints in God's kingdom. Consider other apt Scriptures: Colossians 2:8, "See to it that no one takes you captive through hollow and deceptive philosophy, which depends on human tradition...rather than on Christ." In 2 Corinthians 11, Paul warns Christians that Satan masquerades as an angel of light. A similar contrast is spelled out in Romans between carnality and spirituality.

Well, how do we avoid the kingdom of darkness and live in the kingdom of light? True light? This calls for "spiritual wisdom and understanding," as the passage just read indicates. How that understanding comes about is the substance of this message. There is a popular misconception that God has a special information track for Christians. But no, such a view would deny the clearest teaching of Scripture—that the creation is good and we

Scripture reading
Luke 4:1-13 (NRSV)
Jesus, full of the Holy Spirit, returned from the Jordan and was led by the Spirit in the wilderness, where for forty days he was tempted by the devil. He ate nothing at all during those days, and when they were over, he was famished. The devil said to him, "If you are the Son of God, command this stone to become a loaf of bread." Jesus answered him, "It is written, 'One does not live by bread alone.'" Then the devil led him up and showed him in an instant all the kingdoms of the world. And the devil said to him, "To you I will give their glory and all this authority; for it has been given over to me, and I give it to anyone I please. If you, then, will worship me, it will all be yours." Jesus answered him, "It is written, 'Worship the Lord your God, and serve only him.'" Then the devil took him to Jerusalem, and placed him on the pinnacle of the temple, saying to him, "If you are the Son of God, throw yourself down from here, for it is written, 'He will command his angels concerning you, to protect you,' and 'On their hands they will bear you up, so that you will not dash your foot against a stone.'" Jesus answered him, "It is said, 'Do not put the Lord your God to the test.'" When the devil had finished every test, he departed from him until an opportune time.

My message is based upon Colossians 1:9-14, which reads as follows (NIV in this and subsequent citations):

For this reason, since the day we heard about you, we have not stopped praying for you and asking God to fill you with the knowledge of his will through all spiritual wisdom and understanding. And we pray this in order that you may live a life worthy of the Lord and may please him in every way; bearing fruit in every good work, growing in the knowledge of God, being strengthened with all power according to his glorious might so that you may have great endurance and patience, and joyfully giving thanks to the Father who has qualified you to share in the inheritance of the saints *in the kingdom of light.* For he has rescued us from the domain of darkness, and brought us into the kingdom of the Son he loves, in whom we have redemption, the forgiveness of sins.

---

are created in God's image. Without having ears to hear, eyes to see, hands to feel, a nose to smell, or a tongue to taste, we wouldn't get much information, would we?

Remember Helen Keller's struggle? Blind and deaf she *finally* discovered God through touch. Not much grist for the wisdom mill unless sensory antennae are working! And without having a mind to sort out impressions and make reasonable inferences we wouldn't get very far handling what our senses, as God's messengers, signal to us. And without having intuitive imagination to utilize sense and reason we wouldn't be able to act faithfully upon what our senses receive and our minds organize meaningfully.

In short, as Christians we're to take our bodies seriously as the temple of the Holy Spirit. God doesn't have some special funnel, separate from intelligence, through which he pours knowledge into our heads. So, how does this relate to the kingdom of light? Like this: I am concerned that we not be taken captive through deceptive human traditions or ways of understanding. These deceptions usually assume a special knowledge track (a subtle scam the early church called "Gnosticism" and rightly labeled heresy). In Scripture "light" refers to the illumination, or knowledge, we gain from God. We rightly call this "revelation" to indicate its source outside ourselves. But it's a mistake to think God doesn't use the means he has created in order to reveal truth to us and through us.

The kingdom of light

I have said we know by *sense*, *reason*, and *intuition*. Imagine each of these modes of knowing as continents in a sea of experience, separated from each other, but administered from a central headquarters. Do you see the picture? Or envision planets revolving around a central sun. Such is the kingdom of light. The first realm is sense. Consider how we move from light at the center to darkness at the periphery—from holiness to sinfulness. Note the linguistic descent in this progression: sensible, sensate, sensory, sensual. Our language is telling us something! People *live* in the sensory world, even Christians, although in the Victorian age they pretended not to. Some people are more comfortable here than anywhere else. They like to be physical. Jesus once talked about people who had ears that heard nothing and eyes that didn't see. The Good Samaritan saw and heard, and touched, whereas those who passed by on the other side refused the messages God sent through their senses. They could see the guy was in trouble. They could hear his moans.

Here at North Valley many of you *see* that some caring service needs to be done and respond, "I can do it." Your eyes see what others' eyes may not. You use your senses, as Augustine said, as "the messengers of God." You don't have to conjure up a set of spiritual eyes or ears—you just use the ones you have to learn what's up and what God wants you to do about it.

Now, our bodies can get us into sinful or loving deeds. But so can our minds. So let's talk about the people who feel more at home with the mind—rational types. They would rather solve puzzles than ski. They are at home with computers and spreadsheets. In reading spy stories they are more interested in solving the plot than in the gruesome details. Well, several North Valley people are scholars; and those of us who are know that mental acuity is no more exempt from the temptations of darkness than having sharp eyes and ears.

There is also an intuitive realm. Most of us don't spend so much time here. But occasionally we have special dreams or leadings or promptings—not immediately testable but inwardly convincing, empowering, and often amazingly fruitful. Psychics are sometimes hired to try to find missing children. Are they more spiritual than the others whose spheres of understanding are generally in sense and reason? No. It's wrong to ascribe to such persons greater spirituality than others—as if to be intuitive is the same as being spiritual. It isn't. Intuitive persons aren't any more spiritual than accountants who keep honest books or carpenters who do honest repair on our houses. Common sense tells us that all three ways are important and to be wary of people who hype an exotic "spiritual" way of knowing. God is our creator. He has made our bodies wonderfully complex. Our bodies are his temples. Such is the kingdom of light. The worldly way is to put ourselves at the administrative center of this universe rather than Christ, whom John, the first Christian philosopher, called *logos,* the Word. This word, this light, is the energizing source of all knowledge, not the ego. Christian discipleship means keeping sense, reason, and intuition firmly orbiting this center—tethering all thoughts to Christ.

It is said Jesus was tempted in all points that we are, yet without sin. That's comforting theology to me! I have been tempted and sinned. So have you. It is good to know that on earth Jesus was no magic figure somehow exempt from the real problems of the world. Consider his temptations in the wilderness. They are examples for us. Jesus was tempted to put his body first. He was hungry after a long desert fast and Satan came to him, as an angel of light, in the guise of the apparent good, and said, "Look, you've got the power, turn those stones into bread!" Well, Jesus rejected that temptation to put his body first. He rejected the temptation to let sensual satisfactions control. That sensual road we call lust, and it means more than illicit sex although it includes it. Not tethered to the Light, the senses can fling us into outer darkness. The answer to this threat is not asceticism but letting our bodies be instruments of the Holy Spirit. Think of the good sensuous satisfactions you enjoy: grass on your feet in summertime, a long hot shower, tasty food, pungent cedar boughs, feeling the sun on your back, putting your arm around someone special, hugging a baby. Obviously, love is not abstract, it is very sensory. In this realm, sanctification means letting the Spirit guide our senses and their interactions with others. Kierkegaard said you can't love your neighbor as yourself without having God in the middle.

The second temptation of Jesus had to do with the mind, specifically in respect to power. "Fall down and worship me," Satan said "and I will give you the kingdom—no sweat." Here is a proposition to the mind: Forget all that agony of Golgotha, you can get what you want without suffering on a Roman cross. Although not that dramatically, we are all tempted this way in human relationships—to get power cheaply. You succumb to that temptation when you denigrate others to your advantage, or manipulate another person because you are more clever. Such is reason in the service of self, or on a social scale, in the service of a sovereign state. The world we live in forces logic upon us, but that logic doesn't have to mean nuking your enemies, literally or figuratively. There is nothing wrong with logic but it becomes a Satanic trek to the dark periphery when persons twist reason to support their own quest for power over others and nature. We live in the shadow of a holocaust made possible by those who want the kingdom but not the cross, and are prepared to use terrorism or weapons of mass destruction to get it. To be spiritual is not to forsake reason but follow it—to have the mind of Christ, to think right. To yield your body as an instrument of righteousness also means to set your mind on what is right and true—to bring all thoughts into subjection to Christ.

In the third temptation Satan asked Jesus to cast himself off the temple and let the angels swoop him up just before he hit the ground. A spectacular approach, that's for sure! That seemed more effective than sweating it out in Gethsemane or arguing with the Sadducees. This is a temptation to go the mystic route without rational restrictions—to substitute an emotional high for good thinking. Well, that is a trap too. Satan, as an angel of light, whispers to religious folks that the weirder a proposition is, the more spiritual it is. Now that is a delusion! Don't listen to it! Satan is masquerading before you as an angel of light. Succumbing to this voice leads to priestcraft of all sorts. There are all kinds of psychic highs people can experience—from meth to whipped-up emotions, just as there are all kinds of rationalizations, and all kinds of sensory experiences. Intuition land is no more spiritual than sensory land, or rational land. One territory is no more nor less God's province than the others.

There are many fascinating sights and scenic bypaths on each of these continents. Perhaps you feel more at home in one than the other. Some of you face sensual temptations as well as creative opportunities. Maybe you possess strong artistic talent, or you love music, or stuffing the basketball through the hoop. It's okay to be a sensuous person, but listen to your rational and intuitive friends and keep to the gravitational center—Christ. Some of you are good at managing things, and organizing people. Fine, use your gifts, but let the mechanics and the dreamers keep you from straying into the kingdom of darkness lugging your organizational and theological charts with you. Some people love the psychic territory, fascinated by Ouija boards, the occult, or UFO's. For religious folk this may mean fascination with angels, casting out demons, or drumming up emotional ecstasy. You could worship all night and sleep through work the next day. Well, you better listen to your rational and sensory brothers and sisters, or you, too, will stray over into outer darkness.

I was brought up to assume that demonic forces stayed only among animistic people. But you know, demonic forces lurk in sophisticated as well as primitive cultures. Satan always comes as the angel of light, offering the apparent good. So move around in the territories of the understanding. Don't get trapped into thinking the spiritual is where you are and the unspiritual where the others are in realms of understanding. Live in the kingdom of light. Circulate around. Learn the spiritual joy that comes from solving problems, from doing your work well, from tending flowers, crafting quilts or paintings, hugging family, experiencing mystical contemplation, from following leadings to minister to others.

Some of us may not be psychic enough. Maybe we should pray in solitude more, take time to contemplate, learn to be alone, but always with eyes toward the Center. Some of us may not be sensuous enough. Maybe we should strengthen our ability more fully to sense God's creation—to see with our eyes; to hear with our ears; to taste with our palates; to smell with our noses; to touch with our hands the wonders of creation, including its creatures, human and otherwise. Some of us may not be rational enough. Maybe we should try to be more logical in processing the data we receive and the conclusions we draw about things and people.

For the sake of simplification one can say that in the sensory world lust threatens love, in the rational world deceit threatens truth, and in the intuitive world magic threatens prayer. But darkness cannot put out the Light. Let your bodies be the temples of the Spirit. Draw your power from Christ, the Center and then travel about in the universe of the understanding, open to what God can reveal to you. And don't let pride make you suppose you are more spiritual in one realm of the understanding than another.

Seduction occurs anywhere along the dark edges of the worlds. Don't be seduced. To be sanctified means for the senses to be filled with the glory of the Lord, for reason to focus single-mindedly upon universal Truth, for intuition to discern the will of God for specific situations. This is the true light of wisdom as compared to the light of folly.

Our heavenly Father, we are thankful for Paul's words to us about the kingdom of light, which is also the kingdom of your son, Jesus Christ, in whose name we pray. Lord, we have been tempted, and have sometimes strayed out of your will and into the dark side. We thought the apparent good was the real good. For this we are sorry and repent. Forgive us. Help us not to be lured away by lust of the body. Help us not to succumb to the deceits of the mind and the spirit. Lord, this is hard in a world in which deceit is a way of life and people get paid handsomely for it. You have given us a world that is orderly and you have given us the capacity to see things logically. But we need your Spirit to help us. Forgive us for being blind to insights that come from meditation and prayer. Forgive us for thinking we were more spiritual because we disdained reason and sense, for confusing emotion with spirituality. Teach us, Lord, to distinguish the true Light of Christ from the false light of Satan. Evil lies so close—may we not fall into temptation. May we accept the way of the cross and not try to get into the kingdom like thieves and robbers who won't go in by the door.

Teach us your way of understanding and your way of power. Help us to live with the promise of the resurrection. We offer you our faith. In Jesus' name, amen.

A Call to Holiness

Yachats Community Presbyterian Church, June 9, 2005; Reedwood Friends Church, August 11, 2005; North Valley Friends Church, August 25, 2005

Why we need a new call to holiness

"Be perfect," said Jesus, "as your heavenly Father is perfect" (Matthew 5:48). Jesus' words strike us like a spotlight in the face; they penetrate like a siren to the ear. We'd turn away, but we can't. Holiness haunts us! Deep within our being we hear its soundings. If we cover our ears the divine voice trumpets within us. If we wrap darkness around our souls, the Light shines through the cracks in our psyche. The Lord's love overwhelms us. We can't flee the One who calls! Shall we respond by running away? Resisting? No. We respond by opening hearts and minds, that's how! With fear and trembling we let Jesus illumine and lead us along life's path. Do we trust Jesus' voice? We acknowledge his call in our heads; may we do so in our hearts!

A hunger and thirst for righteousness gnaws at us through culture, politics, commerce, education, and religion. Think about it. You may fudge on *your* words,

Old Testament reading
Psalm 29:1-2 (NIV here and throughout)

Ascribe to the Lord, O mighty ones, ascribe to the Lord glory and strength. Ascribe to the Lord the glory due his name; worship the Lord in the splendor of his holiness.

but from *others* you want truth. *You* may do shoddy work, but you insist upon integrity in the labor of *others*. *You* may be an instrument of evil but you don't want to be its victim. The *good*, the *true*, and the *beautiful*—like doves from the ark of God these ideals circle around you searching for solid ground in a soggy world. Holiness summons your body, your mind, your spirit. Sometimes that call blares like a siren; at other times it wafts gentle as a breeze, or it warms quiet as a summer sun. If you hunger and thirst after righteousness, Jesus said, you will be filled (Matthew 5:6). You hear this call to holiness whoever you are, whatever your maturity, whatever your work—and whether you want

New Testament reading
1 Thessalonians 3:12-13

May the Lord make your love increase and overflow for each other and for everyone else, just as ours does for you. May he strengthen your hearts so that you will be blameless and holy in the presence of our God and Father when our Lord Jesus comes with all his holy ones.

to or not. Resist, and life darkens into despair; heed the call, and life brightens with hope.

Currently churches are pretty quiet about Jesus' call to perfection. In those penitential years following the horrific American civil war, holiness became a major theme. A hunger for holiness launched camp meetings where penitent Methodists and Quakers knelt in sawdust weeping for their sins, then rose to cry "hallelujah" for God's cleansing power! Spiritually thirsty Presbyterians trekked to "deeper life" conferences. Christians from many churches were baptized by the Spirit. They cleaned up wicked lives and redirected energies to missions and social justice, sacrificially, in the name of Jesus. Christian colleges blossomed like daisies in the spring. Drunkenness and violence diminished. Towns became safer.

In their zeal for God, and to distance themselves from "carnal Christians," these folks came to speak of themselves as "holiness people." Sounds smug, doesn't it? It was; and slowly revival fires smoldered to ashes. Some emotional fervor from the old movement lingered, but for much of the contemporary church, that earlier holiness emphasis has been lost. Heart purity and holy living doesn't sell on today's religious market. "Feel good" religion does.

The Holiness Movement provided a great legacy, and gratitude requires more than lamenting its loss. Why is "holiness" no longer high priority? Consider some reasons.

Internally, holiness movements flounder when proponents' failures become conspicuous. People get blindsided by unexpected temptations. Failures occur, and rather than repent, sins get rationalized as mistakes or justified by dubious Bible proofs. One failure is hypocrisy, that is, claims to personal righteousness when evidence is obviously otherwise—for example, revivalists succumbing to adulterous behavior. Another failure is *self*-righteousness, that is, elevating one's own spiritual path and denigrating others. For example, calling other Christians carnal because they haven't experienced a "second blessing" or been "slain in the spirit" or experienced mystical auras. A third is legalism—keeping the letter of the moral law, while neglecting its spirit. For example, scrupulously tithing income but being chintzy with employees or ungenerous toward neighbors. A fourth failure is tokenism, limiting holiness to minor issues, like not shopping on Sunday. A focus on scruples rather than justice and virtue pushed holiness doctrines into an abyss of irrelevancy.

There are external reasons why churches neglect holiness. Accommodation to worldly culture is one. Although leavened by the gospel, culture remains a bastion of the Evil One. Some early holiness movements took a *selective* anticultural stance. Buggies were okay, cars weren't. Books were okay, movies weren't. Stylish dress was okay for men, but women had to look dowdy. People stumbled into hidden cultural traps. People back from "deeper life" conferences or camp meetings got snared by material success—better jobs, new houses, greater respect. Arrogance sneaked onto the path of upward social mobility. Loyalty to God's kingdom got diverted into nationalistic fervor by people opposing "worldly" earrings. *Their children* junked the holiness dress code and attacked worldliness in movies, rock music, and public schools, but supported a worldliness that made their lives comfortable—militarism, class status, political advantage, and economic privilege. *The grandchildren* took a different tack, accommodating to culture by putting Christian labels on rock music, thus maintaining a pious pose while reveling in worldliness. You may be one of these children or grandchildren.

Why were we so vulnerable to cultural entrapment? For one thing, science skewed how we measure things. Zealous Christians began to interpret Bible language too scientifically. To keep the Bible inerrant they scrounged for scraps of scientific evidence, dinosaur tracks in Texas or wood fragments on Mount Ararat. But then, alas, they interpreted Bible language about values *too figuratively*, treating his moral teachings as hyperbole, as if God sets the moral clock ahead so laggards will arrive roughly on time. Or they dodged Jesus' hard teachings about righteousness by postponing them to some millennial future.

So, if one defines perfection in scientific terms, as 100 percent on a line of reality, anything less falls short. If connoted as exaggeration, any reasonable effort suffices. Visions theological have been replaced by visions commercial. Machineried calls to perfection drown out Jesus' call to holiness. Voices and images tug at us—mind, body, and spirit—in advertisements as diverse as cosmetics, pharmaceuticals, and automobiles. Have you heard the Lexus ad: "the passionate pursuit of perfection"? Are *we* asked to be holy? No. We're asked to be clean, muscular, well-oiled, sexy machines. Honing body and psyche to perfection is a high-ticket item. Orthodontists, plastic surgeons, physical therapists, and counselors abound for patching up the blemished. How else to avoid social leprosy among the nerds, the addicts, the aged, and the poor who drag down the economy? Euphemisms sanitize evil. Thus adultery is called a "relationship," the enemy is dubbed a "target," civilian casualties are softened into "collateral damage," greed is camouflaged as "business smarts."

A local church often is no longer a hospital for contrite sinners but a spa for beautiful people. The gospel of health and wealth mimics technological worldliness, and megachurches market socialization, not holiness. Contrary to Reformation insights, salvation is conveyed by fellowship rather than through gospel truth. Christians climbing the social ladder clamor after important people—like athletes and movie stars and military brass. Worshipers join drug addicts in seeking new highs. In this dour analysis, empty ritual replaces worship in spirit and in truth for Quakers as well as for Baptists and Episcopalians, Pentecostals and Catholics. Appearance supplants substance. The aesthetic best becomes the enemy of the moral good. From this scenario we should learn that technology makes a good servant but a deceitful master. If we aren't careful we'll be sold into slavery!

Our global world elevates tolerance to the highest level, beyond truth, integrity, and agape love. In a relativistic culture living virtuously is more antisocial than being pleasantly sinful. A smelly armpit is deemed worse than cheating on a test. Our heroes are gloriously flawed. They point guns at us on TV, they lie, they steal, they seduce. Current culture tolerates every lifestyle except being wholly surrendered to God. The "powers that be" resist the triumph of Christ over their sin management. These powers cling to old rituals for hanging on to sin—the state clings to a warrior cult, business to institutionalized greed, tribes to ethnic superiority, and culture to literary myths extolling endless tragic struggles between good and evil.

Psychology has taught us, rightly, to acknowledge the dark side of the psyche, and not to fantasize about it. To modern ears professions of holiness sound a bit psychotic. We're rightly warned of false claims to holiness. For many modern folks, psychology, unfortunately, has challenged *all* legitimate biblical claims for triumph over sin basic to historic holiness teachings—whether Catholic, Calvinist, Quaker, Wesleyan, Orthodox, or Pentecostal. Ritually confessing one's sin every Sunday—or during Lent—is easier than answering Jesus' call to holiness.

So, how does our world impact Jesus' call to holiness? Positively it exposes poor or fraudulent representations and challenges us to understand better the self that is to be renewed in God's image. Negatively it opposes Jesus' kingdom and offers secular alternatives to the perfection to which God calls us.

Consider a call to holiness that offers a greater hope.

Perhaps God will honor our penitent spirit. Then the earth will yield abundance to folks who commit their bodies to be temples of the Holy Spirit, who rightly care for the earth and all its creatures—including human ones. A hunger for holiness is embedded as software in the soul; it needs to be updated.

This call to holiness acknowledges the power of the cross. Christ's atoning death regenerates. Does God just forgive sin without delivering from its power? No. Without the power to sanctify, the cross loses force and the resurrection loses glory. The gospel is weakened by churches "preaching up sin to the grave," by flakey New Age stuff that strokes the ego, by modish megachurch spirituality, by what Bonhoeffer labeled "cheap grace." *The gospel proclaims victory over sin, inward as well as outward, deliverance from its power as well as from its guilt.* The dark side of human nature has been abundantly evidenced by the violence of our era, and reinforced by the insights of psychology and science. *That we don't have to be trapped in this sinful condition is the good news Jesus brings.* Consider the different ways God delivers us. Consider what holiness means.

First, holiness is a part of conversion crisis. True conversion means facing up to God and saying yes. The penitent, forgiven rebel surrenders to a patient God of love. The self is transformed by the power of the Holy Spirit. As Paul said, we put off the old self and put on the new, "created...in true righteousness and holiness" (see Ephesians 4:21-27).

Considered this way sanctification makes sense. Good attitudes and right actions arise from a cleansed heart. The sanctified self isn't an instant mutant, but rather a recipient of God's baptizing power to redirect one's will from evil to good. *How* this occurs isn't so important. *That* it occurs through a decisive response of the human will to God's will *is* important. Just say yes!

Second, holiness is spiritual discipline, living by deliberate habits of spirituality. Through prayer, contemplation, service, and study, the Spirit shapes the self into Christlikeness. Such discipline is to the soul what aerobic exercise is to the body. Under the Spirit's power the will triumphs over evil desires. Devotional writings ancient and contemporary clearly teach this. Richard Foster's books urge folks to match in the workaday world the monastic vows of poverty, chastity, and obedience. Through sanctifying disciplines applied to the right use of money, sex, and power, the body truly becomes the temple of the Spirit in the *ordinary* ventures of life and *all of life* is blessed by this devotion.

This disciplinary process is in vogue. Universities offer programs in spirituality. Such popularity ought not discredit it, but should put us on guard against a pride that could sabotage its force. *It is a subtle temptation to study spirituality instead of to practice its disciplines*, just as it was a subtle temptation to socialize at camp meetings instead of living in the world under the Spirit's anointing power.

Third, holiness infuses artistic creativity. Our Puritan heritage suspected the arts of all sorts of deviltry. It tried to exclude the aesthetic from the spiritual. As a result the ugly and the mediocre got elevated over the beautiful and the excellent, ostensibly to give God the glory, not humanity. But sanctification also means the restoration of the image of God in humanity and a right stewardship of creation. With the will sanctified, we become coworkers with Christ in renewing the cosmos. The book of Revelation pictures the New Jerusalem as a very livable place—the artificial and the natural in harmony— where God and humanity work together. Creative artistry is not just oratorios like the *Messiah* or frescoes in the Sistine Chapel, or poetry that frames truth with fire, but also machines and tools that ease creature burdens and delight the eye—like bridges along the Oregon coast or comfortable shoes. I warned earlier that the aesthetic best can become an enemy of the moral good. Sanctification prevents this from occurring. It binds aesthetics to the work of the Holy Spirit. Ego submits to Deo, avoiding traps of snobbery or grunge. Human will infused by the Holy Spirit directs aesthetic as well as ethical activities. The senses—smell, hearing, taste, sight, and touch—are antennae for receiving God's signals. The body yields to righteousness, not to unrighteousness. Sanctified senses enable us artfully to share God's creativity. Holiness leads us back through the flaming sword, into the paradise of God, where simplicity blends with elegance, prayer with play, art with worship. Calvin Seerveld, in an apt title, says Christians offer *Rainbows in a Fallen World*.

Fourth, holiness involves right conduct. Those who preach holiness rightly emphasize moral goodness. Clean hands *are* linked with pure heart. Would it make a difference in how you heard Jesus if the following equally accurate translation were given: "Blessed are those who hunger and thirst after *justice* for they shall be satisfied"? Holiness is love in action as well as attitude; it's for groups as well as for individuals.

In saying, "Be perfect, therefore, as your heavenly Father is perfect" (Matthew 5:48), Jesus intended indiscriminate love—the kind that seeks good for neighbor as well as for self, for stranger as well as kin, for the unjust (upon whom God's sun also shines) as well as the just, for enemy as well as friend. This isn't easy. But it's the way of the cross. Jesus' resurrection offers hope, the Holy Spirit's baptism offers power. Holiness isn't for show. It's a call to live morally upright lives. Penitent people understand that God's grace isn't a license to keep on sinning, but a call to moral reformation.

Fifth, holiness is ecstasy. Every charismatic movement since the Montanists of the Roman era has celebrated an ecstatic union of the human and the Divine. This is the case for monks and mystics, Catholics and Orthodox, Presbyterians and Mennonites, Methodists and Quakers, Lutherans and Pentecostals. God leaps over ritual and theology, transcending even the limits of language. God comes as terror to shiver us, as love to draw us, as fire to consume us. Lured by a mystery of bushes unexpectedly aflame yet not consumed, we're caught standing on holy ground! *And God turns that bumbling trespass into a picnic*, visiting us, feeding us, inspiring us! Like Moses we're loath to leave the holy hill. Like Peter we would monument the glory. When will the Spirit thrill us again with such ecstasy? Who knows? Pentecosts aren't scheduled. The Wind blows where it will. So be ready to cherish ecstasy when it comes!

God's Spirit doesn't leave us when emotion fades. Epiphany transmutes into agape service. Heeding Jesus' call to holiness we bow obediently and get to work. In God's name we set captives free, we bind wounds, we teach the good news of Christ in word and deed. We create things beautiful and useful and share them joyfully with others. We discover truth about the universe and its creatures, and act upon what we've learned. We enjoy God's kingdom now, together, anticipating its heavenly fulfillment. God sends us down the holy mountain of ecstatic experience into a world yearning for deliverance from evil. In God's name I urge you: Be faithful and prayerful. Sometime soon you may find yourself standing on holy ground shivering with joy at God's overwhelming presence! Indeed, your day of visitation could start now!

Conclusion

Do you hunger for holiness? Jesus said you are blessed if you do. He promises your hunger will be satisfied. God knocks at the door of your heart, offering conversion, spiritual discipline, artistic creativity, moral goodness, ecstatic presence. Let the Spirit enter! Open the door, my friends. Yes, open the door!

Bible "ABCs"

Yachats Community Presbyterian Church, June 19, 2005

Today is Father's Day. I want to be more inclusive so I'm turning it into Parent's Day! So, a verbal bouquet to parents! We all have parents, from the youngest of us here in worship to the oldest. Some are living; others are not. Some are nearby, some far away. I enjoy looking at the framed pictures of my father and mother. Momma and Papa look a bit stiff, but then ninety years ago people had to hold a pose while a hooded cameraman took the picture. The pictures were taken at the time of their marriage. It's been sixty-six years since my father died from a sudden attack of pneumonia, and left a teenage boy bewildered and heartsick. Sulfa or penicillin could have saved him. Papa was sixty-six years old. Forty-one years ago my mother died in Friendsview Manor, in Newberg, Oregon, where we now reside. She was eighty-one, younger than I am now. She sort of faded from various ailments and slipped off to her heavenly home one night. I like to remember my parents when they were younger. They were good parents, and I loved them. I thank God for my parents and look forward to seeing them in heaven. They were faithful in the words of our scriptural text from Psalm 145:4 (NRSV), which reads: "One generation shall laud your works to another, and shall declare your mighty acts."

My parents passed the torch of faith to us their children. How? In various ways. My Quaker father set an example by saying grace at meals, by reading the Bible and the Congressional Record each evening, by humming hymns to the hogs while slopping them, by being honest in business and generous with neighbors, by being passionate for justice, by taking us to Sunday school and church each week, by teaching us to buy quality stuff but not too much of it, and by teaching us to avoid debt.

My mother cheerfully worked in the home, taught Sunday school classes, taught us to say our bedside prayers, and encouraged our spiritual growth. Reared a Presbyterian she drilled us with a Reformed catechism. I recall one line from the Westminster Confession: "The first duty of man is to honor and glorify God and to enjoy Him forever." We memorized Bible passages and read good books. Mom was a loving person. I remember being disciplined sometimes—never in anger, always in love.

My parents differed on some issues. Papa was more patient than Mom with people who did dumb things or were slow paying for the hay they bought from us. It was a good home, and I tried to convey this to our own family. My parents stood in a succession of generations that passed the covenant of Christian faith to the next ones. On my father's side, staunch seventeenth-century Welsh Quaker farmers with names like Bevan and Ellis had suffered fines for not paying taxes for state-supported ministry, so they sailed for William Penn's colony where they found religious freedom. On my mother's side stood a succession of Mennonite and Reformed believers. In the middle of the nineteenth century two orphaned Jansonius brothers left a crowded Holland and came to the new world to farm its rich soil. One was my great grandfather. In subsequent generations, spoken languages and then prayer languages changed from Welsh and Dutch to English. America became the land of the covenant as God-fearing descendants of these Welsh and Dutch ancestors trekked westward, from the Atlantic to the Midwest; from the Midwest to the far West.

I expect these reminiscences have started a train of thinking in your mind. I hope so. How was the Christian faith passed on to you? How have you passed the Christian faith on to the next generation? To help us ponder these questions prayerfully, I've printed for our worship today the ABCs of the Bible. At my mother's insistence, I learned these when I was eight or ten years old. The first four I remember, the rest I've had to reconstruct, adapting various versions. We will read in unison a few at a time, and then I'll comment. After we've completed the alphabet let's have a bit of Quaker silence, for you to ponder *your* pilgrimage of faith. Prayerfully consider how your parents—or someone else's parents—passed the Christian faith to you, and how you are passing the torch of faith to the next generations. Then ask God how together we can tell succeeding generations the good news of Jesus Christ and God's kingdom, on earth and in heaven. This is a challenge to us all, because "selling cool"—manipulating tastes and values—is a multi-billion-dollar industry. Powerful forces are stuffing other stories into the eyes and ears, down the nostrils and mouths, and into the muscles of our children, grandchildren, and great-grandchildren. It's not easy for one generation to witness the mighty acts of God to the next one. But the Holy Spirit is greater than the spirit of this world.

The ABCs of the Bible (read in unison)
Basic theology

All have sinned and fall short of the glory of God. Romans 3:23

Behold the Lamb of God, who takes away the sin of the world. John 1:29

Come to me, all you who...are carrying heavy burdens, and I will give you rest. Matthew 11:28

Basic Christian morality

Do unto others as you would have them do to you. Luke 6:31

Every good tree bears good fruit, but the bad tree bears bad fruit. Matthew 7:17

Faith comes from what is heard, what is heard comes through the word of Christ. Romans 10:17

God is not mocked, for you reap whatever you sow. Galatians 6:7

Basic attitudes

Honor your father and your mother. Exodus 20:12

In everything by prayer and supplication with thanksgiving let your requests be made known to God. Philippians 4:6

Just as water reflects the face, so one human heart reflects another. Proverbs 27:19

Know that the Lord is God. It is he that made us, and we are his. Psalm 100:3

Basic discipleship

Love the Lord your God with all your heart... and your neighbor as yourself. Luke 10:27

Make a joyful noise to the Lord, all the earth. Psalm 100:1

Now is the acceptable time…now is the day of salvation! 2 Corinthians 6:2

One generation shall laud your works to another, and shall declare your mighty acts. Psalm 145:4

Praise the Lord! I will give thanks to the Lord with my whole heart. Psalm 111:1

Quiet words of the wise are more to be heeded than the shouting of a ruler. Ecclesiastes 9:17

Restore to me the joy of your salvation, and sustain in me a willing spirit. Psalm 51:12

Basic prayers

Search me, O God, and know my heart…. Psalm 139:23

Test me and know my thoughts. Psalm 139:23

Under his wings you will find refuge. Psalm 91:4

Vindicate me, O Lord, for I have walked in my integrity. Psalm 26:1

Basic admonitions

Wisdom is better than jewels. Proverbs 8:11

eXcept the Lord builds the house, those who build it labor in vain. Psalm 127:1

Young lions suffer want …but those who seek the Lord lack no good thing. Psalm 34:10

Basic invitation

Zacchaeus, hurry and come down; for I must stay at your house today. Luke 19:5

In conclusion we will read in unison lines from a first-century Christian writer, Clement of Rome.

Responsive Reading
Clement of Rome (first century)

CHOIR: Lord, we want our children, and our children's children to have Christian training.

CONGREGATION: Let them learn the value God sets on humility.

CHOIR: Let them learn what power pure love has.

CONGREGATION: Let them learn how good and excellent it is to fear God,

CHOIR: and how this means salvation to everyone who lives in fear of the Lord,

CONGREGATION: with holiness and a pure conscience.

CHOIR: For the Lord is the searcher of thoughts and of desires

CONGREGATION AND CHOIR: As the psalmist says, "One generation will commend your works to another; they will tell of your mighty acts."
(adapted from "First Letter," The Library of Christian Classics, Philadelphia: Westminster Press, 1953, vol. 1, p. 54.)

Remembering

Friendsview Retirement Health Center, January 1, 2006

The rainbow signifies that God remembers the creation and so should we. "'Whenever the rainbow appears in the clouds, I will see it and *remember* the everlasting covenant between God and all living creatures of every kind on the earth.' So God said to Noah, 'This is the sign of the covenant I have established between me and all life on the earth'" (Genesis 9:16-17, emphasis mine, NIV here and in subsequent texts).

The faith community reminds us how God delivers people from bondage.

Leviticus 26:45 reads: "But for their sake I will *remember* the covenant with their ancestors whom I brought out of Egypt in the sight of the nations to be their God. I am the Lord" (emphasis mine).

Through the Messiah, Israel's experiences as a people of God are offered to all people, as was promised to Abraham. The church is witness to this new covenant.

Prayer involves sharing our memories with God.

The psalmist prayed: "Remember not the sins of my youth and my rebellious ways; according to your love *remember* me, for you are good, O Lord" (Psalm 25:7, emphasis mine).

Note the wonder of divine forgiveness. The Lord removes guilt, atones, sanctifies us.

"On my bed I *remember* you; I think of you through the watches of the night," vowed the psalmist (63:6, emphasis mine), and with these words urged us to "keep his covenant and *remember* to obey his precepts" (103:18, emphasis mine). "Remember the wonders he has done," he reminds us, "his miracles, and the judgments he pronounced" (105:5). Therefore we will make gratitude a major aspect of our prayer.

Spirituality includes remembering Jesus: birth, life, teaching, death, and resurrection.

Orthodox Christian churches celebrate Christmas January 7, which happens to be my birthday, so I'll share a bit about how some Eastern Europeans celebrate the nativity. The Macedonian Orthodox celebration begins the evening of January 5. Children go from door to door singing Christmas carols, heralding the birth of Jesus, and receiving fruits, nuts, and candy. Later in the evening, people gather around a bonfire and converse about the past year and the year to come. The following evening is Christmas Eve, when a traditional oak log (*badnik*) is brought to the home. This log is cut by the father of the household while the table is being set for the Christmas Eve supper, which usually consists of baked fish. The oak log is cut into three pieces, representing the Holy Trinity. A member of the family receives a piece and places it on the fire while exchanging a greeting: "Good evening and happy Christmas Eve." While the log is being placed on the fire, the mother and the grandmother gather the children together into the room where the dinner is to be served. Each person carries a bundle of straw from outside, and together they spread the straw on the floor, to make the atmosphere more like that of the night Jesus was born. The house is decorated further with oak and pine branches, representing the wish of the family—"health strong as oak, and with a life long as that of the oak" (adapted from http://faq.macedonia.org/).

Egyptian (Coptic) Christians celebrate the three-year stay of Joseph, Mary, and Jesus in their country. Ironically, this flight to Egypt for safety reverses the flight Moses led *away* from Egyptian bondage. I wrote this poem about the trek of the holy family to Egypt (included in *Look Closely at the Child*).

Egypt To and Fro

Clip clop, clip clop,
Clip clop, clip clop,
clippity clip clip clop
plods the brown donkey
through the dark night.

Clip clop, clip clop,
Clip clop, clip clop,
clippity clip clip clop
plods the brown donkey
toward the dawn's light.

Tick tock, tick tock,
Tick tock, tick tock,
tickity tick tick tock
plod harried persons
through the dark night

Tick tock, tick tock,
Tick tock, tick tock,
tickity tick tick tock
God leads the faithful
toward the dawn's light.

We remember and celebrate the resurrection. We exult in this Scripture: "He is not here; he has risen! *Remember* how he told you, while he was still with you in Galilee" (Luke 24:6, emphasis mine). Yes, we remember the crucifixion—how Jesus died for us. Let's remember also the completed salvation story—the resurrection—and rejoice in its hopeful message. (This poem and the next are from *Prayers at Twilight*.)

Swings in Heaven

I went past a school ground today.
Boys and girls were playing. Recess.
I wanted to stop and watch but figured
somebody might think, is that old coot
a predator? So I drove my pickup slow.
Looked at little kids on swings
and teeter totters, or jumping around.
Lord, I hardly remember what it was like
to shoot marbles, skip rope, play tag.
Made me pine for the past, Lord.
Wouldn't mind being a child again.
Are there swings in heaven?

Spirituality includes remembering others, gratefully, prayerfully.

Jesus chided the disciples: "Do you have eyes but fail to see, and ears but fail to hear? And don't you *remember*?" (Mark 8:18, emphasis mine). Basically we remember how Jesus summed up our obligations: love God, love others. "I thank my God every time I *remember* you," wrote Paul to coworkers (Philippians 1:3, emphasis mine). And to the church he wrote: "…night and day I constantly remember you in my prayers" (2 Timothy 1:3).

Conclusion

We conclude with a great-grandmother's reflections about remembering family:

The Really Important Things

Lord, today I'm looking at old albums,
pictures of my children. Here's my boy
with his little red wagon, and there's
the girls in the look-alike dresses
I made them one Easter. Cute, aren't they?
Oh, they're grown up now, grandparents
themselves. But they love me as much
now as they did then. Some things change
but other things, the really important things,
remain. You hold us all in your hand, Lord.

God's Comfort

Waldport Presbyterian Church, May 7, 2006

Introduction

Did you notice how often the word *comfort* was used in the Scripture reading? Eight times. This reading challenges me. I find it difficult to receive the rich significance of that word because of childhood associations with a warm, fuzzy blanket, referred to by my mother as a "comforter." Is that term familiar to you? Well, the word has suffered further erosion of meaning in our culture. Here are some examples. Parents ask small children are you "comfy"? We label certain edibles "comfort food." Euphemistically we dub public toilets "comfort" stations. Can we redeem this badly battered word and glean from it valuable insights about our walk with God? Our Scripture text helps us do this. It's a familiar one.

Scripture text

Psalm 23:4 (NIV, emphasis mine)

Even though I walk through the valley of the shadow of death, I will fear no evil, for you are with me; your rod and your staff, they *comfort* me.

Scripture reading

2 Corinthians 1:3-6 (NIV)

Praise be to the God and Father of our Lord Jesus Christ, the Father of compassion and the God of all comfort, who comforts us in all our troubles, so that we can comfort those in any trouble with the comfort we ourselves have received from God. For just as the sufferings of Christ flow over into our lives, so also through Christ our comfort overflows. If we are distressed, it is for your comfort and salvation; if we are comforted, it is for your comfort, which produces in you patient endurance of the same sufferings we suffer.

Fortunately, during my childhood two things helped preserve integrity for the word *comfort*. The first was having memorized this psalm and having recognized from its pastoral setting a message about God's care. Second, from studying Latin I learned that the word *comfort* means "with strength." In the varied circumstances of our lives, God deals with us "with strength." Given this denotation of the word, let's receive from these Scripture passages truths about God's comfort.

First, name the darkness.

The New Revised Standard Version uses the word *darkness* instead of "shadow of death." This equally valid rendering reads: "Even though I walk through the *darkest valley*, I fear no evil; for you are with me; your rod and your staff—they comfort me" (emphasis mine). In beautiful pastoral imagery, the twenty-third psalm indicates that like a good shepherd God uses a rod to protect us and a staff to guide us in troubled times, in the darkest valley.

Dark valleys vary. Some troubles happen because of natural circumstances, like floods and storms and fires. Others arise from the ignorance, thoughtlessness, or malice of others. Some we heap upon ourselves. "How could I be that stupid?" we mutter, and try to extricate ourselves from a mess we've got ourselves into.

Sometimes these troubles are physical.

We are on an unfamiliar road in a downpour and we're not sure where the edge of the road is and what's around the bend. We're scared to a point of near panic. Or we're overworked and exhausted. Or we bash the car into a tree and remain crippled by the accident. Or we suffer chronic pain from a stroke, which darkens our lives day after day.

Sometimes our troubles are mental.

Facing adverse circumstances related to family, health, or work, we're unsure how to proceed, what choices to make, what words to say, what actions to take. We're not sure how to cope with troubled relationships: with family, with coworkers, with neighbors. Maybe financial problems keep us awake nights, figuring how to cope. For us oldsters, the clock of time tolls louder as life's valleys loom darker. The darkness becomes, indeed, a shadow of death.

Sometimes our troubles are spiritual.

These are the hardest to cope with, Glittering temptations to sin assail us, or funky doubts nag at us; sometimes it seems the Prince of Darkness has snared us in his slimy hands. Maybe we're guilt-ridden for having hurt people and we can't shake the shame, so we mask it to protect the ego and then, alone with ourselves, feel even guiltier. God seems hidden by the darkness, until in despair we cry out: "God, I need your rod to protect me; I need your staff to guide me!" Then the Compassionate One stoops down beside us in the darkness, takes us by the hand and leads us through the valley of the shadow of death. How assuring to hear Christ's words to us as well as to those first disciples: "I will not leave you comfortless" (John 14:18 KJV).

For some of our brothers and sisters in difficult places the darkness is all three: physical, mental, and spiritual. Consider the agony a member of the Christian Peacemaker Teams, Tom Fox, went through before he was tortured and murdered in Iraq this past March. Consider the stress of hostages facing similar fate. Consider the trauma of parents unable to offer their children sufficient food or medical aid. Paul's testimony about comfort arose from real life troubles. God strengthened him all the way to *his* heroic martyr death, as God has for thousands of people in our own times. So when Paul writes about God's comfort he knows what he's talking about. And so did the psalmist, who had his own darkness to grope through.

In all our dark times we move forward with fear and trembling, calling out to our Shepherd for protection and for guidance. We pray for, and receive, God's comfort. It was said that Jesus was "in all points tempted like as we are, yet without sin" (Hebrews 4:15 KJV). On the cross Jesus bore our burdens; with his stripes we are healed. His triumph over death brings us assurance. In the words of Paul, in Christ "we are more than conquerors"; nothing "will be able to separate us from the love of God" (see Romans 8:37-39). Yes, in the world we will have troubles, but Christ has overcome the world. Christ leads us through the darkness into his glorious light.

Second, consider how the rod of God comforts.

What do they look like, these wolves who would destroy us? And how does the rod of God protect us from them? Some who prey upon God's flock are human predators who would harm us with physical force or manipulative guile. Some are faceless corporate structures, the "powers of this world," commercial and/or cultural forces that could destroy us, body, mind, and spirit if we stray from God's fold. The rod of God protects us by alerting our minds, especially through prayer, to *see* wolves (even those in sheep's clothing) by quickening our consciences when Satan comes in the guise of an angel of light. The rod of God raps *us* with guilt when *we* do wrong, when we succumb to the lure of the wolf hidden in the psyche. God's rod drums out metric joy when we do right! The rod of God protects us by judgments upon worldly evil. God is not mocked. Evil collapses into a dark hole from it's own weight. In the end, right prevails. History is God's story. Thus God makes even the wrath of men to praise him. In the midst of violence and war this is difficult to discern, but we hold this truth in faith, hope, and love. Jesus' resurrection is God's pledge to us that in this life, as in the next, Light overcomes darkness, Jerusalem the Golden arises from the ashes of the Babel's towers. The rod of God strengthens; it comforts me. Does it comfort you?

Third, consider how God's staff comforts.

In the psalmist's imagery God's staff directs us to good pasture and clean water. I take this to mean God nudges us to read the Bible, to pray, to feast on good art and literature, to use our senses to interact with God's creation, through gardening, making things, or relishing rainbows and tidepools. In short, God's staff guides us rightly to use of our bodies as temples of his Spirit. We are comfortable when such spirituality occurs.

God's staff helps us discern the work of the Spirit in others. God taps us on the shoulder, as it were, when out of personal pique or rational concern, we're about to bolt the flock, forsake community, or rend it by snobbery or manipulation. The apostle Paul wrote perceptively: "May the God who gives endurance and encouragement give you a spirit of unity among yourselves as you follow Christ Jesus, so that with one heart and mouth you may glorify the God and Father of our Lord Jesus Christ" (Romans 15:5-6 NIV).

God's staff directs us to the needs of others, whether those needs be physical, mental or spiritual. God's staff points out the good paths within a tangle of competing ways by which we can walk along with others in love and in truth, and with prayerful discernment offer through word or deed a testimony to the Christ we love and follow. Such is true empathy. The world looks for ways to divide and conquer. Jesus' followers look for ways to let God conquer and to unite the world Christ died to save.

God's staff guides us through time and space always in the direction of the eternal kingdom, consonant with the words of Jesus: "I have other sheep that are not of this sheep pen. I must bring them also. They too will listen to my voice, and there shall be one flock and one shepherd" (John 10:16 NIV). My dear friends, ours is, indeed, a *comfortable* gospel!

Let the Spirit Soar

Something there is about this May
that nudges me to jump for joy!
If once again I were a boy
I'd vault a fence each lovely day
just like I used to do…oh, well,
as around the town I stride
I now feel real good inside—
Heaven triumphs over hell.

So, I'll sate my soul with beauty
of budding roses and a boon
of sunlit daisies. I'll do each duty
humming a remembered tune,
and let the Spirit soar
like seagulls on my shore.

(from *Let the Spirit Soar*)

"C'mon, Kyle!"

Selection adapted from "Roberts' Reflections," a monthly column for Northwest Friends, March 2000

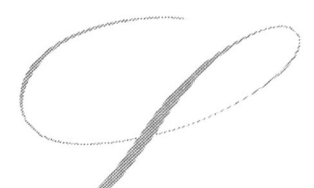

Last month we attended the West Valley League district wrestling match—a two-day affair hosted by a regional high school, Nestucca, located in coastal Cloverdale. Fourteen smaller schools, (e.g., Amity, Warrenton, Culver, and Neahkahnie) competed in rounds of wrestling.

Why endure 12 to 14 hours on butt-numbing benches, being buffeted by bellowing coaches and boisterous fans, watching simultaneous contests on the orange and green mats, and suffering ear-splitting announcements from a high-decibel sound system in a packed gymnasium?

The answer is simple: A grandson was wrestling, his parents were there, and so were we.

The occasion prompted thoughts that I share. You see, the circuit of bouts, weight-ranked from skinny kids at 103 to husky ones at 275, took a lot of time. And the din made conversation difficult to sustain, so mental creativity seemed a way to offset bodily discomfort.

I must mention up front that our grandson did well, winning a respectable three of five matches. We were proud of him, and his grandmother smothered his sweaty face with kisses after the final hard-won victory in the consolation bracket before we headed home.

What has this to do with the church? A lot, as further narration will signify. Bear with me. The host community had knocked itself out preparing for busloads of visitors from 14 schools—the teams and their kinfolk and friends. Local families prepared breakfast and lunches in the cafeteria. Mothers took tickets and their kids stamped our hands with the purple password. Fortyish fathers and mothers, who must have milked the cows early or taken leave of their jobs, came to the gym to keep records, do the announcing, and handle hospitality. Girls in jeans and tank tops posted the names of wrestlers on the score boards and swatted referees with a towel when each round was over (in case they got confused about which buzzer had sounded). EMT volunteers left their daily work to be on hand with first-aid equipment.

Center stage were the wrestlers themselves, scores of boys (and two girls) in wrestling gear, eager to employ energy, skill, and will in a very demanding game. William James once dubbed sports the moral equivalent of war. Perhaps wrestling is as benign a substitute as possible. It sure involves efforts to prevail over another, but within boundaries delineated by rules—by law—to stop force short of violence. I was impressed that few penalties for illegal holds had to be assessed, and referees carefully explained them. Exhausted after their best efforts fell short, a few losing wrestlers came close to tears; but they didn't slug each other, or yell obscenities; rather they shook hands after each bout and received praise from their coaches. Ritual reinforced civility. Each town constituted a strong partisan circle, but when a wrestler wrenched a knee badly, the smaller circles of affinity broke to join in an encompassing periphery of common concern. As John Greenleaf Whittier concluded in his poem "The King's Missive,"...outward Letter and inward Light/Kept the balance of truth aright."

About the struggle itself, with muscles straining and minds whirling, the kids struggled to prevail. Sometimes the bout was short, one opponent quickly pinned the other. At other times points were close and victory not assured until the last seconds of the final round. These contests did not just involve the primary participants. The coaches rose from their ringside seats to call out instructions. The more vociferous fans yelled advice, such as, "turn him over!" "watch that elbow!" "keep your head up!" and repeatedly, "get up!"—advice not really needed by the poor kid who knew what to do, had the will, but not the strength or the skill to do it. The more restrained fans showed empathy by body language, and went home with sore stomach muscles. And of course, we all cheered when our boy (or girl) won.

Some would say, "It's just a game." Of course, but upon reflection, why should this particular expenditure of energy, skill, and will, yielding pleasure, comradeship, and financial gain (motels, merchants, bus drivers, coaches, referees, equipment manufacturers, etc) be demeaned? Is its context of common purpose, common law, and common activity so much different from what goes on daily in the lives of all of us? It's not as essential as the work that provides us with food, clothing, and shelter. But it might be just as important as lots of other activities that make our lives more than meat and drink (music, art, drama, entertainment), that also use our energy, demonstrate skill, and provide community—if we can avoid too much celebrity hype.

Wrestling isn't everyone's cup of tea, but a match does offer a primal metaphor for how we struggle to prevail, and do so in community. The venue may be the schoolhouse, or the office, the farm, the factory, or the home. There are struggles in building a house or a home, in fixing a sewer line, repairing a broken ankle, teaching a student, or healing a broken heart. People struggle against those who, by hook or by crook, would diminish their person, their gifts, or their property, or blunt their skills, or paralyze their wills. Some people are pinned by "corporate downsizing" or litigious suits, others by cultural rot. Others become weary resisting floods or storms or insects or hostile critics or fending off addictions. Without a caring community any one of us may be pinned or beaten down. With a caring community, we may prevail.

The apostle Paul said "For we wrestle not against flesh and blood, but against principalities, against powers, against the rulers of the darkness of this world, against spiritual wickedness in high places" (Ephesians 6:12 KJV). I take this to mean that there are not two distinct spheres—the material and the spiritual—but that the context for all our struggles, including wrestling, is an arena of conflict between good and evil. Law is evident in the rules of wrestling. Grace is demonstrated by the applause of fans, the praise of coaches, the hugs of family, by ice packs on the injured knee. Although not explicitly Christian, one finds in ordinary events intimations of the kingdom that Jesus said "is among you." Luther insisted holiness should be found in the hearth (home), not the cloister. I would add that holiness should mark all the common ventures of life, including games, and that all honest activity, involving energy, skill, and will, can be embraced within the kingdom of God.

This being the case, our worship each Sunday rightly offers to the Lord all our struggles. We dedicate upon the altar of devotion diverse energies and skills. We ask God to strengthen our wills. We accept the sanctifying power of the Holy Spirit on ordinary pursuits. In true worship the community of Christ draws a large circle of love, care, and encouragement around all those little circles to which we belong and which give us a place in the sun, and by which we serve our neighbor. Such is the priesthood of believers: serving each other through our vocations and avocations. If this is so, shouldn't our worship be geared to such affirmations?

At the Nestucca District wrestling match, I "fantasized" about one fan. Shall we call him Jacob? Loudly and passionately, he urged on his favored wrestler (a son, maybe, or nephew?). From the logo on his cap and other garb I took Jacob to be a logger from Willamina. Or maybe an ex-logger, stuck in a low paying job, trying to get on at the mill at forty-eight, even if it's on the green chain. At home a rebellious teenager, a sick and discouraged wife, a heavy mortgage, credit card debt, a pickup needing repairs. Jacob's wrestling with the angel of God is happening vicariously on the green mat. "Get up, Kyle!" he yells, with repeated variation on the theme. Near the end of the match, on his back, Kyle struggles desperately to get up, while the referee scoots from side to side to see if both shoulder blades touch. In a last desperate call before the referee smacks his hand on the mat, Jacob cries out plaintively, "C'mon, Kyle!" "C'mon, Kyle!"

I expect Kyle shrugged off this loss better than Jacob did. Were both present at your church maybe the next day, to experience in the community of faith a circle of encouragement and caring, a supreme loyalty, where wrestling losses and wins gain perspective in a broader context of sin and salvation? Did they gather to hear and heed the word of Christ Jesus, who speaks to their conditions, in whose name the evil powers that would destroy them—whether embedded like demonic viruses within economic, psychological, political, cultural forms—are defeated by Jesus' struggle at Golgotha and validated by the victory of the empty tomb?

"C'mon, Kyle!"
"C'mon, Jacob!"

"Outside the Box"

Selection adapted from "Roberts' Reflections," a monthly column for Northwest Friends, January 2003

Recently I've been hearing an expression: "outside the box." Maybe the phrase is "old hat" to you, but it's new to me—and challenging. After all, philosophers try to keep words "ship shape." We clean up some words, repair some, and part-out others. To do this we diagnose their *denotations* and *connotations*. Denotations refer to how words or phrases ordinarily convey meanings; connotations refer to how original meanings are adapted to special ones, how they get "customized" in the marketplace of linguistic exchange.

Consider denotations

Denotations are straightforward. A box is a container you put things in to keep them in place. Boxes come in handy sizes! Remember at your last move how you scrounged for boxes to put your books or kitchen stuff in? My wife orders shoes from Masseys and they come by mail secured in a box. It's good they're "inside the box," even though, for entrepreneurial purposes, a large carton is used, with foamy chunks of plastic filling the extra space. In any case, boxes keep things from getting misplaced, strayed, damaged, or stolen. A file cabinet is a kind of box too. It contains important documents in an orderly fashion. This way it's easier to locate an important letter in a file than by pawing through papers heaped on the floor. Even my computer has boxes, with little virtual squares on the screen for locating them. What a variety of boxes there are, from a velvety little thing that holds a ring to a huge shipping container stuffed with merchandise for Wal-Mart. Homeless persons sometimes sleep in cardboard containers; but they would much rather occupy a house—a wooden box—where they're not so easily misplaced or damaged. Hmm, is the meetinghouse a box too? Sure.

Consider connotations

Well, I've "toyed" with you long enough; metaphoric subtleties are starting to "kick in" so let's check out connotations. Folks urged to operate outside the box ought to know what they're getting out of—and into. The Internet offers numerous sites to get you outside your box and into theirs, for the price of a few celebrity CDs. It seems somebody is always eager to repackage us whenever we shuck the old box and stand around shivering anxiously in our new freedom.

Obviously, connotative meanings aren't straightforward; they generally flow with prevailing cultural winds. So let's go to the cultural mall to see if freedom is found outside the box. It's one thing to change routine by jogging every morning at six; it's another thing to substitute yoga for prayer. It's one thing to challenge national foreign policy; it's another thing to sabotage the armory. It's one thing to eat only organic vegetables, but it's another thing to sue McDonald's for making you fat. It's one thing to liven up your marriage with a new hobby; it's another thing to trade your spouse for a different model. It's one thing to try new modes of Christian outreach and fellowship; but it's another thing to denounce the institutional church. It's one thing to dress casually in worship, it's another thing to treat God like a beneficent next-door neighbor (which may be why some restless free-form evangelicals are joining the Orthodox Church).

Let's acknowledge that the cry to get outside the box may come from entrepreneurs wanting to sell us something: whether it's gussied-up pickups, nose rings, investments, self-help exercises, or even religious programs. They're not interested in psychic freedom or creativity; they just exploit restlessness of spirit to line their pockets with our money.

Does *restlessness of spirit*, however, suggest a favorable connotation for the phrase, "outside the box"? I think it does. Restlessness of spirit *may* indicate disobedience to God in the face of heavy duties and high moral claims. *But it may also signify an earnest—if ill-defined—desire to be more creative in how we live, in what we do, and in how we love God and neighbor.* In a materially prosperous but spiritually impoverished culture, such restlessness signifies to careful listeners a yearning for renewed faith. When stubborn Pharisees asked Jesus for a special sign, he told them to read the cultural weather (Matthew 16:1-4). A prophetic church correctly reads the signs of the times and responds accordingly. Does this response imply new structures? Secondarily perhaps, but primarily it means inward renewal. It surely doesn't mean cheapening the cost of discipleship, or demoting Jesus to a social reformer, or pushing aside twenty centuries of church history and tradition.

So I ask you, how do persons in your congregations who feel "boxed in" by ordinary routines, traditional beliefs, established systems, standard social structures, and normal personal relationships find new and creative freedom? Does it mean getting outside the box or being changed from within? Can we really get free from structures and relationships? In a well-functioning community of Christ, social boxes aren't traps, they are mansions for the spirit—whether entered through success or suffering. This paraphrase from the "wheels within wheels" passage in Ezekiel (1:19-20) helps make the point: "When the living creatures moved, the *boxes* moved beside them; and when the living creatures rose from the earth, the *boxes* rose. Wherever the spirit would go, they went, and the *boxes* rose along with them; for the spirit of the living creatures was in the *boxes*."

"Kinda"?

Selection adapted from "Roberts' Reflections," a monthly column for Northwest Friends, April 2004

Current culture conveys certain positive values: diminished snobbery, unpretentiousness, openness to new ideas, sensitivity to the feelings of others. There's a down side to these egalitarian values. Consider oral communication. Whether in conversation or public discourse our speech often sacrifices syntax to emotional effect, and refrains from forthright assertions. Accordingly, words such as *kinda* and *sorta* and *you know* often punctuate oral communication. These rhetorical devices can encase propositions in a nurturing nest. If calculatingly chosen, they let a speaker slip ideas in slantwise! As cushioning words they protect the ego from rejection. Does such speech show humility and logical sophistication? Or does it reveal timidity—a culturally induced yen to be politically correct?

Rhetoric is more than syntax, data, analysis, and logic. The "language game" rightly uses emotional overtones and embellished text. But why do *these* reductive and irritating modifiers appear so often in contemporary speech? Because it reflects our cultural ethos, as noted above—we don't want to appear better or to impose definitive judgments on others. Given a current emphasis on relational ecclesiology and narrative theology, feelings claim a higher priority than fact, and so we tousle the words so they flow less didactically. For younger folks, such speech may reflect an educational system so preoccupied with testable outcomes and behavioral problems it hasn't sufficiently taught oral communication skills. Accordingly, children mumble inchoate sentences in tangy voices through poorly exercised vocal cords, and we adults try to be "with it" socially. Alas.

Recently a young newscaster was reporting an explosion that occurred at a Portland oil-recycling plant that engulfed large buildings in a flaming inferno and flung ashy contaminants for blocks. "The blast," she said, "*kinda* spread...." Kinda?

Will your Easter message intone: "The resurrection kinda, you know, conveys a sorta hope for a better spiritual journey"? Of course not! There are occasions when speech should be indirect, tentative, cognizant of variant views, and emotionally relaxing. Easter isn't such an occasion. The most explosive event in all history isn't a "kinda," "sorta" thing. Jesus rose from the dead, and because of his triumph, so shall we. Boldly proclaim this wonderful news! Christ is risen! He is risen indeed! Hallelujah!

www.ingramcontent.com/pod-product-compliance
Lightning Source LLC
Chambersburg PA
CBHW080531170426
43195CB00016B/2530